MW00856796

The Author with McGirr Squirrel Rifle.

THE MUZZLE-LOADING CAP LOCK RIFLE

by

NED H. ROBERTS

ILLUSTRATED WITH PHOTOGRAPHS AND DRAWINGS
BY THE AUTHOR AND OTHERS

Reproduced by

Wolfe Publishing Company
6471 Airpark Drive
Prescott, Arizona 86301

Originally Published
by
The Granite State Press,
Manchester, New Hampshire
1940

Printed in the United States of America

Reprinted August, 1991

ISBN 0-935632-96-4

Wolfe Publishing Company
Prescott, Arizona

THE MUZZLE-LOADING, CAP LOCK RIFLE

By NED H. ROBERTS

Major Commanding the Military Department, Troy Conference Academy, Vermont 1901-'02. Sixteen years service in the National Guard of New Hampshire, New Jersey, Connecticut, New York, and Virginia. Member of State and Regimental Rifle Teams in each of those states. Internationally known expert and author on firearms and hunting since 1912. Sixty years practical experience in the use of rifles from the muzzle-loaders to the latest, high velocity arms. Fifty years experience as big game hunter and wilderness wanderer in Canada and the United States. Honorary member of Victoria Rifle Club, Hamilton, Ontario, Canada, 1900; Life Member of the National Rifle Association of America, and the National Muzzle-Loading Rifle Association. Originator of the well-known "25 Roberts and 257 Roberts" rifle cartridges. Ex-member of the New Hampshire Fish and Game Commission.

PREFACE

With the advent of increased interest in and use of the muzzle-loading cap lock rifles throughout the United States during the past few years, I have been importuned by numerous riflemen, so interested, to write a book on this subject. This book is the answer to these requests.

No book on the muzzle-loading cap lock rifle has been published in the United States since 1848, with the single exception of that most excellent volume, "The Kentucky Rifle," by Captain John G. W. Dillin, in 1924.

The flint-lock rifles were obsolete before I was born, and though I have occasionally shot them I disclaim any knowledge of this type of firearms and leave this subject to those authors better qualified than I, to write about.

I was born on the ancestral farm in Goffstown, New Hampshire, on October 21, 1866. My father, a farmer and agriculturist, after I was about four years old was employed as superintendent of large farms in Vermont and elsewhere, owned by wealthy men. He was superintendent for fourteen years of the, at that time, well-known "Maplehurst Farm" comprising many hundreds of acres, located in Pittsfield, Massachusetts, whose owner was the late Honorable Thomas Allen, Sr., for many years United States Senator from Missouri. Thus I grew up on the farm, for which fact I am very thankful, and as a farmer's son I early learned the use of various tools, carpentry, some forging, and the repairing of furniture, wagons, sleds and farm machinery.

I was educated in the public schools, and was graduated from the Pittsfield, Massachusetts, High School. Later, I was graduated from two of the Bryant &

Stratton Business Colleges as an accountant and teacher of the commercial branches, which subjects I taught in public and private schools in various places in the United States and Canada for forty-six years. My vacations have been largely spent in experimenting with nearly all kinds of rifles and ammunition on the rifle range, and in hunting and fishing in different parts of this country and Canada; which outdoor sports have resulted in giving me far better health than most men enjoy.

On my ninth birthday anniversary, October 21st, 1875, my favorite uncle, the late Alvaro F. Annis who was employed by my father as one of the men on the farm, long since departed to the "Happy Hunting Grounds," gave me a small muzzle-loading percussion lock rifle, and commenced teaching me how to properly load, shoot and care for it, as well as teaching me during the next six or eight years all that he knew about the muzzle-loading rifle, the best methods of casting bullets, making the various kinds of patches from the correct materials, what kinds of oils were considered the best for lubricating the patches, and cleaning and oiling the bore, the best powder to use, the correct charges for the various "gauges," or calibres, then in use; the proper percussion caps for the different rifles and revolvers; and, in short, all the "hundred-and-one little things" that were so necessary for the expert shot with the muzzle-loading rifle to know.

Uncle Alvaro was an experienced rifleman and skillful hunter of all the New England game that was so plentiful in those days. He served with honor for eighteen months during part of the Civil War as a "Sharpshooter" in the famous regiment known as "Berdan's Sharpshooters," and when that regiment, after heavy losses in battles, was disorganized and the remaining members transferred to other regiments, he was sent home as an invalid. He eventually recovered his health, lived for many years and was my constant instructor and adviser in all that pertains to rifles and rifle shooting with both muzzle-loading and breeching-loading arms until his death.

During all these years I have owned one or more muzzle-loading cap lock rifles, and have continued to shoot these as well as using many of the fine rifles of this type that my riflemen friends have owned, and freely allowed me unlimited opportunities of shooting. I have also found time to use about all the different makes and calibres of the various breech-loading rifles as these have appeared on the market up to the present time, during which time, with the assistance of my friend Mr. Fred J. Sage, we developed the 25 calibre Roberts, and the 257 Roberts cartridges adapted to various high velocity arms for vermin shooting and target work at ranges including 600 yards.

I am especially indebted to my dentist friend, P. A. Matteson, D. D. S., of Bennington, Vermont, who has these many years owned a great many of the finest muzzle-loading rifles made by the most noted and skillful of the old-time rifle-makers, all in practically perfect condition—many almost unused when he acquired them—all of which through the doctor's kindness I have been permitted to use as freely as I chose on his private range where we have spent many happy days shooting these fine arms, and on my own range as well. Dr. Matteson has also contributed freely of his fund of knowledge regarding the correct use of the muzzle-loading rifles, much of the history of the various makers of these rifles, and much data that has been of great assistance to me in the preparation of this book; for all of which I again express my sincere thanks. I also desire to express my thanks to my gunsmith friend, Mr. Floyd R. Butler, of Raceville, New York, who has materially assisted me in this publication by furnishing considerable information regarding these old rifles, and for the use of his best muzzle-loaders on the range where we have together made extensive tests of them at various ranges. My sincerest thanks are also due my friend and shooting companion, Fred N. J. Dube, M. D., of Manchester, N. H., for his kindness in editing this manuscript, and to his secretary, Miss Martha Dziengowski, for much assistance in typing it.

Also I wish to express my appreciation to the following riflemen for their assistance in furnishing data for this work: Mr. Frank K. Lucas, Webster, N. Y., for the unlimited use on my own range of his fine Billinghurst, and James & Ferris rifles; Mr. Wm. V. Lowe, Brookline, Mass., for much special data; Mr. Wilfred T. Brodeur, Ludlow, Mass., for valuable information regarding the making of the old "cast steel" barrel blanks used by the old rifle-makers; Mr. Walter Grote, Canton, Ohio, who furnished numerous rare photographs and much data; Mr. E. M. Farris, secretary of the National Muzzle-Loading Rifle Association. Portsmouth, Ohio; Mr. Walter J. Keenan, Cincinnati, Ohio; Mr. Adolph O. Niedner, vice-president of the Niedner Rifle Corporation, Dowagiac, Michigan; Mr. W. A. Luce, Ithaca, New York, for photographs and valuable information; Major W. E. Witsil, ballistic engineer of the Remington Arms Company, Inc., Bridgeport, Conn.; Mr. M. A. Robinson, ballistic engineer of the Winchester Repeating Arms Company, New Haven, Conn.; Mr. H. R. Lunn, Ithaca, New York, The American Rifleman, Washington, D. C.; Mr. L. O. Holman, Trumansburg, New York; Captain John G. W. Dillin, Media, Pennsylvania, Mr. C. B. Shiffer, North Woodstock, N. H. and all others who have assisted in any way in the publication of this book.

It is my honest opinion that no single individual living today can compile a single volume which can be sold at a moderate price that will contain *all the information and data* on the muzzle-loading rifles and their use. With this fact in mind, I have endeavored to give the reader the most important facts, the most useful hints and suggestions, and as many illustrations of rare arms, accessories and equipment as possible in a volume of this size. I fully realize that much which could have been stated has of necessity been omitted in order to prepare a book that can be sold at a popular price. I must apologize for the very frequent use of the word "about" before so many dates; but the fact is that no positive records can be found to positively establish the *exact date* in these cases. I also wish to apologize for any errors and deficiencies in language and composition that may appear herein. If I shall have helped the beginner who is just taking up the shooting of the fine muzzle-loading cap lock rifle to get the best accuracy from his rifle and the most enjoyment out of this fine sport, as well as dropping an occasional hint or bit of information for the experienced user of these arms, I shall have been well repaid for my efforts in preparing this volume, and placing on record numerous data that otherwise might have been lost to the world in a few more years, and after the demise of the few remaining old-time rifle-makers and experts in the use of these fine old rifles.

Goffstown, N. H., July, 1940. N. H. R.

CONTENTS

PAGE

Frontispiece ii

Preface vi

List of Illustrations xiv

Introduction 1

Chapter I. General Construction of the Rifle 10

II. Iron Sights and Telescopic Sights 49

III. Accessories and Equipment 73

IV. Ammunition for the Muzzle-Loading Rifles 135

V. Loading, Cleaning and Care of the Rifle 159

VI. The Target Rifle and Target Shooting 184

VII. The Hunting Rifle 279

VIII. Tools Used by the Old-Time Rifle-Makers 317

IX. Some Noted Makers of Muzzle-Loading Rifles and their Rifles 332

X. The Mountain Riflesmiths 384

XI. Miscellaneous Hints and Suggestions 396

XII. Partial List of Old-Time Makers of Muzzle-Loading Cap Lock Rifles 425

"Shiff the Gunman," North Woodstock, New Hampshire, with his S. Hawken "Plains Rifle."

Carl B. Shiffer, North Woodstock, New Hampshire, generally known as "Shiff the Gunman" throughout this country, was born in a Covered Wagon in Montana Territory, in July 1855.

He grew up in the Rocky Mountains where he hunted and trapped, and on the Great Plains where he hunted buffalo, antelope and other big game and fought the Indians. For many years he was a trader among the old mountain men and trappers in the days when Sharps, Ballard and Winchester rifles and cartridges for these were as staple as gold before Franklin D. Roosevelt's "rubber dollars," depreciated American money, the "A. A. A.," the "W. P. A.," "Sit-down Strikes," the "C. I. O.," etc., became "fashionable" in the United States. In the old days "Shiff" knew the Rockies and the Plains as you know your city's streets today.

For more than 35 years "Shiff" wore a Colt's 45 calibre "Peacemaker" revolver as constantly as his trousers, because if he had dressed without the "Peacemaker" he might soon thereafter have had no further use for his trousers. He was one of the Civil Engineers in building the Northern Pacific Railway, and later on the Georgia Central Railway.

Shiff located in North Woodstock in 1881 where he established his business as a dealer in obsolete and modern firearms, and during these years he has established a reputation for "square dealing" so that today he numbers his customers by the thousands and has handled many thousands of all kinds of firearms. He is recognized today as one of the real authorities on obsolete arms throughout this country and Canada.

Mr. Shiffer is one of the last of the old pioneers and plainsmen, and although he is now 85 years old is still a very hale, hearty and active man and conducts his business and carries on his little farm without assistance. In spite of the fact that he attended school but sixteen weeks he reads Greek, Latin, Spanish and some other languages and is a great student of history.

LIST OF ILLUSTRATIONS

	Page
Frontispiece; the Author	vi
"Shiff the Gunman" with his "Plains Rifle"	xiv
Pioneer Hunter Casting Bullets in the Wilderness	13
Rifling Guides used by John Selvidge and Norman S. Brockway	16
Close-Up View of Rifling Guide and Index	18
Types of Rifling	26
Types of Rifling	28
Sketch of Leading Rod and Leading Bolt	30
Breech and Break-Off of Edwin Wesson Rifle	36
Types of Nipples, or Tubes	39
Brockway Rifle, Primer Ignition	40
Edwin Wesson Target Rifle, Rigby Long Range Rifle used by Irish Rifle Teams	50
G. B. Fogg Rear Sight Leaf	55
A. Leonard, and N. Lewis Rifles	62
Author's E. Anschutz Rifle, and Slotter & Co. Rifle	64
Breech of L. W. Tisdel, and James & Ferris Rifles	72
Bullet Moulds, Colt Type, and Cross Patch Cutter	74
Powder-Horns, F. E. Dunn Collection	76
Powder-Horns, F. E. Dunn Collection	78, 79
Bullet Pouch, Straight Starter and Loading Block	81
Huntoon Bullet Mould and Tisdel Mould	82
G. H. Ferriss Bullet Mould, and Old Bullet Ladle	84
Bullet Moulds	86
Small Powder-Flasks; F. E. Dunn Collection	90
Large Powder-Flasks; F. E. Dunn Collection	92
Flask presented to Buffalo Bill by "Soapy" Smith	92
Hunting Bags; F. E. Dunn Collection	94
Cappers, or Cap Magazines; Dunn Collection	96
Cap Magazines and "Primers"; Dunn Collection	98
Bullet Swages and Millard Split Swage	102
False Muzzle for 3-strip Patch, and Carver Bullet Ladle	103
False Muzzles, Side View and End View	106
Bullet Starters, or Guide Bullet Starters	108
False Muzzle for Huntoon Rifle, and Patch Cutters	110
Types of Bullets	114
Types of Composite Bullets	116
Types of Composite Bullets	118
Nipple Wrenches	122
Sketch of Shooting Bench	128
Machine Rest, Wm. V. Lowe Model	130

Page
Old Pennsylvania Match Rifle and Rest 132
Acorn Shaped Bullet and Sugar-Loaf Boat-Tail 148
Bullets Loaded Incorrectly—Tipping 149
Sketches of Composite Bullets 152
Sketches of Composite Bullets 153
Cartridges for Muzzle-Loading Rifles 156
Cartridges for Muzzle-Loading Rifles 158
Left-Hand Cap Lock Rifle, and A. G. Bagley Rifle 162
Breech of A. G. Bagley Rifle open to Load, and Breech Closed for Firing 164
E. Beerst Dual-Shot Rifle, and B. W. Amsden Double Barreled Rifle 168
Ballard Rifle Converted to Cap Lock, J. M. Caswell Rifle, Confederate Army Alteration of Hall Breech-Loading Flint-Lock Rifle to Cap Lock 174
Billinghurst Buggy Rifle in Case with Accessories 178
Billinghurst, and Edwin Fay "Buggy Rifles" 182
Wm. V. Lowe Shooting from Machine, and Group shot at 40 rods 186
H. J. Huntoon, and N. G. Whitmore Rifles 192
Abe Williams Sharpshooters Rifle, and N. S. Brockway Match Rifle 194
Old Shooting-House and Range at Vernon, Vt. 196
Muzzle-Loaders vs Breech-Loaders at Vernon, Vt. 202
G. H. Ferriss, Long Range Creedmoor Rifle, L. W. Tisdel Target Rifle 204
Colonel Berdan's Rifle, and Exhibition of Rifle Shooting by Berdan's Sharpshooters in 1861 208
Irish Rifle Team of 1874 at Creedmoor 212
Whitworth Hexagonal Bore Long Range Rifle 214
1000 yards Targets of Irish Rifle Team, 1874 230
1000 yards Targets of U. S. Rifle Team, 1874 231
Seth Millard Match Rifle and Edwin Wesson Target Rifle 234
First American Rifle Team to Win Honors Abroad 238
U. S. Rifle Team of 1880 at Dollymount Range 244
Riflemen at Vernon, Vt., Sept. 2, 1896 246
J. Kridder Target Rifle, Unknown Make, Target Rifle, John J. Wurfflein Match Rifle 248
Diagram of 50-shot Group by H. V. Perry; Diagram of 10-shot Group by N. S. Brockway 254
Billinghurst Match Rifle, N. Angel Match Rifle 256
C. Plath and D. H. Hilliard Match Rifles 258
James & Ferriss, and T. Lamson Target Rifles 264
Groups Shot by Morgan James, and J. H. Gardner 268
Groups Shot by N. Lewis, and Horace Warner 272

Page
N. Lewis, and B. W. Amsden Match Rifles 274
40-shot Group at 40 rods by Geo. H. Ferris 275
N. Lewis, and Warren & Steele Rifles 276
Groups with 50 calibre Billinghurst Rifle, shot by John Greer in 1868 277
C. L. Clark, B. W. Amsden, and A. Appleby Rifles 278
Henry Carlile, F. W. White, and B. Musgrove Hunting Rifles 282
N. Lewis Double Barreled Rifle, and A. Cook Rifle 284
N. Lewis Rifle and Shotgun, N. Lewis Double Barreled Rifle, and N. Lewis Match Rifle 286
Revolving 6-shot Rifle, J. Buswell Superposed Rifle, and W. Raymond Side Hammer Rifle 290
L. L. Hepburn 4-Barreled Rifle, Abe Williams Superposed Rifle, and W. Billinghurst Rifle 294
Mule Ear Rifles 296
Jacob Hawken, and Samuel Hawken Plains Rifles 310
Powder-Horn carried by I. Powell at Fort Ticonderoga in 1775 316
A Fine Rifling Guide and Bench used in Virginia 318
Tools used in Boring, Reaming and Rifling Barrels 322
Tools used by the Old Riflesmiths 324
Cherries made and used by N. S. Brockway 326
Billinghurst Target Rifle, and "Seven-Shooter Rifle" ... 334
Norman S. Brockway, and his Last Rifle 344
Horace Warner, and Warner 45 calibre 35-pound Rifle .. 352
H. V. Perry, Rifle-Maker 356
Carlos Gove, Rifle-Maker 360
Carlos Gove Long Range Rifle 362
George H. Ferriss Match Rifle 368
George Schalk Target Rifle 372
John Meunier, and L. W. Tisdel Target Rifles 380
Elmer Wolf's Shop in the Mountains of Maryland 386
Elmer Wolf Rifling a Barrel 388
Elmer Wolf, Riflesmith, and Major Jerome Clark, U. S. Army, Retired 392
Sketch showing Method of Laying Out Roll for Rifling Guide, Uniform Twist 401
Sketch showing Method of Laying Out Roll for Rifling Guide, Gain Twist 402
Merrill Boat-Tail Bullet of 1861 and Paper Patch 404
F. Wasmann Target Rifle 410
Sketch for Making Tools for Floating Out and Recutting Barrels 421
Sketch for Making Tools for Recutting Barrels 422
Group at 40 rods, shot by Walter Grote in Match 424

Introduction

My First Rifle and Early Rifle Training. My first muzzle-loading percussion lock rifle was a small bore, 170 round balls to the pound, or a 30 calibre as we would call it today, had a half-octagon barrel 21 inches long, walnut half stock, brass mountings with small engraved patch-box, brass trigger guard with pistol-grip bow, fine single set trigger, a fine lock with small, nicely curved hammer, a fine hooded "pin-head" front sight, an open V notch rear sight, and a fine rear peep sight with folding disc top, having the stem cut with one hundred turns to the inch, threaded through the upper tang. How I wish I had that little rifle now! I do not even remember the maker's name, but I have a record in an old diary that the barrel was stamped "English Cast Steel" at a point near the breech. Uncle Alvaro, or Uncle "Bub" as he was always called in the family, picked up this rifle on a Southern battlefield. There it lay beside a mere boy in gray who had been killed in the fight, and the barrel, which was some 30 inches long, had a bad dent about a foot from the muzzle where it had apparently been hit by a piece of projectile.

It was evidently a "boy's rifle" of English make, and doubtless the pride of some Southern gentleman's son. Uncle said "it was such a nice little rifle" that he carried it away as a souvenir, later had the barrel cut off at a point below the dent and after the war gave it to me as a birthday present. I sincerely wish I had known enough to have kept it, but after using it some six years, I, fool-like, traded it for a 38 calibre muzzle-loader weighing about fourteen pounds, made by Edwin Wesson, Hartford, Connecticut, as stamped on the full octagon 32 inch barrel, using a "picket," or "sugar-loaf" bullet as they were called in those days, with a paper "cross patch," a false muzzle, bullet starter, double set trigger, walnut half stock, the usual shaded pin-head front sight and rear peep sight with the stem threaded into the upper tang cut with 80 turns to the inch.

A few days after presenting me with the little 30 calibre muzzle-loading rifle, Uncle Bub laid out a course in rifle practice which I carefully followed. First, of course, he taught me how to load the rifle correctly using the round bullet with oiled, linen patch, showed me how to cut these patches with the patch-cutter that came with the rifle, how best to oil these patches using only pure sperm oil. He insisted that patches should be cut from "shirt-bosom linen" only, if the best accuracy was to be obtained. Teaching me how to cast good bullets required several evenings after the day's work was finished. We used old lead pipe, plenty of which could be found on every farm, melted the lead in a small iron pot on the kitchen stove, pouring the lead into the mould with a large, iron spoon with wood handle that he heated and bent so as to form a spout through which the lead was poured much as we use the Ideal bullet dipper today. After the bullets were cast each had to be examined carefully and all that were wrinkled, or had flaws of any kind in them, were rejected and later melted over.

Uncle was very particular to impress upon me the fact that only perfect bullets would give real accuracy in any rifle, and it was only a waste of good powder and caps to use imperfect bullets. When we cast the conical bullets for this rifle, after examining them carefully and rejecting the imperfect ones, the next step was to swage these in the swage that was provided by uncle.

Under his supervision I started shooting the rifle at 10 rods (55 yards), shooting from a rest, at a 2-inch black bull's-eye painted on a piece of wrapping paper. No, we did not have the "classy" printed targets that the rifle-shooters today use, but instead made our own which were often a blackened spot on a piece of board, or shingle. As soon as I was able to keep five successive balls in the 2-inch bull's-eye at this range, uncle reduced the size of the bull's-eye to the size of the cap box in which the "G. D." caps of one hundred were sold, which boxes were about 1 and 3/8 inches in diameter. This small-sized bull's-eye requiring more skill in holding, cleaning, and loading the rifle, was used until I could place five consecutive balls in, or cutting, this spot, and repeating that several times to show that the first "perfect score" was not made by mere luck.

Having mastered the first two stages of this course of instruction, he "promoted" me to shooting in the sitting position at this range using the 2-inch bull until I was able to keep four out of five shots in or cutting this bull's-eye, and repeating this score a number of times. After acquiring the necessary skill this required, I was instructed to shoot off-hand at this range using the same 2-inch bull's-eye and continued this practice until I was able to place four out of five balls in or cutting this bull, and do that repeatedly. Having in a few weeks' practice acquired the necessary skill to qualify as above in this first part of uncle's requirements in rifle-shooting, I was promoted to the 20 rods range where I shot with a rest at a 4-inch bull's-eye until I could hit it five times in succession, and do that repeatedly. Then I was to shoot in the sitting position at this range using the same size bull until I could make four bull's-eyes out of five shots, and make five such groups, all under his supervision. This required a lot of practice on my part, but I acquired the necessary skill to qualify in this stage of the instruction, after which I was again promoted to shooting off-hand at this range using the same bull's-eye, and requiring ten targets showing four out of five consecutive bullets in or cutting that bull. Yes, Uncle Bub thoroughly knew his rifle-shooting, knew how to teach it to a boy, was a strict disciplinarian, and taught me many things that have been of life-long benefit.

During the autumn and winter of 1875-'76, whenever the weather permitted, I diligently and carefully practiced rifle-shooting as outlined, always under Uncle Bub's supervision, so that early in the spring of 1876, I commenced shooting from a rest at 30 rods (165 yards) at a 6-inch bull's eye where I repeated the course followed at 20 rods. That is, shooting first from a rest, second from the sitting position, and last off-hand, until I had "qualified" according to his requirements in each of these positions, after which I was declared by him to be "a damned good shot with the rifle." Uncle Alvaro was then acknowledged to be one of the most skillful riflemen in that county, and such praise coming from him—a man who had been "one of Berdan's Sharpshooters"—was to a boy of those times about equal to the honor of winning a prize at Camp Perry by a boy today.

The year 1876, "The Centennial Year" in the United State, aroused much enthusiasm in rifle-shooting, which was largely occasioned by the visit to this country of the Scotch, Australian, Canadian and Irish Rifle Teams to compete in the International Rifle Match with the United States Rifle Team, which match was shot on the old "Creedmoore Range," on Long Island, New York, at 800, 900 and 1000 yards, in September of that year. Several men who later became some of our most noted expert riflemen had their ambition aroused and commenced practicing long range rifle-shooting that year because of this International Rifle Match, which was won by the United States Rifle Team. Among those who later became internationally noted as expert riflemen was the late Lieutenant W. Milton Farrow, who was, I believe, the first winner of the famous "Wimbledon Cup," now competed for annually at Camp Perry, and I believe the first (or one of the first) rifleman to win the title of "Champion Military Rifleman of the United States," in the match at Creedmoore Range in September, 1882. He also was the inventor of the "Farrow Rifle"—one of the best single shot breech-loading target rifles we have ever had.

The International Rifle Match that year also apparently settled the controversy as to whether the muzzle-loading or the breech-loading rifle was the superior for long range shooting. Each member of the Irish Rifle Team used a muzzle-loading rifle, each being the very best that the most experienced and skillful English rifle-makers could produce, while each man on our team shot a breech-loading rifle, the majority of which were the "Old Reliable" Sharps Model 1874, side hammer, or the Ballard long range rifle, all using the 45 calibre center-fire cartridge loaded with 100 to 120 grains of black powder and a paper patched 500 grain bullet.

I remember that Uncle Alvaro was much disappointed at the results of the International Rifle Match as he had stoutly insisted that the Irish Rifle Team was *sure to win* the match because their fine muzzle-loading rifles were the *most accurate* in the world—far more so than any breech-loading rifle that could be made. He lost a month's wages, or more, in wagers that he had made on the Irish Rifle Team and commenced to look with more favor on the breech-loading Sharps rifle as a result of that match. But he still insisted that the Irish riflemen lost the match "because of their failure to judge the wind conditions correctly, as well as did our riflemen, and the match was, therefore, lost principally on that account even though they had the more accurate rifles." Complete reports of the International Rifle Match with the scores in detail of each member of each team were published in the old *Harper's Weekly* and *Forest and Stream* magazines at that time, all of which uncle and I read and re-read and discussed at length repeatedly. These two magazines then carried advertisements of various models of the Sharps and Ballard long range rifles, with illustrations of these arms, and I became especially interested in them, spending many hours planning how I could earn the necessary $75.00 to purchase one of these rifles.

Early that summer, I commenced practicing at 40 rods rest shooting with my little rifle, which I soon learned did not give nice accuracy at that range because of its small bore, light weight bullet and short barrel. The bullet mould that came with the rifle was of the Colt type with cut-off casting both round and conical bullets, and when I commenced shooting at this range, uncle instructed me to use only the conical bullet weighing about 90 grains as it would "shoot truer" and be less affected by wind than the lighter round balls. However, it did not require much practice to convince me that this small, light bullet was not to be depended upon for good accuracy at 40 rods, and in an attempt to improve the accuracy with this rifle, uncle had a gunsmith make a new bullet mould that cast a longer bullet weighing about 130 grains, which, after we ascertained the correct powder charge, showed better grouping than the 90 grain one and satisfied me for a time. After a few months use of the little rifle with the 130 grain bullet at the 40 rods range, I was convinced that this was not a suitable rifle for use at that range and commenced talking to uncle that "I must have a larger calibre rifle for 40 rods shooting," which finally induced him to let me use his 70 gauge, (40 calibre) Billinghurst hunting and target rifle for this range, which was another "promotion" for me.

He had two muzzle-loading rifles; the above mentioned Wm. Billinghurst 40 calibre rifle with 30-inch octagon barrel which was turned at the muzzle to fit a "guide bullet starter" when used for target work, had double set trigger, walnut half stock, brass mountings and patch-box, a "pin-head" front sight with hood, open V notch rear sight on the barrel and a folding peep sight threaded into the tang of the stock. Also a "knife-blade" front sight that interchanged with the pin-head when the rifle was used for hunting. His second, or target rifle, was made by a man in Ludlow, Vermont, whose name I have forgotten and was very much like the N. S. Brockway rifles. This was a 45 calibre with 32-inch full octagon barrel, used the two-piece cylindrical bullet weighing somewhat over 300 grains, with the oiled paper cross patch, had a false muzzle, bullet starter, fine double set trigger, stocked in the Brockway or N. Lewis manner without fore-end, had the usual shaded pin-head front sight and rear peep sight threaded into the upper tang with the stem cut with one hundred turns to the inch to permit fine adjustments for different ranges and weighed about 19 pounds. There was also a full length telescope made by "L. M. Amidon" of 20 power—so-called at that time—with rear mount that fitted in place of the rear peep sight, which could be used in place of the other sights when desired, a mould that cast a solid lead bullet and another that cast the parts of the two-piece bullet (the butt part of pure lead, the front of hardened lead) a swage for each of these bullets, patch-cutter and all other necessary tools, all contained in a fine rosewood box with racks for the finished bullets, places for each of the accessories, etc.

This was uncle's "pet" rifle that he used for target shooting and turkey shoots at ranges from 40 to 180 rods (990 yards) which was the longest range at which I have any record of his shooting, and seldom at that range, the usual distances being from 40 to 100 rods.

In those days a farmer's boy had mighty little money to spend on "such foolishness as rifle-shooting," as my father called it, worked hard and long for very small pay; consequently it was several years before I was able to save the necessary cash to pay "to boot" (exchange) in trading my small 30 calibre rifle for a muzzle-loader of larger calibre suitable for 40 to 80 rods accurate shooting.

In the autumn of 1877 my parents, through uncle's influence, allowed me to buy my first breech-loading rifle, which was a Frank Wesson 22 calibre rim fire using both the short and long cartridges, with a 24-inch full octagon barrel. This was one of the early models of the "tip-up" action type with two trigger guards, the trigger in the front one being pulled to open the breech, and having a hand-operated extractor on the right-hand side of the breech end of the barrel, which by pulling a small steel knob extracted the fired case, had a fine shaded pin-head front sight, a rear open sight on the barrel with a peep sight screwing into the upper tang, and really was a very accurate shooting rifle for short ranges that partly satisfied me for several years.

The summer before I became fifteen years of age, Uncle Bub found a man who had a 90 gauge—38 calibre—Edwin Wesson rifle that he traded for my little 30 calibre rifle and some cash "to boot," which I earned by picking strawberries and blackberries to sell, and doing other "odd jobs" in addition to doing my regular "chores" at home every day. My father most emphatically did not approve of my interest in rifles and rifle-shooting and refused to buy any rifles, ammunition, or cartridges for me; therefore, I was obliged to earn in some way practically all the money I needed for such purposes, except such as uncle often gave me to spend as I pleased. Good Uncle Alvaro well understood a boy's love for a good rifle and the sport of rifle-shooting, and helped me for many years by carefully teaching me all that he knew about rifles and all that pertained thereto which he had learned by many years experience as a hunter, in target shooting, and as a "Sharpshooter" in the Civil War.*

* The name of Alvaro F. Annis is not found in the roster of Berdan's Sharpshooters Regiment, nor at the War Department in Washington, because when he attempted to enlist in the New Hampshire Company of that Regiment he was rejected on account of failing to pass the physical examination. A year or so later, he enlisted as a substitute for a man who had been drafted and passed the physical examination all right. After he had in this way enlisted it was discovered that he was a very skillful marksman, passed General Berdan's rifle shooting test, was transferred to that regiment and served as before stated. I have been unable to ascertain the name of the drafted man in whose stead Uncle Alvaro served, but I remember that he often told us that for the first few weeks in the Army, he always looked in his cap before roll-call to be sure of answering to the correct name instead of his own.

CHAPTER I

GENERAL CONSTRUCTION OF THE RIFLE, TYPES OF RIFLING

Riflemen in general know that the barrels of the flint-lock guns as well as those used in making the earlier so-called "Kentucky Rifles," with percussion locks, all of which used the round ball of various gauges, were made by hand welding strips of iron in short lengths around a "core rod," driving out this rod so as to prevent its sticking, and repeating this slow, laborious process until a tube of the desired length was formed. Then this rough, welded iron tube was reamed and smoothed inside, the outside smoothed by hand filing or sometimes ground on a grindstone and thus worked into the desired size and shape. The barrel was then straightened, after which it was rifled by cutting therein various numbers and types of grooves with the hand-operated rifling machine. This process of making barrels for the earlier rifles, up to about the year 1830, is so excellently and fully described in Captain John G. W. Dillin's splendid book, *The Kentucky Rifle,* that I shall not waste space by a repetition of it. However, some years after the percussion cap was placed on the open market and displaced the flint-lock, riflemen demanded a rifle that would give accuracy at a much longer range than the round ball rifles that had been in general use up to that time.

The accurate range of the round ball rifle of even as large bore as 15 and 16 to the pound (.695 and .682 inch diameter) was from about 20 to 30 rods (110 to 165 yards) and since so many people were emigrating to the West where buffalo and other game was so very plentiful, and such large, dangerous game as the grizzly bear were found, the hunter-rifleman demanded a rifle of large bore that would shoot accurately at ranges of 60, 80, and 100 rods and have plenty of killing power at those ranges. In order to give good accuracy at these longer ranges it was necessary to use larger charges of black powder with a heavy bullet and cloth patch in the hunting rifle, or a cylindro-conical bullet with paper cross patch in the target rifle. This necessitated the use of a stronger metal for the rifle barrel, with greater tensile strength to withstand the much higher pressure developed by these larger charges of powder behind the heavier, longer bullets, so that about the year 1840 all the best rifle-makers commenced making their barrels of the so-called "cast steel" which had this necessary tensile strength, as well as enabling the barrel makers to furnish a rifle barrel that was free from any roughness and imperfect spots inside the bore.

In the process of making cast steel, iron ore was reduced in the converter to nearly pure iron and cast into small ingots, which with the required amount of carbon were then re-melted in a crucible and cast into small ingots—3 to 4 inches square by 12 to 15 inches long. These were then thoroughly annealed in an air-tight oven, reheated, and passed through rolls that converted the metal into round, octagon or square bars of various sizes and lengths. Cast steel for rifle barrels was not highly carbonized, gave a steel that was tough and durable and not brittle, and really was very excellent barrel steel for muzzle-loaders or breech-loading rifles of low pressure. There appears to have been two different kinds of these cast steel barrel blanks in those days, as Horace Warner, N. S. Brockway and some others, bought this steel in bars of the desired shape, usually octagon, from 12 to 16 feet long, which they cut to the desired lengths and drilled, reamed, straightened and rifled. The second form of cast steel barrel blanks came from the factories in bars of certain lengths with a small hole lengthwise through them. In these last, the ingot, after being annealed, was re-heated and a hole punched lengthwise through it; then a small diameter mandrel was passed through the hole, and the ingot was rolled into the desired size and length. The rifle-makers then bought these blanks with a hole somewhat smaller than the finished bore of the rifle was to be and thus saved the labor of drilling the barrel. The late Norman S. Brockway told me that he had found the barrel blanks that came from the manufacturer with the hole through them did not make as accurate shooting rifles as those that he made from solid bars: therefore, he always bought the best English cast steel solid bars when he could get these, or the solid cast steel bars made by E. Remington & Sons when he could not get the English make, and drilled the barrels himself.

Be that as it may, records show that about 1840 the rifle-makers in the United States began making their barrels of this so-called cast steel in one form or the other, either of which made far better barrels than the old, welded iron ones previously made.

About 1853, after Sir Joseph Whitworth commenced his experiments to determine the best rifle for the British Service he introduced an improved barrel steel, known as the "Whitworth Fluid Compressed Steel," and took out letters of patent on the process of manufacture. In making this steel, an ingot was cast, and while the ingot was still in a fluid state inside, the outside having cooled somewhat, it was placed in the hydraulic press and submitted to many tons pressure which eliminated "blow holes" in the metal, gave it a finer grain and produced a more homogenous barrel steel than any before in use. All barrels made of Whitworth fluid compressed steel have the trade-mark

"Wheatsheaf" stamped on the under side, to distinguish them from other steel.

Soon after the introduction of the Whitworth fluid compressed steel in England, several of the best rifle-makers in this country adopted it for their rifle barrels as it was proven superior to all other barrel steels then known. Among those in this country who adopted this steel for their rifles, we find Morgan James, H. V. Perry, Horace Warner, N. S. Brockway, and doubtless others, who continued to use it for the barrels of their best rifles as long as they made rifles. It was used by many rifle-makers until well along in the 1880's.

Drilling a barrel was the slowest and "toughest" job in making a rifle barrel in those times as they did not have the present type of barrel drills, but used the twist drill for this purpose. It was necessary to withdraw the drill every inch or less, remove the chips and examine the bore with the aid of a mirror and lights so as to be sure the hole was straight, and if it was not, it must be straightened before proceeding with the drilling. This process was repeated again and again until the hole was drilled through the entire length of the barrel, which necessarily required much time and labor and much "cussing" on the part of many rifle-makers. After drilling the barrel, if the rifle was to have a false muzzle, a piece a little longer than the diameter of the barrel was cut off, both ends of this piece and the barrel end were trued in the lathe, then four small holes drilled lengthwise in both. These holes were reamed and fitted with small steel dowels, or pins, which held the false muzzle in place. Then the false muzzle was held in place with a clamp and the barrel was smooth reamed, straightened, rifled and leaded. Here again there appears to have been two different methods of doing this work, as some of the old-time rifle makers cut off the piece for the false muzzle, trued the ends in the lathe, drilled the holes for

A Pioneer Hunter Casting Bullets in the Wilderness.
Illustration from "The Kentucky Rifle," by permission of Captain John G. W. Dillin.

the pins, reamed and fitted these pins, all before drilling the barrel. I understand that this was the method followed by Horace Warner, H. V. Perry, Wm. V. Lowe, and some others; while Brockway told me that he drilled the barrel before cutting off and fitting the piece for the false muzzle and, doubtless, others followed this last method.

After the barrel was drilled and reamed, it was straightened on an anvil by striking with a lead hammer the points at which there was a bend. The oldest method of barrel straightening was to stretch a fine steel wire, kept taut by a light wooden bow, inside the barrel from end to end, touching the inside for the entire length. Spots that did not touch this wire were marked, the wire withdrawn, the barrel laid on a hollow anvil and struck with the lead hammer sufficiently hard to make it straight at that point, the wire again placed inside the barrel and again ex-examined. After one side of the barrel had been straightened in this manner, the wire was moved to the opposite side and if the wire touched the entire length, the barrel was straight. A quicker method is to point the barrel directly toward a window which has a wire stretched across it and clearly visible in front of it. This will throw a shadow distinctly along the bottom of the bore as the barrel is pointed toward it and revolved, and if the shadow appears perfectly straight, the barrel is straight along that surface. If the shadow is crooked or breaks, the barrel is crooked at that point, which is then marked and straightened with the lead hammer as before described. Barrel straightening is an art entirely beyond the ability of about 99.50 per cent. of the so-called "gunsmiths" today, but the best rifle makers of the old days were experts in this work, which was one of the chief reasons for the fine accuracy of their rifles. A rifle

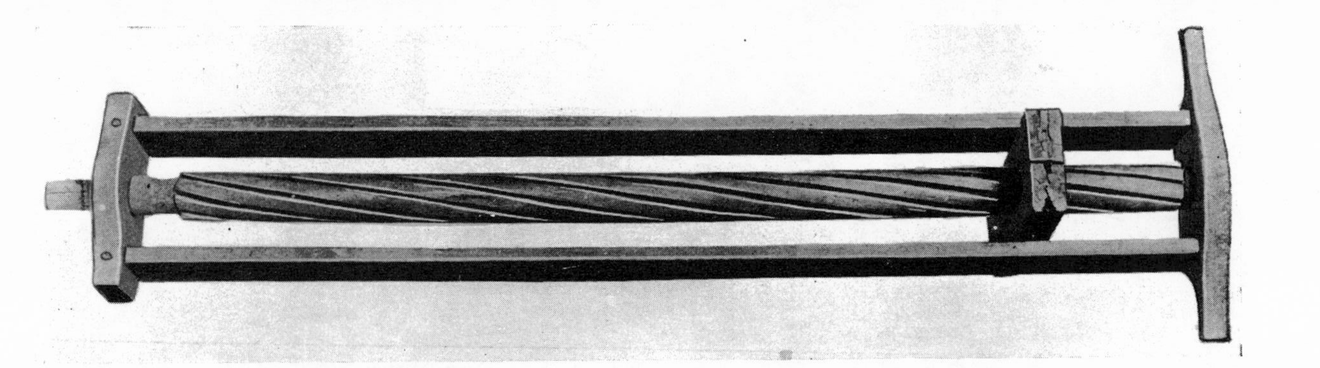

Wooden Rifling Guide used by John Selvidge of Tennessee in 1790-1800.
Illustration from "The Kentucky Rifle," by permission of the Author.

Norman S. Brockway's Rifling Guide. Used many years in rifling his super-accurate barrels.

barrel that is even slightly crooked certainly never can shoot accurately at any range.

After the barrel had been straightened it was ready for rifling which was accomplished by the use of some of the old type, hand-operated, rifling machines of which there are several different kinds. Probably the earliest type of rifling machine used in this country was made entirely from hardwood by the old-time rifle-maker himself who called this the "rifling bench." This consisted of a round bar of hardwood some three inches in diameter and about five feet long, with from four to eight deep radial grooves cut therein, each making one turn in from about twenty inches to four feet or more, extending from end to end of this cylinder. To one end of this bar was fastened a loosely revolving handle and to the other end a clamp for holding the rifling rod which was made of tough, straight-grained hickory. This wooden, grooved cylinder passed through a dialed headpiece the circumference of which was divided by deep rectangular notches into six, seven or eight equal parts, and from the circular central opening two, three, or four iron or brass lugs were fitted into the grooves on the wooden cylinder to hold this in place and cause it to revolve as this was pushed and pulled back and forth by means of the operating handle. The dialed headpiece was fastened to a smooth plank, or bench, with hickory or other hardwood longitudinal guides on either side which would slide smoothly on the bench and the metal index fingers fitting into the grooves caused the rifling guide to revolve. The barrel to be rifled was clamped into two fixtures with its axis directly in line with that of the rifling guide, which carried the rifling rod with the cutter set into it. The cutter, which was kept well oiled, being pushed and pulled back and forth by the rifling guide which passing through the dialed headpiece was

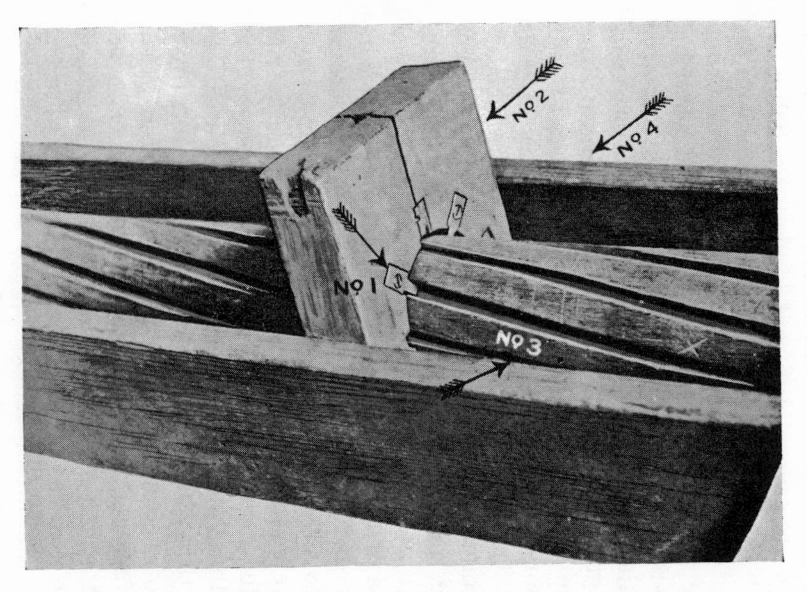

Rifling Guide and Index, used by John Selvidge, Bradley County, Tennessee. No. 1 shows the index fingers that turn the guide. No. 2 is the index and is stationary. No. 3 is the spiral guide that turns the rifling rod. No. 4 is the frame. Illustrated from "The Kentucky Rifle," by permission of the Author.

caused by the index fingers to rotate spirally until the cutter no longer bit into the barrel. The dial was then turned one notch and another groove cut in this same way until all seven or eight grooves had been cut.

The cutter, or "saw" as it was often called, was then taken out of its bed in the hickory rod, and elevated by placing a shim of paper or very thin brass under it, again inserted into a groove in the barrel and the work done over again and again until each of the grooves was as deep as desired. With sharp cutters and smooth working metal a barrel could be rifled in about three hours. It is rather difficult to describe the rifling guide and its operation, but the illustration herewith of a rifling guide makes this quite clear.

At a later period the rifling guides were made from brass or iron cylinders instead of hardwood, and the rifling rod was of steel with a cutter that was adjusted by a screw arrangement in the end. About the time of the Civil War several other types of rifling machines displaced the old rifling guide with its rifling rod and saw. One of these later types is shown in the illustration of the rifling machine used by the late Norman S. Brockway, but, I am unable to state whether he designed this himself, or modeled it after those in use in the Springfield Armory where he was employed during part of the war. All the moving parts of the Brockway rifling machine were made of iron which was more durable than hardwood as well as giving greater precision in operation and adjustments.

Little is really known of the history of rifling: the often-repeated story that rifling had its origin in straight grooves cut in the bore to receive the fouling and facilitate loading, and that one occasion by accident the grooves were given a spiral form and thus the virtues of the spiral grooving discovered, we may dismiss as a fallacy. It hardly could, however, have originated until the manufacturer of firearms had reached some degree in accuracy of workmanship. It appears probable that it was the invention of some individual genius, but the inventor's name is not known with certainty. It has been credited to Gaspard Kollner of Vienna in the 15th century, and to Augustus Kotter of Nuremburg in 1520. There is a record in England of the granting of a patent in 1635 to one Arnold Rotsipen for the invention of the method of rifling small-arms. According to numerous authorities the rifle was quite well known during the 16th century, but the rifles of those times had more disadvantages than advantages since it was then considered necessary to use a tight fitting, round bullet which had to be driven down the barrel by the use of a small wooden mallet and strong iron ramrod. Thus the trouble and labor of loading the rifle was considered as making it inferior to the smooth-bore musket that was so much easier to load; consequently the rifle did not come into general use until about 1750.

An Englishman, Benjamin Robins, experimented extensively with both the musket and various forms of rifling during the years 1707 to 1751 and proved by his experiments that a properly made rifle was much superior in accuracy and range to the musket. In 1742, Robins published a book entitled: *New Principles of Gunnery* in which he set forth the important advantages of the rifled arm as compared with the smooth-bore and showed conclusively that the Nation that should first adopt the rifled small-arms for its Army would thus acquire a superiority over all others. Yet, in spite of this prophecy and the best efforts of eminent military officers of those times, it was more than ninety years before England discarded the Brown Bess musket and adopted a rifle for the entire British Army, in 1854.

In 1800, England organized the "Rifle Brigade" of the 95th Regiment and armed these men with the Baker muzzle-loading, flint-lock rifle with a seven grooved barrel using a round ball about 60 calibre weighing about 350 grains. This was the only rifle used in the British Service until 1836, when it was replaced by the two-grooved Brunswick muzzle-loading, percussion lock rifle using a round ball about 70 calibre weighing approximately 530 grains. But the rifle was not adopted for the entire British Service until 1854, when the Enfield muzzle-loading, percussion lock rifle with a three-grooved barrel of .577 calibre using a cylindro-conoidal, hollow point 530 grain bullet was adopted.

During the years between the invention of the rifle and about 1800, nearly every conceivable form, or type, of rifling had been invented and tested. The deep poly-grooved rifle of the early Austrians and Swiss, the eliptical bored rifle, (which about sixty years later Charles Lancaster of London claimed to have invented) the so-called rachet type of rifling, grooves with rounded corners and rounded top lands, square topped lands with square cornered grooves, square topped lands with rounded cornered grooves, the notched type of lands and grooves—all had been invented and tested during those years. English books record the fact that the gain-twist rifling had also been invented and quite thoroughly tested before 1812, and rifles with various numbers of lands and grooves, from the earliest two-grooved barrel to those with twenty or more, had likewise been tested extensively by that date.

In 1852, Lord Hardinge, Commander-in-Chief of the British Army, being much discouraged with the rifles then used in the Army, commissioned Sir Joseph Whitworth, then the foremost mechanician of the day in fine measurements and accurate manufacture, to make a thorough investigation of the subject of rifling of small-arms in order to discover the best form of rifling and most practical type of rifle for the British Service. After some two years of experimentation he invented and patented in 1854, the Whitworth hexagonal bore rifle with its mechanically made hexagonal bullet fitting the bore of the rifle. This rifle was .450 calibre, the paper patched bullet 1.32 inches long weighing 530 grains, the hexagonal rifling having one turn in twenty inches. The Whitworth rifle was tested by the British Army Ordnance Board early in 1857 in competition with the Enfield rifle, at ranges from 500 to 1800 yards, which shot so wild that no diagram of the shots could be taken, while the Whitworth rifle gave a mean deviation of 4.62 feet at 1400 yards and 11.62 feet at 1800 yards. Yet in spite of the superior accuracy of the Whitworth rifle it was not adopted for the Service arm chiefly on account of prejudice against the hexagonal bore. During Whitworth's experiments he made and tested a rifle having a twist of *one turn in one inch,* and established the interchangeability of small-arms parts manufactured for the British Army, the first person who accomplished this method of manufacture.

During our Civil War the U. S. Government imported quite a number of fine Whitworth rifles and bullets for use by Sharpshooters, after having been equipped with telescopic sights. They were considered among the very finest, most accurate, long range rifles used in that war. The Whitworth rifle was for quite a number of years regarded as possibly the very most accurate long range rifle made, but after some years it gradually went out of use. However, today one of these fine Whitworth rifles in perfect condition is regarded as a great prize and commands a high price.

By about 1840 the majority of our American riflemakers had adopted six, seven, or eight grooves and lands as their standard, but the best shape of these lands and grooves in order to give the very finest accuracy had not been definitely decided. Likewise the matter of whether the gain twist or the uniform spiral gave the better accuracy was a much mooted question in those days. John R. Chapman, in his book, *The Improved American Rifle* (doubtless the best volume on the muzzle-loading rifle heretofore) published in 1848 but written in 1844, states: "I venture to assert that a rifle with a gaining twist, in a windy day at 220 yards, will make a string one-third shorter than a rifle with a regular twist." Therefore, it appears certain that Chapman and Edwin Wesson, then one of the most noted rifle-makers, were staunch believers in the gain twist as giving the finest accuracy, while other expert marksmen and expert rifle-makers were equally as thoroughly positive that the uniform twist was the superior in point of accuracy. Yet, today, in the year of our Lord 1940, expert rifle-makers and expert riflemen are still arguing this same, age-old question which had never, during two centuries, been *fully decided* as regards the lead bullet rifle, either muzzle-loader or breech-loader. Yes, I have heard the most noted rifle-makers now deceased, and the most noted now living, argue this question for hours and hours during the past sixty years, and still I venture to assert that this question as applied to lead bullet rifles, either muzzle-loading or breech-loading, has never been *scientifically and positively decided.* The man now living who has been acknowledged as "The World's best rifle barrel maker"—that master rifle-maker, Mr. Harry M. Pope, claims that the gain twist *is superior in accuracy* to the uniform twist for lead bullet rifles. And, who has ever made *more accurate shooting* target rifles than he?

The late George Schalk, of Pottsville, Pennsylvania, was for many years a noted maker of muzzle-loading rifles that gave exceptionally fine accuracy, and about 1884 in connection with Wm. Hayes, of Newark, New Jersey, who was a very expert marksman, designed the so-called "Schalk system" of rifling with eight wide, flat grooves and eight narrow lands having sharp corners to the grooves and cut with a gain twist. The gain twist rifling was nothing that these men designed, as English records show that it was known and used in Europe before 1750, probably having been designed by Tyrol or Swiss rifle-makers, and was used by Edwin Wesson and other rifle-makers in this country after about 1840. The noted rifle-maker Harry M. Pope, states that his rifling is a modification of the Schalk system and his barrels are cut with the gain twist. Mr. Pope's early catalog, issued when he was in business in Hartford, Connecticut, states: "The advantages of the gain twist are three: 1st—The twist being less at the breech, gives less friction to the bullet; it therefore starts easier and quicker, giving the powder less time to burn on in front of the chamber, which therefore fouls less than in a barrel of uniform twist at the same necessary muzzle pitch. 2nd—The slight change in the angle of rifling, in connection with the choke boring, effectually shuts off any escape of gas and prevents gas cutting. 3rd—It holds a muzzle-loaded bullet in position much better than a uniform twist." Therefore, if Mr. Pope, with all his many years experience in making the most accurate shooting, low pressure rifles in the world, insists that the gain twist is absolutely the *best*, gives the *most accurate shooting*, there must be something to it.

The Pope rifles, again quoting from his catalog mentioned: "The barrels are so bored and rifled as to have a slight, but gradual, taper from breech to muzzle. This, besides keeping the bullet perfectly under control, in connection with the narrow lands (which cut through the bullet easily), makes loading very easy, and very materially increases the accuracy. A bullet pushed through from the breech is tight all the way; there are *no loose places,* and this result is attained by close, careful workmanship; the result is a barrel with a long life."

After a barrel had been correctly leaded, the bore for about two or three inches at the muzzle was a perfect cylinder about .001 or .0015 inch smaller diameter than the rest of the bore, which had a gradual taper from this point to the breech, thus facilitating loading and greatly improved the accuracy of the rifle. The amount of taper in the bore depended, of course, upon the thickness of the patch used; a thick linen patch required more than .0015 inch taper at the breech, but if the rifle used a paper cross patch the bore should not generally have a taper of more than this. A rifle barrel having this shaped bore is correctly known as a "taper bored" barrel, or a "choke bored" rifle. However there is a little difference between a taper bored and a choke bored barrel.

The record of the rifle matches during the years from 1880 to about 1900, show that Horace Warner, Morgan James, H. V. Perry, Wm. V. Lowe, N. S. Brockway and H. M. Pope were the winners in the majority of these matches shot at 40 rods and 200 yards rest. That is, some one of this group of experts made the smallest group, or the group having the shortest "string measure" that were made by anyone during those two decades. Also during this time one or more of these experts made groups at 40 rods, or 200 yards, rest shooting, that are still "world's records" today and have never been equalled or surpassed by any of the modern high power rifles using smokeless powder and metal cased bullets. That is, some of the 10, 11 and 50 shot groups illustrated in chapter VI that were shot by some of these men at 200 yards, or 40 rods, are among the very smallest—

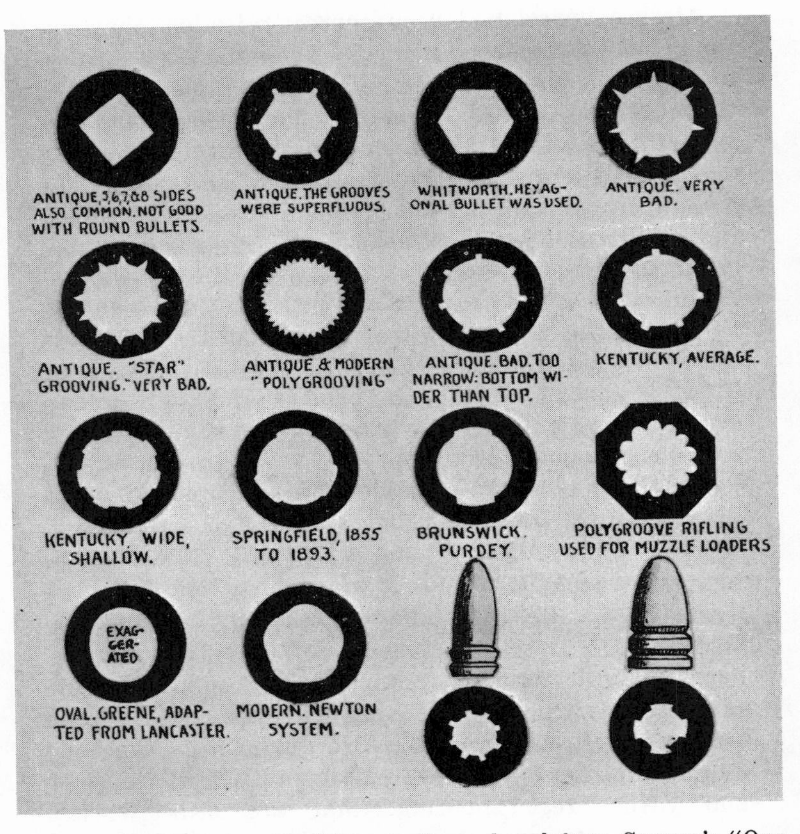

Types of Rifling, part of which are Reproduced from Sawyer's "Our Rifles," by permission of the publishers.

No. 3, Bottom Row, Swiss Rifling and Bullet, Model 1847. No. 4, Austrian Rifling and Bullet, Model 1855.

if not *the smallest*—groups that have ever been made with any rifle, obsolete or most modern.

The rifles used by all these men were either "choke bored" or "taper bored" barrels, which is one of the chief secrets of their superfine accuracy. No one knows who designed the choke bore for the rifle barrel, but Horace Warner was an acknowledged master workman in this matter. Therefore, his method of making the choke bore rifle barrel, as copied from the records of Wm. V. Lowe, is given herewith.

"The barrel after being smooth reamed and rifled is a true cylinder from breech to muzzle, then, with the leading bolt and leading rod, the bore is carefully enlarged about .001 inch from the breech to a point about three inches from the muzzle. Thus the bore from the beginning of the choke—about three inches from the muzzle—to the breech is made a true cylinder about .001 or .0015 inch larger diameter than the three inches at the muzzle. Then lead out this part from the beginning of the choke for a distance of about 1½ inch with a straight taper, leaving the last 1, or 1½ inch of the bore and that of the false muzzle a true cylinder as rifled."

"Stating this another way, a 38 calibre barrel that is, for instance, 30 inches long with a groove diameter of .375 inch, will after being properly leaded and choked, have 27 inches of the barrel from the breech with a diameter of .001 to .002 inch larger than the three inches at the muzzle and the false muzzle; this last 3 inches will be a straight taper from .376 or .377 inch to .375 inch diameter at a point 1½ inches from the muzzle, and from this point to the end of the false muzzle will be a true cylinder .375 inch groove diameter. When the barrel has been correctly choked, a naked bullet—that is a proper fit for the rifle—should *drop freely* of its own weight to the breech as soon as it is pushed past the lower end of the choke.

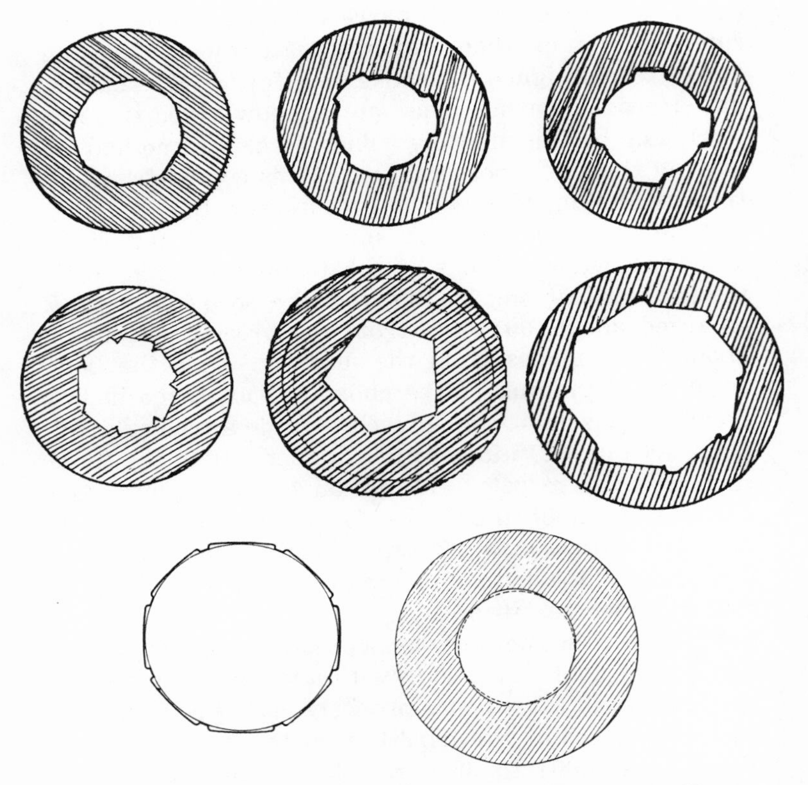

Types of Rifling: Top Row, No. 1, Octagon Bore used by Numerous Old-time Rifle-makers. No. 2, Enfield, English, 3-grooved Model about 1853. Also U. S. Springfield Rifles Models 1873 to 1888. No. 3, 4-Grooved Rifling used by various makers.

Center Row. No. 1, British, Henry type Rifling. No. 2, "5-Square Rifling" used by many Old-time Rifle-makers. No. 3, Major Nuthall's, British, "Rachet Rifling," about 1850. Bottom: No. 1, Pope Rifling. No. 2, Chas. Newton "Parabolic Rifling."

Then take off the false muzzle and work out the front end of the choke, working from the breech end, with the leading bolt until you have made the choke in the barrel enough larger than the diameter of the false muzzle so you can blow a naked bullet out of the end of the barrel with your breath by blowing as hard a puff as possible. The bore of the rifle must be wiped perfectly *clean of all oil and dry* before applying this test."

"When this is done *right,* the naked bullet should *drop freely* from the *end of the choke to the breech* if the rifle is for use with *linen patch.* If the paper patch is to be used, a naked bullet put through the false muzzle to the end of the choke, then it should *drop slowly down the bore without stopping to the breech.* When it works this way, you have the choke *right.* You should *not* be able to blow the bullet in the linen or paper patch out through the choke as there is too much friction, but you *should be able to blow a naked bullet through it when the choke is right.* A rifle using a paper patch requires a little less choke than one using the linen patch."

There are many theories as to why a choke bored barrel increases the accuracy of the rifle, but Warner's theory was that the choke increased the resistance to the bullet, or acted as a restraining force on the bullet just as it left the barrel, thus bringing the axis of the bullet into exact line with that of the bore of the rifle.

Some riflemen confuse the *choke bored* rifle barrel with the *taper bored,* and while there is quite a similarity in these two systems they are *not exactly alike* in the shape of the bore. Each has as its object the improving of the accuracy of a rifle as well as facilitating the loading of the bullet into the barrel. H. M. Pope's rifles have *taper bored* barrels with very slight choke, while Horace Warner's are *choke bored* without taper in the main part of the bore. One thing

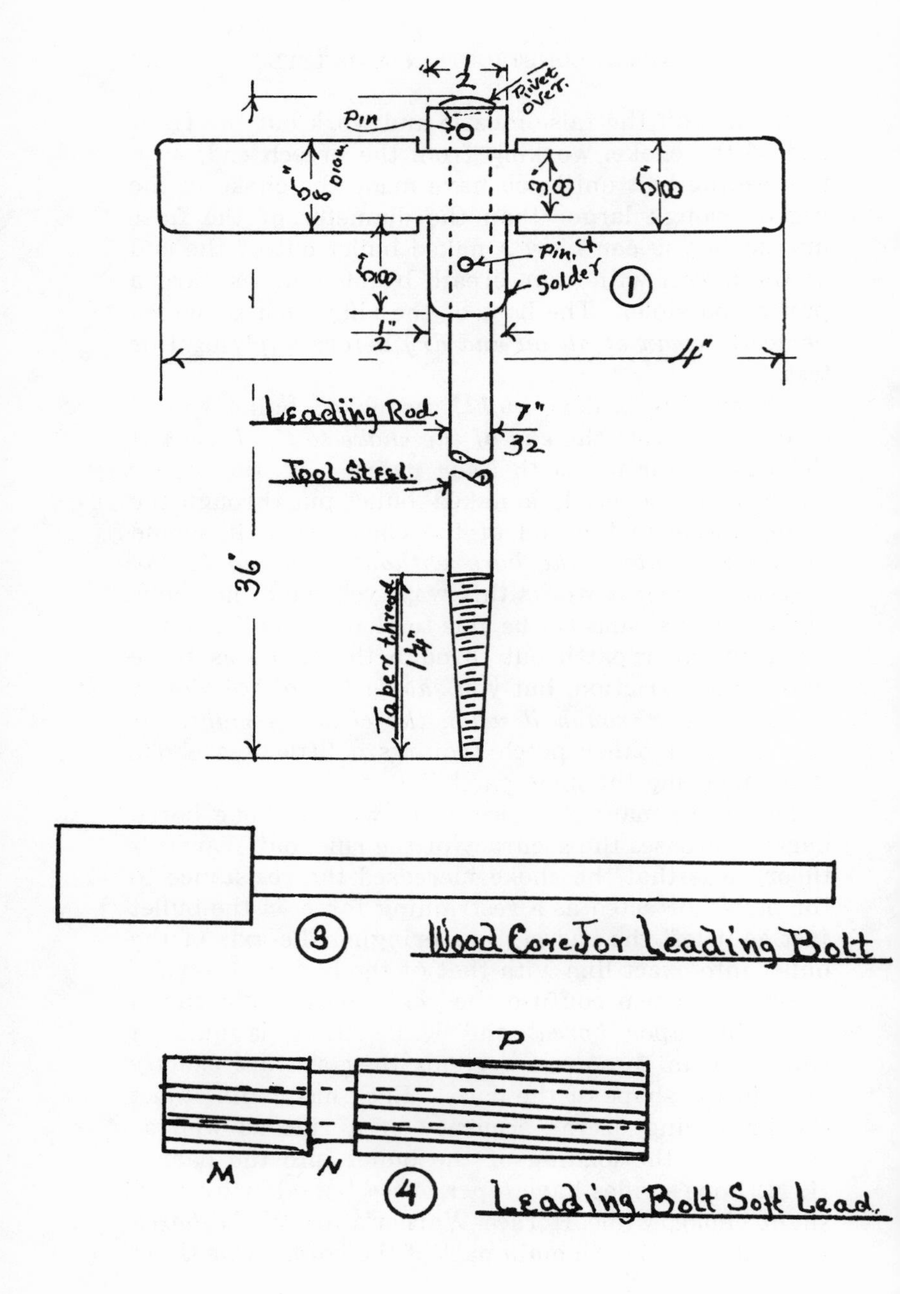
Pin
Rivet over.
Pin.
Solder
1
4"
Leading Rod
7"/32
Tool Steel.
36"
Taper thread
1 1/4"
3
Wood Core for Leading Bolt
P
M
N
4
Leading Bolt Soft Lead.

is certain; that is all the *most accurate shooting* muzzle-loading rifles as well as *super-accurate* breech-loading target rifles are made with a taper bore, or a choke bore, regardless of all theories. As will be seen, the Warner barrels were so made that after a bullet had been loaded through the false muzzle and pushed down the bore about three inches would, by its own weight, *slowly drop down* the bore to the breech; while with the Pope barrel, a bullet *would not* thus drop down the *tapered bore,* but was easily pushed down with the loading rod held between the thumb and fore-finger. Furthermore, we *know* that Harry Pope *never leaded a barrel,* but rifled, or cut, it so carefully and took such a very thin "cut" at each stroke of the rifling cutter that the bore was *perfectly shaped and finished* during the process of rifling. If you want to get Harry Pope good and *mad* and take a chance of getting thrown out of his shop, just ask him if he leads, or emerys, his barrels.

However, all the old makers of muzzle-loading rifles always leaded their barrels and regarded it as absolutely necessary in order to obtain the best accuracy.

After the barrel was rifled, the next very important operation was to "lead" it so as to remove any burrs left by the rifling cutter and to slightly "free" the bore from the breech to a point some three or four inches from the muzzle, thus making it easier to push the bullet down the barrel with the loading rod after it had been inserted some three inches into the bore from the muzzle by the use of the false muzzle and bullet starter in the target rifle, or with the "straight starter" used with the hunting rifle.

The first step in leading the bore was to turn a core of soft wood some four inches long with one end a cylinder about an inch long the same diameter as the bore of the rifle and the rest considerably smaller in diameter. Then all oil and dirt was carefully wiped from the muzzle and the wooden core inserted into the bore leaving about 1/4 inch extending beyond the muzzle. The muzzle was then warmed carefully until it was too hot to hold comfortably in the hand, the barrel was fastened upright in the vise and melted soft lead was poured in until the bore was filled even with the muzzle. After the lead had cooled, this bolt was carefully pushed out, the ends squared and a recess about 1/4 inch wide by 1/8 deep turned about 3/4 inch from the end. The smaller diameter part of the wood core when withdrawn from the lead bolt left a hole about 1/4 inch diameter which fitted the end of the leading rod—which was made of tool steel that would straighten itself if sprung out of true—with a tapering thread cut on the front end and screwed into the leading bolt. After the leading bolt was prepared as above described, it was lightly oiled, a little very fine emery powder was sprinkled on a steel plate and the longer end of the leading bolt was rolled between a file and the steel plate to imbed the emery in the bolt. The bore was then lightly oiled, the leading bolt carefully inserted into the bore fitting the lands and grooves, and very carefully pushed back and forth with the leading rod from the breech nearly to the muzzle.

This was repeated until the bore had been given a straight taper, or enlarged, from a point about three inches from the muzzle to the breech which was about .0015 inch larger than at the muzzle. In use as the leading bolt wore away, the leading rod was screwed farther into the shorter part to take up the wear and keep the bolt tight in the bore, while the recess between the two parts prevented expanding the longer part which did the lapping.

After the barrel had been properly leaded, the breech plug, or "patent breech," was made and fitted to the breech of the barrel by cutting a suitable thread in the rear of the barrel into which the breech plug, or patent breech, was screwed and served to close the rear end of the barrel as well as to provide means for attaching the barrel to the stock. The flint-lock rifles and all the earlier Kentucky type percussion lock rifles were fitted with the breech plug, made of wrought iron or steel and having an extension which formed the upper tang and fitted into the stock. However, about 1840, when the rifles with cast steel barrels using heavier charges of powder with long, heavy bullets came into use, all the better grade rifles were fitted with the so-called "patent breech," which was made of wrought iron, or wrought steel, case-hardened, drilled out somewhat cone-shaped in front and fitted with a thread which screwed into the female thread cut in the rear end of the barrel, thus closing the breech and having a hook which engaged a corresponding recess cut into the steel mounting, or break-off, on the forward end of the stock.

Who invented this so-called "patent breech?" I have never know a man, living or dead, who could answer this question, and all of the books, with just one exception, are silent on this matter. W. W. Greener in his book: *The Gun And Its Development,* states: "The patent breech was invented by Nock (an English gunmaker) in 1787 with the object of getting front ignition of the powder charge. Prior to that date barrels had been made with a plain breech-plug screwed in the end; by hollowing out this plug so that part at least of the powder charge should be behind the touch-hole (or nipple) Nock expected to get better ignition and stronger shooting." During the process of improving the percussion lock rifle, the patent breech was utilized with the nipple placed at the rear end and has proven superior to the old breech-plug.

There are numerous theories regarding the interior shape of the patent breech and the effect of these upon the recoil of the rifle, most of which are mere "theories" without real foundation. It is claimed by some rifle-makers that if the patent breech, or breech-plug, is made with a cylindrical shaped interior the square bottom of this induces additional rearward pressure, or, in other words, increases the recoil of the rifle. Some forty years ago I had a 48 calibre muzzle-loading rifle by G. B. Fogg, of Manchester, N. H., with 30-inch barrel weighing 16 pounds, one of his "turkey," or "match" rifles with false muzzle, bullet starter and other accessories, using a paper cross patched flat point picket bullet weighing about 350 grains backed by 90 to 100 grains of powder. This rifle in spite of its weight had a severe recoil, and a certain rifle-maker told me that by changing the shape of the interior of the patent breech, the recoil could be materially reduced. The patent breech had a slightly tapering cylindrical shape with square bottom about 3/8 inch in diameter originally, which this rifle-maker filled in and reshaped so that it was cone shaped with the bottom about 3/16 inch diameter and rounded instead of square. What was the result? The rifle "kicked" just as hard as before the change in the shape of the patent breech, and the only way in which I was able to reduce the recoil was by using a lighter weight bullet with 75 to 80 grains of powder. This experience convinced me that the interior shape of the patent breech, or breech-plug, has no real effect on the recoil of a rifle.

I believe that the interior shape of the breech plug, or patent breech, certainly affects the ignition of the powder charge and the accuracy of the rifle, but I do NOT believe it has any effect on the recoil.

Some rifle-makers fashioned their patent breech with a projecting lug of rectangular shape having a small hole horizontally, or vertically, through it which fitted a recess cut into the steel mounting of the stock, or break-off, and was held to the stock by a hardened steel, taper pin instead of the hook. N. Lewis, Horace Warner, H. V. Perry, N. S. Brockway, W. Billinghurst and the majority of the best rifle-makers used this taper steel pin method of attaching the barrel to the stock by means of the patent breech instead of using the breech plug with upper tang; therefore, they must have considered this the better method. Edwin Wesson employed still another method of connecting the barrel to the front mounting of the stock, or "break-off." In his rifles a square-headed machine bolt was threaded through the bottom of the break-off into the hook of the patent breech securing the barrel to the stock instead of using the taper steel pin for that purpose. By loosening this bolt with a small spanner, much like the old-fashioned clock key furnished with each rifle, the barrel of the Edwin Wesson rifles were easily detached from the break-off and stock. It has always seemed strange to me that other rifle-makers did not employ the Edwin Wesson method of attaching the barrel and stock as it was so much more symmetrical, fully as strong as the taper steel pin method of attaching as well as presenting a more pleasing appearance to the eye, as shown by illustrations herewith.

If the rifle was fitted with the old breech-plug, the tube, or nipple, was threaded into the top, side or bottom of the barrel just in front of the forward end of the breech-plug. Certain rifle-makers always preferred to fit the tube into a small steel "drum" which was threaded into the right-hand side of the barrel so placed that the hammer would strike the cap, while others fitted the tube to the top a little to the right-hand side of the center of the barrel so as not to interfere with the sighting line, and still others who favored the bottom, or "under-striker" method, fitted the nipple into the under part of the barrel in such a

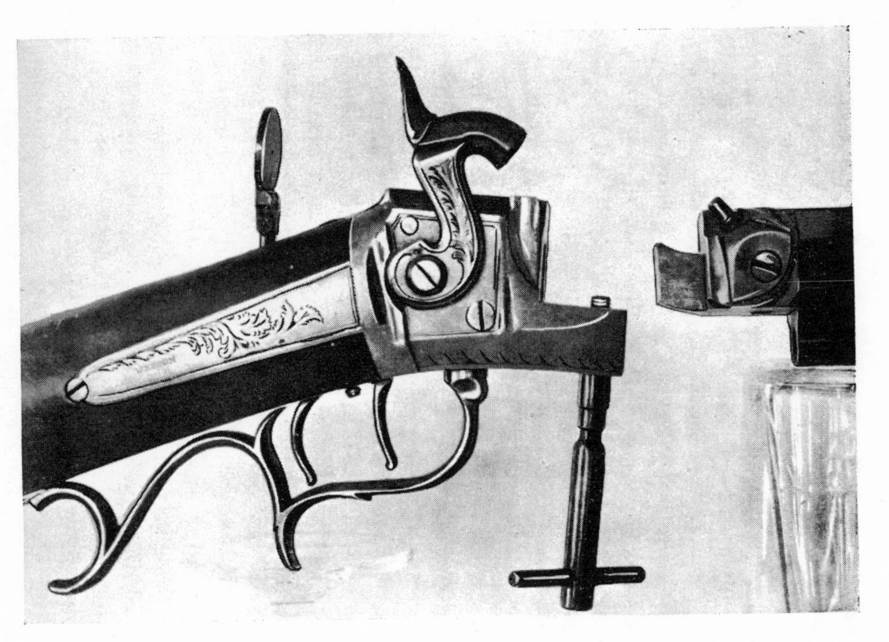

Edwin Wesson Rifle. Showing the Method of Attaching the Patent Breech to the Break-Off.

position that the hammer would fall onto the cap. Some rifle-makers favored the "side-striker" and fitted the nipple horizontally into the right-hand side of the barrel where it lined up with the side hammer. Thus there were in use at least four different methods of fitting the tube, or nipple, to the barrel in which the breech-plug was used. When the rifle was fitted with the patent breech, the tube was threaded into a more or less ornamentally shaped lump projecting from the right-hand side and connected with the powder chamber in the rear end of the patent breech. This gave the breech of the rifle a far more symmetrical and pleasing appearance than the other methods of attaching the tube, or nipple, and was generally considered as giving better ignition, or more "sure-fire." I have spent many hours listening to the arguments between the old-time riflemen regarding the better method of attaching the nipple so as to give the very best ignition when the rifle was fired and this is still an unsettled question today. One maker insists that the nipple in the bottom of the barrel with the "under-striker" type of hammer is absolutely the "surest-fire" and the best and advances numerous claims to prove that he is right in this matter; while another equally noted rifle-maker insists that the correct place for the nipple is in the right-hand side of the barrel, but the third noted maker stubbornly claims that the *only correct place* for the nipple is a little to the right-hand of the center line in the top of the barrel.

The purpose of the nipple in the rifle is to insure the ignition of the powder charge from the percussion cap on this nipple, and if the rifle be properly loaded with the correct size grain of powder, it matters not at all whether the nipple be placed in the bottom, side or top of the barrel. My personal opinion is that the very *worst place* for the nipple is in the bottom of the barrel, since in off-hand shooting if the left hand is placed well back near the breech, the fire from the cap is sure to burn the wrist when the rifle is fired. Or in the case of the hunting rifle, the cap may possibly fall off unnoticed when the hammer is carried in the half-cock notch and result in the loss of game because of the miss-fire of the rifle on account of the absence of the cap, which would have been promptly noticed had the nipple been on the side or top of the barrel. So far as can be learned, no Government has ever approved a percussion lock arm for its army that has the nipple in any place except slightly to the right of the center of the top of the barrel, or set obliquely sloping to the rear in the right-hand side of the barrel: which would indicate that these two are the correct positions of the nipple for sure-fire ignition and most practical use of the rifle.

The best nipples, or tubes, are of English make, lined with platinum which was not affected by the corrosive percussion caps of the early days, consequently were more expensive than the American made ones, but were far more durable. I have a record showing that in 1882, I paid $1.75 for an English made, platinum lined nipple for my Edwin Wesson muzzle-loader that after five years continuous use was as good as new, while another muzzle-loader owned by a friend required a new American made nipple every two or three months, at a cost of 50c to 75c. Nipples were made in three forms of interior shape, known as the "regular or taper bored," "reverse bored," and the "double reverse, or double taper bored." The first type was bored with the hole small at the top tapering larger at the bottom; the second had the hole large at the top and tapering smaller at the bottom; the third type had the hole large at the top tapering to small size in the middle of the nipple then tapering larger at the bottom. Each form of nipple had, of course, its enthusiastic advocates who had numerous reasons to "prove" that their preferred type was the best, gave the better ignition, etc. However, it has always appeared to me that the reverse bored nipple—that with the hole larger at top and tapering smaller at the bottom—was the better type, gave the better ignition and in case of mis-fire the wider opening at top allows one to prick grains of powder into it to better advantage than with the regular bored nipples having the smaller opening at top. I never could see any advantage in the double taper bored type of nipple.

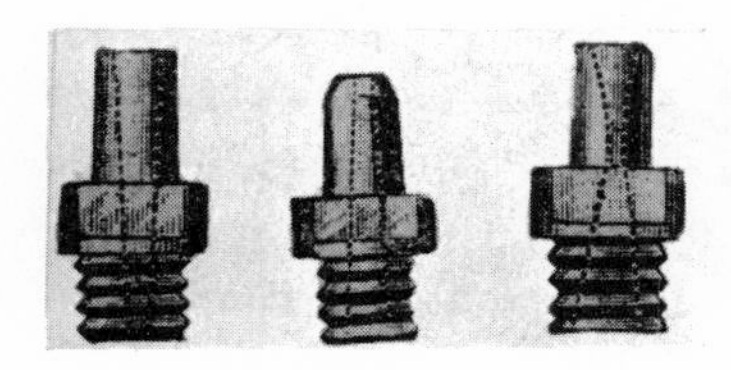

Early in the 1880's in their efforts to improve the long range accuracy of their rifles Horace Warner, Wm. V. Lowe, and N. S. Brockway decided that better ignition of the powder through the medium of a stronger flame would improve the accuracy. Accordingly these makers devised a method of replacing the ordinary nipple with a steel fitting and cap, or top, with a firing-pin therein which used a shot-gun primer, or large sized rifle cartridge primer, in place of the percussion cap and gave a stronger flame resulting in much improved ignition of the powder charge, which, in turn, considerably increased the accuracy of their rifles at all ranges. Illustrations are shown herewith of the method employed by Wm. V. Lowe and N. S. Brockway in using the primer instead of the percussion cap for ignition of the Horace Warner, the Warner & Lowe and N. S. Brockway muzzle-loading rifles.

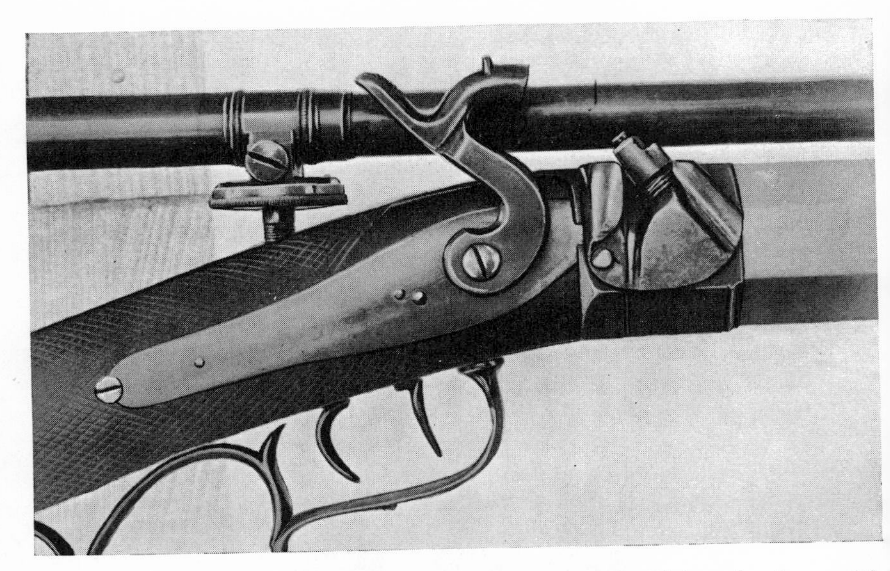

Brockway Rifle with Primer Ignition. Primer and Firing-pin in positic ready to shoot.

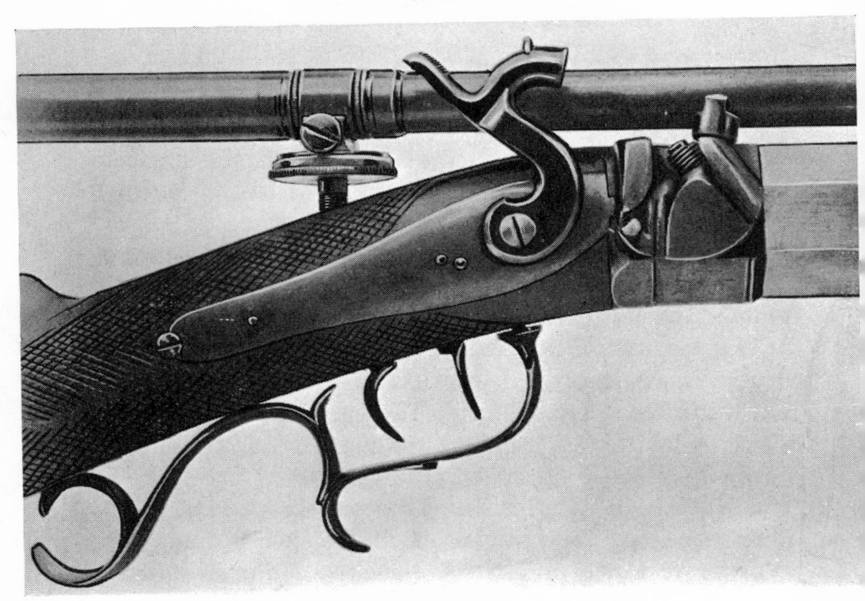

Brockway Rifle with Primer Ignition, showing Primer in place and Firing-Pin Cap off.

This well illustrates the difference of opinion on the subject of ignition as applied to rifles. In *The Improved American Rifle,* by Chapman, published in 1848, he advised the use of the French "G. D." caps for the finest accuracy with the rifle since these gave *weak ignition,* and quoting his words: "It is obvious that the weaker the detonating charge of the cap be, the better, provided it have heat enough to ignite the powder at the bottom of the cone, and on this account alone I use the French G. D. caps split and ribbed, in preference to the English sporting caps." "They can be purchased in New York at about fifty cents a thousand, and when genuine are better adapted for fine target practice than any other with which I am acquainted."

Making the stock of the desired wood, making and fitting the mountings for it, fitting the lock and trigger into the stock, and accurately and carefully fitting the stock to the barrel was the next operation in completing the rifle, all of which required considerable time and skill. The early "Kentucky rifles," the great majority of which were made in Pennsylvania—not Kentucky—were generally stocked to the muzzle, "full-stocked," with tiger-flame maple, plenty of which of the finest grain was to be found in the near-by forests, and a nice grained, well finished, tiger-flame maple stock has a certain rich, velvety appearance and feel that is not equalled by any other kind of wood. But this wood went out of "fashion" for rifle stocks by most makers before 1840 and after about that date the great majority of rifles were stocked with American grown black walnut varying from plain straight grain to "stump walnut" or "crotch walnut" which had beautiful "figure," or fern-like grain, that is extremely beautiful in a stock. Also, some makers often stocked their rifles with wood from the root just above the ground, or from the crotch, of an apple tree.

The outer wood of the apple tree is nearly white when cut, but the wood near the heart is a rich reddish-brown, very hard and dense with very fine grain, or figure, and is one of the most durable woods known. However, it is difficult to obtain in pieces suitable for stocks, requires several years of seasoning and is difficult to season without cracking or checking. One of the most beautiful rifle stocks I have ever seen was made from crotch apple wood with remarkable fern-like figure on both sides, by Mr. J. E. Gage, an old-time rifle-maker and master workman of Concord, New Hampshire. Many of you "gun bugs" would trade your last shirt for a rifle stock having such beautiful grain and figure as this one, which surpassed in beauty any Circassian Walnut stock that I have ever seen—and I have seen many of the finest, presentation grades of these.

Sometimes the old-time rifle-maker stocked a rifle with cherry, from the heart of the tree which is quite hard, dense and strong and often has nice grain, but the reddish color of this wood was not well liked by the majority of riflemen. Occasionally we find muzzle-loading rifles with stocks made from our American beech which is a heavy, tough, strong wood, but rather coarse grained ranging in color from almost white to light brown. Once the grain is filled it takes a very smooth and fine polish, but it has never been popular for stocks. Regardless of the kind of wood used for the stock of the muzzle-loading rifle, practically all makers finished them with raw or boiled linseed oil applied and thoroughly rubbed in much the same as we find in our high grade custom rifle stocks today. Rarely did the old-time makers finish their stocks with varnish, but occasionally we find a target rifle with a stock that has a varnish finish rubbed down to a piano polish.

Some of the rifle-makers made their own locks,

while others bought them from large firms in the cities who carried in stock various grades and makes for sale to rifle-makers. Two principal types of percussion locks were in general use; the back action and the bar action, and each rifle-maker, of course, had a preference. Some claimed that the bar action was the superior while others preferred the back action. It is probable that one form of these locks was equally as good as the other when correctly and skillfully made, and the method of stocking the arm determined the type of lock to be used. Rifles that were stocked after the method of N. S. Brockway, Edwin Wesson and some of the N. Lewis arms permitted the use of a back action lock only, since there was no wood in front of the break-off to which a lock could be attached, while rifles with full length, or half length, stocks with a forearm afforded a place for attaching a bar action lock if the customer, or the maker, preferred that type.

Of course, with the under-striker, or side-striker, type of rifle, the maker of such arms always made his own lock, and there was a great variety of these in regard to their construction. Possibly the simplest locks ever devised—those having the fewest and strongest parts—were the under-striker type where the main-spring formed the trigger guard as W. Billinghurst and Horace Warner made these. The side-striker locks were also very simple in construction and used very few and strong parts that were easy to make and very durable. The trigger and sear was usually made by the maker of the rifle since these parts were easy and simple to make, especially the single trigger, or single set, but large firms in the cities who carried rifle-makers' supplies imported different kinds and makes of triggers and sears, mostly of English or Austrian make, which were preferred by some rifle-makers. The double set triggers found on many of these old muzzle-loading target rifles were of splendid workmanship, the parts simple, strong and durable, and always functioned properly (which cannot truthfully be stated of the present double set trigger) ; those made by Billinghurst, Warner, Brockway, Morgan James, H. V. Perry and others were of simple construction, very durable, could be set for a very light touch if desired, or used without being set, gave a pull of any desired weight for which it had been adjusted, and rarely gave trouble after long years of use. In my gun-room now is a James & Ferris muzzle-loading rifle made in the early 1870's, fitted with one of these fine single set triggers, which after all these years of use works perfectly under all conditions either as a three-pound pull, or with medium or very light set as desired. These are far superior to any of this type made in America today, and it is to be regretted that our great arms manufacturing companies today do not furnish such excellent single set triggers. This appears to have become one of the "lost arts" in rifle-making in this country at present, although the German, Swiss, French and English makers of high grade rifles still equip their arms with these splendid durable single set triggers when so ordered.

Sights of various kinds were made and affixed to the rifle during the process of completing the arm, from the simplest knife-blade type front and open rear sight on the barrel, to the very fine shaded "pin-head" and the tang "peep sight" on the small of the stock. I shall discuss them in a separate chapter.

Browning or blueing the barrel is an operation that was done at various stages in the process of completing the rifle as hardly any two of the old makers did this work at the same stage. With rifles stocked after the method of Brockway, Edwin Wesson, and some others, the barrel was blued, or browned, after the leading operation, the fitting of the patent breech and before the sights had been installed. Other makers who made their stock with a forearm, browned or blued the barrel after the rifle had been fully completed and tested on the range, if the accuracy was satisfactory. If the accuracy was not satisfactory, the barrel could be "worked over" and made to shoot accurately without fear of scratching or marring the browning, while if the barrel could not be made to give the desired accuracy at the target; "We just threw the cussed thing in the scrap heap and made a new one," as one old maker told me, thus saving the labor of browning a useless barrel. Many of the muzzle-loading rifles made before about 1840 have barrels that were left bright with no attempt at any kind of browning, while others were browned by some of the simple, old-time processes then used. Probably the oldest method of browning the barrel was by rusting the outside by repeated applications of very strong vinegar, rubbing this down with a wire brush, repeating this process until the desired brown was obtained and then oiling the barrel and letting it stand a few days before using. A quicker and better method was by applying "aqua fortis" or full strength nitric acid to the outside of the barrel, letting it stand until rusted, rubbing it down with the wire brush, repeating this a number of times and then oiling to stop further rusting.

Some of the makers finished their barrels with a most beautiful butternut brown which is very pleasing to the eye and appears to have been more durable than most of our present day blueing. In chapter XI will be found the chemical formula that Reuben Harwood, who wrote under the pen name of "Iron Ramrod," used to produce this beautiful brown finish on rifle barrels.

Personally, I am very fond of the rich, velvety, butternut brown finish on target rifle barrels that were made by James & Ferris, Schoyen, and some others; to my way of thinking this harmonizes with the walnut stock and makes a nicer appearing rifle than one with the blued barrel on the rifles today. Also, it is more durable than the majority of our blued barrels. The James & Ferris rifle before mentioned, owned by my friend Frank K. Lucas, has been in use for about seventy years and the barrel still has this butternut brown finish looking as if the rifle had been made within the past few years. My George C. Schoyen 25-21 calibre breech-loading rifle with its browned barrel was made more than thirty years ago, has passed through the hands of three former owners, and after all these years that beautiful brown polish is in far finer condition than the blued barrels on several of my custom made rifles, that have not yet seen five years of use.

While the great majority of the muzzle-loading percussion lock rifles were used with the linen, bed-ticking, or other kinds of cloth, or various types of paper patches, about 1880, certain rifle-makers commenced making their muzzle-loaders for use with a cannelured, or grooved, lubricated bullet and thus eliminated the use of the patch. Of course, it is possible that the lubricated grooved bullet in the muzzle-loading rifle, without any patch, may have been tried out many years before that date, but I have failed to find any earlier record of this.

John Meunier, of Milwaukee, Wisconsin, was an extraordinarily fine workman and rifle-maker and made many fine muzzle-loading percussion lock rifles for use with a lubricated grooved bullet of practically the same shape as those that were later used in the fine single shot breech-loading target rifles. He made a remarkably fine rifle of this type that was awarded one of the highest prizes at the Centennial Exposition in 1876, which was later purchased by Mr. A. O. Niedner and owned by him when he lived in Malden, Massachusetts. This rifle was *wonderful workmaship,* it and all the accessories were *marvelously engraved*—the very finest I have ever seen on any muzzle-loading rifle—and Mr. Niedner claimed that it gave especially fine accuracy at 200 yards. One of the *very finest* muzzle-loaders that Dr. P. A. Matteson, of Bennington, Vermont, owned is the John Meunier 38 calibre rifle illustrated in chapter VII. This rifle also uses a grooved lubricated bullet weighing 330 grains, without any patch, is very accurate and of *very fine workmanship*—probably the very finest of all the fine muzzle-loading rifles that the doctor has owned.

As before stated George Schalk, sometime in 1884, made a 33 calibre muzzle-loading rifle for Wm. Hayes which proved to be the *most accurate* shooting rifle that this expert marksman ever used. This rifle had a 30-inch barrel with false muzzle, double set trigger, aperture front sight, rear peep sight and weighed 16 pounds. The 33 calibre grooved bullet weighed 162 grains, was 3/4 inch long and was used with 40 grains of Hazzard's F. F. g. powder. Mr. Hayes stated that after firing several hundred shots from this rifle without cleaning between shots, the last shot was as accurate as the first, and he was always one of the winners, or high score men, in the German "Schutzenfest" and "Bundesfest" matches of those days—the late 1880's and early 1890's.

During the past forty years or more, as the majority of riflemen know, H. M. Pope has made his breech-muzzle-loading rifles for use with the grooved lubricated lead bullet, used without patch and without cleaning between shots, which for several hundred consecutive shots will give as fine accuracy with the last shot as with the first. The Pope rifle is used as a muzzle-loader similar to the cap-lock rifles when so desired, by inserting the primed case into the chamber, closing the breech-block and loading the powder, followed by the lubricated bullet, from the muzzle in *exactly the same way* as with the cap-lock muzzle-loader. After firing, the case is de-capped, re-primed and again loaded as explained; after a day's shooting there are no dirty cases to wash, the bore is not wiped or cleaned between shots, thus saving this labor, as the process of loading the flat base bullet through the false muzzle and seating it with the loading rod at the muzzle of the case containing the powder, effectually cleans the bore of the rifle each time and does this *exactly alike each time.* Managed in this way, the Pope rifle will give finer accuracy for a long series of shots than can be obtained with the cap-lock, muzzle-loading rifle and saves the trouble of cutting and using the patch as well as all the labor of cleaning after each shot.

Furthermore, the Pope breech-muzzle-loading rifle and the Schalk and Meunier muzzle-loading rifles that use the lubricated bullet, without any patch, retain their *gilt-edge accuracy* for many years of constant use. Some of these rifles after 20,000 to 30,000 shots have been fired with them are as accurate as when new since there is no patch to wear out the bore. The linen, cloth or paper patch used with the other types of muzzle-loading rifles is the chief cause of the wearing out, or "shooting out," of the bore after a comparatively few years' use, according to the opinion of many experienced, expert rifle-makers and marksmen.

CHAPTER II

IRON SIGHTS AND TELESCOPIC SIGHTS

The question of what is the *best* kind, or type, of sights for the rifle is as old as the rifle itself. No one has ever invented, or designed, a front sight or a rear sight that *exactly suited every rifleman* for every purpose, and doubtless this is an impossibility, since during the centuries in which the rifle has been in use, practically every conceivable form of both front and rear sights have been thoroughly tested. However, the pioneer hunter-riflemen during the years preceding and during the Revolutionary War apparently were easier satisfied in this respect, or had much better eye-sight, than the generations of riflemen who have succeeded them. As all riflemen know, Daniel Boone and contemporary pioneers and Indian fighters using the so-called Kentucky flint-lock rifles, were actually very skillful marksmen even though their rifles were equipped with the simplest kind of "knife-blade" type front sights, always set very low on the long octagon barrel, and usually a very low flat-topped, V notched rear sight set into the rear of the barrel at varying distances from the break-off.

Of course, the ranges at which these pioneers usually shot game or Indians was generally well under 100 yards, but occasionally they killed deer at 40 rods or more, and we have authentic records of their having killed or disabled individual Indians at even longer ranges. It must be remembered that these pioneers learned to shoot the rifle when they were young boys, grew into manhood with the rifle almost constantly in their hands, were dependent on it for the larger part of their daily food, and must be at all times prepared to defend the lives of their families and themselves

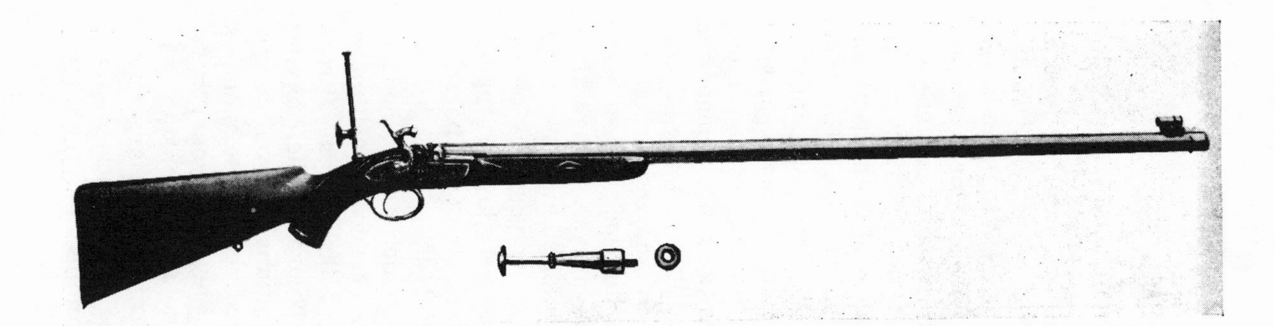

J. Rigby, Muzzle-Loading "Long Range Rifle," 45 calibre, used by the Irish Rifle Teams in the International Rifle Matches of 1874, 1875 and 1876, at the "Creedmoor Range," Long Island.

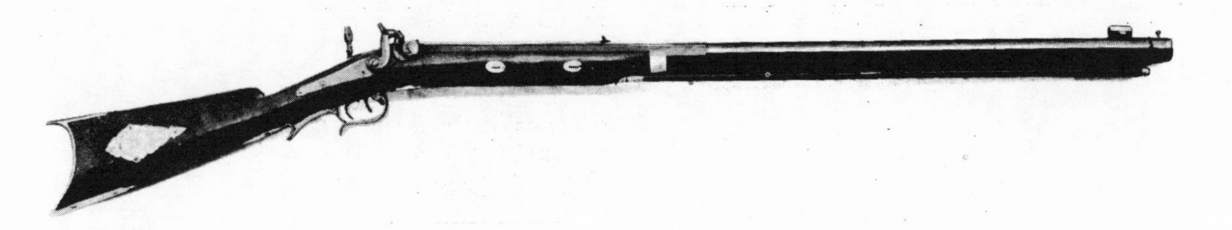

Edwin Wesson Muzzle-Loading Target Rifle, from Floyd R. Butler's Collection. My Target Rifle for 40 rods Shooting in 1881 was like this.

against hostile Indians. The pioneer who did not early become a skillful marksman with the rifle was generally short-lived, or a politician who let others do the fighting necessary to establish and defend the settlements—and even that type was scarce in those times.

However, after the percussion, cap-lock rifle came into general use—along about 1830—the average range of the rifle was increased through the medium of better ignition afforded by the percussion cap and the improvements in gunpowder, which, in turn, made it possible to do accurate shooting with the rifle at considerably longer ranges than formerly, and thus the necessity for better sights became apparent. Practically all the flint-lock and percussion-lock hunting rifles that had been in use by the pioneer hunter-riflemen up to about 1840, were fitted with the simple open front and rear sights mentioned. The earliest attempt that I have found to improve these sights was on a Pennsylvania made rifle by John Henry, bearing the date of 1835, which had a low silver bead front sight, about 1/16 inch diameter, with a very dark blue steel stem and a two-leaf rear sight with U shaped notches having one leaf stamped "10" and the other higher one marked "20." Evidently this rifle was made for a man who had adopted the English idea of having a rear sight which provided correct adjustment for shooting at 10 rods with the lower leaf and 20 rods with the higher one.

Previous to about 1840, very few strictly target rifles had been made in this country as the demand for rifles up to that time had been for practical "all around" arms chiefly for use in hunting or war, and for this purpose the plain open sights appears to have been generally satisfactory. After about this date the rifle having been further improved, further improvements made in the manufacture of gunpowder, the flat point "picket," or "sugar-loaf," bullet with considerably increased range in general use instead of the old round ball, we find various improved forms of front and rear sights on the rifles by the best makers. The so-called "California buck-horn" rear sight with its various modifications came into use on hunting rifles, and hunting and target rifles, during this decade. After about 1840 in this country we had five different kinds, or types, of rifles in more or less general use which I shall classify as: First, Hunting Rifles; Second, Army Rifles; Third, Hunting and Target Rifles; Fourth, Target Rifles; Fifth, Machine Rest Rifles.

The hunting rifles, designed strictly for that purpose, were of various "gauges," or calibres, using the round ball or the flat end picket with cloth patch, generally had long octagon barrel with the various open sights mentioned, and weighed from about 8 to 14 pounds. The Army rifles, designed for war purposes, were of large calibre—50 to 65—with plain modified "barley-corn" front sight and an open rear sight with several leaves providing elevation for ranges up to 500 or 600 yards, had round barrels, stocked nearly to the muzzle, and those for the infantry were provided with triangular, or sabre, bayonet. All Army rifles were well known to be much inferior in accuracy to all other classes of rifles at that time.

The hunting and target rifles by the various makers, intended for the use their title denotes, had the octagon barrel turned cylindrically at the muzzle for about one inch to fit the guide bullet starter which was used in loading the rifle when used for target work, were especially rifled for the short "picket," or sugar-loaf, bullet with cloth patch, weighed from about 9 to 14 pounds, and had a longer accuracy range than the hunting rifles as well as being more accurate. These were also provided with a "straight starter," much lighter than the other, for use when hunting with these rifles and had various combinations of sights.

The target rifles were designed by the makers strictly for the *finest accuracy* in target shooting at ranges of 40 to 100 rods, the barrels were usually full octagon, fitted with the false muzzle, guide bullet starter, rifled especially for the long cylindrical, or cylindro-conoidal, bullet using the oiled linen patch, the oiled paper cross patch, or the two-strip, or three-strip, oiled paper patches according to the preference of the maker or the customer's order. They had fine double set, or single set, trigger as ordered, weighed from about 10 to 20 pounds, and were used for off-hand or bench rest shooting according to the weight of the rifle or its design, and were fitted with various types of sights especially for fine target shooting, or the telescope sight. The machine rest rifles had long, heavy octagon barrels often 2½ inches or more across the flats, had the false muzzle, guide bullet starter, fine double, or single, set trigger, and weighed from 25 to 50 or even 60 pounds. They were of large bore—from 45 to 56 calibre—having the barrel especially rifled, often with the gain twist, to give the *very finest accuracy* with the long cylindrical, or cylindro-conoidal, bullet which was generally cast in two parts and swaged together. The patch was of oiled linen, the oiled paper cross patch, the two-strip oiled paper, or three-strip oiled paper patch, while the powder charge was from 100 to 150 grains of black powder. Such rifles were generally stocked without a fore-arm, sometimes without any stock but simply a large knob to be held in the hand, were shot from machine rests of various types, used special sights or the telescope sight, and were intended solely to give the *maximum possible accuracy* at ranges of 40 to 200 rods.

Having described on the preceding pages the sights

in general use on the hunting and army rifles, I shall give a detailed description of those then usually found on the other three classes of rifles.

The hunting and target rifles in calibres from 28 to 45 as made by Wm. Billinghurst, N. Lewis, James and Ferris, Edwin Wesson, D. H. Hillard, and others, were very popular in New York and New England states, from about 1840 until many years after the Civil War, among men who wanted a rifle suitable for killing any game found in this section as well as for target shooting at 40 to 60 rods, and for "turkey shoots" which were then popular. These were fitted with the usual shaded pin-head front, an open V notch rear sight, and a peep sight with folding disc top screwing into the upper tang of the arm, thus making them as near an "all around" rifle as possible. Occasionally we find them fitted with a plain knife-blade, or low, small silver bead front sight, instead of the shaded pin-head, or interchangeable with it when this rifle was used for hunting, while the open rear sight was adjustable for different ranges by means of the small steel "steps" now in general use with our sights of this kind. Sometimes we find these rifles with very peculiar, or "freak," types of open rear sights, too numerous to mention here, which might have been home-made by the owner of the rifle, or a kind that the maker of the arm considered especially good.

A rifle of this type of 36 calibre that I once owned, made by G. B. Fogg of Manchester, New Hampshire, before the Civil War, had a rear sight leaf of peculiar shape that always appeared especially practical to me. The general design of this was quite like the full California buck-horn sight, except that the opening in the sight leaf was shaped like the "spade" on playing cards, having a narrow opening, about 1/8 inch, at the top of the leaf. The front sight was a small silver bead with a black steel stem standing about 5/16 inch above the octagon barrel, which, when shooting at 110 yards, was held so that the top of the bead was just above the square corners of the bottom notch in the opening, and when shooting at 220 yards the bead was held just above the top of this spade-shaped opening. Thus when shooting at these two ranges one always knew just where to hold the bead in relation to the rear sight opening in order to land the bullet in the desired spot. Of course, this is but a modification of the California buck-horn rear sight, but quite likely this sight was made by Mr. Fogg before the latter was in use in the eastern part of this country. A sketch herewith illustrates this rear sight leaf.

There was quite a variety of folding disc top peep sights in use on rifles of this kind, each maker having a design that he, personally, considered the best. However, they were all made so as to permit folding the disc top down toward the muzzle, to allow the unobstructed use of the open rear sight in connection with the front sight when using the rifle for hunting purposes. Certain makers instead of threading the peep sight through the upper tang of the stock, and possibly weakening that, attached it to the breach of the barrel with small screws let into it the long end of an L shaped piece of steel with the other vertical end extending some four inches back of the break-off, having a small peep hole in the center of it, through which aim was taken when using the rifle for target work. Adjustments for elevation were made by a small screw threaded through the long part of this sight and bearing on the barrel, which was turned in with a screw-driver to raise the elevation, or by the use of the steel "step-piece," now used in open rear sights. N. Lewis obtained the elevations with this form of peep sight by attaching with a hinge joint on the under side of the rear end a small wedge-shaped steel brace with the bottom end fitting into small notches filed in the upper tang. By pushing forward on this brace so as to engage another notch, the peep plate was elevated, or lowered by placing the bottom of the brace in another notch nearer the butt. When the rifle was used for hunting, these sights were removed by unscrewing the attaching screws, leaving the small of the stock and rear of the barrel free of any obstructions. I have never yet seen one of these hunting and target rifles that was originally fitted with a telescope sight, because in those times the hunting telescope had not been invented, or at least had not come into use in this country.

About 1840, in the eastern part of the United States, there were quite a number of men who were interested in target shooting with the rifle at ranges of 40 to 100 rods, which created a demand for rifles with better sights that would shoot more accurately at these longer ranges. No person who is well informed would be so unwise as to state positively that the shaded pin-head, or globe, front sight was *never used* before about 1840, but among the many hundreds of flint-lock and percussion-lock rifles examined by me, I have never found one that was originally fitted with this type of front sight, while after that date we find practically all the target rifles, and hunting and target rifles, with this sight. The makers of the heavy, octagon barrel target rifles of those days fitted them with a very small bead, or pin-head, front sight, the making of which is almost one of the "lost arts" today. In making this a bead somewhat smaller than the head of a pin is filed on a piece of steel wire with the stalk left as small and thin as possible, standing up from the base about ¼ inch, shaded by a tube, or thimble, about ⅜ inch diameter by one inch long.

This pin-head and shade are attached to a beveled steel base which fits a dovetail slot across the barrel about 1½ inches from the muzzle, having a small pointer filed on the front end of the shade at the bottom to serve as an index and show how much the front sight has been moved from the center of the barrel when adjusting for windage. The top octagon flat of the barrel in front of the sight is cut with longitudinal lines 1/32 inch apart on each side of a zero mark in the center of the barrel, thus enabling the marksman to know, and record if desired, just how many divisions from either side of the zero the sight has been moved to counteract for the deviation of the bullet by the wind, in its flight to the target.

It is really surprising that anyone could file so perfectly by hand these extremely small and thin pin-head front sights, usually not over 1/32 inch in diameter, but we know that they were so made. When I inquired about making these extremely fine pin-head front sights from Norman S. Brockway, he told me; "I did not always make the very fine pin-heads out of steel or iron, but made them from a pig's bristle." He further explained that a small bristle from a hog or pig may be cut off and one end slightly burned with a red-hot iron which will cause a very small bead to form—much smaller than anyone can file out of steel with the aid of a magnifying glass—which was then set into a soft pine plug in the sight base, and secured with shellac or waterproof cement. Other makers years ago told me the same thing, which must have been one of their "trade secrets" used in making the pin-head front sights found on many of the fine old target rifles.

The target rifle almost never had an open rear sight, but instead a peep sight was threaded into the upper tang just back of the break-off. This was made of steel with a flattened circular top having a small hole in the exact center, countersunk on each side to take away reflections of light, with the stem, or stalk, about 1/4 inch diameter by 2 1/2 or 3 inches long, cut with threads of 64, 80 or 100 turns to the inch according to the maker's practice or the customer's order. Please remember that there was no such thing as standardization in the making of any part of the rifle in those days; each rifle-maker had his own ideas in regard to the best way of making every part of his rifle, and he always followed his own design unless the customer specifically ordered it otherwise. Therefore, three fine target rifles, each by a noted maker, would probably have the stem of the peep sight cut with different threads, and no two having the same number of turns to the inch. Some makers slightly flatted one side of the peep sight stem so that the owner of the rifle could make thereon, with a knife or file, marks indicating the correct adjustment for different ranges, which was made by screwing the peep up or down through the female thread cut in the upper tang.

Many of these sights were made with a short steel tube, or shade, brazed to the back side of the peep disc to prevent reflections of light when aiming, but the objection to these was that the rifleman was obliged to make full turns of the sight stem when adjusting for elevation instead of half turns which could be made when the peep disc was without the shade. In order to compensate for this, the stem of the peep sight with shade must be cut with finer threads, having a greater number of turns to the inch, than those without the shade. Some makers of target rifles made the top of the peep sight stem in the form of a hollow cylinder about 3/8 inch long by 5/8 inch diameter, into which was fitted a small steel shade some two or three inches long, with one end closed by a steel disc having a small peep hole brazed inside this shade and the rear of the shade of disc shape about 1 1/2 inches in diameter, somewhat concaved towards the rear, which is held in place in the peep sight stem by a small set screw in the top. Thus arranged, the rifleman could make half turns of the sight stem, loosen the set screw, remove the shade and replace it so that the large disc end was towards the rear; then tightening the set screw secured all in proper place for shooting. The illustration of the J. Meunier and F. Wassmann's target rifles show this type of rear peep sight, which is an improvement over the thin, flat disc with peep hole having no shade.

Another type of target rifle, once very popular in the Kentucky-Tennessee-Carolina section of the country and now again coming into favor, is the extremely long octagon barreled rifle with plain open front and V notched rear sights having very long sheet-metal shades held friction tight over both front and rear sights in order to improve the definition of the sights and target. Some of these rifles have barrels from 48 to 60 inches long, usually full stocked with tiger-flame maple, and often having a rectangular piece of the stock some six or eight inches long by about two inches thick projecting from the under side of the muzzle end some six inches back of it for the purpose of affording a muzzle-rest for the rifle in target shooting. These arms were of large bore, from about 52 to 22 round balls to the pound, or about .453 to .609 inch diameter, using a patch of cotton sheeting or bed-ticking generally moistened with saliva before loading. The muzzle of these rifles is generally slightly enlarged or beveled for a fraction of an inch to facilitate starting the ball into the bore by pressing with the thumb. Then a straight starter of various shapes is used in pushing the ball some two of three inches into the bore after which it is pushed home with the loading rod.

This type of rifle never was popular in the New

England States and New York since the accurate range of these is limited to about 30 rods, or less, and generally give their best accuracy at 60 to 100 yards, which were popular ranges for target shooting in that section, while in the eastern states the popular range for target shooting was 40 rods—220 yards. This southern type of rifle made by the most skillful makers in that section was extremely accurate at 60 yards rest shooting, and often placed three or five balls practically in one hole, when the rifle was shot by an expert marksman experienced in its use.

Another form of sight for target rifles, which is known as the "tube sight," came into use during the decade from 1840 to 1850. This consists of a sheet-iron or brass tube about 3/8 or 1/2 inch diameter extending from a point about three inches back of the break-off to the front sight slot near the muzzle. The rear end of this tube is funnel-shaped, with the large end towards the eye, and having a metal disc with small peep hole in the center affixed inside about 1 1/2 inches from the rear end, while the front end of this tube is connected to the shade of the pin-head front sight thus affording a shaded tube from the rear peep to the front sight. This eliminates all light reflection between the sights and assists in defining the front sight and the target. The tube sight, used in connection with an aperture front sight having the aperture and rim of the right size for the bulls-eye at each different range is, doubtless, the nearest approach to the telescope sight ever devised, and again appears to be coming into favor in matches where the telescope is barred.

Strange as it may appear, the expert marksmen during the years from about 1835 to the 1870's, who were continually seeking to devise some form of front sight that would enable them to make smaller groups at the target, never thought of using a small stem with disc top having a hole in the center surrounded by a narrow rim through which the bulls-eye could be centered instead of trying to hold the pin-head front sight on the bulls-eye or at 6 o'clock under it. Finally some "bright" individual thought of this form of front sight surrounded by the usual shade, and thus invented the so-called "aperture" front sight that is so well known today, but, as far as can be learned, no target rifle made in any section of this country before 1870, or possibly 1880, was originally fitted with an aperture front sight. All the available reports of the International Rifle Match between the foreign rifle teams and the United States Rifle Team, during the centennial year of 1876, indicate that each member of the foreign teams used the globe, or pin-head, front sight, while some members of our team used an aperture front sight. This is the earliest record we have found of the use of this type of front sight in a rifle match. Mr. Wm. V. Lowe, who was in partnership with the late Horace Warner from 1886 until June, 1888, stated in a letter to me, dated January 9, 1940: "I cannot say as to the origin of the aperture sight; I remember that when I was shooting in 1880 or 1883, the aperture sight was spoken of as something new, and an improvement over the pin-head, so I think it came into use about that time." Mr. Lowe is a recognized authority on matters pertaining to the finest muzzle-loading target rifles, and we may safely accept his statement regarding this matter as doubtless correct.

There is not the least doubt that some of the old-time riflemen having especially good eye-sight, with their fine heavy muzzle-loading target rifles with extremely fine shaded pin-head front and rear peep sights, using the best load for the individual rifle, were able to make remarkably small 10-shot groups at 40 rods rest shooting under favorable weather conditions.

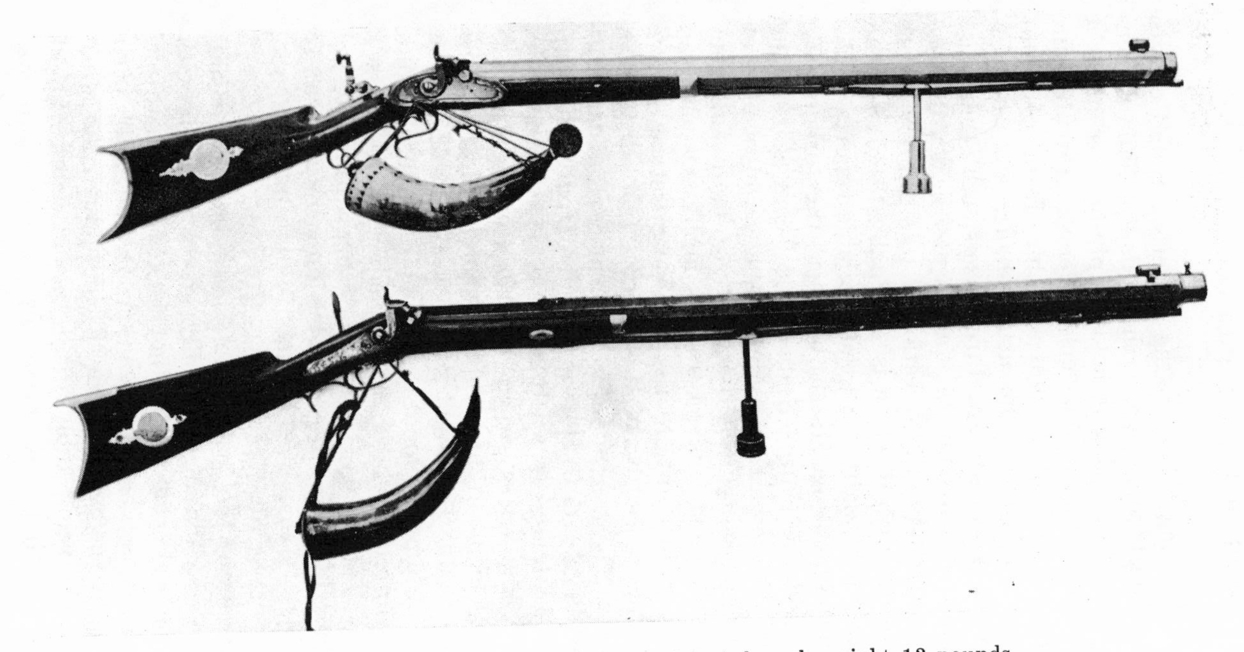

Top. A. Leonard 42-calibre Rifle, 32-inch barrel, weight 13 pounds.
Bottom. N. Lewis 45 calibre Rifle, 35-inch barrel, weight 15 pounds.
From Dr. P. A. Matteson's Collection.

But the great majority of men, lacking this almost telescopic eye-sight, were constantly endeavoring to find some form of front and rear sights that would enable them to "place all the bullets in one hole at 40 rods rest shooting," as they so often stated. However, no form of iron sights has ever been invented that will enable the man with average eye-sight to accomplish the feat, since it is absolutely beyond the possibilities of the average unaided human eye.

Since riflemen who practiced shooting at 40 rods or more had long been familar with the Galilean telescope of high power which they used in spotting the bullet-holes in the target at such range, some ingenious rifleman who had, doubtless, devoted much thought to the improvement of rifle sights finally conceived the idea of fixing in the tube sight the necessary sets of lenses to give a telescopic view of the target, with a set of cross-hairs placed at the focal point of the eye-piece for use in aligning the telescope on the bull's-eye, and thus invented the telescope sight for rifles. We have been unable to find any positive record of the original inventor of the telescopic rifle sight, but records have been found which show that the first telescope sights came into use on rifles in this country between 1835 and 1840.

Records are available that show that the Continental Congress, in 1776, authorized the purchase of telescope sights for rifles, but it is practically certain that these sights were *not telescopic,* because no records can be found to show that the telescope sight had been invented at that time. It is probable that the sights ordered by the Continental Congress were merely tube sights, and not true telescopic sights.

Of course, the first of these sights were crude affairs, doubtless made from spectacle lenses, having many optical defects, and were really inferior to the pin-head and peep sights in affording an accurate aim.

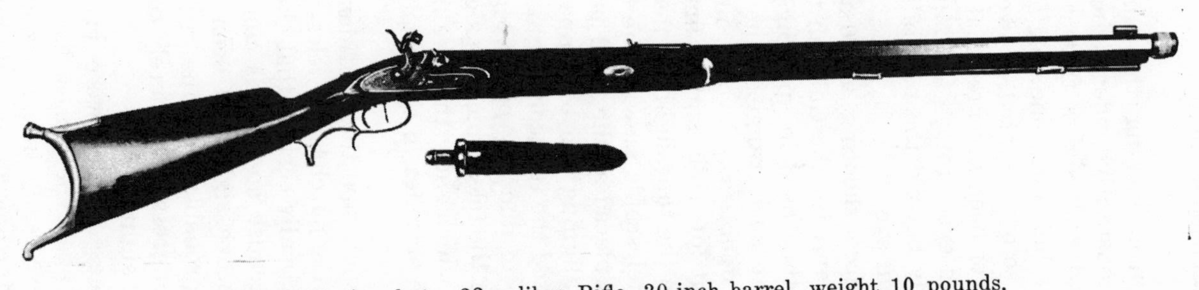

Author's E. Anschutz, 33 calibre Rifle, 30-inch barrel, weight 10 pounds.

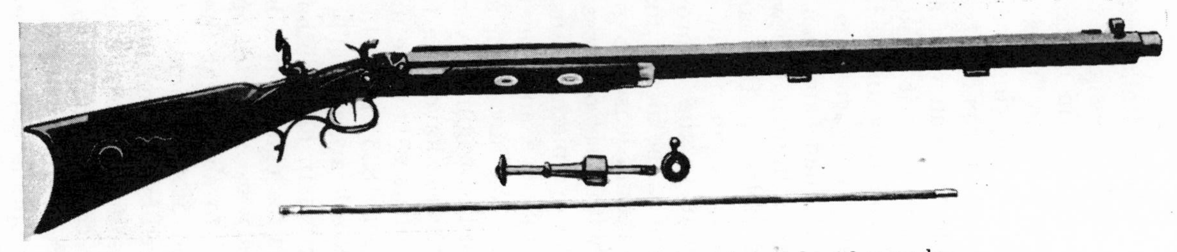

Slotter & Co., 38 calibre Rifle, 34-inch barrel, weight 16 pounds.

John R. Chapman, in his book, *The Improved American Rifle,* which was written in 1844, states: "I am aware that telescopes have been in use for some time, but to my cost, I know that they never did perform so well as the globe sight, until made and used as above described, and which I once thought of securing by a patent, but found that the trouble and expense would over-balance the profit." On the preceding page of the book, Chapman states: "I shall now proceed to describe such improvements in sighting which I have lately effected by the introduction of a telescopic sight and movements connected therewith, which perform perfect at all times. The tube in which the lenses are fixed is 3 feet 1 inch long, ⅝ths of an inch diameter outside, 1/20th of an inch thick, weighing 10 ounces. It can be made very good and stiff from sheet-iron, brazed at the joint, floated and leaded out true; however, sheet-steel is preferable. To the front end a saddle of steel is firmly fitted and brazed; and a narrow flat rib is soldered over the brazed joint of the tube, the object to be attained being stiffness combined with lightness; for when fixed on the rifle, a discharge has the tendency to pitch it forward, and break out the dovetail or neck off the pivot screws; and this tendency increases as the charges of powder increases. A carriage is made to slide through the bead sight dovetail, furnished with two standards, through which two screws pass into the saddle, serving as axes or pivots of elevation or depression. The back movement for elevating or depressing without taking out the telescope is designed to adapt itself for all ranges, keeping the charges of powder and the sighting always alike, a property which the globe sight does not possess, for with it no nearer approach can be made than half turns, and I have never seen one work truly with half turns; consequently, you cannot work nearer than one turn."

Again on page 55 of the book mentioned, he states: "These target telescopes are made by Morgan James, rifle-maker, Utica, N. Y., and with front and back movements (mountings) cost about $20.00. A pair of cross-hairs are fixed in the telescope for the purpose of sighting at a mark, and are fastened on a new plan invented by James, which cannot be affected by the vibration of the weapon, and particular attention is paid to the *seating of the lenses*, and the fastening and fitting of the tubes in which they are set, to the tube of the telescope." The italics above are mine, just to call attention to the fact that the early telescope makers like Morgan James fully realized the importance of this matter.

From these statements, and in view of the fact that Chapman was an experienced English civil engineer who had long been accustomed to the use of the surveyor's transit with its fine cross-hairs, precision lenses, and fine definition of distant objects, as well as being an expert rifleman of long experience in the use of all the other kinds of rifle sights, it therefore is quite certain that the first practical telescopic rifle sight in this country was invented by John Ratcliffe Chapman, C. E., about 1840, or at least prior to 1844, and that instead of taking out a patent on this invention he gave the specifications, and all details of the construction of the telescope, and its mounts to Morgan James and authorized him to manufacture and sell this telescope sight.

Since Chapman had not patented the telescope sight and mounts, it was not long before other rifle-makers copied, as best they could, the Chapman-James telescope and mounts as made by Morgan James, but as these other makers were not well informed in optical principles their telescopes were generally so poorly constructed and defective that they were unsatisfactory to the expert rifleman. It therefore follows that from about 1835 or 1840 to about 1855 the best rifle telescopes made in this country were those by Morgan James.

Some time in 1855 the late Wm. Malcolm, of Syracuse, New York, established the first rifle telescope manufacturing business in this country, and furnished riflemen an instrument that was much superior to the Chapman-James and all other rifle telescopes then made. Before he commenced business all the rifle telescopes that were made by the various rifle-makers who, with the exception of Morgan James, knew little or nothing about optical construction, were so made that the rifleman could not adjust the telescope correctly for different ranges nor properly focus it for his individual eyes. While the telescopes that were on the market before those made by Wm. Malcolm were of high power, from 10 to 20 as then rated, they all had the lenses ground for the normal eye, or for the eyes of the individual for whom the telescope was made, and these lenses in their cells were held in place by small screws through the tube and were not adjustable in any way. Therefore the telescope could generally be used only by the owner for whose eyes it was made and adjusted, which was, of course, a great disadvantage.

The Wm. Malcolm telescopes were made from steel tubes without joint or seam—a distinct improvement over all former makes—furnished in various grades and powers from 3 to 20 or more; the tube was some six inches longer than the rifle barrel, 3/4 inch outside diameter, about 19/32 inch inside, with lenses 1/2 inch diameter. All lenses were set in brass cells held in place by small screws through the main tube so they could not change adjustment by the recoil of the rifle, while the ocular and objective lenses likewise held in brass cells were retained in place by small set screws through the main tube which had small slots in it so that these screws could be loosened and the cells moved forward or back until properly focused. Tightening these set screws held the lenses in correct adjustment for any eyes. The rear mounting of the Malcolm telescope was practically the same as that designed by Chapman, but the front mount was considerably improved. In order to adjust the other makes of telescopes for deflection of the bullet by wind, it was necessary to drive the front mount base to the right or left, with a small hammer, through the dovetail slot in the barrel the required number of divisions marked on the top of the barrel. This was difficult to accomplish, battered the dovetail base after repeated changes with a hammer as well as being a "make-shift" method of adjustment. Therefore Wm. Malcolm made the front mount of his telescopes in two separate parts with a lateral screw for making windage adjustments.

The bottom part of this mount was a dovetail piece of steel fitting the slot in the muzzle of the rifle barrel, with another dovetail cut in the top of this bottom base which had a small lump of metal at the left end with a female thread through it. The top piece consisted of a dovetail piece to fit the slot in the bottom part, with a transverse screw having a knurled head that fitted the female thread in the other part, and having a ring, or hoop, formed in the top of this sliding base which fitted the outside of the telescope tube, while a flat spring in the bottom of this ring supported the telescope against the top of the mount. Thus the upper section of the front mount, sliding in the dovetail cut in the top of the fixed base, was adjustable to the right or left of the zero point by turning the knurled head of the adjusting screw. This permitted making fine windage adjustments uniformly by the use of the division lines 1/50 inch apart cut in the face (muzzle side) of the sliding part of the mount.

As far as can be learned, the first telescopes made in this country with achromatic lenses were the Wm. Malcolm, while all the other earlier makes were fitted with plain non-achromatic lenses that gave a color fringe around the circumference. Thus the Wm. Malcolm telescopes with their full achromatic lenses gave much better definition of the target without the objectionable color fringe, had a flatter field of view, and gave clear definition at the edge of the objective, which advantages made them far superior to any other on the market for many years.

During the Civil War, Mr. L. M. Amidon, of Bellows Falls, Vermont, made full length telescopes of various grades, but we have never seen one of his make that had achromatic lenses. They were considered good instruments in those days and we find many of them today on the old target rifles. After the Civil War, the late Norman S. Brockway moved to Bellows Falls, Vermont, and established his shop where he made the fine Brockway target rifles, most of which were fitted with telescope sights, many of which were Amidon's make. However, after a few years, as his business increased, Brockway started making his own telescopes. When I inquired about this matter, he said: "I bought a book on telescopes, studied it all up thoroughly, then went to New York City, where I spent a month with one of the large firms that made telescopes and learned how to make good telescopes—better than those made by Amidon—and thereafter I made my own telescopes for my rifles unless the customer especially ordered the Amidon or some other make."

However, in spite of their "crude manufacture," as many would call it today, I have seen many of the old, long, Wm. Malcolm telescopes of the so-called "20 power" that gave very nice definition of the bull's-eye at 40 rods. Often under good light conditions these would show 45 calibre bullet holes in the black of the target, but the field of view was, of course, quite small, and would not at all suit the present day "rifle cranks." Yet with the handicaps of small diameter lenses, small field of view, and definition that would today be classed as "very poor," those old-time expert rest-shots made 5 and 10-shot groups at 40 rods (220 yards) with these telescopes on their fine muzzle-loading 16 to 20 pounds target rifles that none of our modern high velocity rifles, except the so-called "bull guns," can equal today with all our boasted improvements in rifles, smokeless powders, metal cased bullets, non-corrosive primers and "latest fashion" telescope sights. Therefore the old-time rifle and telescope makers are certainly entitled to much credit for their skill and fine workmanship. The great majority of the old, full length telescopes that we find today on the target rifles have damaged lenses, or covered with many years accumulation of dust, or cross-hairs broken or gone. These telescopes can be restored to good, serviceable condition by a telescope maker who is familiar with their construction, and as the Malcolm Rifle Telescope Company, of Auburn, New York, have very satisfactorily performed this work for me on several occasions, I can recommend them to others for repairing these old telescopes, with the assurance that the work will be properly done at moderate prices. Or if new, full-length telescopes are desired, I believe this firm are prepared to furnish the same with suitable mountings.

If any of our modern, short tube telescopes are installed on these old, muzzle-loading target rifles, it is advisable to attach the rear base block from four to five inches in front of the nipple in order that the fouling from the cap will not deface the rear mount, and obscure the micrometer divisions of the elevation and windage adjusting screws. Our modern extremely short tube telescopes, like the old Winchester and Lyman 5-A scopes, are much too short to be practical on the muzzle-loading, cap lock rifles. Those with 18 or 19 inch tubes are about as short as can be used to good advantage on such rifles, and the mountings should be of the Lyman type so that the telescope tube will slide forward with the recoil of the rifle instead of punching one in the eye, or on the forehead, as is the case with telescopes having the old types of mountings in which the telescope is rigidly secured. Many serious accidents have occurred to shooters when using rifles with the old, long telescopes having short eye relief, on muzzle-loading rifles having much recoil, which violently drives the telescope backward breaking the shooter's glasses, injuring the eye, or even putting it out. I have known of several deaths that were caused in this way, and regard it as my duty to warn riflemen about this.

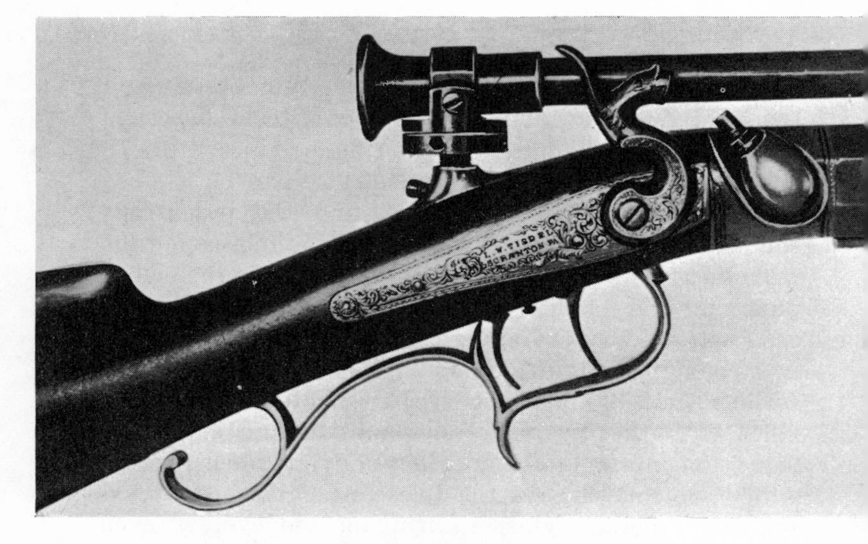

L. W. Tisdel Rifle, showing Breech, Rear Mount for and Rear of Tub
Sight.

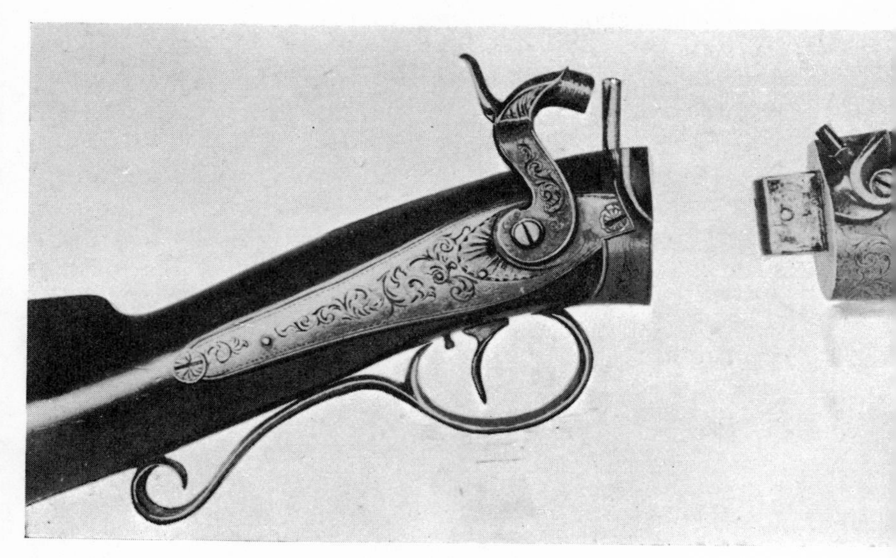

James & Ferriss Rifle, showing Patent Breech and Method of Attaching t
Break-Off. Single Set Trigger.

CHAPTER III

ACCESSORIES AND EQUIPMENT

The accessories for the hunting rifle generally comprised a bullet mould, powder-horn or powder-flask, charger, bullet pouch, hunting bag, priming wire, which when used with the flint-lock is called a "frizzen-pick," patch cutter, wormer, loading block for patched balls, bullet starter, also called a straight starter, and nipple wrench. With the exception of the powder-horn or powder-flask, and the bullet pouch these accessories were all small and light, and, except the charger, were carried in the hunting bag where they were instantly available when needed.

The old-time bullet moulds casting the various sizes of round balls were generally quite small, made from bronze or iron without any cut-off, but having a small projection on each handle near the joint somewhat like the blades of shears, bevel-edged, and sharpened for use in trimming off the sprue of lead left on each bullet in casting. Some of the very earliest bullet moulds in this country were made from rectangular blocks of soapstone with the cavity for casting the ball or bullet worked out by hand, probably by the use of small chisels and a bent file. Two hard-wood dowels set into one-half of the mould fitting corresponding holes in the other half held the two parts of these moulds together when in use. Sometimes the two halves of these soapstone bullet moulds were set into larger pieces of hard-wood so as to be cooler in handling. Surprisingly good round balls and bullets were cast in these crude bullet moulds, as will be seen by the illustrations herewith showing one of these very old bullet moulds and the bullets cast in it. Many of these old moulds had no bullet trimmer attached, and

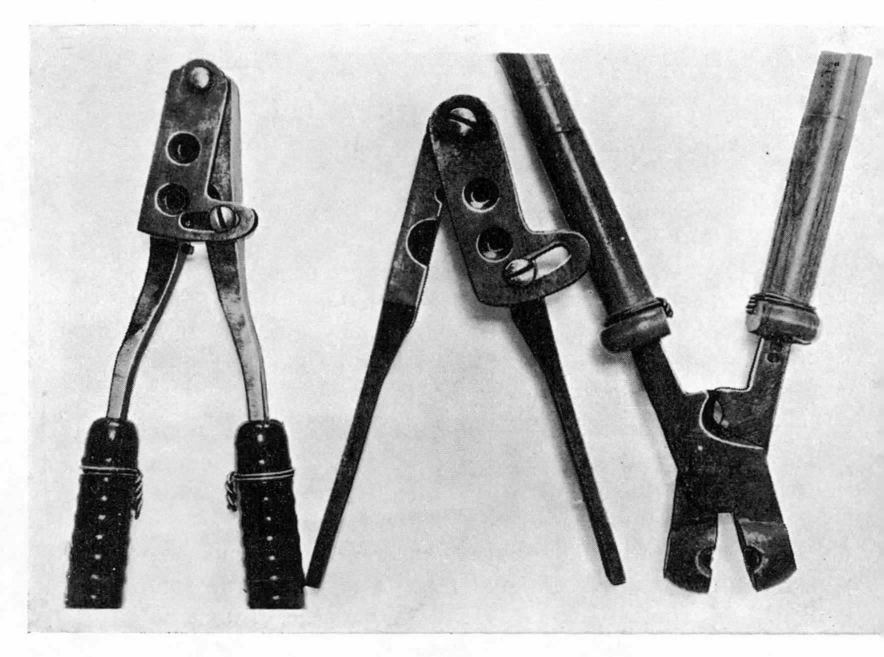

Left and center, Colt 36 and 31 calibre Bullet Mounds. Wood Handle fitt
by Author. Right, Mould for 36 calibre Round Ball.

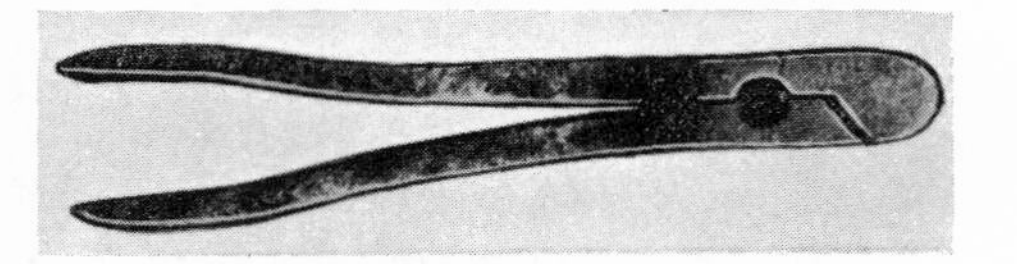

One of Author's Bullet Moulds for his first 30 calibre Rifle.

Patch Cutter for Paper Cross Patches.

the rifleman cut off the sprue with his hunting knife, or with a separate sprue trimmer. They almost invariably had small plier-shaped iron handles, and I have sometimes wondered if the old pioneers had asbestos covered hands to enable them to handle these hot iron moulds when casting bullets. When I was a boy, old hunters told me that they wrapped the handles of the bullet mould with wet buckskin, or cloth, and dipped these frequently in water to keep the handles cool enough to work with. Having cast a quantity of balls, the next operation was to cut off from each ball the excess lead, or sprue, left in casting, which was easily done with the bullet trimmer made as an integral part of the handles.

About 1837, after the famous Colt revolvers were placed on the market, the Colt bullet mould, casting a round ball and a conical bullet at the same time, with a steel cut-off plate pivoted near the joint at the top of the mould with which the sprue of the two bullets was cut off before opening the mould, soon appeared on the market. These may have been the first bullet moulds having an attached cut-off that were made in this country. Rifle-makers quickly adopted the Colt design, and made the bullet moulds with swinging cut-off for their rifles, but most of these were still made with iron handles and of small size for the hunting rifles, so as to be easily carried in the wilderness.

Bullet Casting. In the early times the pioneer-rifleman used a small iron ladle with a pouring spout for melting the lead for his bullets and turning it into the bullet mould after melting the lead in the coals in the fire-place. One old hunter that I knew as a boy often showed me his bullet ladle of this type that he carried across the continent to California and back in the early 1850's, and told me how he had cast many hundred bullets for his 50 calibre Hawken's rifle with it using "buffalo chips" as fuel for melting the lead.

Powder Horns from F. E. Dunn Collection. Second from bottom, at right, was used in

When the early pioneer, while traveling in the wilderness, had exhausted his supply of round balls with which he set forth, he melted lead in a similar small iron ladle by means of a good bed of hard wood coals, and cast more balls from the lead that he had recovered from the animals he had shot. More than sixty years ago, my Uncle Alvaro taught me how to cast bullets in the wilderness with the small ladle, and I have cast many bullets for my muzzle-loading rifle in this way when many miles from any habitation.

Before the Civil War, someone invented a small bullet-melting ladle having three short legs, one of which was hollow and shaped outside to fit the pouring hole in a bullet mould; depressing a lever opened the top of this hollow leg through which the lead was poured into the mould. I do not know who invented this, but the one illustrated is stamped: "Patented April 24th, 1860," and these were quite common when I was a boy.

The old powder-horn, once so common in every family, was made from the hollow shell of a cow's or steer's horn scraped thin and smooth with a knife, a thin wooden bottom affixed in the larger end, the point of the horn cut off leaving a small hole through which it was filled and the charge poured out, a soft-wood plug whittled to serve as a stopper for it, and a shallow groove cut around the horn about an inch from the small end. A buckskin thong, or cord, long enough to pass over the shoulder as a sling was attached by one end to the wooden bottom of the horn, and the other, tied in the groove around the small end, held the horn against the right, or left, side of the body where it could be quickly grasped when needed. The wooden stopper was also tied to the small end of the horn, or to the sling, to prevent losing it. A small charger to contain the proper charge of powder for the rifle was made from a small piece of bone

Powder-Horns from F. E. Dunn Collection. Note Powder-Horn used by Lieut. Burnett of the Texas

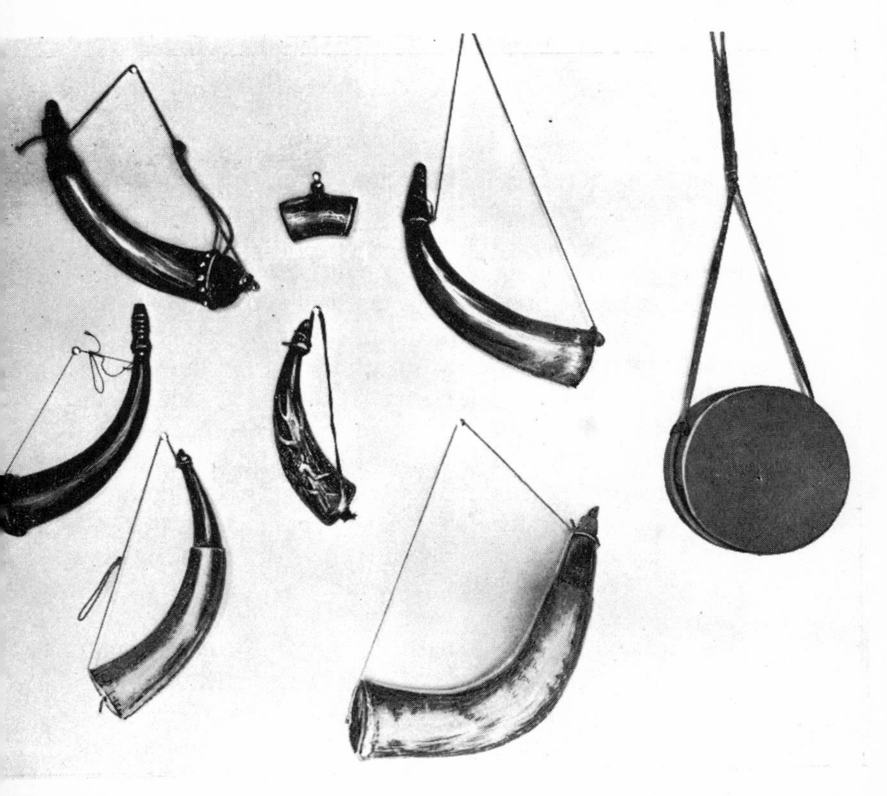

wder-Horns from F. E. Dunn Collection. Wooden Canteen at right and Horn at right top were used by Aaron Burr.

all horn at top center is a "Salt Horn" used by the Pioneers for carrying salt as the horn is impervious to moisture and salt in it never hardens or cakes.

hollowed out, or from the tip of a small horn, with a hole bored through the small end into which was tied one end of a buckskin thong and the other attached to the powder-horn. This afforded the hunter a measure which when evenly filled from the horn gave fairly uniform charges of powder with which to load the rifle.

About 1836 when the Colt revolver was placed on the market, powder-flasks made from zinc, copper or brass, with a charger having a spring operated cut-off, came into use, and gradually displaced the old powder-horn with its separate charger. The very first of these powder-flasks were made with a non-adjustable charger the right size and length to hold the correct charge for the different bores, or calibres, of revolvers, rifles and shotguns. Later, along in the early 1840's, the charger was improved so that it could be adjusted to throw several different bulk quantities, or charges, of powder, thus enabling the rifleman to use lighter or heavier charges than normal as desired, as well as enabling one to load the rifle much quicker than was possible with the old powder-horn and separate charger.

The bullet-pouch, generally made from tanned buckskin, was simply a bottle-shaped bag with the neck tightly tied around a hollow piece of horn or wood having a hole through it somewhat larger than the round ball that fitted the rifle, and having a soft-wood plug as a stopper attached to the bullet-pouch by a thong. A buckskin thong long enough to pass over the shoulder as a sling, was attached at each end to the sides of the bullet-pouch and suspended it against the left, or right, side of the body, where it could be easily reached when needed. A right-handed man always wore the powder-horn suspended from the opposite shoulder by the leather thong, against the right side usually just above the hip; while the bullet-

Bullet Pouch that came with Author's First Rifle 65 years ago. Straight Starter and Loading Block for Patched Balls, showing 4 balls in place.

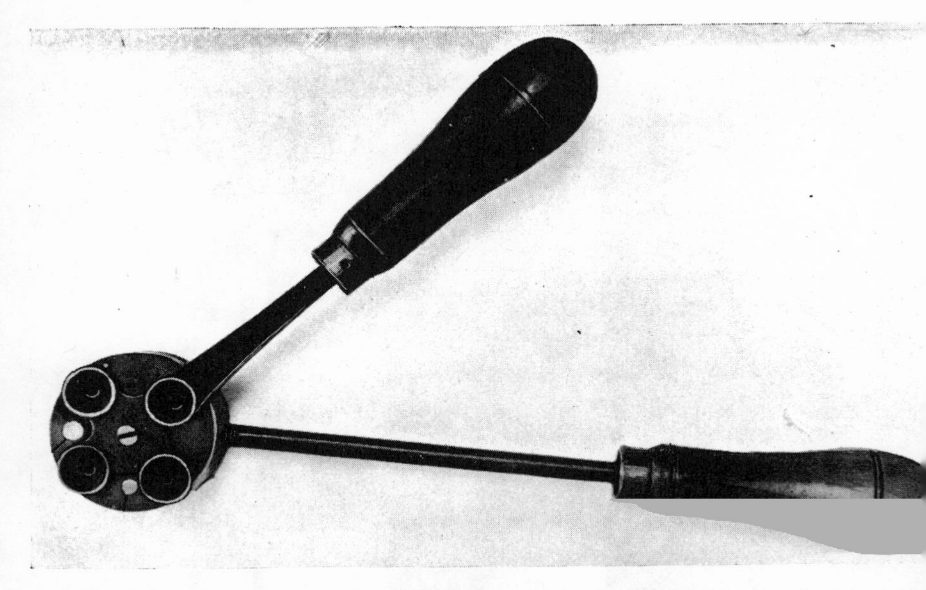

J. H. Huntoon 6-cavity Bullet Mould that casts five 32 calibre Cylindrical B
and one 28 calibre.

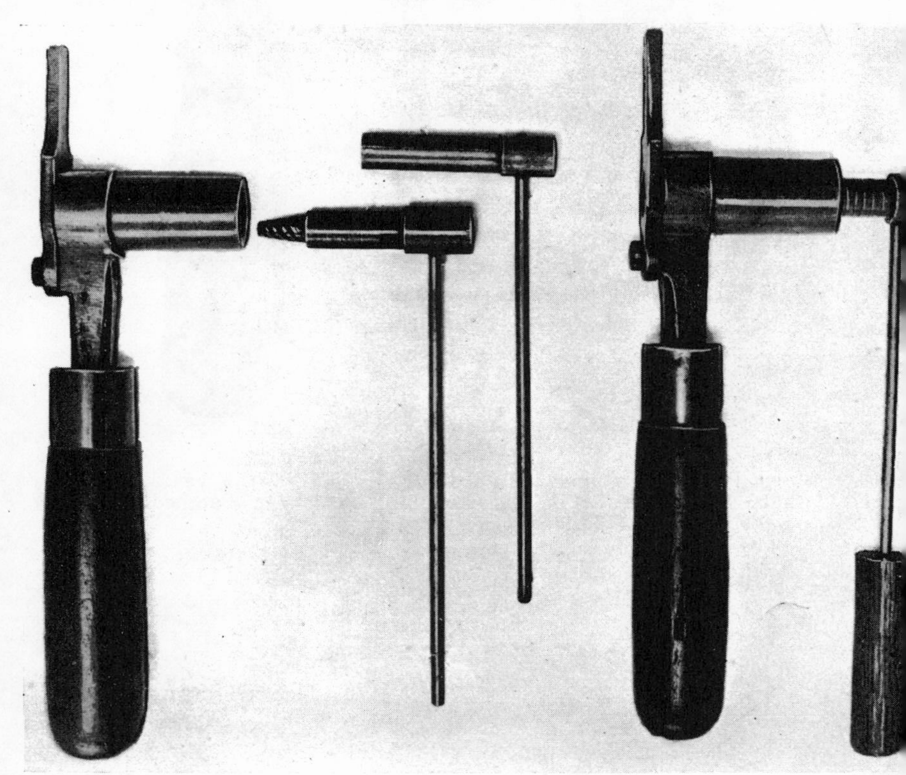

L. W. Tisdel Bullet Moulds for casting 40 calibre, two-piece Cylindrical Bull

pouch was similarly worn against the left side. Of course, the left-handed man reversed this, wearing the powder-horn on the left side, and the bullet-pouch on the right side of the body.

Many hunters did not carry a bullet-pouch, but instead carried their bullets in one of the pockets of the hunting bag which was suspended by its leather sling against the side of the body, and from which the bullets could be quickly taken when loading the rifle. The objection to carrying the bullets in the hunting bag was that since this was closed only by a flap over the top, held in place by a horn or wooden button when closed, if one stumbled or fell to the ground the balls might spill out, and thus be lost, which with the pioneer in the Indian days was certainly a very serious matter, and might cost the unfortunate man his life. The majority of the old, experienced hunters that I knew when I was a boy, expressed a decided preference for the bullet-pouch as a means of carrying the round balls when in the wilderness. Patches cut and lightly oiled were always carried in the patch-box, set into the side of the stock near the butt plate where they were quickly reached; but as the patch-box was of small capacity a larger quantity was carred in a tin box in one of the compartments of the hunting-bag, or in a pocket in the hunting coat. Old hunters have repeatedly told me that they, and the pioneers generally, used the oiled cloth patch in preference to the wet one. Bears were numerous in most parts of the country in the early days, the pioneers and hunters always killed them so as to have a supply of bear's oil on hand for oiling the patches for the rifle and lubricating the barrel after cleaning, as well as having bear's grease for use in cooking. It is generally well known by riflemen that an oiled patch enables one to load a somewhat tighter fitting ball, or bullet, than can be used with a patch wet with saliva. Also when

Top, 40 calibre Bullet Mould by Geo. H. Ferris.
Bottom, Seth Millard Mould for 45 calibre Composite Bullets.

Bullet Ladle Patented in 1860. From F. E. Dunn's Collection.

loading hurriedly, or in very cold weather, one is less likely to have a ball stick partly down the barrel with an oiled patch than with a wet one; hence the old hunters preference for the oiled or greased patch.

Patches for the hunting rifle were cut with the steel patch-cutter that was furnished with the rifle, the hunting knife or shears. The easiest way was with the patch-cutter, which was simply a steel wad-cutter having a circular beveled edge, well sharpened, of the proper diameter for the individual rifle. When cutting patches, several thicknesses of linen, or other cloth, are folded and placed over the sawed-off end of a block of wood with a piece of cardboard, or paper, under the cloth, the patch-cutter is placed on the cloth and struck with a wooden mallet, thus cutting half a dozen or more patches at once. Or having no patch-cutter, the cloth is folded and cut into narrow strips with the hunting knife, these strips again folded and cut cross-wise making small squares of the desired size; then several thicknesses of these squares are laid on a board, and the hunting knife used in cutting off each corner so as to form octagon-shaped patches instead of round ones. Shears may be used in this same way in making these octagon-shaped patches instead of round ones.

It is often stated that the pioneers made their patches from thin parts of tanned buckskin. They may have done so in emergencies during long wilderness trips after all their cloth patches had been used. Even if the rifle was made for use with bed-ticking patches, which average about 15/1000 inch in thickness, it is difficult to work buckskin down to this same thickness, and it is impossible to use a much thicker patch in the round ball hunting rifle unless a smaller size ball is used, which could not well be done when the hunter or pioneer was in the wilderness with but one bullet mould casting only one size ball.

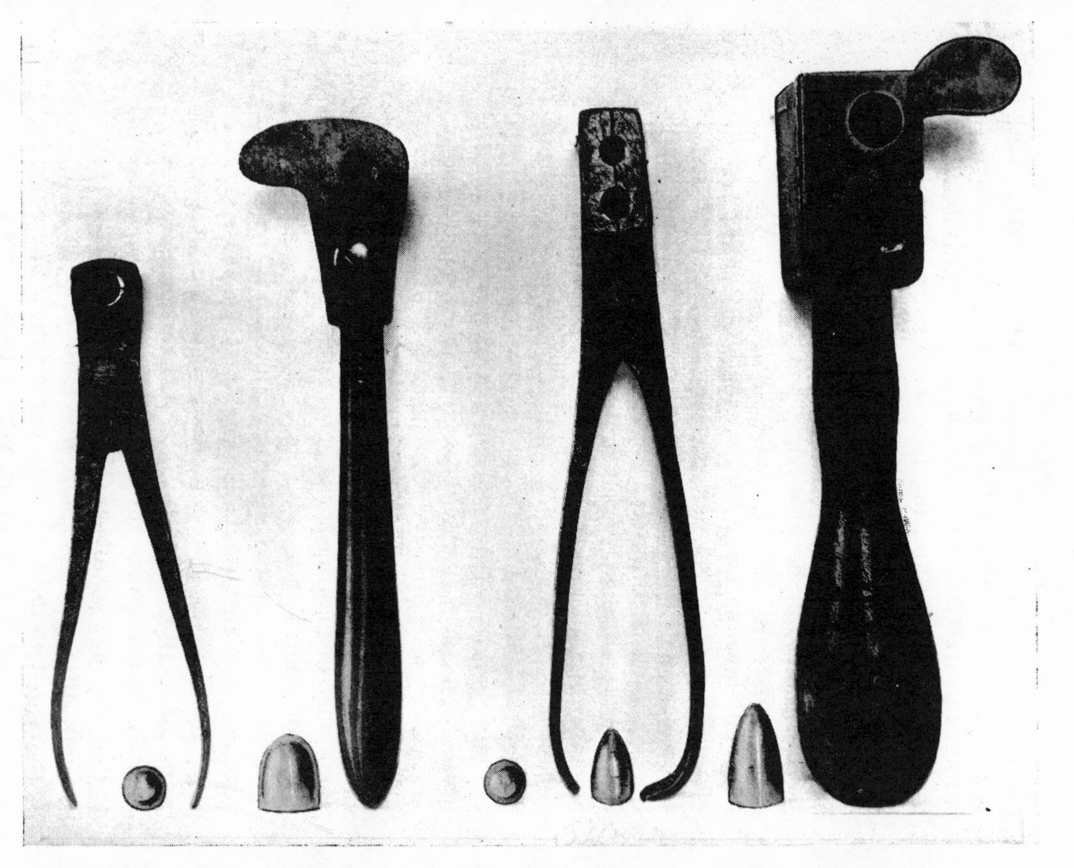

Old Bullet Moulds. Left to right 30 calibre Round Ball, 36 calibre Bronze Mould, Double

In certain sections of this country it was customary to use bed-ticking for patching the balls of the hunting rifle, which were cut with the patch-cutter, or by the other methods described above. Instead of using the ready cut patches, many riflemen and hunters in that section cut the patches as needed. In this case a piece of bed-ticking about a foot square is oiled, greased, or wet with saliva, placed over the muzzle of the rifle after pouring the powder charge into the barrel, a ball placed on the cloth, pressed down with the thumb even with the muzzle, then, with the hunting knife, the cloth is cut off even with the muzzle of the rifle, and the ball pushed down the barrel with the ramrod. Sometimes the straight starter is first used, with which the ball is pushed some three inches down the bore and then pushed home with the ramrod.

The priming wire is a short piece of small sized steel or iron wire usually having a small ring formed at one end, the other filed taper-pointed for use in picking out the opening of the nipple, or tube, when it becomes clogged. This was usually carried thrust into a piece of oiled buckskin, or cloth, in a pocket of the hunting bag, or sometimes stuck into the sling strap of the powder-horn where it was handy when needed.

The "wormer," or "worm," is simply a screw, or cork-screw, shaped piece of steel with a hollow shank which is fitted to the small end of the ramrod, held in place by an iron pin through ramrod and both sides of the shank, and is used for holding the cloth in cleaning the rifle, or in removing a cleaning patch that slipped off the button-shaped end of the cleaning rod. I have been told that by the use of the wormer, a ball or bullet could be removed from the bore of the rifle in case one forgot to put any powder into the barrel before loading the bullet or ball. After all the years in which I have used muzzle-loading rifles, I have never been able to do this with any wormer that I have ever seen or used; neither have I ever seen this done by anyone. I do not say this is impossible if the ball fits very loosely in the bore and if the wormer is of the screw type and real strong, and if the wormer is strongly attached to the ramrod; also if the ramrod is strong, and some six inches longer than the barrel. You will note there are many IFS in regard to removeing a ball from the bore of the rifle by the use of the wormer, and you will find several more ifs before you accomplish this trick.

Back in the pioneer times they used "tow"—a short, coarse hemp or flax fibre—for cleaning and oiling the rifle; this was merely twisted around the worm which held it in place while swabbing the bore to clean the residue left by the black powder, as well as for holding the oiled or greased tow used in lubricating the bore after cleaning. It was also the habitual practice of many of the old-time riflemen to leave a well-oiled swab of tow pushed clear down to the breech of the rifle when not in use. However, this is a practice that I, personally, do NOT approve as I have seen many nice rifles that had been left with the oiled wad of tow in the bore for a long time, the oil evaporated and dried out, and the breech of the bore badly rusted when the rifle was again wiped out previous to using.

The loading-block for patched balls is a piece of hickory, or other hardwood, about ¾ inch thick, 2 inches wide and 6 inches long, having from two to five holes bored through it of a size that tightly fits the round ball in its cloth patch. It is prepared for use by placing an oiled patch well centered over each hole and pushing a ball into each on top of the patch until even with the surface of the wood, thus holding each ball in its patch friction tight until needed. Sometimes these loading-blocks had octagon holes of a size that just fitted the octagon muzzle of the rifle, cut about 1/4 inch deep in the bottom of the loading-block with a ball hole in the center of each octagon. In loading the rifle, an octagon hole in the loading-block is placed over the muzzle, thus quickly and accurately centering both the patch and ball over the bore. The small end of the straight starter is next placed over the ball in its patch and pressing down on the knob of the starter forces a ball and patch into the bore the length of the starter rod, the starter removed, and the ramrod used to push the bullet down the bore until it rests on the powder. A man accustomed to the use of the loading-block and straight starter can load the rifle much more rapidly than when using the patch and ball separately.

The straight starter, used with or without the loading-block, is made from hickory, or other close gained hardwood, and consists of a cylindrical plug 3 or 4 inches long, about 1/16 inch smaller than the bore of the rifle with a flattened knob on the top which is held in the palm of the hand when applying pressure to start the ball or bullet into the muzzle of the rifle, then by striking the knob with the ball of the hand, the ball is forced down the bore the length of the starter rod. The starter is then removed and the ramrod used in pushing the ball down onto the powder. The end of the starter rod should be shaped to accurately fit the point of the bullet, or surface of the round ball, and a copper ferrule should be tightly fitted to the end of the rod to prevent splitting it in use. The straight starter was generally suspended from the shoulder by a buckskin thong or cord, or carried in the hunting bag.

The hunting bag in the pioneer times was usually made from tanned buckskin, but sometimes from a tanned fox or raccoon skin, of various sizes and shapes, having several pockets inside with a flap to cover the top and prevent spilling the articles out of it

Small Powder-Flasks from F. E. Dunn's Collection.

as well as to keep out water and snow. A buckskin thong, sewed at each end to the ends or back of the bag, and long enough to serve as a sling, held the bag in place at the side of the body with the sling passing diagonally across the body and over the shoulder. These hunting bags were often more or less ornamented outside with Indian bead work, colored porcupine quills, fancy stitching or silver ornaments sewed on with raw-hide thongs. When made from the fox or raccoon skin tanned with the hair on, the nose and part of the animal's head was often used to form the flap of the hunting bag. When the bag was closed the flap was held in place by a horn or wooden button and a loop of thong, or thongs attached to both body and flap of the bag and tied together to fasten the flap.

These hunting bags were usually rectangular shaped about 5 inches deep by 7 or 8 inches long, but were often of other sizes and shapes according to the fancy of the owner or maker. It was a very useful accessory to the pioneer and hunter, and in it were carried all the small necessaries for the rifle such as the bullet mould, tow for cleaning and oiling the rifle, extra patches, caps, nipple wrench, etc. These genuine old-time hunting bags are today highly prized by the devotees of the muzzle-loading rifle and collectors, and often command a cash price equal to about a month's wages in the pioneer days.

The nipple wrench for the hunting rifle was often an L-shaped piece of 3/8 inch round steel with the short end about 2 inches long and the other about 4 inches. The short part was drilled and shaped as a wrench to fit over the nipple and its base, while the longer part which served as a handle in unscrewing a broken nipple or in turning in a new one, was usually flattened and the end shaped as a screw-driver to fit the screws that held the lock plate in place. The T-shaped nipple

Large Powder-Flasks from F. E. Dunn Collection. One presented to "Buffalo Bill" by

wrench, described on another page with the accessories for the target rifles, was also sometimes furnished with the hunting rifles. As a nipple was liable to break almost any time after considerable use, a nipple wrench of some kind was a very necessary accessory for the hunting rifle, and was always carried in the hunting bag, or pocket, when on hunting trips.

Caps, the last thing used in loading the muzzle-loading rifle, were carried in a small pocket in the hunting coat, in a separate pocket in the hunting bag, or in a small receptacle in the butt of the rifle for this purpose, according to the preference of the rifleman. Occasionally we find one of the old-timers who used a separate small buckskin or leather bag worn on the belt, or attached to the sling strap of the powder-horn, or fastened to the coat, for carrying the caps. Almost any place, or any way, where they would be handy when needed, not get lost or spill out when running, was satisfactory. The "capper," "cap primer," or "cap magazine," as described with the accessories for the target rifles, was sometimes used with the hunting rifles after these came on the market about 1837, and were very convenient in cold weather when the fingers were numb with the cold. The capper being somewhat larger than a silver dollar, was easier to handle with cold fingers than the single cap.

The accessories for the hunting and target rifles, were the same as those for the hunting rifles, except that these arms were usually furnished with several not needed with the hunting rifles. This type of rifles require both the guide bullet starter and the straight starter, a bullet swage, swege, or swedge (three different approved ways of spelling the same word, and all mean exactly the same, which I shall spell the first way in this volume), an ammunition box for use in target shooting, and often two bullet moulds casting different shaped bullets—one for hunting use and the

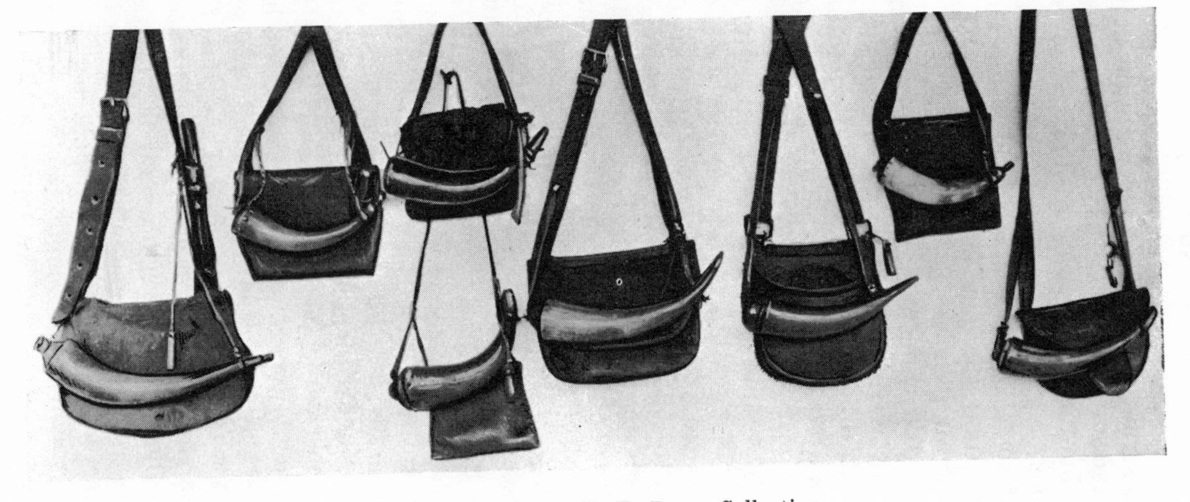

Hunting Bags from F. E. Dunn Collection.

other for target shooting. The straight starter was the same design as that for the hunting rifles, while the guide starter is the same as that used with the target rifles as described and fully illustrated on the following pages with the target rifle accessories.

When the hunting and target rifles became popular, about 1840, the old powder-horn and hunting bag were going "out of fashion," the metal powder-flask with adjustable charger having displaced the former, and in the eastern part of this country very few hunting bags were in use as the majority of the owners of rifles of this kind did not take the long wilderness hunting and exploring trips that the early pioneers made. Of course, those who in 1849 and early 1850's emigrated to California and other western territories, taking with them these rifles for defence and hunting, found the hunting bag a useful part of their equipment. When hunting with these rifles the straight starter was always used as it was lighter to carry and easier to use than the guide starter.

The majority of these arms were especially rifled, often with the gain twist, to use the conical, or flat point "picket" bullets instead of the round ball, which being heavier had a longer accuracy range and better killing power. The bullets for these rifles were cast and then swaged, which trued them up to more exact size, somewhat re-shaped them and at the same time condensed the lead, all of which considerably improved the accuracy at the target or game. The swage used with these rifles is the same type and construction as that used with the target rifles, and a full description of it with illustrations will be found on other pages.

"Cappers," "cap primers," or "cap magazines," are small, peculiarly shaped magazines, a little thicker inside than the over-all length of a percussion cap, made from copper or bronze, holding one hundred caps, and

"Cappers" or Cap Magazines from F. E. Dunn Collection. Capper at top handles Musket Caps used in the Civil War.

having a narrow end about 1/4 inch wide into which the caps are forced by a spring, one at a time, and held while being placed on the nipple of the rifle. Several different shapes of cappers were in use years ago, principally with revolvers, occasionally used with rifles of this type, but were not used with the earlier cap-lock hunting rifles in use before about 1837, as they had not been invented, or I can find no record of their earlier invention and use.

Herewith are illustrated two small accessories, the correct name of which neither the owner nor I know, but for want of a better name I shall call "primers." As will be seen, these consist of a small brass cylinder filled with fine powder, with a plunger at the top. Projecting from the side of the main cylinder is a short, funnel-shaped tube having one end of the right size to fit closely over the top of the nipple of the rifle, and connected to the main cylinder by a small opening through which the powder was forced by pressure on the plunger at the top of the cylinder. When the rifle mis-fired, the small tube of the "primer" was placed over the nipple, held down tight against it, and then pressure applied to the plunger at the top of the cylinder, forced by compression, the fine powder into the nipple of the rifle making it ready to fire after a cap was placed on it.

These "primers" were never in general use in this country; I had never heard of such a thing until a few weeks before this book was published, when I found these two that are illustrated, in the collection owned by Mr. F. E. Dunn, of Glenns Falls, New York. I know of no other person who owns one of these and believe them to be very rare. These were not marked with the name of the maker, but we think they were of foreign make — possibly French workmanship. Whether they were really effective and practical in actual use is a question that we cannot answer; but if

Cap Magazines or "Cappers" from Collection of F. E. Dunn. The two small accessories with Funnel-shaped parts are "Primers"; these contain FFF g. powder for priming rifle when it misfires.

they were practical, why did they not come into general use?

During my early boyhood days these hunting and target rifles were very popular in the New England States and New York, especially those by certain makers. The man who owned a Wm. Billinghurst rifle of this type with all its accessories, and ammunition box was regarded as having the *finest all-around rifle* obtainable. They were of very high-grade workmanship, especially accurate and thoroughly dependable arms. Those made by N. Lewis, James & Ferris, and D. H. Hilliard, were next in popularity.

The target rifle, because of the greater refinement in manufacture in order to give superior accuracy, required a larger number of accessories than the two preceding classes of rifles. These were especially rifled, many of them with a gain twist, for use with the long cylindrical, or cylindro-conoidal, bullet which required a certain kind of patch. Four different kinds of patches, known as the oiled linen, the oiled paper cross patch, the two-strip oiled paper, and the three-strip oiled paper patches, which were not usually interchangeable in the same rifle, were in general use with these rifles. Each noted maker had a preference for one certain type of patch in order to secure the very finest accuracy at 40 rods or more, although they made rifles to use any kind of patch that the customer desired. The target rifles were all made with the false muzzle and guide bullet starter, as these are all absolutely necessary in order to obtain the finest accuracy.

The false muzzle was invented by Mr. Alvan Clark, of Cambridge, Massachusetts, the noted maker of telescope lenses, who was granted a patent on it in 1840, and granted to Edwin Wesson then located in Northboro, Massachusetts, then one of the leading riflemakers, the sole right to make and sell rifles with a false muzzle on a royalty basis of $2.00 for each false muzzle made. The object of the false muzzle is to serve as a funnel to insure the entrance of the bullet and patch without damage into the bore of the rifle when loading; while the object of the bullet starter is to start the bullet and patch down the bore of the rifle, bearing uniformly on the lands with its long axis perfectly coinciding with the axis of the bore. The false muzzle is a piece of the barrel a little longer than the diameter of the barrel, which is cut off either before drilling the barrel or after it has been drilled, but *before* it has been *reamed and rifled.* Before cutting off this piece for the false muzzle, the octagon barrel is placed in the lathe and the muzzle end turned cylindrically about 1½ inches in length, or about ¼ inch longer than the false muzzle will be when finished. After the piece for the false muzzle has been cut off, from the muzzle end and close to the perimeter, four holes about ⅛ inch in diameter are drilled parallel to the bore and smooth reamed to fit the four steel pins that have been tightly fitted into *exactly corresponding* holes drilled into the rear end of the false muzzle. These steel pins project about ⅞ of an inch beyond the end of the false muzzle to fit the corresponding holes in the muzzle of the barrel, and hold the false muzzle in place when loading the rifle. After this piece for the false muzzle has been cut off, and the holding pins fitted to it and the barrel, it is held in place by clamps while the barrel is *reamed and rifled as one piece.* Thus the grooves and lands in the false muzzle *exactly coincide* with those of the barrel. The forward end of the false muzzle is slightly enlarged, and the lands slightly beveled off for about ¼ inch to facilitate entering the patch and bullet into the bore without tearing the patch.

For several years after the invention of the "Clark's patent false muzzle," Edwin Wesson was the only rifle-maker in the United States who could furnish rifles with the false muzzle, but about 1848 he sold to other prominent rifle-makers the right to make these on payment to him of $3.00 each; $2.00 of which Edwin Wesson paid to Mr. Clark.

In the old *Shooting and Fishing* magazine, issue of February 11, 1904, is an article stating that the false muzzle was invented by Carlos C. Clark, in 1836, while he was employed as a gunsmith by Ripley Brothers, Windsor, Vermont. This article recites at some length this invention by Mr. Clark, and states that he, Carlos C. Clark, was granted a patent on it in 1839 or '40. However, it is very certain that the writer of that article, who signed it as "E. I. P," made a mistake in the first name of the inventor, because the U. S. Patent Office granted a patent on this to Alvan Clark, of Boston, or Cambridge, Massachusetts, in 1840.

The kind of patch to be used with the rifle must be decided upon before making the false muzzle for each rifle, since it is necessary to turn in the lathe a shallow, circular recess, the same size as the cloth patch, in the muzzle end of the false muzzle if the rifle is to be used with the circular linen patch. If the oiled paper cross patch, or the two-strip oiled paper patch is to be used, it is necessary to cut shallow grooves the same width as the strips of the patch at right angles across the muzzle end of the false muzzle. If it is desired to use the three-strip oiled paper patch, three shallow grooves are cut across the muzzle fitting each of the strips of the patch. Thus it will be seen that a false muzzle which was made for use with the two-strip or three-strip oiled paper patch could not be used with the oiled linen or other cloth patch, which being thicker than the paper patch would make it impossible to load the rifle unless a smaller diameter bullet was used.

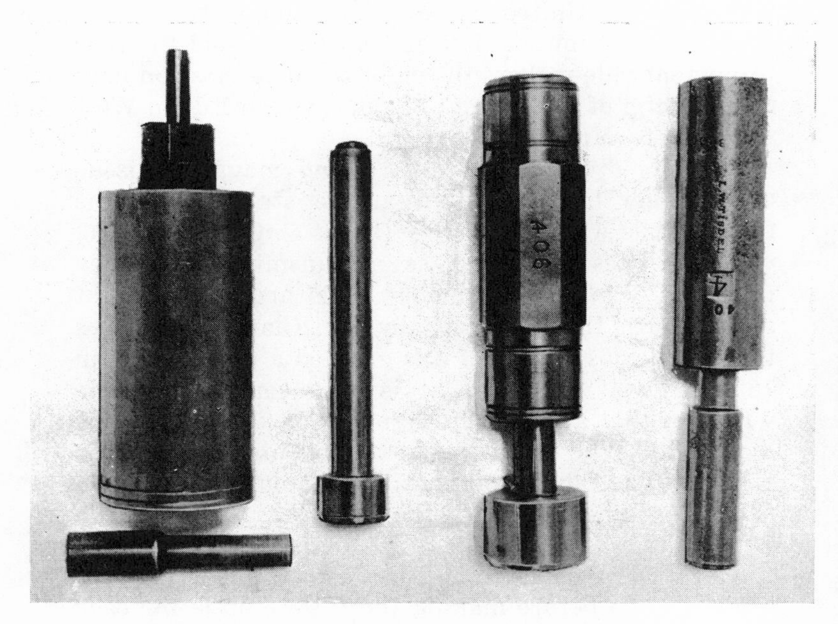

Bullet Swages. Left, Brockway Swage with Plunger for Expelling Bullet. Center, Carver type Swage and Plunger, by F. R. Butler. Right, L. W. Tisdel, old type Swage and Plunger.

Seth Millard Split-Swage and Plunger, from W. A. Luce collection.

.lse Muzzle, Cap for 3-Strip Paper Patch with strips and Bullet in position for loading, 38 calibre Cylindrical Bullet and Bullet Starter for J. H. Huntoon Rifle.

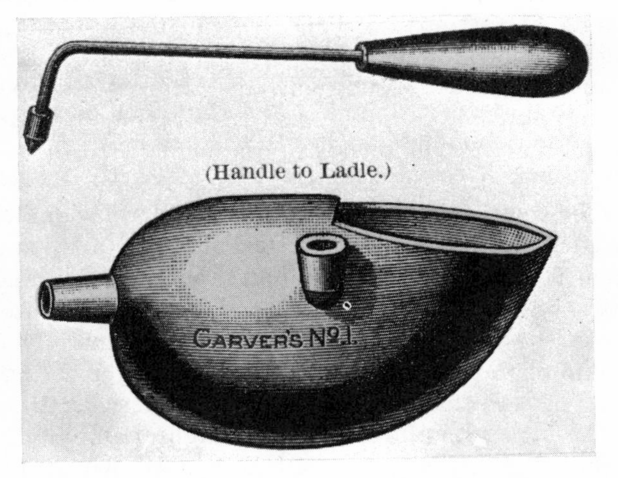

Bullet Ladle Invented and Patented by James W. Carver, Windsor, Vermont.

A small steel post about one inch high with a ball or disc about ½ inch in diameter should be screwed into the top of the false muzzle to block the front sight, or prevent seeing through the telescope when aiming, to assure the removal of the false muzzle before firing, in order that it may not be shot away and lost or injured.

The bullet starter, also called the guide starter, is required with the false muzzle of the target rifle in order to enter the patch and bullet through the false muzzle into the bore of the rifle with the *axis of the bullet exactly in line with that of the bore.* The bullet starter consists of a bronze body about three inches long, having the base about ¼ inch larger diameter than the false muzzle, and about ¾ inch long, is turned in the lathe with a recess that accurately and closely fits over the false muzzle. The other longer part is turned a tapering cylindrical shape with a hole about the diameter of the bore of the rifle drilled lengthwise through it and the base, with the axis of this hole *exactly coinciding with that of the bore of the rifle.* A plunger of soft steel or bronze about five or six inches long is turned in the lathe to accurately fit and slide through the body, having one end accurately shaped to fit the point of the bullet, and the other end having a flat knob about 1¼ inches in diameter fitted to it.

In using the bullet starter, after the charge of powder has been poured down the barrel, a patch is placed in the recess in the top of the false muzzle which is held to the muzzle of the rifle by the holding pins, a bullet is centered in it, and just started into the bore of it, the bullet starter is placed carefully over the end of the false muzzle with the plunger fitting the point of the bullet, held tightly to it with the left hand while with the ball of the right hand the knob of the plunger is struck ONE BLOW which forces the bullet in its patch through the false muzzle into the bore of the rifle the length of the starter plunger. The starter is then removed, and the loading rod used to push the bullet down onto the powder. It is of the *utmost importance* that the bullet in its patch shall be *uniformly and accurately* entered into the bore of the rifle in such a manner that the bullet shall not be even slightly canted or tipped, but that *the axis of the bullet shall exactly coincide with that of the bore of the rifle.* The only way of doing this *uniformly the same each time* is by the use of the false muzzle and bullet starter, also called the guide starter. Further details regarding this will be found in chapter VI.

The patch-cutters for these rifles were of various types in order to cut the form of patch required for the individual rifle; that for the oiled linen or cloth patch was merely a steel wad-cutter with the proper diameter cutting edge hardened and ground sharp to cut the correct size patch from this material. Rifles that used the oiled paper cross patch required a cutter made from hardened steel in the form of a cross having each part of equal length, with the beveled edges ground sharp in order to cut the thin paper, and were the most difficult and expensive to make. The two-strip and three-strip paper patches were rectangular pieces of thin paper about 5/16 inch wide by 1⅜ inches long, larger or smaller depending upon the calibre of the rifle and length of the bullet, which were cut by the use of a steel patch-cutter of this shape, having the beveled edges hardened and ground sharp so as to cut this thin paper. Sometimes they were made with a cutter much like a small trimming board used for trimming photographs, either type of which were easily made and not expensive. Illustrations of various patch-cutters are shown herewith.

In cutting cloth patches, several thicknesses of the desired cloth, or linen, are placed over the sawed-off

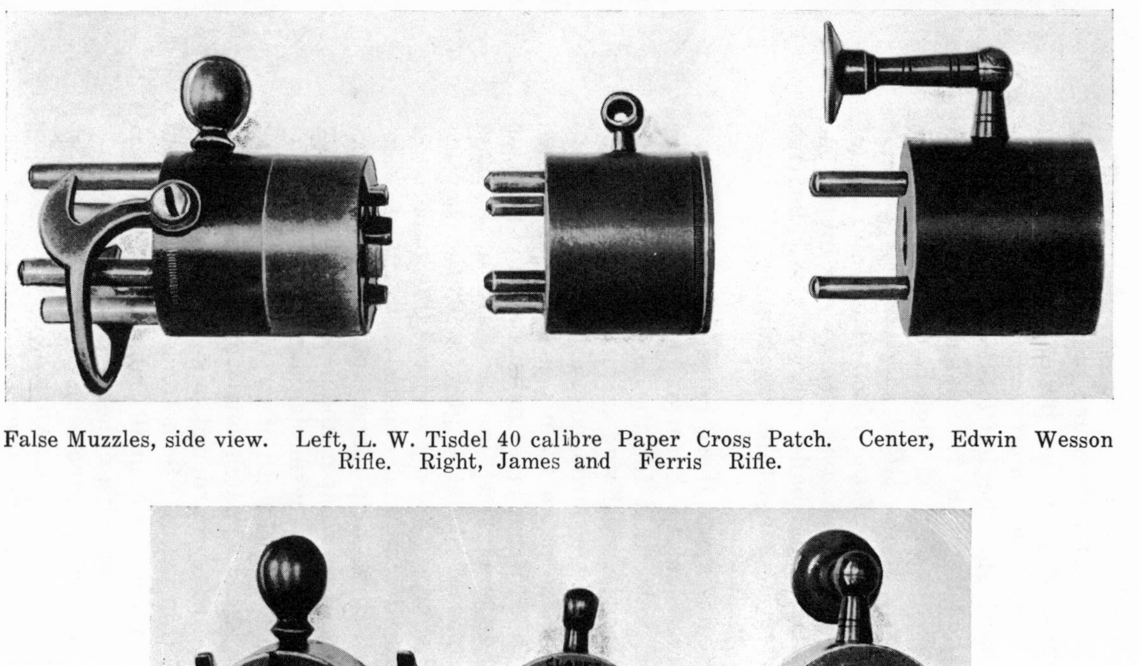

False Muzzles, side view. Left, L. W. Tisdel 40 calibre Paper Cross Patch. Center, Edwin Wesson Rifle. Right, James and Ferris Rifle.

end of a block of wood, with a piece of cardboard underneath, the patch-cutter is placed on the cloth, and struck with a wooden or hard rubber mallet, thus cutting six or more patches at once. The various types of paper patches are cut from thin, tough, bond paper about .001 or .002 inch thick in the same manner as the cloth patches. In cutting these thin paper patches it is especially important to have a piece of cardboard, or thick paper, under the several thicknesses of patch paper in order that the edges of the patches will be cleanly cut, and not left ragged or torn. After the paper patches have been cut they should be lightly oiled with pure sperm oil uniformly applied to the entire patch. The linen or cloth patches are similarly oiled, unless it is desired to use the patch wet with saliva, in which case the patches are, of course, not wet until loading the rifle. Regardless of whether the patch be of paper, linen or other cloth, it is very important that all should be *uniformly* and lightly oiled, because if one patch is lightly oiled, the next one heavily, these two bullets will have a *different point of impact* on the target at 220 yards even though the point of aim was exactly the same for each.

The target rifle requires both a loading rod, or ramrod, and a cleaning rod in order to obtain the best accuracy. Years ago these were both made from tough, straight-grained hickory, white oak, or other close-grained, tough wood. The loading rod is usually made with the wormer attached to one end, and the other hollowed out to fit the point of the bullet, and has a copper ferrule tightly fitted to this end to prevent splitting the wood when forcing the bullet down the bore. The cleaning rod is made of the same kinds of hardwood, somewhat longer than the loading rod, one end having a small knob with square under-cut, and a narrow tapering shank, like the sketch herewith, to hold the square or round cleaning patches. The

Bullet Starters, also called Guide Bullet Starters, of various makes. One at right, by H. M. Pope.

other end should have a rectangular slot about one inch long by 1/8 inch wide cut lengthwise in it to hold the dampened patches for cleaning the bore after each shot. The old-time rifle-makers often made the loading and cleaning rods with a spiral stripe around the entire length of the rods, which was sometimes done by winding a tarred cord spirally around the rod and then burning off the cord, which left a charred spiral the length of the rod; then the rod was smoothed with fine sandpaper and oiled. Others made the spiral on these rods by staining with aqua fortis—now known as nitric acid—applied with a narrow, chisel-shaped piece of hardwood used like a paint brush and applying several coats; then wet the rod with ammonia and sandpapered it smooth. Or a strong saturated solution of potassium permanganate may be applied in the same way spirally around the rod until the desired shade is secured, dried a short time, and then sandpapered smooth and oiled.

Another method of spirally staining the rod is as follows: Electricians' waterproof tape while in the roll is split with a safety razor blade to about 3/8 inch in width, and wound spirally around the entire length of the rod leaving a space of the bare wood about the same width between the spirals of the tape. The exposed wood is then carefully stained with nitric acid applied with a piece of hardwood having a chisel-shaped end and used as a paint brush. In this way apply two or three coats of the nitric acid to the exposed wood. When this is dry, the tape is pulled off, the rod wiped with a cloth wet with stronger household ammonia, again dried, then smoothed with fine sandpaper, and well oiled with raw linseed oil.

Practically all the expert riflemen today prefer both the cleaning and loading rods made from hard, highly polished, drill-rod steel instead of wood. The pores of wood are quite apt to become filled with grit after

False Muzzle, Cap for holding 3-Strip Paper Patch and Bullet Starter for J. H. Huntoon 38 calibre Rifle.

Patch Cutters of various makes from W. A. Luce Collection.

much use, which acts as an abrasive and wears the muzzle of the rifle, while the hard steel rod with its high polish, never holds grit to thus wear the muzzle. Also when pushing a tight-fitting bullet down the bore with the hickory, or other hardwood, rod it often becomes bent, or breaks, while the polished steel rod never breaks and remains straight regardless of tight-fitting bullets. The smaller the calibre of the rifle the more difficult it becomes to load it with a tight-fitting bullet when using the wood rod, while the small polished steel rod does the work easily without bending or breaking. The English swivel-handle, celluloid covered steel rods are also excellent loading rods after having a tip that fits the point of the bullet made for them. The stiff bristle brushes that come with these rods are fine for cleaning the bore of the rifle, and the tips known as "wool mops" that fit these rods are excellent for oiling the bore after cleaning. The celluloid covering of these rods does not carry grit to wear the muzzle of the rifle, and are preferred to the steel rod by some riflemen who hesitate about using the hard steel cleaning rod.

Chargers. Years ago all the target rifles were furnished with one or more chargers with which the correct charge, or charges, of black powder were measured. These chargers were merely a small brass, or tin, tube of various lengths according to the calibre of the rifle, with a cork tightly fitted into one end, then the tube cut to such a length that when filled with powder and stricken off even with the end, held the correct bulk of black powder, or charge, for that particular rifle and bullet. The old-time rifle-makers' method of making the rifle of a pre-determined gauge, or calibre, and then the charge of powder and most accurate shooting bullet determined by experimentation, is doubtless "shocking" to our present-day ballistic engineers. Be that as it may, this method produced results — *accuracy* — that our modern rifles rarely approach and seldom exceed. Often the old-time rifle-maker after having completed the rifle, was obliged to spend several days on the rifle range with it in testing out several different charges of powder, and possibly several different shaped, or weights, of bullets in order to determine the *right charge* of powder and the *most accurate shooting bullet* for that individual rifle. Having determined these two essentials, the charger, or chargers, holding the correct bulk of powder for use with each different bullet could be made, but not before.

During and after the Civil War many rifle-makers discarded the separate charger, and furnished a metal powder-flask with adjustable charger with their target rifles; however, many of the most noted rifle-makers insisted that the separate charger, which was filled from the powder-flask and stricken off, gave more uniform charges and resulted in better accuracy than was obtainable with the powder-flask only. A small funnel, preferably of aluminum, having a top about 2 inches in diameter and the spout, or tube, a little smaller than the bore of the rifle, about 3 inches long, should be included in the accessories for the target rifle. After firing the rifle and wiping the bore before loading, this funnel is placed in the bore of the false muzzle after attaching it to the barrel; then holding the rifle with the barrel in a vertical position, the charge of powder is poured through the funnel into the barrel. This prevents the grains of powder from sticking to the sides of the bore when loading, and improves the accuracy.

In order to cast good bullets the rifleman needs some kind of a small, iron kettle in which to melt the lead, and a bullet dipper for pouring it into the bullet mould, or one of the electric bullet melting furnaces, or a similiar melting pot for use on a gas or gasoline stove. The least expensive of these is the well-known Ideal Melting Pot and Bullet Dipper, made by the Lyman Gun Sight Corporation, of Middlefield, Connecticut. They were not the originators of this bullet dipper; neither was it invented by the late John H. Barlow, the proprietor of the old Ideal Manufacturing Company. Long before that company was in existence, the late James W. Carver, an expert rifleman and a Vermont Yankee inventor, designed the "Carver Bullet Ladle," illustrated herewith, and applied for a patent on it. Whether or not the patent was ever granted, I am unable to state, but the Ideal Bullet Dipper is but a modification of Carver's ladle. Possibly Mr. Barlow purchased Carver's patent on this and re-designed it in a smaller size. During the past forty odd years thousands of shooters all over the world have used the Ideal Melting Pot and Bullet Dipper, and by their use in connection with a hundred or more different kinds of bullet moulds, literally millions of different calibres and types of excellent bullets have been cast. A person who is experienced in casting bullets can cast as perfect bullets with this outfit as is possible with any other method or bullet casting outfit. It is possible that bullets cannot be cast as rapidly in this way as with the electric bullet melting pot.

Of course, the Ideal Bullet Dipper and Melting Pot does not "harmonize" so nicely with the electric cooking stove, electric coffee-maker, electric refrigerator, electric flatiron, electric toaster that "shoots" the toast onto one's plate, almost, electric curling iron, electric washing machine, and other electric "contraptions" that are now so "fashionable." But if one must be "in the latest fashion," and cast his bullets with the electric bullet casting outfit, the Potter Electric Bullet Furnace, made by the Potter Engineering Company, of Syracuse, New York, will be found satisfactory for casting small quantities of bullets. Its chief defect is

No. 1, 35 calibre Brockway; 2, 38 calibre Brockway; 3, 45 calibre Whitworth; 4 and 5, 50 calibre Billinghurst; 6, 45 calibre Brockway before Swaging; 7, 45 calibre Brockway, Swaged.

No. 1, 35 calibre Lewis; 2, 32 calibre Appleby; 3, 36 calibre Lewis; 4, 45 calibre Hexagonal Bullet for Granger Rifle, left-hand twist; 5, 48 calibre 650 grain Cylindrical Bullet for Billinghurst 60-pound "Sharpshooters" Rifle; 6, 22 calibre Conical for Lewis Rifle; 7, 22 calibre Round Ball for Lewis Rifle; 8, 60 calibre Musgrove; 9 and 10, 36 calibre Bullets cast in Old Soapstone Mould; 11 and 12, [illegible] calibre Lubricated Bullets for Schalk Rifle.

its very small capacity, as it holds but 2½ pounds of metal. The Merit Melting Pot, made by the Merit Gun Sight Company, of Oakland, California, for use on a gas or gasoline stove, is larger, holds 20 pounds of metal, costs less than the electric bullet furnace, is less expensive in operation, and the more practical, according to my experience. With this, or the electric melting pot, one can turn out perfect bullets more rapidly than with the older melting pot and bullet dipper method, but this is the only advantage that I find.

Bullet moulds for the target rifles were of many different sizes, shapes, and designs, since many different types of bullets were used. Many rifles were made to use a bullet that was cast in two separate parts: the base of pure lead, the front part of hardened lead and tin alloy, and the two parts swaged together, while others used a soft lead bullet cast in one piece and then swaged. The purpose of the composite bullet is that the soft lead butt part positively upsets and fills the grooves of the rifling, while the hardened lead front part limits the length of upset, thus keeping the fit on the bore, and consequently the friction, the same for each shot. Whereas, if the bullet is a long cylindrical one, cast whole from soft lead, the length of the upset may vary somewhat from shot to shot, consequently increasing or decreasing the friction in the barrel, which, in turn, causes a difference in the point of impact on the target, thereby more or less enlarging the group. Regardless of whether the bullets are cast in one piece or two, it is necessary to swage them before using, which operation with the bullet cast whole trues it up, slightly enlarges the diameter, forms it perfectly into the desired finished shape of base and point, and at the same time condenses the lead; all of which much improves the accuracy. The separate parts of the two-piece, composite bullets were almost

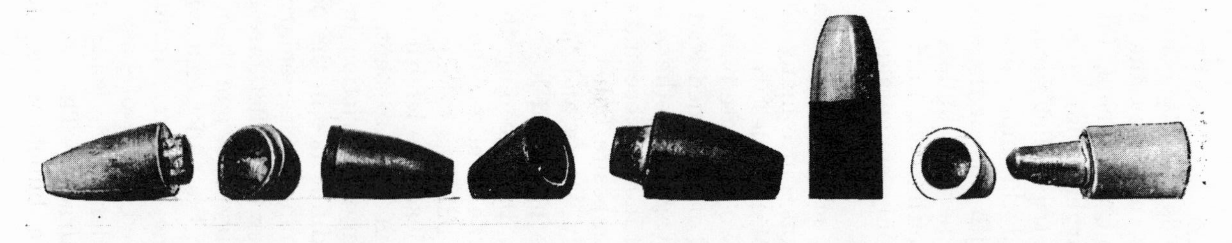

Composite Bullets. Left to right: Nos. 1 and 2, Parts as Cast for 45 calibre Base-Band Bullet No. 3, used in Lewis Rifle. Nos. 4 and 5, Cast Parts for 50 calibre Bullet for Billinghurst Rifle. No. 6, 45 calibre Bullet for Brockway Rifle after Swaging. Nos. 7 and 8, Cast Parts for Bullet No. 7.

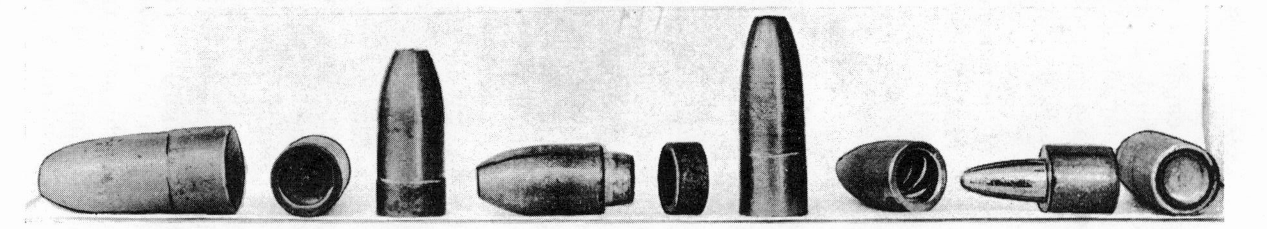

Left to right. No. 1, 50 calibre Lewis Base-Band Bullet. No. 2, Showing base of 40 calibre Base-Band Bullet No. 3. Nos. 4 and 5, Cast Parts before Swaging for Bullet No. 3. No. 6, Swaged Bullet for 40 calibre Tisdel Rifle. Nos. 7 and 8, Cast Parts for No. 6. No. 9, Showing base of Bullet No. 6.

never cast perfectly; therefore it is necessary to place these parts together and swage them into the desired diameter, shape the base and point, and firmly join the two parts together with the least possible line of demarcation between them.

As will be seen by the illustrations, the two pieces of the composite bullets before being swaged are quite different in shape and size from the finished bullets as they come from the swage. This is also true of the one-piece bullet, which comes from the mould with a square base that is in the process of swaging generally somewhat rounded, or countersunk, as well as usually changing the shape of the point at the same time. The cherries used in the old days were not as perfectly made as those today, and it was impossible to cut a mould with them that would cast the almost perfect bullets that we get with our moulds now. The base of the composite bullet was very seldom cast in the shape desired, but was so shaped by swaging. Also, different shaped punches could be used in the swage by means of which several different shaped bases could be made from one shape of base part as cast, and swaging a bullet greatly improves the homogeniety of the metal from which it is cast, which alone will improve the accuracy of any bullet.

Swages are of many different sizes and designs in order to swage the various types of bullets used with the target rifles. The simplest type consists of a cylindrical piece of tool steel about one inch in diameter by three or four long, having a hole drilled lengthwise nearly through it, with the end of this hole reamed to the exact shape desired for the finished bullet. This hole, or bore, is then smooth-reamed so as to make it a true cylinder and perfectly round, of the exact size required and the shape of the point desired in the finished bullet, and then carefully polished inside to facilitate the removal of the bullet after

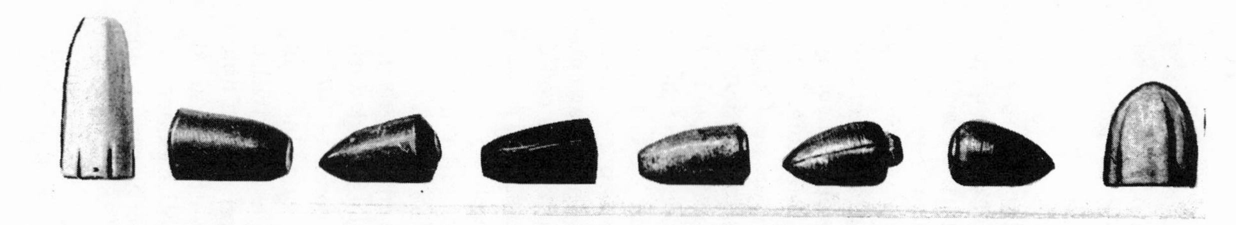

Left to right. No. 1, 45 calibre 295 grain Bullet for Brockway Rifle, showing Rifling after putting through False Muzzle. No. 2, 42 calibre 198 grain Picket Bullet. No. 3, 39 calibre 150 grain Pointed Picket Bullet. No. 4, 35 calibre 150 grain Flat Point Picket Bullet. No. 5, 36 calibre 145 grain Lewis "Sugar Loaf" Bullet. No. 6, 38 calibre 130 grain Boat-Tail Bullet used in Carlos Clark Rifles in 1835. How come that our Modern Boat-Tail Bullets are *something new?* No. 7, 35 calibre 120 grain Pointed Picket Bullet for N. Whitmore Rifle about 1830. No. 8, 55 calibre "half-breed" Bullet. So called because it is half of a Round Ball and part of a Cylindrical one.

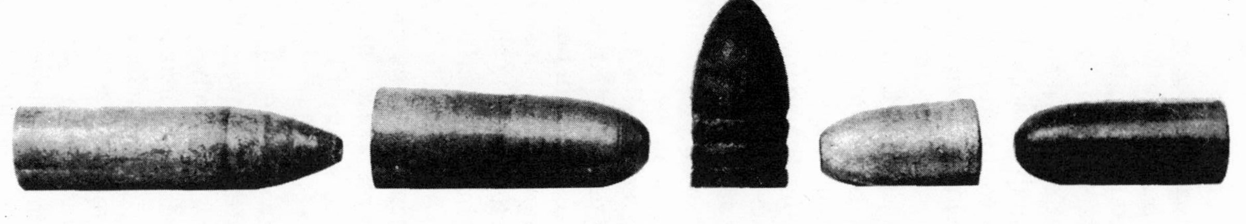

Left to Right: No. 1, 45 calibre 600 grain Bullet used in Billinghurst 50-pound "Sharpshooters Rifle." No. 2, 65 calibre 870 grain Two-piece Bullet for Abe Williams, 65-pound. "Sharpshooters Rifle." No. 3, 58 calibre Civil War "Minnie" Bullet. No. 4, 50 calibre Base-Band Bullet for Lewis Rifle. No. 5, 48 calibre Two-Piece Bullet for Billinghurst Rifle.

swaging. A steel cylindrical punch is then turned in the lathe about .0003 inch smaller diameter than the finished bore of the swage, with one end turned to the exact shape as the base desired for the finished bullet and the other somewhat enlarged for striking with the hammer or mallet. This punch is then smoothed and polished to the exact size of the bore of the swage, and then hardened so as not to be deformed in use.

In using this swage, the cast bullet lightly oiled is dropped point down into the bore, the punch inserted behind it, and with the base of the swage resting on the bench, or block of wood, the large end of the punch is struck a certain number of times with the hammer. This compresses the lead, gives the base and point the desired shape, and makes the bullet the exact diameter required. The punch is then withdrawn, the swage turned bottom up and struck smartly with the mallet which is supposed to cause the bullet to drop out of it, but frequently does not. When the bullet fails to drop out of the swage, the muzzle is struck with the mallet or lead hammer to jar the bullet out, and after repeated attempts the bullet comes out. This is the *worst* type of swage made, as generally the bullet fails to drop out properly after swaging, then repeated blows are struck with the lead hammer to jar the bullet out, which finally drops out. This old two-piece swage has caused more trouble and profanity than any and all other accessories for the muzzle-loading rifles.

Before swaging, the bullets should be slightly oiled by rolling on a piece of cloth, or buckskin, that is lightly and uniformly oiled with light oil, or between the lightly oiled palms of the hands, which is supposed to cause them to drop out of the swage easier: but neither method will cause them to *always* do so. At last an improved bullet swage as made by N. S. Brockway and some others was designed, which consists of the body of the swage having the bore clear through lengthwise, and having screwed into one end a steel point-forming part with a sliding plunger the size and inside shape of the desired point of the bullet, and a punch as in the other type of swage. In using this swage, the lightly oiled bullet is dropped point down into the bore of the swage, and rests against the plunger in the point-former, the punch is inserted and struck a certain number of blows with the hammer, or mallet, while the base of the swage rests on a block of wood having a hole bored in it a little larger and deeper than the point-former and its plunger. The punch is then withdrawn, the swage turned bottom up, and a light tap with the mallet on the plunger of the point-former easily expells the bullet without deforming it in any way. This was really a *great improvement* over the old two-piece swage, and saves the rifleman a lot of trouble, time and "cussing" in swaging bullets.

Another type of swage known as the "Carver Swage," is made in three pieces; the body having the hole clear through it, the separate point-forming piece closely and accurately fitted inside one end and the punch fitting the other. After swaging a bullet, the point-forming piece is pulled out of the body, and lightly tapping the punch with the mallet easily expells the bullet uninjured. Everything considered, the Carver swage is the easier to use, but requires more careful workmanship in making, is more expensive and because of the very slight burr left on the body of the bullet at the junction of the point-former and the body of the swage, is not generally as desirable for swaging the long cylindrical bullets as the Brockway type of swage. Illustrations showing the various types of bullet swages will be found on another page.

Nipple Wrenches. A nipple wrench of some kind is very necessary for use with the target rifle as even the best nipples break after having been in use for a long time. The percussion caps of the early days contained fulminate of mercury which was very corrosive and erosive; this corroded the nipple quite rapidly unless it was made of the best steel and platinum lined, and even these sometimes broke. A badly corroded nipple is liable to break at any time, and it is quite important to have at hand a tool with which the broken nipple may be easily removed, and a new one inserted. The simplest kind of nipple wrench and the lightest, is the L-shaped one as described under the accessories for the hunting rifle on a preceding page. However, the nipple wrench shaped like the inverted T was usually furnished with the target rifle. The vertical part of this is made from 3/8 inch diameter steel about three inches long, having about a 3/16 inch hole drilled 1/2 inch deep into one end and a slot cut crosswise the same width as the base of the nipple so as to fit closely over the nipple. The other end has a 1/4 inch hole drilled horizontally through it into which is fitted a piece of steel about three inches long so as to extend equally on each side and serve as a handle in unscrewing a broken nipple or putting in a new one. Then the end having the slot that fits over the nipple should be hardened so as to make it tough, but not brittle which would cause it to break off in use.

Some nipple wrenches of this type are made with a wooden handle fitted over and securely fastened to the steel piece that fits the nipple, which are efficient if the handle is quite strong and rigidly fastened to the steel part. Some nipple wrenches are made with a wooden handle like a screw-driver, but these are not as efficient in use as the other types mentioned since this handle does not afford a good grip for the hand, or have as much leverage when unscrewing a badly corroded nipple as the other types. Illustrations

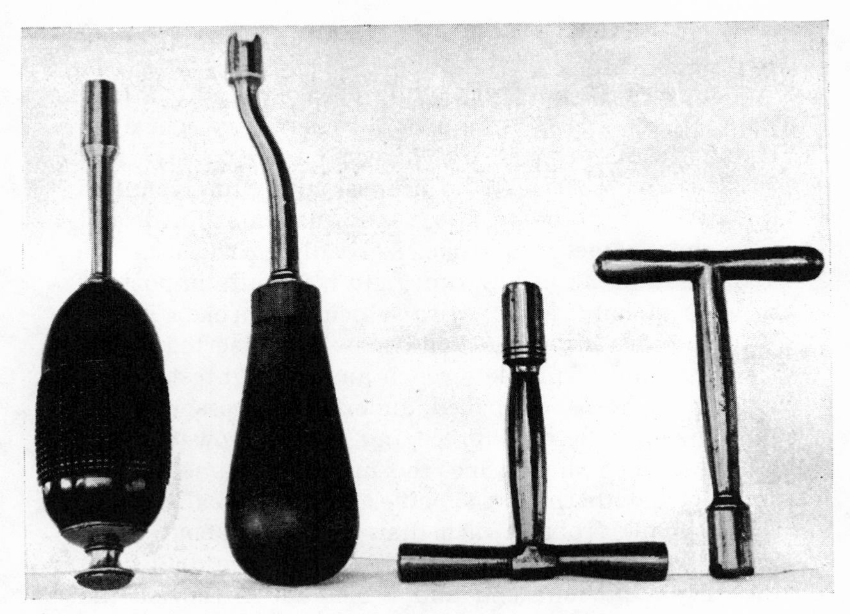

Nipple Wrenches from W. A. Luce Collection.

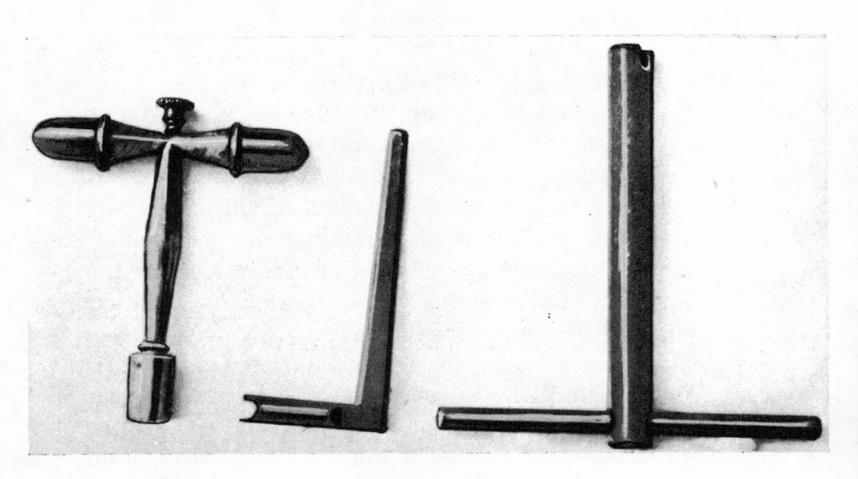

Nipple Wrenches from F. E. Dunn Collection. Left-hand Wrench has places for extra nipples by unscrewing ends of the T-shaped handle. Wire for picking out nipple in top.

showing the different nipple wrenches are given on another page.

Ammunition Boxes. A well-made, rigidly constructed ammunition box having several compartments in which to carry the powder-flask, charger, caps, patches for the bullets, cleaning patches, oil and other equipment, and one or two wooden bullet racks in which the bullets are carried, is an essential piece of equipment for the target rifle. This box should be made of black walnut, mahogany, or similar wood, with the bottom very securely fastened in place, the top secured by small bronze or steel hinges of good strength, and two strong bronze or steel hasps with a lock and key attached to the front. The top should have a folding bronze handle for carrying the box attached by small bolts (not screws) through the wood and secured by washers and nuts inside. These boxes vary in size and shape according to the individual's fancy or the calibre of the rifle for which it is made. Usually they are about 9 to 10 inches wide by 11 or 12 inches long, and 3 or 4 inches deep, with a felt lining glued to the inside. The bullet rack fitting one of the compartments may be round, square or rectangular in shape, usually of soft, well-seasoned pine or spruce about 1¼ inches thick with holes the size and shape of the point of the bullet drilled into it about one-half the length of the bullets for the purpose of carrying these point down in these holes. After the labor expended in casting and swaging the bullets it is essential that they should be carried in such a manner that they will not be damaged in any way before use, and the best method is by means of the properly-made bullet racks fitting the ammunition box. Years ago these boxes, thoroughly well made, could be had for about three or four dollars, but today are quite expensive as it requires a skillful cabinet maker to construct these in a satisfactory manner.

The various types of metal fishing tackle boxes sold by sporting good dealers, having one or more trays inside with several compartments in each, are really quite superior to the wooden boxes for this purpose. They have the advantages of being stronger, lighter and less expensive than the wooden ammunition boxes, as well as having plenty of room inside for carrying one or two bullet racks, powder-flask, cleaning solvent, oil, cleaning patches, patches for the bullets, and all other small articles needed on the range.

A spotting telescope of high power is a very essential accessory for use with the target rifle in spotting the bullet holes in the target at 200 yards or more. During the past sixty odd years I have used many makes, types and power of telescopes for this purpose, and while the modern prism spotting telescope is shorter and more convenient to carry, I still believe that the large objective draw-tube telescope gives the better definition of the target at 200 or 220 yards. I have yet to see any prism spotting telescope that can be purchased for $150.00 or less that gives as fine definition at these ranges as can be obtained with a high-grade draw-tube telescope having a power of 50 to 70. The English made, "Lord Bury" telescope in 50 power is the finest spotting telescope that I have yet owned, and gives most excellent definition at all ranges.

John R. Chapman stated in his book, *The Improved American Rifle,* which was published in 1848, as follows: "The refracting telescope of considerable power is requisite to observe the bullet holes in the target, making the marksman independent of a marker. These can be purchased at from $10.00 to $20.00 each, although the one I use cost $45.00, made by Lerebours of Paris, with a power of 77 times, is beautifully clear, with which at 40 rods a pin's head may be seen."

Now, Chapman was a civil engineer of long experience, a *reliable and truthful* man, and when he stated that his 77 power draw-tube telescope would show the head of a pin at 40 rods (220 yards) *he meant just what he stated.* Very well, just show me any prism spotting telescope that can be purchased today at $150.00 or less that in good light will show the head of a common pin at 220 yards. As the farmer said about the giraffe: "There aint no such animile." Of course, if you are willing to pay from about $250.00 to $500.00 for one of the large, heavy so-called "Team Captain's Spotting Scopes" advertised by various optical instruments manufacturers, you will have a telescope that equals the performance of that used by Mr. Chapman: but how many of you gun bugs are willing to pay that sum for a telescope? If, on the other hand, you can content yourself with one of those "old-fashioned," long draw-tube telescopes of 50 to 70 power, you will find that it gives such definition as Chapman described, if the instrument is strictly high-grade workmanship.

A tripod for the spotting telescope is also quite necessary, and we have these of various makes and designs, constructed of aluminum or aluminum alloy that are light, strong and durable, selling from about $3.50 to any price you care to pay. Be sure that whatever make you select is rigid when set up, else your powerful telescope will be of little use in spotting the bullet holes in the target at 200 yards or more because of the excessive vibration of the tripod.

In order to obtain the best accuracy — make the smallest groups—in rest shooting with either type of the target rifle, a muzzle rest of bronze or cast aluminum about six inches long should be attached crosswise to the under part of the barrel about 6 or 8 inches from the muzzle and held in place by a small set screw tapped through it and about ¼ inch into the barrel. This was the customary method of attaching the muzzle rest by the old-time rifle-makers, but many riflemen object to tapping a hole in the barrel near the muzzle, which is wholly unnecessary when using the aluminium type herewith illustrated. As will be seen by the illustration, the top clamp of this rest fits over the octagon top of the barrel and is secured in place by a cap-screw in each end threaded into the base part. When the rifle has a full length telescope, the top part of this muzzle rest must be made of sheet aluminum about 1/4 inch thick, bent in the proper shape to fit the top of the barrel and held in place by cap-screws at each end.

I, personally, prefer the aluminum muzzle rest to those of bronze or iron, as they are lighter to carry in the ammunition box and in every way fully as efficient in use as any other kind. If the aluminum muzzle rest is to be used with a very heavy target rifle having a barrel some two inches across the octagon flats, it would, of course, be necessary to make it much larger than the illustration shows, but otherwise would be the same design.

A well-constructed shooting bench, or bench rest, is an essential part of the equipment for use with the target rifle if rest shooting is to be practiced and without which the machine rest rifle cannot be used. We now have on the market several different types of folding, portable shooting benches, most of which are all right for testing hunting rifles and 22 calibre rim fire rifles, but unsatisfactory for use with the target rifles because they are too small size, and not rigid or firm enough. If a portable shooting bench must be used, one made according to the following plan, if properly made, will prove as good as any. The top should be made from clear spruce or fir, 2 inches thick, shaped like the diagram herewith. The main part of the top is 2 feet 6 inches wide by 2 feet 8 inches long:

the right-hand piece is 11 inches wide and 4 feet long in order that 16 inches may extend back of the other part to afford a rest for the butt of the rifle, and a support for the right arm. The top should be securely fastened together by cross cleats 1½ inches thick by 3 inches wide, attached with 3-inch wood screws at each end and at the end of the arm rest. The five legs each 3 inches square by 28 inches long—one for each corner of the top and one at the end of the arm rest—should be attached to the underside of the cross cleats by wrought-iron strap hinges about 6 inches long by 2 inches wide held in place by 2-inch screws, so that the legs will fold against the under side of the top when transporting it. Also five braces 1½ inches thick by 2 inches wide will be required to hold the legs in position when the bench is in use. These braces are attached to the front and back legs firmly, but the two sides braces and that for the leg of the arm rest should be attached by ¼ inch bolts through these legs and ends of the braces, held in place by washers and wing-nuts so that they may be easily removed when folding the legs for transportation.

A small stool or bench of chair height, or a folding camp chair, is necessary as a seat for the rifleman when shooting with this rest.

A rectangular box without ends, 7½ inches high by 6 inches wide and 9 inches long, should be made from 1-inch spruce or fir, well smoothed on the top and sides, on which the muzzle cross piece, or aluminum muzzle rest attached about 6 inches back of the muzzle of the rifle is rested when shooting, is necessary in order to hold uniformly and make small groups on the target. Also a wedge-shaped block of hardwood about 9 inches long by 2 inches wide and 1½ inches thick at the thick end should be made and smoothed on top for use as a rest under the butt of the rifle in

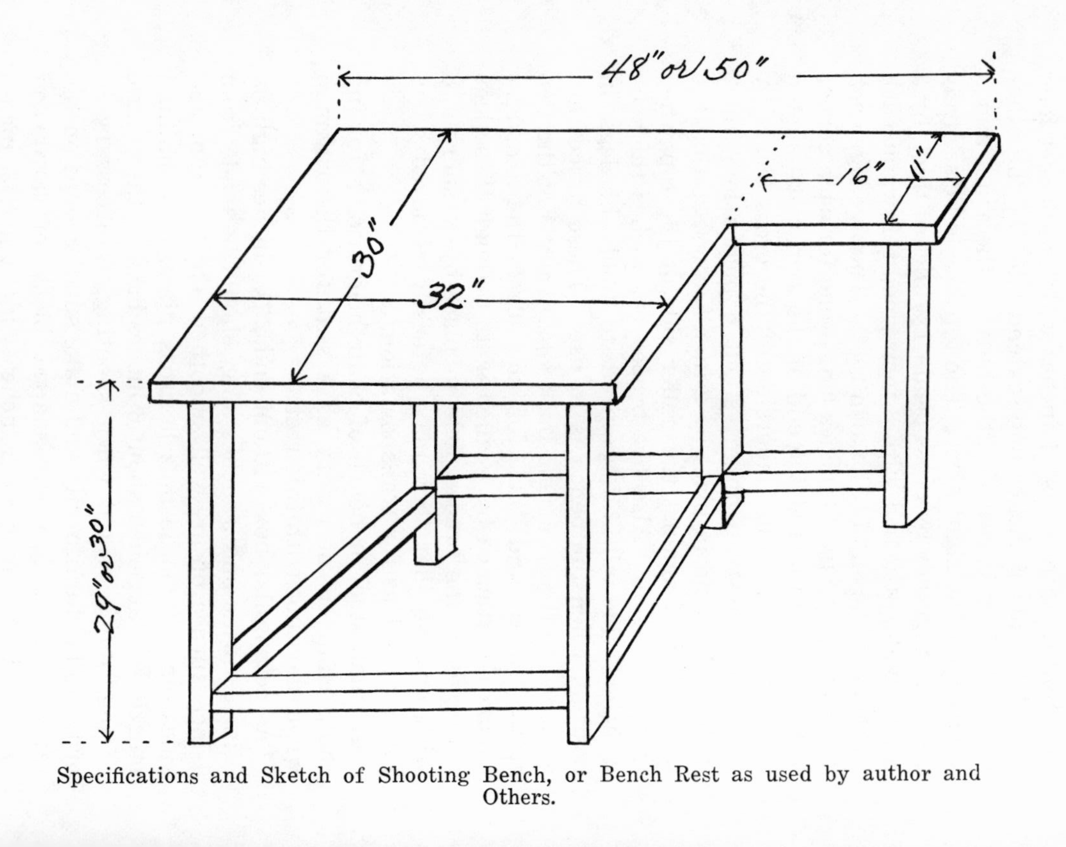

Specifications and Sketch of Shooting Bench, or Bench Rest as used by author and Others.

order to maintain uniform elevation when shooting from the rest described.

If one has a permanent range where he practices shooting, it is advisable to build this bench rest in a more substantial and solid manner, having the legs 4 inches square by 36 inches long, set 7 or 8 inches into the ground so that the bench will be solid and rigid. In this case it is advisable to make the top 36 inches wide by 40 inches long for the main part, with the arm rest 11 inches wide and extending back 18 inches to the rear. A top this size gives more room for setting up the tripod of the spotting telescope, and for powder-flask, bullets, patches, etc., used in loading the rifle. Also the fixed bench rest built in this way should have pieces 1½ inches thick by 4 inches wide firmly nailed to the top of the legs under the top of the bench as top braces for the legs which are spiked to the top of the bench instead of being hinged. The braces near the bottom of the legs should also be nailed to them, thus making the bench far more strong and solid than any portable rest.

If it is desired to shoot from machine rest it will be necessary to first construct a solid, tapering concrete base 20 inches wide at the bottom, 8 or 9 inches wide at the top, 24 inches long and about 44 inches high. The bottom of this base should be set about 15 inches into the ground leaving it about table height above and held in place by rubble and cement. The top of this base should have a bolt 8 inches long by ½ inch diameter set 5 inches deep into the cement at each corner with 3 inches of each bolt extending above and washers and wing-nuts for each bolt. A piece of clear spruce or fir plank 2½ inches thick and the same size as the concrete top, planed smooth on top, with ½ inch holes bored in each corner fits over these four bolts set into the corners of the cement top, and is secured in place by washers and wing-nuts. This provides a

Machine Rest designed and used by Wm. V. Lowe, Horace Warner and other Expert Rifle-men.

solid and substantial base to which the machine rest is fastened, by lag screws or bolts, to the plank top. After the day's shooting, the wing-nuts are removed and the plank top with the machine rest attached is easily removed for safe keeping until again needed.

There are numerous types and makes of machine rests on the market, some of which are not well adapted for use with the muzzle-loading rifle, that can be purchased for about $25.00. The best of these is that made by the noted rifle-maker, Harry M. Pope, 18 Morris Street, Jersey City, New Jersey, and two formerly made by Wm. V. Lowe, which are not now on the market, but can be made by any good machinist from the description and illustrations herewith through the courtesy of Mr. Lowe. The Simplified Machine Rest shown in Figure 3 is a most excellent device for controlling the rifle, and is one of the simplest, reliable rest for the purpose. The main portion is a brass casting, the slide and screws being of machine steel. The slide should be fitted very closely, as should in fact all the moving parts, to avoid any tipping when the adjusting screws are moved. The front cross level is usually made of brass, and has a notch in the front which is pushed into contact with a screw in the stand. The method of operation is the same as with the improved machine rest, described below.

The Improved Machine Rest, shown in the illustrations on another page, is the best device from many different designs evolved to overcome various difficulties. One difficulty was that when the strength of the wind changed suddenly, and a new windage setting was made with other rests, a wild shot resulted because other changes, not intended, took place. In this rest, all this is eliminated by having powerful springs oppose the action of the adjusting screws, thus taking up all back-lash, or lost motion. One spring holds the

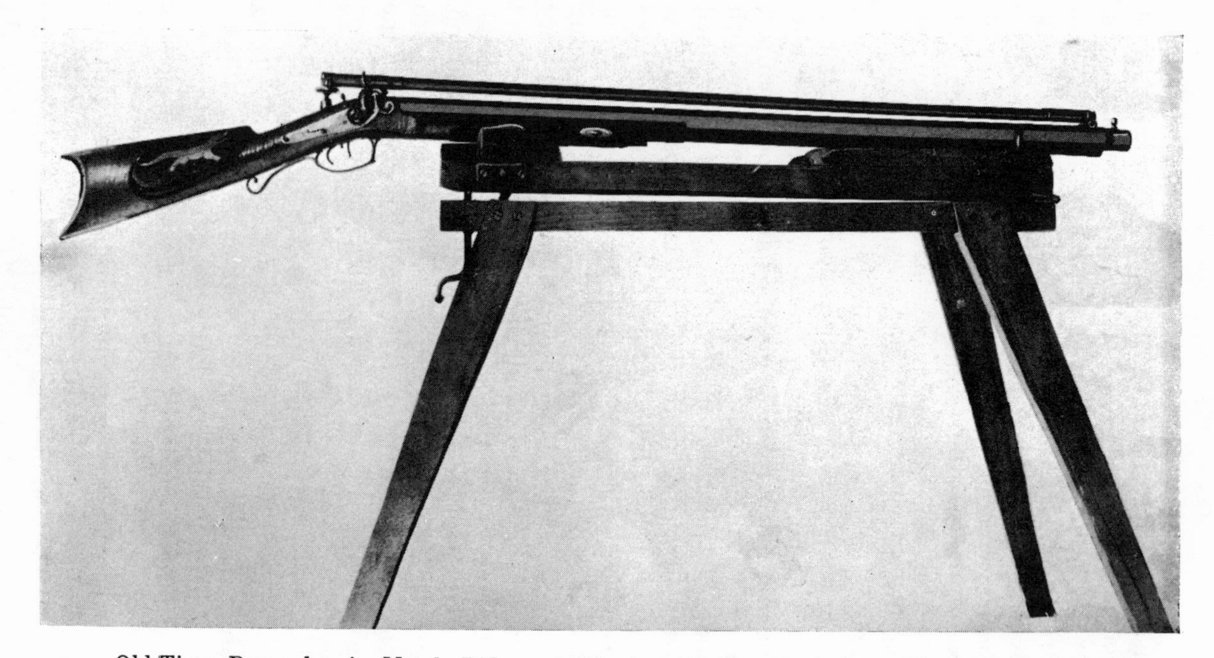

Old-Time Pennsylvania Match Rifle and Wooden Machine Rest, from W. A. Luce Collection.

rest down, and springs on the cross level prevent tipping until the rifle has recoiled an inch or more, and the bullet has left the muzzle. In the case of very heavy recoil these holding down springs can be tightened, giving more resistance. The cross level should stop on the hold-down springs in front before the action strikes the rear supporting V. The fore-end is, of course, removed so that the barrel will rest in the rear support.

All parts of this rest must be fitted very closely, as a movement of the rest is magnified more than two hundred times at the target. In firing a rifle from either this rest or the one previously described, the finger of one hand is placed on the trigger, with the thumb on the guard, and the trigger "pinched" of. The other hand is rested lightly on the butt. This is shown by the photograph of the shooter in the actual firing position. This method allows the shooter full opportunity to watch the flags and wind conditions generally; which is quite difficult to do if the rifle is held at the shoulder.

The accessories and equipment for the machine rest rifles are the same as those for the target rifles, except that more are required—often having half a dozen different bullet moulds with swages for each bullet and other impedimenta. Often these rifles weigh from 40 to 60 pounds, or more, although the largest and heaviest that I, myself, have seen, with its false muzzle and telescope sight, tipped the scales at this latter weight. These are really but scientists' instruments, of little practical use, usually built for the purpose of testing some theory regarding a form of rifling, a certain turn of rifling, or the length and shape of a bullet, or some other pet idea of the rifle-maker. Some of these machine rest rifles have shown remarkable accuracy at extremely long ranges—a mile or more as surveyed, not "guessed at." According to the late

Colonel Charles Winthrop Sawyer, the War Department Records at Washington, show that during the Civil War, Captain John Metcalf, 3D, of the U. S. Army Engineer Corps, using one of these extremely heavy, super-accurate machine rest rifles, which was shot from a camouflaged blind on the top of a high hill, picked off a Confederate general at a range of one mile, one hundred eighty-seven feet with the first shot. This range had, of course, been ascertained by triangulation by our engineers before the shot was fired, and the angle of elevation was thus found to be 87 degrees 57 minutes 8¼ seconds. Therefore, Captain Metcalf knew exactly what elevation was required, but the deflection and retardation of the bullet by wind and atmosphere over that very long range had, of course, to be very carefully estimated. No one really knows the important effects of that one shot on the future events during that battle. A full account of this may be found on pages 91 to 102 of Sawyer's book, *Our Rifles,* by those who wish to read all the particulars of this matter. The rifle used by Captain Metcalf in this case was made by "Abe Williams, Oswego, N. Y.," as stamped on the barrel and weighed between 50 and 60 pounds. I saw this rifle with a copy of the War Department record on exhibition some years ago and I am quite sure it was 50 calibre. The bullet used in it was a long, cylindrical, composite one with three-strip paper patch. The telescope was said to have been made by Morgan James, but was not marked with the marker's name.

CHAPTER IV

AMMUNITION FOR THE MUZZLE-LOADING RIFLES

The most important factors in securing fine accuracy with an accurate shooting muzzle-loading rifle of any type are a *suitable powder* and the *right bullet.* When I was a boy learning to shoot the rifle under my uncle's instructions at least nine out of every ten riflemen regarded the English, Curtis & Harvey, "Diamond Grain" black powder as the *very best,* and Hazzard's "Kentucky Rifle" as the second best. A black powder made at Schaghticoke, New York, was also used by numerous riflemen in those days, but it did not burn as clean as and did not give the accuracy that was obtained with either of the other kinds mentioned. It was cheaper in price than any of the others, which somewhat accounted for its use. About 1879 or 1880, Uncle Alvaro purchased in Boston several cans of the "American Dead Shot" F. g and F. F. g, black powder made by the American Powder Company, which we found to be nearly equal to the Curtis & Harvey "Diamond Grain" and sold at a lower price than the English powder. Still another that was preferred by some riflemen was the "Orange Extra" that was made by the old Laflin & Rand Powder Company at that time, I believe.

The essentials of a first-class black rifle powder are: First, it must be a moist burning powder so as to easily wipe out and not cake onto the bore at the breech. Second, it must be of uniform strength and every "lot" of the same strength. Third, it should not be an extremely rapid burning powder—such as is best for shotguns—as this causes too much upsetting of the lead bullet and results in poor accuracy. All these essentials of a superior black rifle powder are best combined in the Curtis & Harvey Diamond Grain powder as this always burns quite moist, easily wipes out of the bore after each shot, does not "burn on" at the breech, every different "lot" appears to be of the same uniform strength and the rate of burning is just *right* for the muzzle-loading rifles. This powder has been manufactured in England for two centuries, or more, and I understand that the chief reason for its superiority is in the charcoal used in its manufacture, which is made from the English willow trees. This charcoal appears to be superior to any made in this country, or from any other wood, which with their other especially pure and highly refined chemicals produces a black rifle powder that is of the highest quality known. This Diamond Grain powder was usually carried in stock by the leading dealers in arms and ammunition in the larger cities and towns in this country until about 1900, but since that date has not been imported by our dealers and is now difficult to obtain.

However, I have used this powder for many years and have never yet found its equal for use in the muzzle-loading rifles; also it is excellent for loading cartridges with black powder and low pressure smokeless priming for use in the breech-loading single shot target rifles. The records kept by Mr. Wm. V. Lowe while he was in the rifle-making business and shooting in rifle matches, which through the kindness of Mr. Walter Grote, I have recently read, show that he also found the Curtis & Harvey Diamond Grain black powder gave excellent accuracy in the majority of the rifles that he made or used.

Generally speaking, a very fine grain black powder should not be used in muzzle-loading rifles unless they are of small calibre. Rifles of 38 calibre and larger usually give the best accuracy with F. g. powder, while those of smaller bore do best with F. F. g. However, there are, of course, exceptions to this rule and we occasionally find muzzle-loaders of 40 to 45 calibre that require the F. F. g., powder to make their smallest groups. Of late years the Kings Semi-Smokeless powder is quite popular among the users of these rifles and usually gives good accuracy in most calibres. It has a tendency to burn on at the breech in some rifles, especially in hot weather, and I, myself, have never been able to secure as good accuracy with this powder in any muzzle-loading rifle as I get with the Curtis & Harvey Diamond Grain and the "American Dead Shot" black powders. Under NO CIRCUMSTANCES should any of the smokeless powders now on the market be used in any muzzle-loading rifle, as its use is SURE to ruin the barrel, or it may even burst it and injure or kill the shooter. Also NEVER MIX any of the so-called low pressure, or bulk smokeless powder with black powder, or Kings Semi-Smokeless as DANGEROUS PRESSURES are sure to result.

Patches. These are of many kinds, shapes and materials. As a boy, I was taught by Uncle Alvaro that only "shirt bosom linen" should be used for making the circular patches for the target rifle when the best accuracy was desired. We often cut patches for the hunting rifles from good quality bleached cotton sheeting after it had been thoroughly *washed twice* in order to remove all starch or other chemicals from it. We used this simply because it was cheaper than the linen, which cost a dollar a yard or more. Within the past few years a cloth known as "broadcloth shirting" has appeared on the market, which makes excellent patches for the muzzle-loading rifles. This is obtainable in several different grades and thicknesses, costs much less than linen, and appears to be equally as good, in point of accuracy, in the majority of the muzzle-loaders. In the Kentucky-Tennessee-

Carolina section of the country many of the long, round ball rifles are made especially for use with bed-ticking patches, quite likely because this material was cheap in price and always handy to obtain. Doubtless strong unbleached cotton sheeting of the same thickness would serve equally as well for patches with these rifles, but might not have been as easily obtained by those mountaineer riflemen as the bed-ticking.

Paper patches of different shapes and sizes are cut from thin, tough bond paper, or some makes of thin typewriter paper such as is used in making several copies at once. These papers may be obtained in different thicknesses from about one-half thousandth inch to 1/1000 or 2/1000 inch. Years ago there was a paper on the market known as "patch paper," made especially for making the patches for the paper patched bullets that were used in the fine single shot breech-loading target rifles. This came in different grades and thicknesses, and was the best we have ever had for making paper patches for the muzzle-loading rifles, as even the very thinnest was very tough and not easily torn in seating the bullet from the muzzle of the rifle.

When cutting the various shapes of paper patches, it is especially important to keep the edges of the patch-cutter very sharp, and keep a piece of cardboard, or thick paper, under the paper from which the patches are cut in order to have the edges of the patches smoothly and evenly cut. These patches of whatever shape should always be uniformly and lightly oiled with pure sperm oil several hours before using. The various linen or cloth patches are oiled with this same kind of oil, or wet with saliva, before using. If patches are to be oiled it is advisable to apply it a day or two before using in order that the fabric will be uniformly saturated. When patches are oiled immediately before using it is difficult to get them all uniformly oiled, and if one patch be heavily oiled, the next lightly, the bullets will have different points of impact on the target even though the point of aim was exactly alike for each shot.

Whether the finest accuracy is obtained with the cloth patch wet with saliva or oiled has been an endless source of argument for—no one knows how long. One expert rifle-maker, or marksman, claims that the patch wet with saliva *positively does give the best accuracy* as he has *repeatedly proven.* Another equally expert rifleman, or rifle-maker, will insist that the *very best accuracy* can be secured *only* by the use of the *oiled patch,* which fact he has *proved hundreds of times.* Probably the real truth of this is that it is a matter of individuality with each rifle; some giving their best accuracy with the oiled patch and others with the patch wet with saliva. The muzzle-loading target rifles are apt to be quite "cranky"; each is a distinctly individual product and we seldom find any two *exactly alike,* even by the same maker, or that can be managed precisely the same way and get the best accuracy.

Percussion Caps. According to the records, back in 1848 the most expert riflemen believed that the best accuracy with the target rifle was secured by the use of a *weak cap.* John R. Chapman, in *The Improved American Rifle,* stated that he had found the French "G. D." caps gave the finest accuracy because they gave a *weak ignition* of the powder charge. Quoting his statement: "It is obvious that the weaker the detonating charge of the cap be, the better, provided it have heat enough to ignite the powder at the bottom of the cone." In later years—along in the 1880's and 1890's—Horace Warner, Wm. V. Lowe and a few other rifle-makers insisted that we should use a cap that gave *strong ignition,* and they even went so far as to use the Berdan primer and various shotgun primers in specially constructed nipples of their rifles in order to get stronger, or hotter, ignition. Far be it from me to attempt to state which of these theories is the correct one; but it appears reasonable to suppose that these are the two extremes and that a middle ground may be the best. A cap surely should have sufficient flame to ignite the powder charge *uniformly alike each and every time,* and it may be possible that too strong ignition may cause a deterioration in the accuracy, especially if the barrel is a light one. Black powder, as we all know, ignites very easily and the whole charge is ignited almost *instantaneously,* which is very different from our modern smokeless powders that burn comparatively slowly and require a strong, hot flame to ignite them. Therefore, it is possible that the cap for the muzzle-loading rifle need not give an intensely hot flame in order to *uniformly ignite* the black powder.

Years ago when I learned to shoot the rifle, practically all experienced riflemen considered the English, Eley Brothers percussion caps as the highest quality and the *best.* Those made by the old Union Metallic Cartridge Company, the Winchester Repeating Arms Company and the old U. S. Cartridge Company were good quality and were used in greater quantities than the Eley Brothers' caps simply because the American-made caps were the cheaper. However, the majority of riflemen in those days always insisted in using the Eley Brothers' caps on the hunting rifles, especially when hunting deer, bear, or similar game, as these were absolutely *sure-fire* and nearer perfectly waterproof than any other make. During my experience with the rifle, I have used many, many thousands of Eley Brothers' caps of various sizes on hunting rifles, target rifles, shotguns and revolvers of many different makes, and during all these years under nearly all kinds of weather conditions, *very seldom if ever* did

I have a misfire with them. Also, more than fifty years ago I spent nearly a year in the Hudson's Bay Country of Canada, where the Indians and half-breed trappers used principally the "H. B. C. trade guns"—percussion lock 20 gauge smooth-bore arms—and the ONLY caps carried by the different "posts" were Eley Brothers. These caps in spite of the intense cold of winter or heavy rains in spring—extremely cold or hot, wet or dry—very seldom misfired even in the hands of these trappers in this far-northern wilderness.

Years ago Eley Brothers' caps of different sizes were carried in stock by nearly all arms and ammunition dealers in the United States and sold at about 60c for a box of 250 in the "Double Waterproof" grade, but are not stocked by our dealers today. Their "Anti-corrosive" caps of different sizes can be purchased from dealers in arms and ammunition in the cities and larger towns in Canada, from the Dominion Ammunition Company, of Montreal, and the "H. B. C. Trading Posts" in the most remote wilderness sections carry no other kind of caps. Yes, in those far-flung wilderness territories many Indians and half-breeds still use the muzzle-loading guns, usually of 20 gauge, with which they kill ducks, geese and similar game with the different sizes of shot, and these same guns when loaded with a proper charge of good black powder with one or two 20 gauge round balls on top are sure "bad medicine" for moose or bear at the ranges at which these men generally kill them. This is the "fashion" in the Year of Our Lord 1940—not one hundred years ago—as I know from a friend who is the "factor" of an Hudson's Bay Company Post at the mouth of the Great Whale River in the James Bay country, about nine hundred miles from the nearest postoffice and railroad station.

With all other makes of caps, I have had plenty of

misfires; the worst I can remember of using were the famous ? "G. D." caps that I used during my boyhood days. These were notorious for misfires and Uncle Alvaro often said that their trade name "G. D." was but the abbreviation of well-known profanity. They were lower in price than any others, and a farmer's boy was obliged to be as economical as any Scotchman in order to be able to do much shooting. Why, I even made the greater part of the shot for my 14 gauge muzzle-loading shotgun after I acquired that, and when I actually used "boughten" shot in that gun, I felt "pretty classy." Quite different from the present day boy, who would feel insulted by the present of "an old muzzle-loading shotgun," which he would doubtless call "an archaic piece of junk."

At present the Winchester Repeating Arms Company and the Remington Arms Company make the different sizes of percussion caps; the best being those of the first mentioned make, which are primed with a non-corrosive mixture that does not erode or corrode the nipple or breech of the barrel and are sure-fire. The caps made by the latter company are all chlorate primed, very corrosive, but quite sure-fire. F. Joyce & Company, Ltd., of London, England, and Kynoch, Ltd., of Birmingham, England, also make various sizes of percussion caps, but I have never used either of these makes and know nothing about them. The French made caps in the various sizes and brands that were so popular from about 1830 to 1880, are no longer carried by our ammunition dealers, which is no loss to our riflemen. Do not mourn because you cannot get the famous ? "G. D." caps now, even if Chapman did state that they were the best. There were also American made "G. D." caps in the old days, but these were even worse than the imported ones.

The devotees of the muzzle-loading cap lock rifle are indebted to Mr. Edwin Pugsley, vice-president of the Winchester Repeating Arms Company, for inducing that company to furnish us the excellent Winchester "Staynless" percussion caps that are made with their most improved non-corrosive priming. Mr. Pugsley has a very extensive collection of firearms, is much interested in the percussion, or cap lock arms, and knows the damage done to the nipple and breech of these arms by the old corrosive caps formerly made in this country. His interest in the muzzle-loading cap lock arms and his desire to assist those who shoot these, has resulted in the manufacture of the best percussion cap we have ever had. I find them superior in every way to the Eley Brothers' caps, or any others that I have yet used.

The following table shows the dimensions and sizes of the different caps that are now generally obtainable:

DIMENSIONS OF PERCUSSION CAPS OF VARIOUS MANUFACTURE

Manufactured by WINCHESTER REPEATING ARMS CO., New Haven, Conn.

All Non-Corrostive

Trade Name "Staynless"	Inside Diam. at Top	Inside Diam. at Bottom	Outside Length
F. L. No. 9	.152 inch	.163 inch	.200-.210 inch
F. L. No. 10	.159 "	.170 "	.205-.215 "
F. L. No. 11	.165 "	.175 "	.205-.215. "
F. L. No. 12	.168 "	.178 "	.205-.215 "
F. L. No. 13	.174 "	.184 "	.205-.215 "
Split Musket No. 4	.220 "	.228 "	.215-.225 "

Manufactured by REMINGTON ARMS CO., Bridgeport, Conn.

9 F. C. & 9 Hicks F. L.	.152 inch	.160 inch	.200 inch
10 F. C. & 10 Hicks F. L. & 11 Hicks F. L.	.163 "	.166 "	.200 "
12 F. C. & 12 Hicks F. L. & 13 Hicks F. L.	.172 "	.174 "	.200 "
Musket & Hicks Musket	.223 "	.230 "	.200 "

All Chlorate Priming; Corrosive.

Manufactured by ELEY BROTHERS, LTD.,
London, W. C., England

ELEY BROS. "ANTI-CORROSIVE" PERCUSSION CAPS

Trade Name, and Size	Inside Diam. at Top	Inside Diam. at Bottom	Outside Length	Corrosive or Non-Corrosive
No. 10	.156 inch	.17 inch	.217 inch	Corrosive
No. 11	.16 "	.17 "	.217 "	"
No. 12	.162 "	.176 "	.226 "	"
No. 13	.172 "	.185 "	.226 "	"
No. 14	.176 "	.186 "	.226 "	"
No. 18	.161 "	.174 "	.226 "	"
No. 24	.150 "	.165 "	.217 "	"
No. 26	.217 "	.225 "	.270 "	"

Bullets. There are actually a greater number of different shapes and designs of bullets for the muzzle-loading rifles than we have in Heinz Pickles—he only claims "57 varieties," you know. Bullets may be classified according to their form, or shape, as the round ball, the conical, cylindro-conoidal and cylindrical.

The simplest and oldest type of bullets for the rifle is the spherical, or round, ball, which in the various bores, or gauges, has been in use from the invention of the rifle until the present day, and was the only type of bullet used from the earliest times to about 1835. In the early times the various sizes of the round balls were designated as a certain number to the pound; as for instance, "90 to the pound," "120 to the pound," etc., instead of calling them a certain calibre as we now do. This method of stating the gauge of the rifle, or size of the round ball, was not very accurate, but has served its purpose for more than two centuries. A rifle that gauged "70 to the pound" could be used with a ball 71, 72, 73, or 74 to the pound depending upon the thickness of the patch used, and the nominal size of the bore was that of the *ball only, without the patch,* that fitted the bore of the rifle. The late George Schalk, of Pottsville, Pennsylvania, was one of the best rifle-makers in America and made many very fine muzzle-loading rifles. He was very skillful and very accurate in all his work, and the micrometer measurements of the different gauges of round balls as published in *The Kentucky Rifle,* which we may accept as correct, are given herewith by permission of the author, Captain John G. W. Dillin.

No. of balls to pound.	Measurements in inches and decimals of inch.	No. of balls to pound.	Measurements in decimals of inch.
5	1.15	40	.485
6	.954	42*	.4805
7	.900	44	.474
8	.861	48	.463
9	.823	50*	.458
10	.790	52	.453
11	.760	56	.442
12	.748	60*	.437
13	.727	64	.416
14	.708	70	.400
15	.695	80	.388
16	.682	90	.383
17	.665	100	.364
18	.647	110	.350
19	.637	120	.340
20	.628	130	.332
21	.618	140	.324
22	.609	150	.318
23	.601	160	.310
24	.588	170	.305
25	.585	180	.298
26	.575	190	.292
27	.572	200	.290
28	.559	210	.288
29	.549	220	.284
30	.533	230	.282
32	.530	240	.280
34	.519	250	.278
36	.506	260	.274
38	.491	270	.2715
		280	.269

* The measurements for 42, 50 and 60 to the pound are the average micrometer diameter of four round balls of each of these gauges as I measured them: not Mr. Schalk's.

The earliest attempt in improving the round ball was the so-called "belted bullet" which was made with a belt about ¼ inch wide by 1/16 inch thick around the circumference to fit the two grooves of the Brunswick rifle. According to the English records the Brunswick two-grooved rifle and belted bullet was a flat failure as this combination gave even poorer accuracy than the smooth-bore and round ball. The next improvement was a short cylindrical bullet with four longitudinal bands equidistant on its circumference to fit the four grooved bore of the "Jacobs Rifle," which was developed in 1846 by General Jacobs of the British Army in India. This rifle and bullet proved much superior in accuracy and range to any before invented, but evidently General Jacobs was not "in the political ring" as his rifle was rejected by the Government on the grounds that the Brunswick rifle and two-grooved bullet was "good enough for His Majesty's Service in India."

In 1855 before Sir Joseph Whitworth had perfected his hexagonal bore rifle, the late W. Greener (father of W. W. Greener), of London, invented the "Cape Rifle" and its mechanically fitting bullet. This was a short cylindrical bullet with two longitudinal bands placed equidistant on its circumference that fitted the two-grooved bore of the rifle, which was a double barreled arm, having the barrel rifled with a twist of one turn in twenty inches, and was considered a very "radical" idea in those times. The Cape rifle was made in 45 and 50 calibre, gave good accuracy and had the extreme range of 2000 yards without the bullets key-holing or stripping, as the mechanically fitting bullets even in that quick twist were kept point-on by the two grooved bore. Quite a large number of the Cape Rifles were sold to sportsmen who made hunting trips to South Africa in those days and these were considered as very satisfactory rifles for big game shooting.

In 1854 Sir Joseph Whitworth was granted a patent on his hexagonal bore muzzle-loading rifle with its mechanically fitting bullet, but it required nearly two years to make the machinery for producing this rifle in quantities, so that the Whitworth rifle with its hexagonal bullet was not officially tested by the British War Office until 1857. When this rifle was placed on the market it created quite a "furore" and this long, peculiarly shaped bullet was hailed as "the perfect rifle bullet." In the official tests in England this bullet and rifle gave considerably finer accuracy at all ranges including 2000 yards than any ever before tested; the mean deviation at 500 yards being but 37/100 foot while the smallest deviation at that range with any other rifle up to that time—the Enfield—was 2.42 feet. However it eventually proved that the mechanically fitting bullet was expensive to make, the bore of the rifle fouled excessively and showed excessive wear after being in use a short time. Thus the Whitworth hexagonal bore rifle and bullet failed to prove "the perfect rifle and bullet" and went off the market in about a decade.

In the United States about 1835, someone in an attempt to secure a longer accuracy range designed a bullet with the main part shaped like an acorn with rounded base, similar to the sketch herewith. (Figure 1). This was probably the earliest improvement made in this country on the round ball, but it is very doubtful whether it gave any better accuracy than the round ball. Our records are very silent on this point, and it hardly seems possible that this bullet could have been at all accurate on account of its very rounded base, very short bearing on the bore and difficulty in seating it perfectly central in the bore of the rifle when loading. However, it soon went out of use.

The first real improvement over the round ball in our American rifles, known as the "sugar-loaf," or

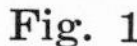

Fig. 1

Fig. 2

"picket," bullet was designed by some unknown rifleman about 1835. This was a conical shaped bullet with a more or less rounded base and a flat point, or carried to a sharp point much like the Springfield 30-06-150 grain "Spitzer" bullet adopted by the U. S. Army in 1906 and regarded as "something new" at that time. Actually it was such an *old type* bullet that the majority of the men who had used it in this country were dead or had forgotten all about it. There were several different shapes of these sugar-loaf, or picket, bullets; some having almost a boat-tail shaped base, others slightly rounded, or square, or like the sketch herewith of a bullet used in an N. Lewis 36 calibre "squirrel rifle" made during the Civil War, which I once had. (Figure 2). The sugar-loaf and picket bullets when well made and used with the right patch in a properly made rifle having a guide bullet starter, were far superior in accuracy, range and killing power to the round ball. As a result of this, all the best rifle-makers soon commenced making their rifles for this type of bullets instead of the round ball and the accuracy range was increased from about 30 rods to 40, 60 or 80 according to the bore, or calibre, of the rifle.

In 1848 when John R. Chapman published *The Improved American Rifle,* all the expert marksmen used rifles especially made for this type of bullets. The chief defects in the sugar-loaf, or picket, bullets are that it has a very short bearing on the bore of the rifle, is very easily seated in the bore in such a way that the axis of the bullet is not *exactly in line with that of the bore,* consequently it leaves the muzzle of the rifle in a slightly tipped position, which gives poor accuracy at the target. This is shown by the sketches herewith; one of which shows the bullet at the breech put down crooked, and the other showing this same bullet as it leaves the muzzle slightly canted off center.

It is extremely doubtful if anyone can possibly seat ten consecutive bullets of the conical type in a rifle

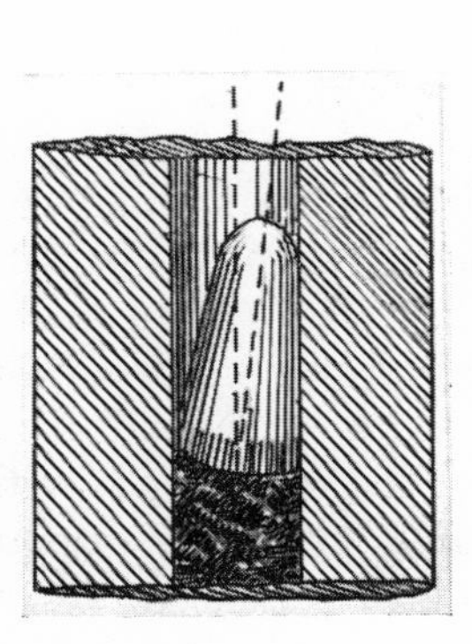

Bullet loaded with axis not coinciding with that of bore.

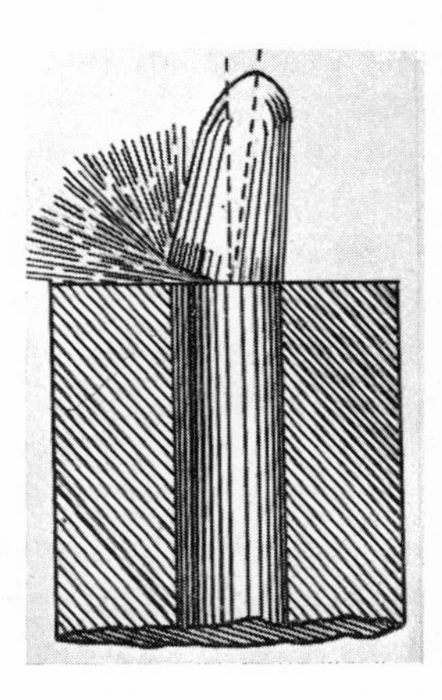

Incorrectly loaded Bullet leaving muzzle of rifle.

barrel without the use of the false muzzle and bullet starter and have *every bullet with its axis exactly coinciding with that of the bore.* Even by the use of the false muzzle and bullet starter these picket bullets are sometimes entered into the bore in a slight tipped, or canted, position which results in an "of shot" on the target.

This fault of the conical bullets resulted in improving it by making a short cylindrical base connected to a conical front part having either a flat point, or a sharp one, and is known as the cylindro-conoidal bullet. With the introduction of this type of bullet the long range accuracy of the target rifle equipped with false muzzle and bullet starter was greatly increased, and at the same time the accuracy at any range was much improved. For instance, the best target rifle using any shape of conical bullet would give good accuracy—make quite small groups—at 40 rods when shot by an expert rifleman, but would in spite of the greatest care in loading give an occasional "off shot" that greatly enlarged the group, and 60 rods was about the limit of range for nice accuracy with this type of bullet. An equally accurate rifle using the cylindro-conoidal bullet gave nice accuracy at 100 rods, or more, depending upon the calibre and weight of the bullet, and would make considerable smaller 10-shot groups at 40 and 60 rods than was possible with any kind of conical bullets.

In times past many remarkably small groups have been made at 40 rods rest shooting with the most accurate muzzle-loading target rifle, equipped with false muzzle and telescope sight, using the various calibres of cylindro-conoidal bullets. Even at 60 to 100 rods these rifles and bullets when handled by expert rest shots would make groups that very few of our modern high power rifles today can equal. However, the "rifle crank" is never satisfied, always seeking a more accurate rifle or bullet, which resulted in designing by some progressive rifleman in the old days, the long, cylindrical bullet with which, in a fine target rifle, the accuracy at 40, 60, 80 and 100 rods was considerably finer than with the cylindro-conoidal bullets, and at the same time the accuracy range was increased to 1000 yards or more. As an illustration of this, a fine 16 or 20 pound target rifle with false muzzle and bullet starter, and telescope sight, using the long cylindrical bullet with two-strip, or three-strip, paper patch, when used by an expert rest shot, will make as small groups at 60 rods as the rifles using the other types of bullets will average at 40 rods rest shooting.

There are several different methods of making these last two types of bullets, either of which may be cast whole, or in two pieces. If cast whole, the bullet will not be perfect as it comes from the bullet mould, but must be swaged to the correct diameter and shape, and the lead compressed at the same time. The base, or butt, of the composite, cylindro-conoidal and cylindrical bullets is cast from pure lead and the front part from quite hard lead and tin alloy, the object being to produce a better balanced bullet, or one that will shoot more accurately than one cast in one piece. The parts of these composite bullets come from the mould in a somewhat rough form and not correctly shaped; then each piece should be carefully weighed on accurate powder scales and all parts that are 1 grain over or under weight are rejected. Then the good parts after being lightly oiled are assembled together and swaged. In this operation the bullets are brought up to the correct diameter, the base given the desired shape, the point shaped correctly and the lead compressed so as to be free from flaws and internal hollows, thus making the bullet as nearly perfect as possible. It is impossible to cast a lead or lead alloy bullet as perfectly as can be produced by swaging.

The best shape of the base and the point of the cylindro-conoidal and cylindrical bullets, as well as the best shape of the separate parts of these composite bullets, has led to much experimentation in the past. Some rifle-makers and expert riflemen claim that the soft lead base should be cast integral with the shank that fits into a corresponding hollow in the hardened lead point, as shown by this sketch (Figure 3). Other equally expert makers and marks-

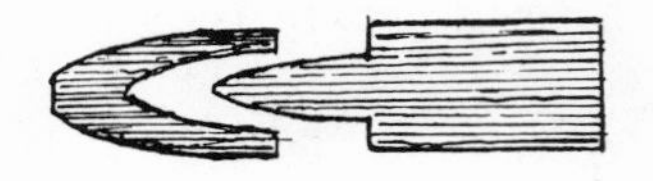

Fig. 3

Fig. 4

men claim that this is all wrong; that the soft lead base should be cast with a hollow into which the shank of the hardened lead point fits, as shown by this second sketch (Figure 4). According to the records of Mr. Wm. V. Lowe when he was in business with Horace Warner, the better — more accurate shooting—bullet is that cast according to the second method; that is, the hardened front part of the bullet should be cast with the shank as an integral part of it and fits into a corresponding hollow in the soft lead butt. As to the best shape of the base of the bullet in order to obtain the best accuracy, it is claimed by some experts that the bullet swaged with a perfectly square, or flat, base forming a perfect right angle with the body of the bullet always gives the best accuracy. Other experts insist that the base should have a slight hollow—concaved— in order to get the best accuracy; while others insist that the base should be slightly convex when it comes from the swage; yet another experienced expert claims that these two shapes of the base is all wrong, and that it should be shaped like the following sketch if the best accuracy is desired. (Figure 5). I have known several expert riflemen who demanded that their bullets be swaged into a boat-tail shape like this sketch (Figure 6) which they claimed was the most accurate shooting bullet they had ever used; while another old, experienced rifleman would use only a bullet having a deep V shaped hollow in the base of the bullet, like Figure 7. Therefore, as the old adage reads: "When doctors disagree, who shall decide?"

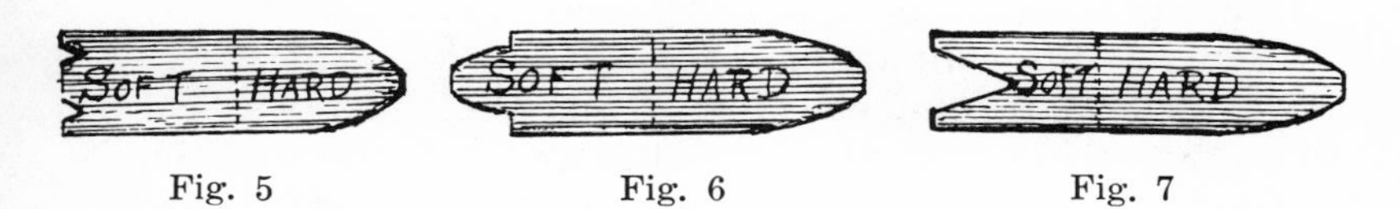

Fig. 5 Fig. 6 Fig. 7

Many of our modern riflemen believe that the boat-tail bullets give the very best accuracy in the high power rifles of today; if that be true, it is possible that these old-timers who insisted in having a boat-tail shaped base of their lead bullets may have been correct in this matter, although the great majority of the expert shots with the muzzle-loading target rifle used a bullet having some form of a hollow, convex, or flat base in order to get the best accuracy. But, who really *knows* which is actually the *best shape* of the base of the bullet in order to get the very *finest accuracy* with the muzzle-loading target rifle? I, personally, only know that the most *accurate shooting* muzzle-loading target rifle *I have ever owned,* used a long cylindrical bullet that had a *hollow base* after it was swaged; and the *most accurate rifle* of this kind that *I have ever* shot, used a long, cylindrical bullet that had a *perfectly square base* after swaging. There you are; take your choice. Here is a great field for experimentation on the part of the experts in the use of the muzzle-loading target rifles.

Cartridges for the Muzzle-loading Rifles. Yes, they made cartridges for some of these rifles, especially for certain hunting rifles and nearly all Army rifles. When I was about eleven years old, Uncle Alvaro showed me how to make cartridges for my 170 gauge (30 calibre) rifle according to the following method: First a hard-wood cylinder about six inches long was turned and smoothed in the lathe, with a diameter about .012 or

.014 inch smaller than the bore of the rifle measured on top of the lands. A piece of wrapping paper about .003 inch thick by 3½ inches long was rolled tightly around this cylinder and marked at the point where it made two complete laps. Then the paper was cut off at this point, unrolled and placed on a piece of tin, which was then cut to the same shape and size to serve as a pattern for cutting a supply of these pieces of paper for making the "tubes" for these cartridges.

By the use of this tin pattern and a sharp knife, six or eight thicknesses of wrapping paper could be cut at once into rectangular pieces about 2⅛ inches wide by 3½ long. A piece of this paper was tightly rolled around the wooden cylinder and the edge pasted down with gum arabic mucilage; then this paper tube was carefully slipped off the cylinder and set aside to dry while making other similar tubes. After a supply of these tubes had been made, one was slipped back onto the wooden cylinder nearly to the end and a round ball with the sprue end up was placed inside the tube which projected over the ball about ⅜ inch. This end was then twisted and tied with a piece of white thread, and the cylinder withdrawn leaving the ball in the front end of the tube. With a proper size steel wad-cutter, we cut from an old hat a quantity of felt wads which were then soaked in a hot mixture of beeswax and sperm oil, then dried for about 24 hours. After the ball had been secured in the front end of the paper tube, one of these lubricated felt wads was placed in the tube and carefully pushed down onto the ball; then we poured a measured charge of powder into the tube behind the wad and bullet, and finished the cartridge by twisting the end of the paper cylinder together and tying it with a piece of red thread. Then with a small brush, we applied a light coat of the melted beeswax mixture to the front end of the cartridge in which the ball was held, in order to facilitate loading and take the place of the usual oiled cloth patch.

When loading the rifle, one of the cartridges was taken from the cartridge box, or hunting bag, the end that was tied with the RED thread was grasped in the teeth, the end of the paper torn off, the powder poured down the bore, and the rest of the cartridge pushed down onto the powder with the ramrod. Placing a cap on the nipple completed the loading, which by the use of this home-made cartridge could be done more rapidly than when using the loose powder, patch and ball separately. When loading these cartridges with the conical bullet for this rifle, the end of the tube was attached with gum arabic mucilage to the base of the bullet and dried with the point of the bullet extending from the tube instead of having the paper tube tied over it, and the rest of the process of loading the cartridge was as above explained.

In this same way, by the use of a larger wooden cylinder and larger pieces of wrapping paper, I loaded hundreds of cartridges with different sizes of shot for my 14 gauge double barreled shotgun and seldom used the loose powder and shot.

It is generally well known that during the Civil War our soldiers were supplied with paper cartridges for the muzzle-loading Springfield, Enfield, Remington and other rifled muskets and carbines used by the Army and Navy before any of the various breech-loading arms were adopted for the service. The English manufacturers of the Whitworth hexagonal bore rifle furnished cartridges having a paper case containing the bullet and powder for that muzzle-loader, and the British, French and other foreign nations used paper cartridges for their Army and Navy rifles and muskets. It is believed that King Gustavus Adolphus of Sweden originated this type of "cartridge" early in 1600 when he ordered his soldiers

1 2 3 4 5 6 7

Cartridges for the Muzzle-Loading Rifles during Civil War. No. 1, 50 calibre Smith-Poultney Carbine; 2, 577 calibre Enfield Rifle; 3, Harper's Ferry Rifle 58 calibre; 4, Whitworth Rifle 45-85 calibre. Nos. 5, 6, 7, for Unknown Makes of Civil War Rifles or Carbines. From John Baker's Collection.

to carry their powder and ball together in paper cylinders with the ends twisted over the ball and powder.

The "Combustible Envelope" cartridge was made by the Colt's Patent Fire Arms Manufacturing Company, of Hartford, Connecticut, for their "Revolving Rifles, Muskets and Carbines" from about 1850 until after the Civil War. This consisted of a thin paper envelope, thoroughly impregnated with nitrate of potassium, containing the powder charge and attached to the base of the bullet. This envelope was somewhat waterproof; that is, it would stand a slight wetting, could be handled with wet hands as during a rain storm, and was completely consumed when the arm was fired, thus leaving no residue in the breech or chamber. They were, however, extremely fragile and the bullet had a tendency to separate from the combustible envelope in transportation, but in that case the cartridge could be used by first loading the envelope containing the powder and then the bullet. These cartridges were also furnished by this company for all the various calibres of Colt, Remington, Whitney, and other makes of revolvers that used the percussion cap, and by their use these revolvers and revolving rifles could be loaded much more rapidly than with the loose powder and bullet. Illustrations of many of these old paper cartridges for the different muzzle-loading rifles are shown herewith.

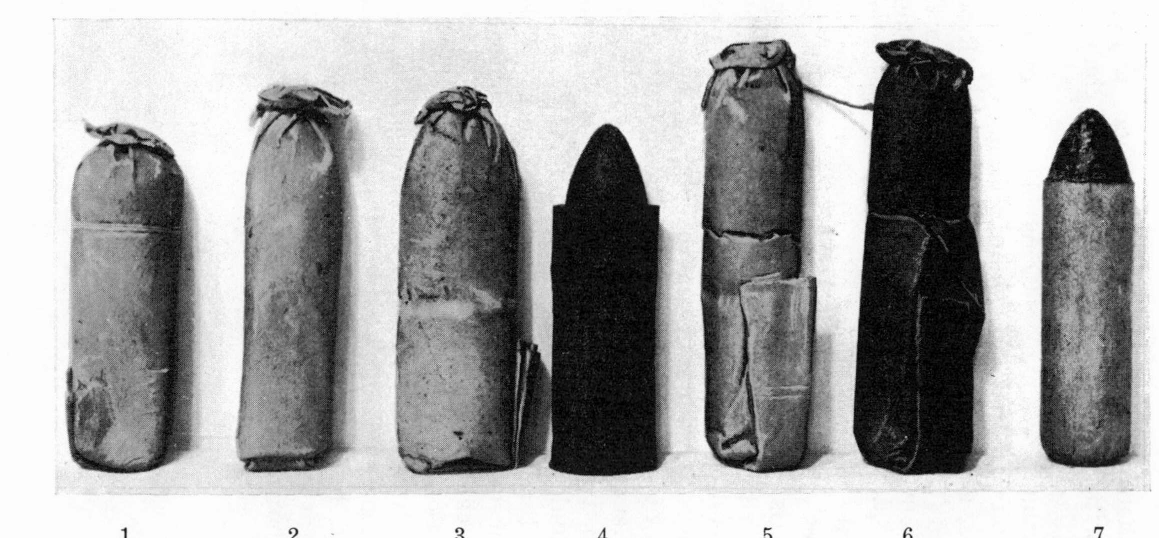

1 2 3 4 5 6 7

Cartridges for Muzzle-Loading, Civil War Rifles and Carbines. No. 1, Musket 58 calibre; 2, Musket "Buck and Ball" 58 calibre; 3, Musket 69 calibre; 4, Smith Carbine, Rubber Case Ctdg.; 5, Musket 58 calibre "Minnie Ball; 6, Confederate Rifle 58 calibre 7, Gallagher Carbine 50 calibre. From John Baker's Collection.

CHAPTER V

LOADING, CLEANING AND CARE OF THE RIFLE

In the days of long ago, it was customary for the rifle-maker to send each customer, in the box with the rifle and its accessories, one or more test targets that were made with the rifle at 20 or 40 rods, or sometimes groups that were shot at both these ranges, with notations on these targets showing the kind, size of grain and charge of powder, the kind of patch and the type and weight of ball or bullet that was used in making these test groups. The makers generally sent a piece of the linen used as patch material for the rifle, or if it was a target rifle using a paper patch, several sheets of the paper from which the patches were cut, were sent so that the purchaser would know exactly what thickness of linen, or paper, to use in making patches for his rifle. Horace Warner, N. Lewis, N. S. Brockway, Wm. Billinghurst, Edwin Wesson and other makers of high-grade arms usually sent with each rifle, written or printed instructions for its management in order that the customer, if inexperienced in the use of that make of rifle, would be able to obtain the best results with it, as well as to prevent damaging the rifle or any of the accessories by misuse.

I have before me a small pamphlet by N. Lewis, Troy, New York, dated 1876, entitled, *Directions for Managing a Rifle to Do Good Shooting,* which he sent with each of his rifles, and from which I give a few quotations: "In the first place you must use coarse powder; it is much better than fine. I have given the Laflin & Rand Powder Co.'s Powder a thorough trial, and I find that their Orange Rifle Powder manufactured at Schaghticoke, New York, and Newburg,

New York, is as good as any I have ever used. *It is very strong, clean and does not foul the gun,* and is well adapted for my guns. I can fully recommend their F. g. and F. F. g., Orange Rifle Powder for good sporting and Rifle Shooting." The word "sporting" in this case means hunting. On another page, Lewis states: "Always use a linen patch. In all cases, I send a sample of linen for patches and the size you want to use on the ball to do good shooting. For immediate shooting, always use a very wet patch on the ball. In case you are hunting and want to keep your gun loaded for any length of time, I should prefer a greased patch, as a wet one will corrode the gun by leaving it loaded any length of time. For fine shooting, a wet patch is better than a greased one. For fine shooting always wipe your gun every time before loading it again with a wet patch. In all cases, always raise the hammer half-cocked when you are putting down the ball. In all cases, I send a charger with the gun that is right for the slug ball. The round ball does not require more than two-thirds as much powder as the slug ball. Always use the charger as I fit it, if you wish to do good shooting from one rod to one hundred. It will do no harm to add a little more powder for a longer distance."

On another page he states: "When you load your gun you must always put your ball down one time as hard as another; if you push it one time harder than another, it will shoot one time higher than the other. When you hold your gun against your shoulder, you must hold it as firm one time as another, or you will shoot one time higher than another." On page 18 of this pamplet, under the heading, "How to Manage a Patent Muzzle Rifle," he stated: "Be careful in putting the muzzles together, and not rap them too hard as it upsets the muzzle and spoils fine shooting of the gun. Never wipe or clean your gun unless the muzzle is on.

When you put the ball down on the powder the more sensitive you can put it there, the better you can shoot." By the words "Patent Muzzle," Lewis meant the false muzzle, since that was patented by Alvan Clark and for many years was known as "Clark's patent muzzle," "the patent muzzle," or the false muzzle, as we now know it—three different terms that all mean exactly the same thing. Also, years ago, a rifle having a false muzzle was frequently termed a "muzzled rifle."

Lewis' instructions for casting bullets read: "For balls for a target gun, I prefer mixed lead, to make it harder, as it does not upset as much and shoots better. I use it as follows: Take four pounds of soft lead and one ounce of block tin, melt and mix them well together, and you will find they shoot better than soft lead. I prefer soft lead for a sporting gun." Here again, "sporting gun" means a hunting rifle. He further stated: "After you run the balls ready for swedging, put two or three drops of oil on your hands and rub the balls through them before swedging, and it will make them come out of the swedge easy. Put the balls in the swedge, take a hammer and strike the follower two or three good taps, and it will swedge the ball."

On page 19 of this pamphlet, Lewis gives a *very important* piece of advice in the following language: "I will here give you a little advice how to use a gun and not injure yourself or others. In the first place handle a gun that is not loaded the same as though it was—never point it towards yourself or others when you are working the lock, capping or un-capping it in any shape—then if it accidentally goes off it will not injure any one." That is all he had to say about that—simple, isn't it? Again he stated: "Ninety-nine accidents out of every hundred with a gun are caused by carelessness. To speak within bounds, I

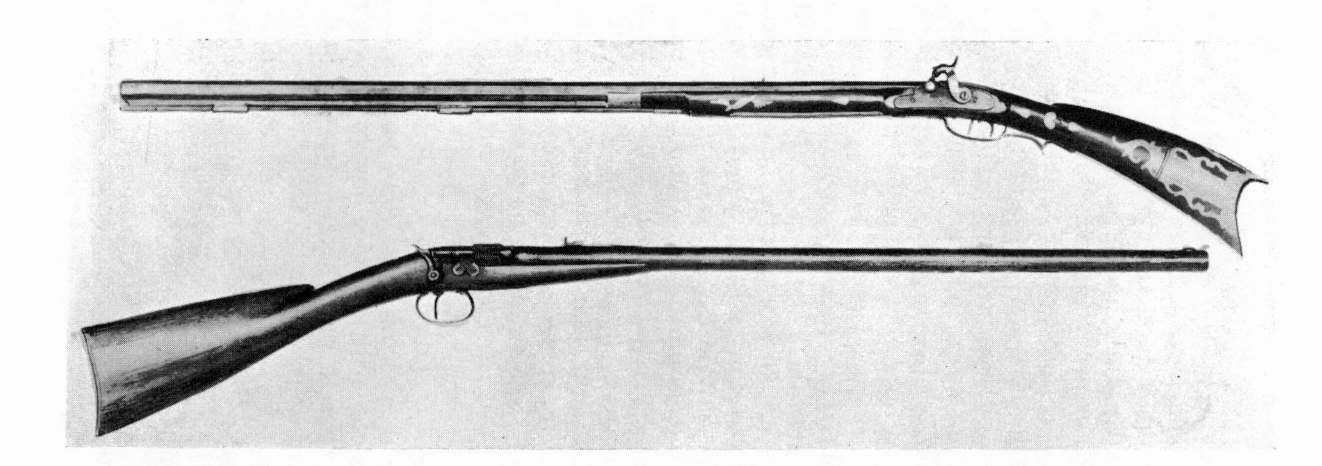

Top: Left-hand Cap Lock "Squirrel Rifle," Unknown Maker, 29 calibre, 37-inch Barrel, weight 7¾ pounds.
Bottom: Albert G. Bagley, Cap Lock Rifle, patented 1852, 40 calibre Round Ball, 29½-inch Barrel. From W. A. Luce Collection.

have shot away over fifteen tons of lead. I have shot every rifle I ever made from twenty-five to two hundred shots with nearly double the quantity of powder used in the charger sent with the gun. I never bursted a gun, nor ever made a scratch on one, or received one myself. My motto has always been; 'An ounce of prevention is worth a pound of cure.' These directions are got up solely for those who use my rifles. Please preserve them as such and you will oblige, Your Friend, Nelson Lewis."

Judging from some of the foregoing instructions, they had "accidents" with "unloaded guns" in those days, and the "I didn't know it was loaded" *idiot* had been causing trouble even in those "good old days."

Assuming that you have had little experience in using the round ball hunting rifle which has been kept with the bore well oiled for some time, and which you now wish to "shoot at a mark," as we used to say; the bore should first be wiped of all oil and grease. Then with the hammer at half-cock, blow through the barrel to ascertain if the nipple is open; if it is stopped with oil, grease or dirt, remove the nipple with the nipple wrench and clean out the vent. Also examine the vent into the patent breech, or breech-plug, and be sure this is free of dirt or oil so as to insure good ignition of the powder charge from the cap. The nipple will often be difficult to remove because it has become rusted in, and in such case the patent breech and nipple should be soaked an hour or more in some of the penetrating oils used in garages for removing rusted nuts, which will generally start the rust enough so that the nipple can be removed. DO NOT heat the patent breech as it is case-hardened, and heating it hot enough to loosen a rusted nipple would spoil it. After the vent in the nipple has been cleaned and the vent from the nipple to the cone in the patent breech, or breech-plug, is opened, replace the nipple and snap

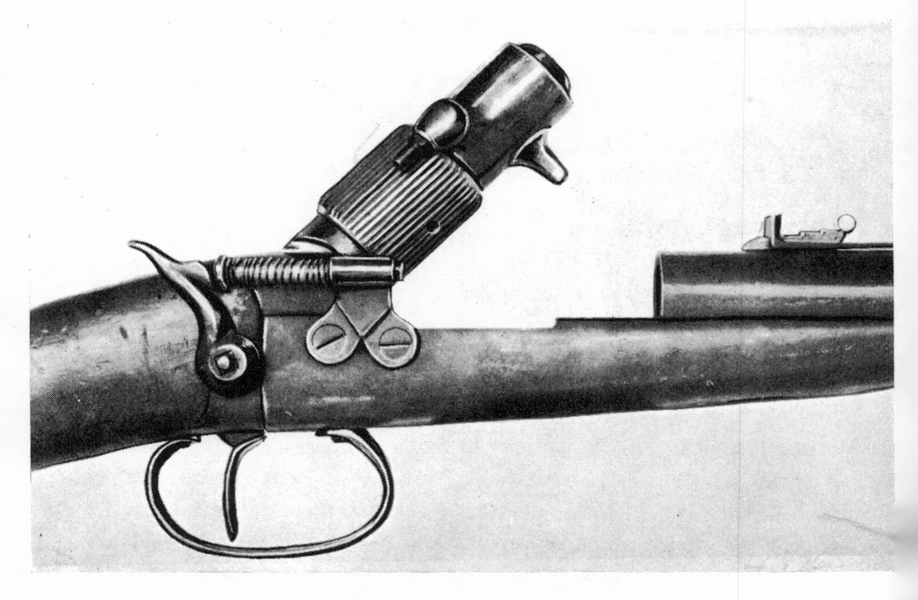

Albert G. Bagley, Cap Lock Rifle, showing Action Open ready for Loading

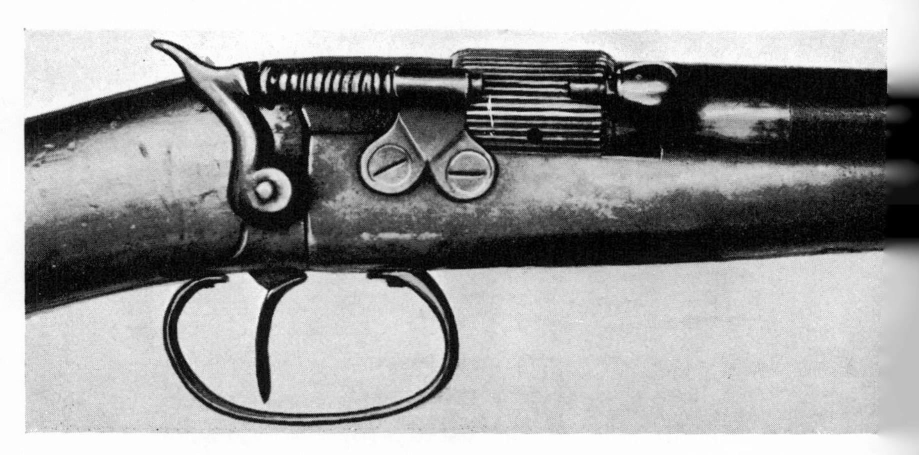

Albert G. Gagley, Cap Lock Rifle, showing Action Closed ready for Firin
From W. A. Luce Collection.

several caps on it to clean the vent of all oil and moisture. Then put in a small charge of *powder only* with a wad of cloth or paper and fire that. If the rifle fires all right with the charge of powder only, you are ready to load the rifle with powder and ball.

The pioneer rule for ascertaining the correct charge of powder for a round ball rifle was: place a ball in the palm of the hand and pour out from the powder-horn enough powder to completely cover the ball. Then make from a piece of bone hollowed out, or the tip of a small horn, or from a brass tube with a cork in one end, a charger which this quantity of powder exactly fills even with the top—"stricken measure." This method is still the best for ascertaining the correct charges for the different gauges of round ball rifles, and gives charges that average in weight about as follows:

150	balls	per	pound,	31	calibre,	25	grains	weight	of powder
100	"	"	"	36	"	40	"	"	" "
56	"	"	"	44	"	60	"	"	" "
18	"	"	"	60	"	85	"	"	" "

Another old-time rule for this purpose was: use 3 grains weight of powder for each 7 grains weight of ball, which applied to the above calibre round balls works out very nearly the same charges as above. Thus, 31 calibre round ball, weight 60 grains, divided by 7 equals 8, 4/7 x 3 equals 25, 5/7 grains powder; 36 calibre round ball, weight 90 grains, divided by 7 equals 12, 6/7 x 3 equals 38, 4/7 grains of powder; 44 calibre round ball, weight 118 grains, divided by 7 equals 16, 6/7 x 3 equals 50, 2/7 grains powder, or nearly 10 grains less than by the other rule.

Nearly all round ball hunting rifles were cut with a slow twist of rifling and quite deep grooves to use a heavy charge of powder in proportion to the weight of the ball and are "express rifles," as they were called years ago, thus they gave a low trajectory over ordinary hunting ranges—20 to 30 rods—which is so desirable when shooting at unknown ranges, with high velocity for those times, and consequently good killing power.

Having decided upon the approximate charge of powder for the rifle and made a charger with which to measure this bulk charge, we are ready to load the rifle. Holding the barrel in as nearly vertical position as possible and having filled the charger even full from the powder-horn, pour the charge carefully into the barrel; then place an oiled linen, or other cloth, patch over the muzzle being careful to center it over the bore. Next place a round ball, *with the sprue up,* in the center of the patch—be sure that the ball is truly centered in the patch—press the ball down with the thumb even with the muzzle, then apply the straight starter holding the left hand around the muzzle and the starter and strike the knob of the starter with the ball of the right hand thus forcing the ball down the bore the length of the starter rod. Remove the starter and holding the ramrod short with both hands push hard and straight to start the bullet some six or eight inches down the bore, from which point the ball should be easily pushed down onto the powder. DO NOT ram, or pound, the ball down the bore, and DO NOT "whang" the ball with the ramrod onto the powder—simply seat the ball firmly on the powder with a light pressure on the ramrod. If the ball and patch does not slide fairly easy down the bore from a point about six inches from the muzzle by applying pressure to the ramrod, the patch is too thick, or the ball too large for the rifle, and *ramming* or *pounding* the ball down the bore will upset it making it merely a slug of lead instead of a sphere and thus destroy all accuracy.

Be careful to seat the ball on the powder with *uniform pressure* each and every time, because if you seat it very lightly one time and very hard the next, these two balls will have quite different points of impact on the target. Be sure to keep the hammer *half-cocked* when loading the rifle, and this should be a *safety notch* from which the rifle cannot be fired by pulling the trigger. Never load the rifle with the hammer down on the nipple, as the air pressure in the barrel might cause you to not seat the ball clear down on the powder. Never load with the hammer fully cocked as a jar against the stock might cause the hammer to fall onto the nipple and break it. Be sure that the ball is actually seated down on the powder and not left some distance above it, because if the rifle be fired with the ball partly down, you will spoil the barrel by enlarging the bore, or making a "ring" in it, at the point of the obstruction. A rifle with a properly made barrel has the bore somewhat "freed," or slightly enlarged, from a point about three to six inches from the muzzle to the breech in order that the ball may be easily pushed down onto the powder without upsetting it or battering it out of shape.

One of the *greatest essentials of accuracy* is that the ball, or bullet, be delivered from the muzzle of the rifle as *perfectly* as possible, and if the ball or bullet is "whanged" out of shape in loading, it is impossible to deliver it from the muzzle in perfect condition. This was the chief reason for the notorious *inaccuracy* of the rifles in use in 1600 and early 1700 before the American, or Kentucky, rifles were designed with its "freed" or tapered bore. With those early rifles, the naked round ball was driven, or rammed, down the bore onto the powder thus forcing the bullet into the deep grooves by expanding it and deforming it. This required a strong iron rod to *pound* or *ram* the bullet down and expand it, and gave this rod the name "ramrod."

After the ball has been loaded as described, a cap is

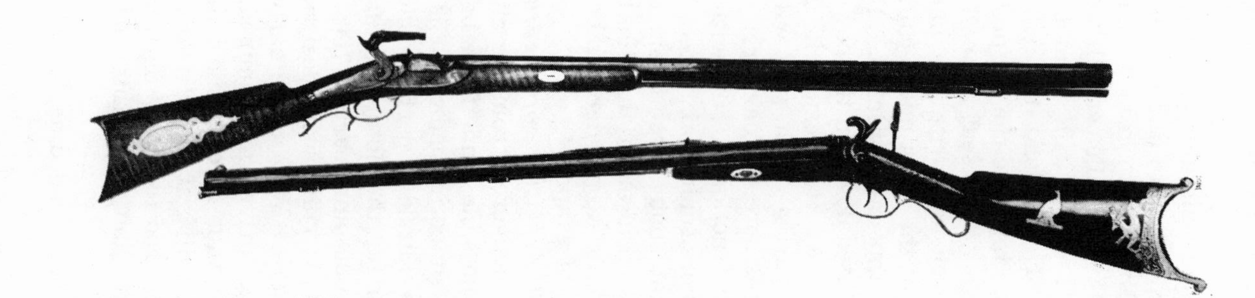

Top: E. Beerst, Dual Shot Rifle. Two charges fired from a Single Barrel. Hammer in Position to Fire the Forward charge, Double Set Trigger.
Bottom: B. W. Amsden, "Combination" Rifle and Shotgun, 44 calibre Round Ball, 14 gauge Shot Barrel. From W. A. Luce Collection.

placed on the nipple and we are ready to shoot. After firing, place the hammer at half-cock, remove any part of the cap that may stick to the nipple and blow through the bore to help soften the powder residue and clear the vent in the nipple before loading again. With good, clean, moist-burning powder it is unnecessary to wipe, or clean, the bore of the round ball hunting rifle after each shot, because as the Dutchman said: "Ven der negxt vun you loadts, der last vun gedts viped." However, when shooting "at a mark," or target shooting, with this type of rifle the accuracy is generally much improved by wiping the bore with a slightly wet cloth followed by a dry one after each shot.

The round balls for this type of rifles should be cast from pure lead—not hardened, then the sprue cut should be smoothed or rounded with a small file, or pocket knife, if the best accuracy is desired. I have heard old riflemen, years ago, say that it mattered not whether the sprue surface of the ball is placed at the bottom or top when loading the round ball rifle, but this is not reasonable and does not agree with my experience and that of the majority of experienced riflemen who use the muzzle-loading rifles. All experienced riflemen who use the modern high power rifles, as well as the most expert marksmen with the target or Schuetzen breech-loading single shot rifles, know that the *base of the bullet* which rests against the powder and is first acted upon by the powder gas must be as *perfect as possible* and each bullet have the *same shape of base,* in order to give good, uniform accuracy. Of course, these same conditions obtain in rifles using the round ball; therefore, as almost no two cast round balls have *exactly the same shape at the point where the sprue was cut off*—one ball having a decidedly flat place at this point, the next one cut obliquely and the third having an inverted V cut sprue end—it is beyond all reason to expect these three balls to group closely on the target. Experienced experts agree that better accuracy with the round ball rifles will be secured by *always loading the sprue surface of the ball at the top,* or towards the muzzle. I was taught by Uncle Alvaro that this is the *only correct way* to load the round ball; thus it became a habit with me that I have always followed, and have seen no reason to change this method.

Commercial "Buckshot" and Round Balls. While the commercial buckshot and round balls appear to have their surface completely covered with minute flat spots, as seen under the magnifying glass, they appear to give fully as good accuracy as the best cast round balls in the majority of rifles. In some rifles they have actually given considerably smaller groups than could be obtained with the most perfect balls we could cast. I would not hazard a guess at the number of pounds of buckshot and lead balls that I have used in round ball rifles during my experience with such rifles, but I may safely say that I have used several hundred pounds of the following Eastern size buckshot and round balls: No. 1, 30 calibre; No. 0, 32 calibre; No. 000, 36 calibre buckshot, and 44 and 45 calibre round balls in various muzzle-loading rifles and cap-lock revolvers, in all of which these gave the best of accuracy as well as saving the trouble of casting these bullets. The only trouble that I have ever had with these buckshot and round balls has been that sometimes these were too hard, appeared to have been made from an alloy of lead and tin, or lead hardened in some way, instead of being of pure, soft lead. While some particular rifleman may think that these small flats on the surface of these buckshot and round balls *absolutely must* affect the accuracy, I do not believe any one can hold close enough when using bench rest and iron sights to detect the difference in accuracy between these and the very best cast round balls when used in the same rifle. Only a machine rest would enable one to ascertain exactly which actually gives the better average accuracy in an accurate shooting round ball rifle at 60 and 100 yards.

The hunting and target rifles that became popular about 1835 or 1840 were nearly all made to use some type of the sugar-loaf, or short, flat-point picket bullet instead of the round ball, although many of these rifles by N. Lewis were so rifled that either the round ball or the sugar-loaf or picket bullets gave equally as good accuracy, according to his claims, but which I, personally, doubt very much.

Geo. O. Leonard, Wm. Billinghurst, James & Ferris, D. H. Hilliard, and others who specialized in this type of rifles often rifled these with a gain twist in order to give superior accuracy with the picket or sugar-loaf bullet for target shooting and turkey shoots. Edwin Wesson and N. Lewis always cut these rifles with the gain twist. The gain twist barrel is rifled with a slow pitch of rifling at the breech which gradually increases to a quicker twist at the muzzle. For instance, a Wm. Billinghurst 36 calibre rifle of this type having a gain twist barrel cut with one turn of rifling in 30 inches at the breech gradually increasing to one turn in 12 inches at the muzzle, using a flat point picket bullet .760 inch long weighing 165 grains, with oiled linen patch, and 65 grains of powder, would average 1 to 1¼ inch 10-shot groups at 100 yards rest and 3 to 3½ inches at 200 yards. Loading this same rifle with the correct size round ball, oiled linen patch and the correct charge of powder, gave 10-shot groups at 100 yards rest that averaged 2½ to 3 inches and 6 to 8 inches at 200 yards, which simply shows that the gain twist while being the best for the picket bullet was all wrong for the round ball.

Practically all the hunting and target rifles by the

different makers were intended to use the linen, or cloth, patch since the paper patch would have been impractical when using the rifle for hunting, especially in rain or snow. However, I once had a 36 calibre rifle of this type made by W. W. Wetmore, of Windsor, Vermont, that had but one bullet mould for casting a picket bullet, but had two swages. One swage gave the finished bullet the correct diameter for use with an oiled linen patch .008 inch thick for use in hunting, while the other swage left the bullet the correct diameter for use with an oiled paper cross patch .002 inch thick for target shooting. This rifle was cut with a grain twist and gave nice accuracy at 40 and 60 rods with either the linen patched bullet or the oiled paper cross patch bullet, although at these ranges the rifle made somewhat smaller groups when using the bullet with the paper patch.

The hunting and target rifles usually were cut with shallower grooves than the hunting rifles and generally required wiping with a damp cloth followed by a dry one after each shot in order to secure the best accuracy in target shooting, but gave satisfactory accuracy for an entire day's hunting without thus cleaning the bore, provided the right powder was used—a moist burning one. Regardless of the type of rifle, one should always wipe all oil out of the bore and clean out the vent in the nipple, and snap several caps on the rifle before loading it. It is also advisable to always load the rifle first with about half a charge of powder ONLY and fire that, so as to be SURE that the vent in the nipple and into the patent breech is open, before loading with a bullet and the full charge of powder and attemping to shoot at the target, only to find that the rifle fails to fire because of oil or obstructions in these vents.

The various makers of the hunting and target rifles always sent a charger with each rifle that held the correct charge of powder for the rifle, which charge had been ascertained by the maker in his range tests as giving the best accuracy. These chargers were usually simply a brass, or tin, tube about the same diameter as the bore of the rifle with a stopper in one end, and when filled level full—stricken measure—held the right charge for that particular rifle. Various rules were used by the old-time makers for ascertaining the correct charge for these hunting and target rifles, but practically all of these gave only the "approximately" correct charge. Each rifle has its own individual characteristics so that in order to ascertain the best charge, the one that will give the very *best accuracy* in any individual rifle of this type, it is necessary to test the rifle on the range with several different charges. In this way, we generally find that the charge that gives the best accuracy is a little more, or less, that than determined by any rule.

One of the old-time rules for deciding the powder charge is: "Use 1½ calibres of powder for rifles under 70 gauge (40 calibre) and 2 calibres for those over that gauge." Here is how that works out: a 32 calibre rifle should use 32 plus 16, or 48 grains of powder; a 36 calibre rifle would use 36 plus 18, or 54 grains; a 90 gauge—38 calibre—would use 38 plus 19, or 57 grains powder; a 70 gauge (40 calibre) needs 40 plus 40, or 80 grains powder; a 52 gauge—45 calibre—should have 45 plus 45, or 90 grains powder. Actual tests on the range show that the majority of charges determined by this rule are very nearly correct for the best accuracy at 40 rods, but certain rifles often require slightly more powder in the calibres above 38, and less in the smaller calibres.

Another rule is: "Use 1 inch of powder for each foot of barrel." That means, a 90 gauge—38 calibre—rifle with a barrel 30 inches long should use 2½ inches length of the bore of powder, which equals 72 grains

Top: Ballard Presentation Rifle, 44 calibre Rim Fire using Nipple and Cap to fire R. F. Cartridge having hole punched in center of rim.

Center: J. M. Caswell Kentucky Cap Lock Rifle, 45 calibre Round Ball, 36½-inch barrel, weight 8 pounds.

Bottom: Confederate Alteration of Hall Breech-Loading Flint-lock Rifle. Original breech action cut off. Breech-plug installed with nipple to use Musket Cap, 16 groove Rifling, 32½-inch barrel, weight, 8 pounds. Captured and brought home by Wm. Bailey of the 118th New York Regiment. From F. E. Dunn Collection.

weight; a 40 calibre of same length barrel gives 82 grains weight and a 45 calibre with same barrel length equals 94 grains weight, as the *average* of five charges of each as weighed on my Fairbanks Powder Scales. This rule gives somewhat heavier charges than the foregoing one, as you will note, and with the majority of the rifles under 40 calibre that I have used are too heavy for the best accuracy, while with those of 40 calibre and larger these charges are practically the same as those that have given the best accuracy in the rifles that I have tested.

All the old-time makers were very particular to carefully test each of their rifles, usually at 20 and 40 rods rest shooting, in order to be sure that the rifle gave the best accuracy as well as to determine the best powder charge, the correct thickness of patch and the correct diameter and shape of bullet for each rifle. The test targets were sent with each rifle so that the customer could see just what degree of accuracy the maker obtained with it in his tests on the range. Only recently, I examined several test targets that D. H. Hilliard shot with one of his top hammer 36 calibre hunting and target rifles that he made for a customer in 1865, and read the pen-written instructions for its use that accompanied it. From these instructions and Hilliard's letter, it seems that the civilian rifleman in those days had trouble in getting powder for his rifle and Hilliard wrote this customer as follows regarding this: "I can furnish a 25-pound can of the Hazzard's F. g. Kentucky Rifle powder for $20.00, but it will be shipped by freight as LARD (not gunpowder) in a 50-pound lard tierce, from a grocer friend, and you will have to pay for about 20 pounds of lard as well as the powder in order to get it. It will be packed in this way: A 50-pound lard tierce will have a false bottom set in 7 inches deep under the true bottom and this space is filled with lard. The can of powder is put in and a false top set in snugly to hold the powder in place, then the 7 inch space between the false top and the real top is filled with lard, the top fastened in and you receive the shipment of LARD with your powder in the middle. The Government inspectors use a 'lard-tester' with a 6-inch blade; therefore a 7-inch depth of lard in each end of the tierce will pass the inspector's lard-tester all right even if both ends of the tierce are tested."

So you see, the rifle cranks had their powder troubles even in those "good old days."

When loading this type of rifle for target shooting it is advisable to pour the powder through a small funnel placed in the bore, to prevent the powder grains from sticking to the sides of the bore; then the funnel is removed and the oiled or wet patch should be carefully and accurately centered on the muzzle, the bullet placed on the center of the patch and started partly into the bore with the fingers before applying the "guide starter," or bullet starter. Be sure to place this starter squarely over the muzzle of the rifle and see that the plunger is fitted over the point of the bullet; then hold the bullet starter down tightly with the left hand while striking the knob of the starter plunger with the ball of the right hand—NOT the palm—ONE BLOW sufficiently hard to force the bullet and patch down the bore the length of the starter plunger. Remove the bullet starter and with the loading rod, or ramrod, *push the bullet down the bore* until it rests on the powder. DO NOT strike the starter plunger more than ONCE, as every time you do so you slightly upset the front and point of the bullet, thus *decreasing the accuracy.*

If the bullet cannot be forced down the length of the starter plunger with one smart blow of the ball of the hand, the patch is too thick for that bullet, or the bullet is a trifle too large. That noted rifle-maker

Harry M. Pope, states in his instructions to purchasers of the Pope muzzle-loading rifles as follows: "Hold the starter down tight onto the false muzzle with the left hand and drive the bullet in the length of the starter plunger with ONE BLOW with the ball of the right hand. Strike in line with the plunger and do NOT strike with the palm as that will make your hand sore. DO NOT strike several blows as the bullet upsets each time and goes with difficulty. Get the knack of the exact strength required and *strike but once.*"

Always wipe off the muzzle of the rifle before loading again and see that no grains of powder are spilled on it before applying false muzzle, the patch, the bullet and the bullet starter. Otherwise a grain or two of powder adhering to the muzzle will cause the bullet starter to rest unevenly on it, which will cause the plunger to be out of exact alignment with the bore and result in seating the bullet in a slightly tipped position, as shown in the illustration in chapter V. Thus the axis of the bullet is not coinciding with the axis of the bore and results in poor accuracy at the target. Be sure that the bullet is exactly centered in the patch, because if it is not, the groups at any range will be considerably enlarged; and use only perfectly cut patches for target shooting. In other words, if the patch is much out of shape—has a piece cut out of its circumference—it should not be used as it is certain to cause an off shot by tipping the bullet slightly off center as it leaves the muzzle of the rifle.

Cleaning the Rifle. This is most important with any kind or type of rifle and many a fine muzzle-loader has been ruined by failing to clean it after use, or by improperly doing so. As a boy I was taught that the *only right way* to clean a rifle is as follows: Place the hammer in the half-cock notch, place a small funnel in the muzzle, hold the rifle in a vertical position by means of a towel or cloth around the barrel near the

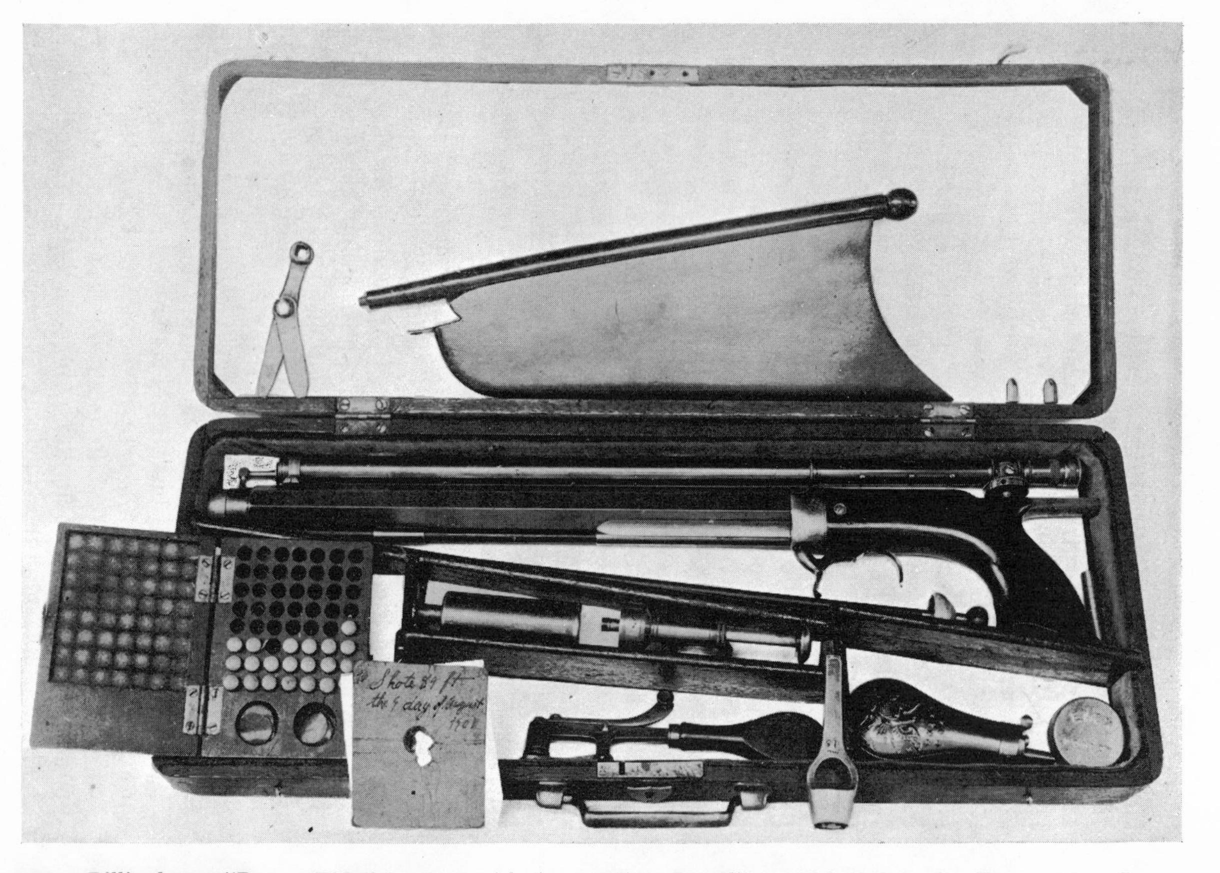

... "... Rifle" in Case with Accessories, 32 calibre, 15-inch barrel. From W. A. Luce

muzzle which is twisted so as to form a handle to prevent burning the hand in case the hot water is spilled. Then with a basin set on the floor to catch the water from the nipple, pour about two quarts of boiling water slowly through the barrel letting it run out of the nipple. Here is where the twisted towel comes into play, so that you will not scald your hand in case any water is spilled as you are pouring it into the funnel. Then stand the rifle in a corner with the muzzle down for about ten minutes so the barrel will cool somewhat, but *do not* let it stand long enough to get *cold;* then with a piece of outing flannel, or canton flannel, in the slotted end of the cleaning rod, swab out the bore using six or eight pieces of the cloth until you have apparently wiped the bore *dry.* Then with a proper sized cleaning patch of this material, wet with pure sperm oil, used on the notched end of the cleaning rod, swab out the bore with three or four oiled patches; wipe out with a dry patch to be sure that all powder residue has been removed, then with a smaller piece of the cleaning material in the slotted end of the rod, well wet with the sperm oil, wipe the bore slowly the whole length and leave this oil in the bore until the rifle is again used. Wipe off the nipple, hammer, lock-plate, barrel and the muzzle with another piece of cloth wet with the sperm oil; also wipe over the stock and fore-arm with this oiled cloth and with the muzzle pointed obliquely towards the floor, place several drops of sperm oil in the vent of the nipple. Keep the rifle after thus oiling it in a dry place until again needed.

Even when hunting in the wilderness, one can easily get hot water in camp and clean the rifle after the day's hunt, and oil it as described. I well remember that on my first deer hunting trip in Northern New Hampshire with Uncle Alvaro when I was about twelve years old, that after an all day's hard trip in a mountainous country, on arriving back at camp about dark, tired and hungry, the very *first thing* was to heat some water and clean my rifle while uncle cleaned his, oil it and hang it on pegs in one side of the camp, before making any attempt to get something to eat, or to rest. Uncle's instructions were: "On arriving at camp, no matter what time of day or night, whether you are wet or dry, warm or cold, the FIRST THING TO BE DONE is to feed and care for your horse (if you are riding one), *next* clean, oil and, if necessary, load your rifle; then get your supper, or meal, wash your dishes, get wood for your next fire, if needed, and then you have time to rest yourself. If you *absolutely must neglect* any of these things, go without your victuals, but *care for your horse and rifle first,* else you may not need any more victuals."

As before stated, the old way of cleaning the rifle by the hot water method as described, if *properly done,* cleans the rifle *thoroughly* and it will not rust. However, riflemen are often careless in cleaning the rifle in this way; they set the rifle aside after using the hot water and let it get stone cold, which allows *slight rust* to form in the bore. Whereas had the barrel been thoroughly wiped while it was still warm, and the bore thoroughly dried with cleaning patches, then oiled thoroughly and the vent in the nipple oiled with the sperm oil, the rifle would have kept all right for several weeks in perfect condition. With all the good cleaning solvents that we have today, I find the following method of cleaning the muzzle-loading rifle more convenient than and equally as effective as the hot water method. After the day's shooting, a stiff bristle brush (not wire) is attached to the hard steel, or celluloid covered rod, the brush dipped into Hoppe's No. 9, or the "J. L. N. Nitro-Solvent," and, with the hammer at half-cock, the bore is scrubbed its entire length. This brush is removed and a second, clean one wet with the nitro-solvent is used in the same way; then with a cleaning patch of outing flannel, or canton flannel, used in the slotted end of the cleaning rod, the residue and solvent is carefully and thoroughly wiped out of the bore. Next with the proper sized patch wet with the solvent and used on the notched end of the cleaning rod, the bore is well swabbed with several such patches; the bore wiped dry and clean and then with a loosely fitting cleaning patch saturated with "Rust Veto, No. 3" oil, the "B. S. A. Safetipaste," or "Rig," used in the slotted end of the rod, the bore is thoroughly coated. Wipe over the outside of the barrel and all metal parts with this same patch, and the rifle may then be set aside for several weeks without fear of rusting.

When a rifle is not likely to be used again for several months, I coat the bore liberally with the "B. S. A. Safetipaste," give the outside of the barrel and all metal parts a heavy coat of this, put the arm in my gun cabinet and it will keep perfectly for a year or more. In fact, I set one muzzle-loading rifle, that was treated in this way, aside in a sheepskin case for five years and at the end of that time the rifle was in as perfect condition as when set away. I presume that the gun-grease known as "Rig" may be equally as good as the B. S. A. Safetipaste, but I, personally, prefer the latter as it has given such perfect results in my rifles. I now have a rifle barrel that was thoroughly greased with this Safetipaste, tightly wrapped in paraffine coated paper which was laid away in January, 1930, and on wiping this barrel out in February, 1940, I found the bore and the outside of the barrel in absolutely perfect condition—the same as when laid away. Any gun-grease that will do this is *good enough* for me.

When the rifle is not in use, if it is not kept in the gun cabinet, I find that the sheepskin gun cases sold

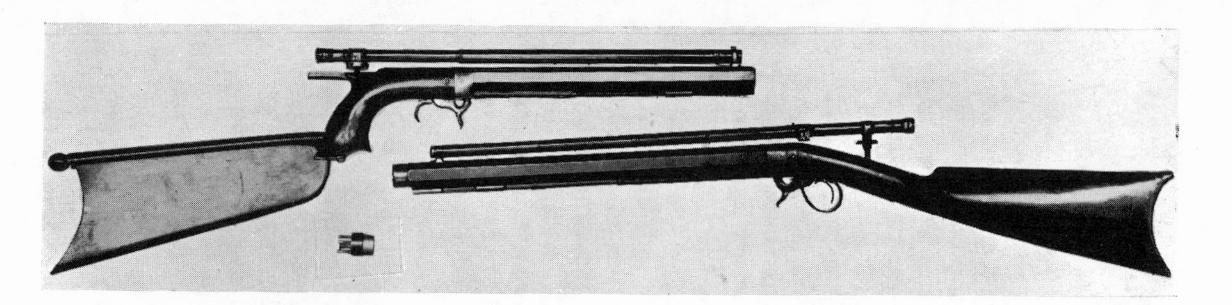

Wm. Billinghurst, "Buggy Rifles." Top: Same rifle shown in Case on page 178. Bottom: Underhammer Model 32 calibre. 18-inch Barrel. Wm. Malcolm Telescope Sight on this. Billinghurst Telescope on Rifle at top. From W. A. Luce Collection.

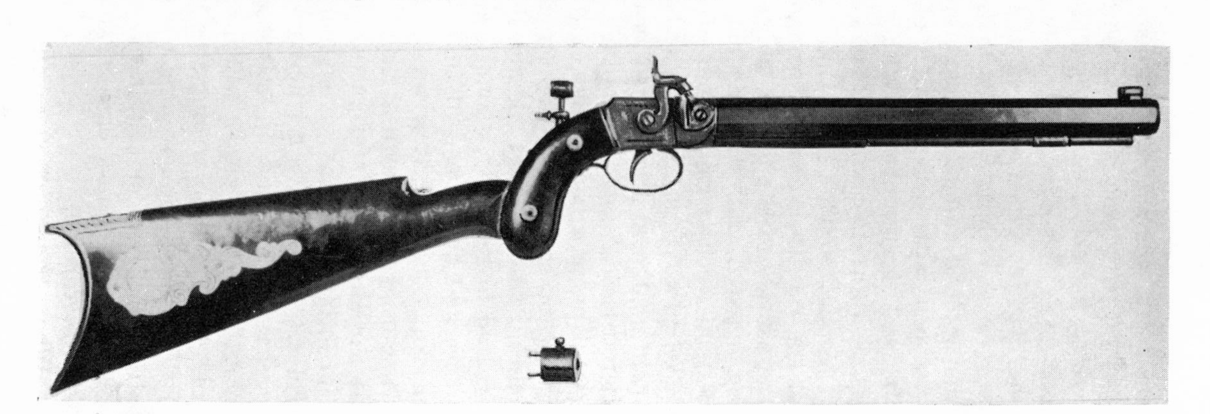

Edwin Fay, "Buggy Rifle," or "Pocket Rifle," 31-calibre, 12-inch Barrel, Silver Mountings. Single Set Trigger. From Shiff the Gunman's Collection.

by R. C. Nichols, of Yarmouth, Maine, or L. L. Bean, Inc., of Freeport, Maine, are the very BEST in which it can be kept as the heavy lamb's wool on the inside prevents rust and tarnish to the metal and provides an oily substance that preserves a fine rifle in perfect condition for long periods of time. My experience has been that a well lubricated rifle will keep in better condition in one of these sheepskin gun cases, stored in a dry place, than in any gun cabinet that I have ever seen.

Some riflemen have a habit of leaving an oily patch in the muzzle of the rifle when setting it aside, but this is a practice that should NOT be recommended as the oil sometimes evaporates from the cloth, that then absorbs moisture and after a considerable time causes the bore to rust at the muzzle, which is the very WORST place for this to happen. Other riflemen leave the cleaning rod with an oiled patch pushed down to the breech of the bore, which is another way in which NOT to keep a rifle, because sooner or later the oil will evaporate, the cloth will absorb moisture and a bad rust spot will form at the breech of the bore—possibly ruining the rifle. No good reason can be assigned for this habit of leaving the cleaning rod with an oiled patch pushed down to the breech when the arm is not in use; no experienced rifleman would do this with a modern, breech-loading rifle and even the inexperienced shooter would not think of so doing. Then why do this with the muzzle-loading rifle? If the bore of the rifle is well coated with a suitable oil, the "B. S. A. Safetipaste," or "Rig," it may be set aside for a long time without fear of rust forming in the bore, and it is NOT ADVISABLE to leave the cleaning rod in the barrel when the arm is not in use.

CHAPTER VI

THE TARGET RIFLE AND TARGET SHOOTING

"Shooting at a mark," or as we say today target shooting with the rifle has been a popular pastime or sport in the United States for fully two centuries. On account of the clumsy, unwieldy stock and the uncertain ignition of the match-lock and wheel-lock arms and their inaccurate shooting, there could have been no shooting at a mark even at short ranges with these arms—unless the mark was a large one. However, the invention of the flint-lock combined with better shaped stocks and reduction in weight, gave these rifles a better balance for off-hand shooting. The flint-lock with its improved ignition, improvements in the types of rifling and its "freed" bore that loaded easily, in connection with a better quality of gunpowder, resulted in an improvement in the ability to hit an object aimed at with these rifles; thus accuracy was developed and "shooting at a mark" soon thereafter became a popular sport in this country as well as abroad.

The American flint-lock rifle with its slender stock, its long, carefully rifled barrel using the patched round ball, came into use in this country early in 1700 and gave a degree of accuracy that had never before been known. The rifles that had been made in Europe during the preceding century, principally by the German and Swiss rifle-makers, failed absolutely to meet the requirements of the American pioneer who was then attempting to conquer a great wilderness. Those arms were too heavy, too large bore which was wasteful of both powder and lead, difficult to load as it required an iron ramrod and a mallet with which to drive home the naked round ball. After a few shots they fouled and leaded so badly that no one could guarantee to hit a man at 50 yards the first shot with them. They were really inferior as a practical arm and less accurate than a well-made smooth-bore using the round ball. What our pioneer needed was a comparatively small-bore rifle using a ball weighing about half an ounce that would shoot ACCURATELY, have good killing power up to about 150 yards, not waste powder which was scarce in the Colonies, that could be easily and quickly loaded, would have a light report when fired so that the sound would not reach the ears of lurking Indians, and an arm that balanced well so as to make accurate off-hand shooting as easy as possible.

This meant that the rifle must have a long barrel containing as much metal as possible to absorb the sound when fired, the bullet must be lubricated in some way to facilitate easy and rapid loading and the rifle must use small charges of powder and lead as a sufficient quantity of these must be carried upon the person to last for long periods of time when in the wilderness and many miles from a source of supply. About 1710 there came to the eastern part of Pennsylvania many German and Palatine Swiss, many of whom at home had been rifle-makers and were ingenious, skillful workmen in both iron and wood fabrication. They soon grasped the idea of the type of rifle that was needed for use in the Colonies; the pioneers and these gunsmiths consulted and experimented, making changes and improvements here and there as experimentation suggested, until about 1730 there appeared an American rifle so far superior to any that the world had before known that it was in a class by itself, and for about one hundred years maintained its superiority as the most practical, most deadly accurate rifle at ranges up to about 150 yards that had been produced.

Wm. V. Lowe shooting from machine rest.

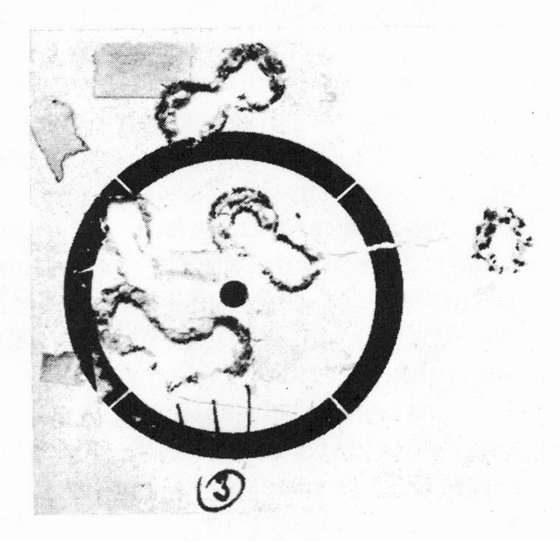

Group shot by Wm. V. Lowe in National Rifle Club Match at Vernon, Vt., May 26, 1887, with 38 calibre Horace Warner Muzzle-Loading Rifle. String measure 6 13/16 inches.

But, does some reader say, what has this to do with target shooting and the target rifle? I answer, EVERYTHING. Never before had the world known a *really accurate,* practical rifle for use in hunting, or war, or by the pioneer settler in the wilderness. Here was the birth of the rifle that was destined to later make history, to conquer the great wilderness from the savage Indians and wild beasts, to establish eventually a new, independent nation and still later to be developed into the superbly accurate target rifle of 1845 to 1895. And even today, 1940, in spite of all our boasted improvements in smokeless powders, metal cased bullets and high velocity arms, we have yet to produce a more accurate rifle.

Who invented or designed the "patch" for the rifle bullet? No one knows just who this person was, but it certainly was a master-stroke in the improvement of the accuracy and ballistics of the rifle, as well as ease of loading the arm. More improvements were gradually made in the construction of the rifle, particularly in the shape of the lands and grooves and the fitting of the patched ball to the bore so that it was easily loaded without deforming it, which combined to bring the typical American flint-lock rifle, later called in the dialect the "Kaintuck," or properly the Kentucky, to its highest development by about 1760.

The major part of this country, then a wilderness inhabited by hostile Indians and wild animals, was slowly being explored and settlements made therein by the pioneers who were constantly dependent on their rifles for defense against their enemies as well as for the greater part of their daily food. Thus it became a necessity for these pioneers to be expert marksmen with their rifle, and soon after a settlement had been established in the wilderness, the father commenced training his son in rifle shooting through the medium of "shooting at a mark." This "mark" usually was a charred or blackened chip from a log, or a block of wood, or a knot on a tree, until a sufficient degree of accuracy had been attained to enable the boy to kill small game for the family table. In this way, under the instruction of the father, the pioneer boy became an expert marksman at an early age and retained this skill by the daily use of the rifle in shooting deer, turkey, bear, wolves and similar game. In those days there were no "sports," as we know them today because these men and boys, women and girls, all had their individual daily work that kept them busy from sun-up to sun-set in clearing the land, planting and tilling the crops, harvesting them, the various household duties, and maintaining a living in the wilderness. However, as the population of the settlements increased and homes became established, it was customary for the men and older boys to have "shooting matches"—especially if there were several men who were considered expert shots with the rifle. Much rivalry often existed among the men in these frontier settlements, and we often read of feasts of marksmanship by some of these pioneer-riflemen that excite our admiration or our doubts even today.

When I was a young boy I frequently visited an old pioneer relative of my grandmother's who was one of the old settlers in Dunbarton, New Hampshire, when it was a wilderness inhabited by wolves, "catamounts" (panthers), bear, deer and other wild animals,—in the days when "Rogers Rangers" were trying to protect the settlers along the Merrimack and Connecticut rivers from the Indian raids,—and listen to his stories of hunting and "turkey shoots" that were held every autumn and at Thanksgiving at "Clifford's Tavern" in that town. Dunbarton is the town in which Kenneth Roberts in his book, "Northwest Passage," located the imaginary "Flint's Tavern" with its sign "No More Rum for 54 Miles," which is an interesting scene in the motion picture but not according to the real history of that town.

I was so interested in these stories that I made notes of them in a small book, from which I quote: "The ranges were usually 15 rods off-hand or 20 rods rest shooting, at a live turkey tied to a stake, and if one drew blood on the turkey he won it. These turkey shoots were largely attended and there was much rivalry among the best shots to see who could win the greater number of turkeys in a given number of shots. Sometimes there were shoots in the autumn for steers, or "beef shoots," in which case each marksman had his own "board" (target) having a cross in the center, or a blackened board with a piece of white paper tacked in the center of it as an aiming point. The fee was usually two shillings (33, 1/3c) a shot; each man fired one shot at his own board and the man who placed his ball nearest the exact center, as determined by measuring with a piece of string from the center of the cross to the center of the bullet hole, was the winner of the "first choice" of the parts of the steer. Then all fired a second round of one shot each to decide the winner of the "second choice," and so continued shooting until all the "choices," or parts, of the animal had been won."

This old gentleman had a fine, full stocked "Kaintuck" flint-lock rifle of 50 to the pound gauge, with silver patch-box and many silver inlays in the stock and fore-stock, that I greatly admired. He had a splendidly carved powder-horn with Indians, animals and a map cut in it, a horn charger, a smaller horn containing "priming powder," and a finely ornamented hunting bag that also excited my admiration. Frequently after telling me about some of the fine shots that he had made at game, he would give a demonstration of his ability as a marksman by shooting at a mark, or a woodchuck or crow, and I have often seen him kill these at ranges of 20 rods or more. No "guess work" about these ranges, either, as in those days all New England farms were measured in rods and the owner knew exactly the length and width in rods of every field and pasture that he owned. Therefore if he shot a crow out of an apple tree in a certain field he knew the exact distance from where he stood to the tree. This old pioneer, William Story, often called his rifle "Hannah" and at other times "Kaintuck"; he pronounced bear as "bar," and in another chapter, I shall relate one of the hunting experiences of this man during the early days in Dunbarton, as he told it to me more than sixty years ago.

Between 1790 and 1800 there was developed in certain parts of this country a typical flint-lock "match rifle," or "turkey rifle," with quite heavy full octagon barrel about 38 to 40 inches long, full stocked, double set trigger and with various types of tube sights, but all using the round ball with linen patch. It is sometimes stated that about 1800 some of these rifles had telescope sights, but I am sure that this was a mistake as the rifle telescope sight had not then been invented. They were all simply tube sights, but mounted like the long telescope sights of later years. In years past, I have examined a large number of these flint-lock match rifles, but have never yet found one that had a sight containing lenses, or glass, of any kind. Captain Dillin in his book, *The Kentucky Rifle,* also states that he has never seen a flint-lock with a real telescope sight of any type, but has found many with tube sights of various kinds.

The percussion cap was invented about 1813 by Joshua Shaw, of Lincolnshire, England, but was kept secret by him until he came to Philadelphia in 1814, when he applied for a patent on this invention, which was refused because he was an alien and our patent laws forbade granting patents to aliens at that time.

Improvements were made by him in the composition of the fulminate and methods of manufacture so that by about 1825 the percussion cap had practically been perfected and adopted in place of the flint as the means of ignition for fire-arms by the rifle-makers in this country, those in foreign countries and the Governments of many foreign countries. Since the United States had refused to grant Shaw a patent on the percussion cap which they had later adopted for use on the Army and Navy rifles they evidently felt somewhat guilty and in 1846, when Shaw was over seventy years old, Congress awarded him an honorarium of $25,000 for his discovery and invention.

The percussion cap was, of course, a great improvement over the flint-lock as it afforded better, quicker and more certain ignition of the powder charge, as well as being unaffected by rain or snow. This latter feature was an especially important improvement over the flint-lock which could not be depended upon to give proper ignition in wet weather, and after the percussion cap had been perfected many of the flint-lock rifles were changed to cap lock which improved the efficiency and accuracy of these arms. The perfection of the percussion cap was the last thing needed to bring the round ball hunting rifle to a degree of perfection and accuracy that made it much superior as a practical arm to any rifle ever before known, so that this type of rifle reached its highest development between about 1830 and 1850.

About 1835 a muzzle-loading percussion lock rifle with heavy, full octagon barrel 30 to 36 inches long, using the flat point picket bullet with linen patch, with the end of the muzzle turned cylindrical to fit the guide starter or bullet starter, usually called a "turkey rifle" or "match rifle," became popular in the eastern part of the United States. These were usually 36, 38, 40 or 42 calibre, although some were 45 or 50 calibre;

H. J. Huntoon, Primer Ignition Match Rifle, 38 calibre, Cylindrical Bullet, 3-strip patch, 30-inch barrel, weight 18 pounds. Owned by W. T. Brodeur.

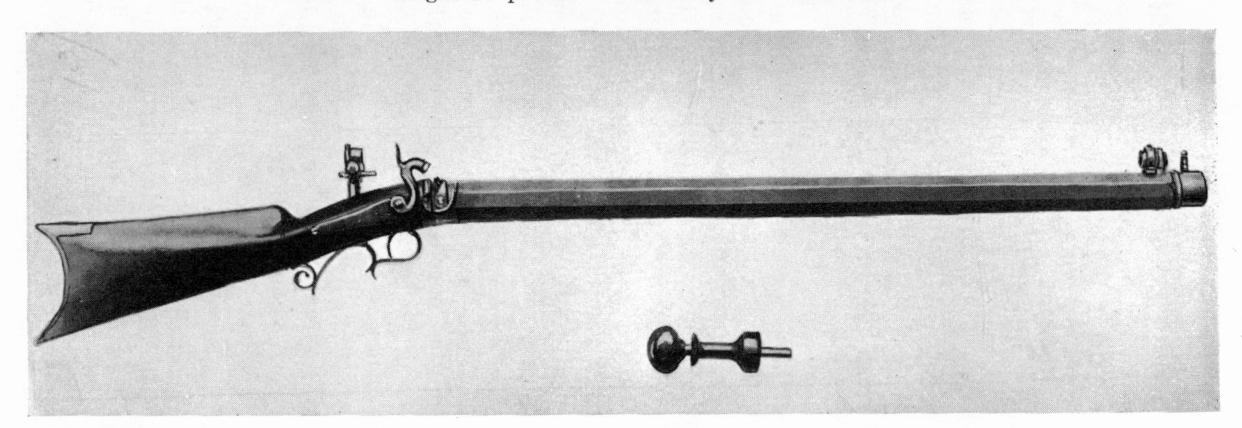

N. G. Whitmore, 40 calibre Match Rifle, Picket Bullet, 30-inch barrel, weight 19 pounds. Owned by Howard M. Irish.

were fitted with single or double set trigger, fine shaded pin-head front, an open rear sight on the barrel with a rear peep sight screwing through the upper tang, and gave considerably finer accuracy at 40 to 60 rods than any other rifles before in use. These usually weighed from about 9 to 15 pounds and were designed for men who wanted a rifle principally for use in turkey shoots and "shooting matches," but which would also be suitable for shooting deer, bear and similar big game. The most widely known makers of these turkey or match rifles were Wm. Billinghurst, N. Lewis, Edwin Wesson, James & Ferris, D. H. Hilliard and P. A. Reinhart.

The Billinghurst rifles were largely used in the Mid-West and Western parts of the country, while those of Edwin Wesson, N. Lewis, James & Ferris, and Hilliard were used in large numbers in New York State and the New England States. P. A. Reinhart of Loudonville, Ohio, learned rifle-making under Wm. Billinghurst and after becoming a master rifle-maker, returned to Loudonville, re-established his business there and made hunting and target rifles that were used chiefly by Ohio and Pennsylvania riflemen.

The majority of these turkey or match rifles were, I believe, cut with the gain twist, although we find many that have the uniform twist of rfling; because, as before stated, these rifles were intended for target shooting chiefly and for that purpose there is little doubt that the gain twist rifling gives the better accuracy with the picket or conical bullet. They were considered the *most accurate* rifles for 40 rods shooting that could be made before 1840, when Alvan Clark invented the false muzzle which resulted in the development of the special target rifle with the "Clark patent muzzle," or false muzzle. The groups shown herewith that were shot with various makes of these turkey or match rifles illustrate the accuracy that can

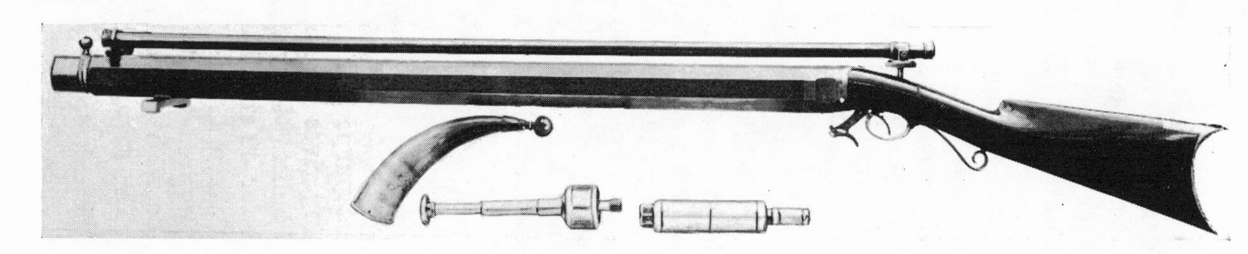

Abe Williams "Sharpshooters Rifle," 56 calibre, 31-inch barrel, weight 28 pounds. From Dr. P. A. Matteson's Collection.

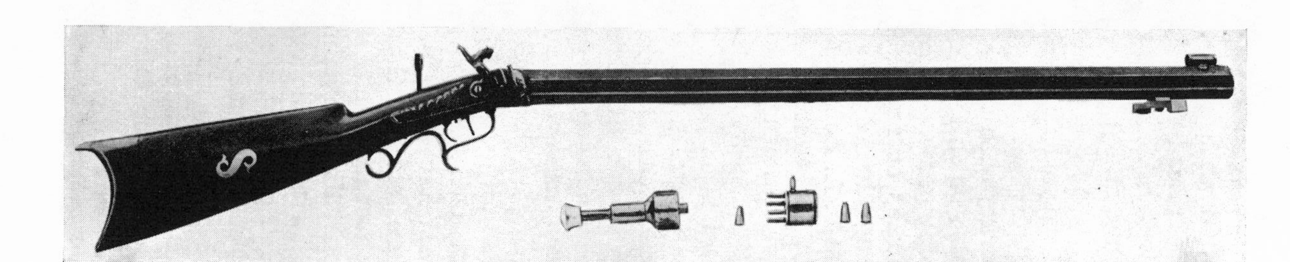

N. S. Brockway Rifle, 45 calibre, 32-inch barrel, weight 16 pounds. Uses Picket Bullet with Cloth Patch. Very Accurate. From Dr. Matteson's Collection.

reasonably be expected from one of these rifles by the best makers, if the bore is in perfect condition and the shooting is done by an expert marksman who is experienced in the use of the muzzle-loading rifle. We know from experience that the man who is today an expert in the use of our modern, high velocity rifles with which all he has to do is to insert a factory-made cartridge, aim and pull the trigger, will find himself only a *poor shot* with the best muzzle-loading target rifle and will find that he has *a lot to learn* before he is able to make fine groups with these latter rifles.

It is impossible to secure as fine accuracy with the hunting and target rifles as with the target rifles having the false muzzle, because the bullets used in the former were not as well shaped and do not have as long bearing in the bore of the rifle as the bullets used in the latter rifles. It is also an impossibility to load a considerable number of consecutive bullets of the short picket type as perfectly into any rifle without the false muzzle as is easily done with this accessory. In using any rifle that does not have a false muzzle, the most experienced, careful rifleman will, in spite of the greatest care in loading, frequently get a bullet seated in the barrel in a slightly tipped position so that the axis of the bullet does not exactly coincide with that of the bore of the rifle. This is illustrated in chapter V, and shows clearly how the tipping bullet leaves the muzzle of the rifle and why it does not have the same point of impact on the target as does a perfectly loaded one. Since the so-called "picket," or conical, bullet has such a short bearing on the lands and grooves of the rifle, it is especially difficult to load it perfectly and uniformly every time even by the use of the guide starter, or bullet starter, *without the false muzzle* as can be done with a rifle having *both the false muzzle and the bullet starter* with which the target rifle is equipped. If the bullet can not be loaded

Old Shooting House and Range at Vernon, Vt. Where the Matches of the National Rifle Club were held from about 1868 to 1896. Reproduced from "The American Rifleman," by Permission of the Editor.

as perfectly in any rifle without the false muzzle, it is simply *impossible* to secure as fine accuracy—make as small groups—at 40 rods or more with any rifle that does not have both these *very essential parts*.

We therefore find that the "match rifles" which were made before 1840, regardless of who made them, never gave as fine accuracy, or made as small groups at 40 rods or more, as those made after that date and fitted with the false muzzle. Also, after the invention of this false muzzle we find that the accuracy range of the best target rifles was increased to more than twice that of the best rifles without the false muzzle. This increase in the accuracy range was the result of the use of the long cylindrical, and cylindro-conoidal, bullets using the oiled paper patch of various types, combined with the further improvements in the manufacture of gunpowder, improved percussion caps and the ability to load these long bullets with their paper patch perfectly by means of the false muzzle and bullet starter. In addition to the above improvements, we had in this country from about 1840 to 1890 a large number of riflemen who used the muzzle-loading target rifle for their target shooting and who made a very careful study of these rifles, developed the compound type of bullets, improved the moulds for casting the parts of these bullets and the swages for perfectly shaping these in order to improve the ballistics, range and accuracy of these rifles. If you doubt that statement, just show me where and when any rifle matches were shot and high scores made with any muzzle-loading rifles at 1000 yards before 1840.

As an illustration of this increased accuracy range of the target rifles, we have been unable to find any records of match shooting at ranges of 80 rods (440 yards) with the very best rifles made before 1840, while after that date with the introduction of the target rifle having the Clark's patent muzzle—false muzzle—we find frequent records of matches at ranges of 100 to 200 rods (550 to 1100 yards), and the popular range for target shooting was increased from 20 to 40 rods. I remember that when Uncle Alvaro was teaching me to shoot the rifle, he frequently told me that the "real rifleman should be able to keep his bullets in an 8 inch bulls-eye at 40 rods off-hand shooting, or in a 4 inch ring at that range when shooting with a rest, using the rear peep and pin-head front sights, *if the rifle was really an accurate one.* Or if the rifle had a telescope sight, the sharpshooter should keep his bullets in a 2½ inch circle at that range when shooting from a rest, using a rifle with a false muzzle, of course."

Before I had become sufficiently skilled to shoot at this range, it was one of my greatest pleasures to attend with Uncle Alvaro, the bi-weekly shoots of the rifle club to which he belonged and see him and numerous other riflemen shoot at 40 rods. The club had three targets at that range, two of which were generally used by the off-hand shooters while the bench rest shooters used the third target. At that time—1878 to 1880—many of the club members used muzzle-loading target rifles of 40, 42 or 45 calibre weighing from about 12 to 16 pounds. The majority of the members used the then "new fashioned" Sharps, Ballard or Remington single shot breech-loading arms, nearly all chambered for the 40 calibre "Sharps straight," or the bottle-necked, cartridges with long, paper patched bullets. I remember one man in particular—Mr. George Pierce—who used a Ballard for the 44-77 bottle-necked cartridge with a 470 grain paper patched bullet, and a Mr. "Jim" Henry who used a Remington rolling block rifle for this same cartridge, who sometimes were in the "high score" list and occasionally made higher scores off-hand than the muzzle-loaders. However, in the rest shooting these rifles did not make as high scores—as small groups—as the best muzzle-loaders even though the breech-loaders were cleaned after each shot. This club used a 4 by 6 foot target for off-hand shooting at 40 rods, with a bulls-eye 8 inches in diameter then known as the "Creedmoor" target—which is the same as the Army "A" target for 200 yards—but the rest shooting was scored by "string measure" usually, although they sometimes used the German ring target for this shooting. The off-hand matches of this club were frequently shot at 200 yards instead of 40 rods during the summer and autumn if the weather was pleasant, but in stormy and cold weather the shooting was at 40 rods as that was the distance from the shooting house to the targets. This house had windows opening horizontally that faced the targets from which the members could shoot in comfort during cold weather as it was heated by a wood-burning stove. Sometimes I sawed and brought in wood for the stove, and in lieu of compensation I was allowed the privilege of shooting a score with uncle's rifle, or one of the breech-loaders, on the rest target. If I made a good group—short string measure—uncle often rewarded me by the present of a powder-flask full of his Curtis & Harvey powder, but if I made a poor group he scolded me all the way home.

The National Rifle Club which was one of the first rifle clubs—possibly *the first*—in the United States was organized in June 1858, according to the records in the secretary's book of that club. The late Norman S. Brockway was for many years the secretary of that club, and from this book I quote the following: "Organization of the National Rifle Club at Framingham, Mass., on June 16th, 1858. We, the undersigned, this day form ourselves together into a body to be known as the National Rifle Club, and made choice of officers as follows: viz. John Williamson, President,

58½ Division Street, New York City; Hiram W. Smith, Secretary, 29 Washington Street, Boston, Mass.; A. Haven, Treasurer, South Framingham, Mass. Present at the meeting in addition to the above; L. Amidon, Bellows Falls, Vt., William Gleason, East Lexington, Mass., W. W. Wetmore, Lebanon, N. H., W. B. Farrington, Lebanon, N. H. Adjourned to meet at Waltham, Mass., on Oct. 5th, 6th, and 7th, 1858."

"Signed, Hiram W. Smith, Secretary."

This secretary's book also contains the following record: "First Annual Meeting of the National Rifle Club, at Waltham, Mass., Oct. 5th, 6th and 7th, with the following attending and shooting in the matches; Wm. Gleason, John Williamson, W. G. Langdon, H. P. Minot, G. Leonard, T. Spencer, A. Haven, L. Amidon, H. W. Smith. The conditions of the match were 50 shots at 40 rods rest, and the man making the shortest string for the 50 shots to be the winner of the Club's medal in addition to the cash prizes." "The old officers were re-elected for another year. Adjourned to meet at Waltham, Mass., on Oct. 4th, 5th and 6th, 1859." "Signed, Hiram W. Smith, Secretary." There was no record of the make, calibre or weight of the rifles used nor any statement regarding the kind of sights used by the different shooters, but stated: "The Medal was won by T. Spencer with a string measure of 54 inches for the 50 shots." This shows that the rifle used by Mr. Spencer was a very accurate one as his average is but 1.08 inches per shot from the center of the target, and very few indeed of our boasted .30-06 Springfield rifles can show such a record for 50 consecutive shots with our most modern smokeless powder and metal cased bullets as used in the National Matches at Camp Perry in recent years.

Soon after the close of the Civil War, Norman S. Brockway was elected secretary of the National Rifle

Club and held that office as long as the club was in existence. In 1868, as near as I can learn, the place for holding their annual match was changed to Vernon, Vermont, and continued to be shot there until the close of their last match in September 1896. In these matches the rules of the club stated: "Match to be 5 strings of 10 shots each. Any style rest allowed that does not confine the rifle or add weight to it. Sights, Any. Time Rules. String Measure. Distance 40 rods." Their "standard" weight of rifle was 20 pounds; all over that weight had 1/8 inch per pound deducted from each 10-shot string, while rifles under 20 pounds weight had 1/8 inch per pound added to each 10-shot string, in order to equalize the weight of the rifles above or below their "standard," and appears to have been a perfectly satisfactory method of handicapping competitors in rifle matches of this kind. The club and its members undoubtedly did more to promote interest in the development of super-accurate rifles for shooting at 40 rods than any other rifle club in this country. The members of the Massachusetts Rifle Association, at the famous "Walnut Hill Range," near Boston, almost without any exception, used breech-loading rifles of various calibres and makes, and the first time I visited that range, in 1883, I did not see a single muzzle-loading rifle in use by any member or shooter. While this club has undoubtedly done more in years past to develop the super-accurate, single shot breech-loading target rifle, and the Walnut Hill Range is more widely known both in this country and abroad than any other rifle club in the United States, they have not accomplished nearly as much in improving and developing *the most accurate shooting muzzle-loading rifles* as the old National Rifle Club at Vernon, Vermont, accomplished during its existence.

As some of the younger riflemen of today may not understand the "string measure" method of scoring

Muzzle-Loaders vs. Breech-Loaders, Vernon, Vt., May 26-27, 1886. Left to right—front row: Hiram W. Smith, Norman S. Brockway, David H. Cox, D. A. Brown, B. Stephenson.
Back row: C. W. Hinman, D. Park, R. C. Cressy, J. N. Frye, Frank I. Fenn, C. F. Fletcher, William V. Lowe, William Maynard, F. J. Rabbeth, W. Milton Farrow, unidentified visitor, George F. Ellsworth.

Photograph taken by A. C. Gould. Copied from "The American Rifleman," by permission of the Editor.

the groups in rifle matches, I may explain by stating that, according to information given me when I was a boy, it was customary in the shooting matches of pioneer days for each man to provide his own "mark," "board" or target as we call it today. This was usually a charred piece of board—charred by burning as that makes an especially black color—about a foot square, with a piece of white paper in the center having a cross marked in the middle of it. After the required number of shots had been fired by a man at his own board, it was brought to the firing point, a wooden plug was placed in each bullet hole, a piece of string was held by one end at the center of the cross mark, the string carried around the wooden plugs in the bullet holes, back to the center spot and cut off. This string was then measured and the man whose string measured the shortest was the winner. This was the old, pioneer method of string measure, but at some later period the method was changed and thereafter they measured with a piece of string from the center of the cross mark to the center of half of a round ball which each man provided and which was placed in each bullet in his board. The string was measured, the length set down on a piece of paper, the distance of the center of each half bullet from the center of the cross was measured in the same way and set down; then by adding these measurements the total length of the string was ascertained and the man having the shortest total was the winner. I believe this second is the method still in use by the riflemen in the mountain sections of Kentucky, Tennessee and the Carolinas today.

The third method of "string measure" as practiced in most parts of this country since about 1840, or earlier, is as follows: After a shooter has fired the required number of shots on his own target, it is brought to the firing point where some man who has

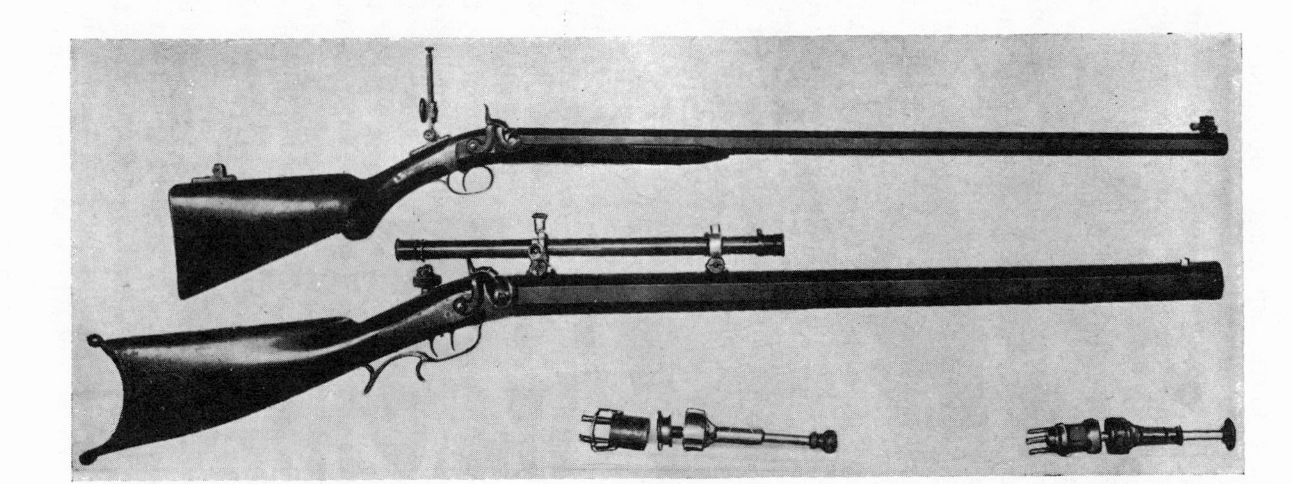

Top: Geo. H. Ferriss, "Creedmoor" Long Range Rifle, 45 calibre 550 grain Cylindrical Bullet, Paper Patch, 31-inch barrel, weight 10 pounds.
Bottom: L. W. Tisdel, 47 calibre Match Rifle, 28-inch barrel, weight 17 pounds. From W. A. Luce Collection.

been chosen as the "Measurer of Targets," places the target over a piece of paper, pricks a hole with a small "scriber" through the center of the "bud," or center spot, and in the same way marks the center of each bullet hole. Then a pair of dividers are used in measuring the distance from the center of the "bud" to the center of each bullet hole, these distances recorded in inches, eighths and sixteenths, these measurements are added and the total is the "string measurement" of the group of shots. This is the most accurate method of measuring, or scoring, groups shot with any calibre of rifle, but is too slow in operation to permit using it in matches where there are many contestants who each fire five shots or more, and is only occasionally used today by the men who shoot the muzzle-loading rifles.

The target that affords the most accurate method of scoring is, undoubtedly, the German Ring which has a center ring 1½ inches in diameter counting 25 in the center of a black bull 12 inches in diameter and surrounded by rings ½ inch apart to the circumference of this bull, counting 24, 23, 22, 21, 20, 19 and 18 respectively. Thus by the use of this target, if a bullet cuts the 23 ring the shooter knows that his bullet is approximately 2¼ inches from the exact center of the bull, or if it cuts the 22 ring it is 2¾ inches from the center. This target was very popular during the 1880's and 1890's in the Schuetzen rifle matches with those fine single shot target rifles, and is, I am glad to note, again being adopted by clubs whose members have again taken up the shooting of these single shot breech-loading rifles. It should be adopted today by the National Muzzle-Loading Rifle Association for use in their outdoor rifle matches, as it is a far more equitable method of scoring than the National Rifle Association Targets now used in their matches.

The first method of string measure as here given does NOT give the same results, or measurement, as the other two, as can easily be determined by trial with any group of shots on any target; but when I was a boy, I frequently saw old riflemen and hunters measure groups in this way and they assured me that this was the usual method followed by the early rifle-makers and pioneers in the days of the flint-lock rifle.

The targets used in the matches of the National Rifle Club, as well as in nearly all the other muzzle-loading rifle matches, consisted of a piece of card-board about a foot square with a black, or other color, circular paster called the "bud" in the center and having diagonally crossed lines indicating the center of the "bud," which was usually one inch in diameter. When you consider that the range was 40 measured rods from the muzzle of the rifle to the target, it will become apparent that in order to sight accurately on such a small spot, the old, long telescopes then in use certainly gave excellent definition even though they had a quite small field of view. Experienced riflemen today know that one cannot do really fine shooting on such a small bull with our present 8 power, modern telescopes having 1¼ or 1½ inch objectives that give much wider field than the old-time, full length telescopes in use before, during and for some time after, the Civil War. Therefore, these old-time telescopes could not have been as bad and deficient optically as some of our present day "authorities" and "experts" would have one believe, else the marksmen could not have sighted accurately on such a small diameter bud, or mark.

On the 7th of August, 1861, according to the old *Harper's Weekly* from which I quote: "Colonel Berdan and His Sharpshooters." "We illustrate herewith the exploits of Colonel Berdan and his famous sharp-shooting regiment, which will shortly be heard of at the war. On the 7th, the Colonel gave an exhibition of his skill at Weehawken, New Jersey, in the presence of a large crowd of spectators. The "man target," christened Jeff Davis was set up at a distance of a little more than 200 yards. Colonel Berdan inaugurated the firing. In an easy, business-like way, he loaded his rifle, an ordinary target piece with a telescopic sight, and approached the "rest." The visitors crowded around him in every direction, excepting, of course, that occupied by the muzzle of the rifle. A sense of personal danger preserved a small opening there. The wind blew quite heavily. It will be conceded that these circumstances were not particularly conducive to careful and unerring aim, but Colonel Berdan is a man of wonderful nerve. The crowd did not at all disturb him. Balancing his rifle for a moment, he fired at the head of the figure. When the smoke had cleared away, the hole made by the bullet was observed by the aid of the telescope, in the cheek, near the nose."

"Again the Colonel loaded and quickly fired at the head, hitting it just over the frontispiece of the cap which was painted upon it. The third shot was fired. "Put his eye out," remarked the Colonel. The ball had struck near enough to that organ to destroy its use had it been a real one. The fourth shot hit the face. "I'll try nature's rest," said the Colonel, and he proceeded to a knoll nearby, and throwing himself at its side, accommodated his person to its shape, and took aim, but the percussion cap only exploded. "Davis is safe this time," he remarked. "We will try him again." Another cap was provided, and the image was struck just below the front piece of the cap. The aim was quite as accurate as he had previously obtained. The sixth shot hit about two inches lower than the fifth. The seventh hit the top of the head. Loading again, the Colonel made ready to fire.

Colonel Berdan's Rifle and Exhibition Rifle shooting by "Berdan's Sharpshooters" at Weehawken, New Jersey, August 7th, 1861. From "Harper's Weekly," August 24, 1861. Rifle is 48 calibre, 31-inch barrel,

"Where will you have this shot?" he inquired of a bystander. "In the end of the nose," was the answer. "Between the eyes," suggested another. At this moment the rifle was discharged. "You spoke too late," quietly remarked the Colonel. "He has another nostril." A gentleman was called to witness the effect of the shot, and afterwards our reporter. "Where shall I put the next shot?" the Colonel inquired of the man who had requested that he spoil the nose of the image. "Try the right eye," was the answer. No sooner said than it was done, and the ball entered the lower part of that eye. The effect of this shot was carefully noted by several persons through the glass. "Will you tell me where to hit him again?" once more asked the Colonel, of the person who had called the last two shots. That individual declined as he was satisfied that the Colonel could hit anything and it was not worth while to fire at the image, whose face was riddled. "We will hit him in the heart now," remarked the Colonel as he fired the tenth shot, and the bullet was accurately placed in the heart region of the image. In this manner, the Colonel proceeded to shoot at the buttons on the coat, the right or left arm, or wherever directed by the spectators until the entire heart and chest region of the image was well riddled with bullet holes."

This same magazine reports that; "The requirements are that no man is admitted to the Regiment who does not shoot, at 600 feet distance, ten consecutive shots at an average of five inches from the bulls-eye. Remarkable though it may seem, many of the men excel this proficiency. Colonel Berdan himself has, on a windy day with a strange rifle, put ten balls within an average of 1 and 1/10 inches each from the center of the bulls-eye, at 600 feet. At 1000 feet the Colonel made a string of 22 inches for ten shots. The American riflemen proved generally superior, especially the hunters of New England and the West. The uniform of the Sharp-shooters will be green in summer and gray at other seasons, to assimilate as nearly as possible with the colors of nature. They will be armed with the most improved Springfield rifle, with a plain silver pin sight at the muzzle, and a notched sight, or the globe sight at the breech for long range shooting. It was first intended to arm them with the Northern target rifle, but it was found that there were not enough in the country. Each man may take his own rifle if he wishes. Colonel Berdan has invented a ball which is superior to the old Springfield rifle ball, and will carry with great accuracy a distance of 3000 feet. It is a grooved and conical ball, and is almost certain for a horse at the distance of three-fifths of a mile. It is the first regiment ever formed worthy of the name—i. e., that subjected each member to the rifle-shooting test. Colonel Berdan comes of Huguenot stock; his ancestry came to this country after the Revocation of the Edict of Nantes. He was born in the western part of New York."

Illustrations herewith show Colonel Berdan's rifle that he used in this shooting and the "Jeff Davis" target well peppered with his bullets, which I photographed from the *Harper's Weekly* of August 24, 1861.

From the *Harper's Weekly* issue of October 5, 1861, I quote the following extract: "The New Hampshire Sharp-Shooters." "We publish herewith several illustrations of the New Hampshire Company of Berdan's Sharp-Shooters Regiment, including a portrait of Captain Jones. These New Hampshire marksmen are all men of excellent moral character, more than ordinary intelligence, and of good social position. Quite one-third are farmers, the remainder being composed of mechanics and artisans who earn their $2.00 a day the year around. They are led by Captain A. B. Jones, a stalwart, handsome young man, who was offered the commission by the Governor on his graduation-day at college, and who sprang with alacrity from the study of Euclid and Herodotus to that of Hardee and Scott. He is a wonderful rifle-shot himself, having made a ten-shot string of *seven inches* from a rest in a recent public trial of the men. This almost equals the marvelous exploit of Colonel Berdan himself at the Weehawken exhibition, and is actually better than the champion string made in Kentucky in '48. Let the Colonel look to his laurels! The next best shot in the Company is one Brown from Bow, New Hampshire, whose string measured fifteen inches; but the average of the whole hundred men is under thirty inches." "Captain Jones in recruiting the New Hampshire Company, advertised for candidates to come to headquarters at Concord, bringing with them satisfactory certificates of good character and habits as their second qualification for admission. The result was that over 250 applications were made, nearly all of them by men who could "pass the string test." So that the 100 taken being deducted, there is material for another company of riflemen from the Old Granite State. New Hampshire has done well in this war in a good many ways, but she has nothing to be prouder of than the 100 whom she has sent to operate on the wings of an army under young Captain Jones. If they don't give a good account of themselves, we shall hereafter have no faith in strong arms, steady nerves, clear sight, or 40-pound rifles."

The First International Rifle Match in the United States. One of the chief features of the Wimbledon, England, matches for many years has been and still is, the match for the Elcho shield, which is annually competed for by teams of eight men from England, Scotland, Canada, Australia, Ireland and other countries, at 800, 900 and 1000 yards with match rifles. In 1873, the Irish team had won this match by a previously un-

The Irish Rifle Team, First International Rifle Match at Creedmore Range, September 28, 1874.

Dr. J. B. Hamilton, Maj. A. B. Leach, James Walker, in front row. Second row: J. K. Milner, Edmund Johnson. Back row: Captain P. Walker, John Rigby.

paralleled score. Fired by their success, their captain, Major Arthur B. Leach, published in the New York *Herald*, a challenge to the riflemen of America, to shoot a similar match in this country in 1874 for the championship of the world. A stake of 100 pounds sterling a side was to be put up, not for the sake of pecuniary gain, but as guarantee that the Irish team would meet the representative shots of America. The directors of the National Rifle Association of America were far too dignified a body to entertain a newspaper challenge not addressed to it, and did nothing about the challenge. Doubtless the Irish Rifle Team did not know of the existence of the National Rifle Association of America, else they would have sent the challenge direct to them. However, the Amateur Rifle Club, of New York City, having neither the dignity nor the scruples of the National Rifle Association, took up the challenge in February 1874, and in so doing showed a "nerve" which can only be correctly described as audacious.

The Irish Rifle Team had just defeated the best long range riflemen of England and Scotland by an unprecedented score, they were provided with the *finest match rifles* having Vernier elevation and wind gauge scales and were veteran riflemen who had been practicing long range shooting for many years. The Amateur Rifle Club had been organized but a short time, had a total membership of less than seventy and during 1873, had held but five matches, all of which were at 500 yards. *Not a member of the club had ever fired a shot at 600 yards.* Neither were there any riflemen outside the club who were more experienced in long range rifle-shooting. Therefore, it was audacious indeed for this young club to accept the challenge of the Irish Rifle Team. The rifles then in use in this country were without Vernier scales on the rear sights and without accurately adjustable wind

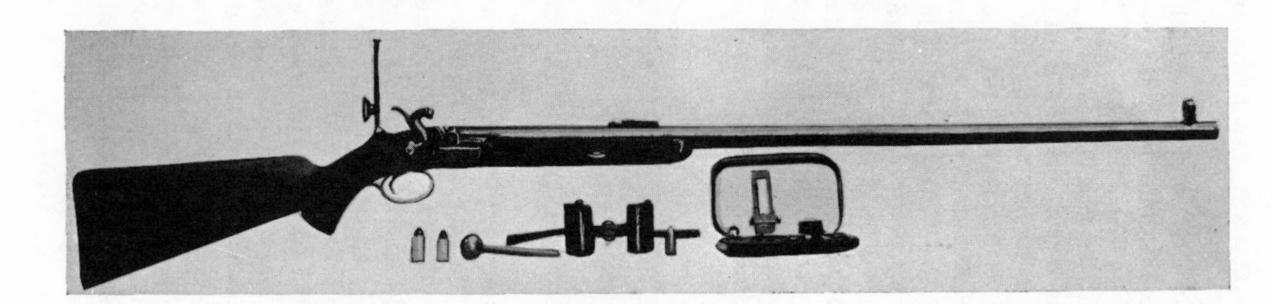

Whitworth, Hexagonal Bore, Muzzle Loading Long Range Rifle, 45 calibre, 120 grains powder, 530 grain Paper Patched Bullet. Shot without cleaning, Weight of rifle, just under 10 pounds, 32-inch Barrel. Bullets, Bullet Mould, and Extra Sights in Morocco Case.

gauge front sights. L. L. Hepburn, who was a skilled machinist, excited the envy of his competitors by his ability to supply the lack of a wind guage on his rifle by tapping his front sight with a hammer to one side or the other the proper distance to counteract the deviation of the bullet by the wind. The rifles had crescent shaped butt plates instead of flat ones that when firing in the prone position bruised the shoulder and raised a lump on the collar bone of the shooter. Neither the bullets nor any of the rifles then in use here could be relied upon to do accurate shooting at the long ranges stated in the challenge. Worst of all, the club that accepted the challenge lacked the financial ability to meet the heavy expense of organizing and training a rifle team, and the management of such a match. Acting, however, upon the maxim, "Nothing venture nothing win," it proceeded to qualify itself to at least make a creditable effort to sustain the honor of America even if they lost the match—which they fully expected to do, as they had been much ridiculed for having accepted the challenge.

The E. Remington & Sons and the Sharps Rifle Company each agreed to contribute one half of the $500.00 which was required to be put up towards the prize, and each guaranteed to turn out an American breech-loading rifle, which in point of accuracy would be the equal, if not superior to, the muzzle-loading rifles used by the Irish Team. Few if any riflemen in this country believed the claims of these rifle manufacturers to turn out a breech-loading rifle that would prove accurate at such ranges. Up to this time it had been the general belief by riflemen and others that no breech-loader could be made that would be equal in accuracy to a correctly made muzzle-loading rifle. Therefore, this match was a contest not only of Americans agains Irishmen, but of the breech-loading rifle against the Rigby muzzle-loading, long range rifles.

Early in the spring of 1874, the promised breech-loading rifles were delivered to the competitors. All were 44 calibre using 90 to 100 grains of black powder with a 550 grain bullet slightly hardened (probably about 1 to 50) and proved to be marvelously accurate. It has never been fully settled which were the better, the Remington or the Sharps; but both were doubtless more accurate than the men could hold. The major part of the foregoing account is taken from "Recollections of the National Rifle Association," by General George W. Wingate, as published in the "Arms And The Man" in 1907.

Arrangements were completed for holding the match on the Creedmoor Range, on Long Island, during the latter part of September 1874, which range then was about like a cow-pasture compared with the fine range at Dollymount, Ireland, on which the Irish Team were accustomed to shoot. In 1871, the New York Legislature passed the bill authorizing the purchase of the land and the construction of the Creedmoor Range. General Wingate appears to have had charge of the laying out and the construction of this range, which was the first real rifle range in this country. The name of the range was suggested by Colonel Henry G. Shaw, of the New York *Sun,* then one of the directors of the National Rifle Association, and had its origin in the fact that the land had formerly been known as "Creed Farm," and was level and flat; hence the name "Creedmoor." The National Rifle Association furnished $5,000.00 for the construction of this range, and the City of New York and the City of Brooklyn each contributed equal sums, while the State of New York purchased the land.

Throughout the spring and summer of 1874, try-outs were held frequently at Creedmoor which resulted eventually in the selection of the American team comprising Lieutenant Henry Fulton, G. W. Yale, an employee of the Sharps Rifle Company, Colonel John Bodine, later nicknamed "Old Reliable," Colonel H. A. Gildersleeve, L. L. Hepburn, an employee of E. Remington & Sons, and General T. S. Dakin.

The story of this First International Rifle Match as published in the New York *Herald,* Monday, September 28, 1874, is quoted as follows: "THE GREAT RIFLE MATCH. Ireland and America Struggle for the Championship. AMERICA'S VICTORY. Magnificent Scores at Half-Mile Ranges. Honour Reaped, even in Defeat. The Battle of the Rifles—Muzzle-Loaders v. Breech-Loaders. Diagrams showing the Position of every Shot that Struck the Target." That was the display heading. "Those who stood on the Creedmoor rifle range on Saturday, to witness the great trial of skill between the famed Irish marksmen who had carried off the Elcho Shield from the best shots of England and Scotland, and the comparatively unknown representatives of American marksmanship, are not likely to soon forget a contest that is destined to remain a landmark in the history of rifle shooting. When the challenge to a trial of skill was accepted it was not thought possible that America could furnish a team of long range marksmen capable of competing successfully with the victors of Wimbledon. And it must be confessed that to good luck as much as superior skill do we owe our success in the very close contest. The error of making a bull's-eye on the wrong target made by one of the Irish team gave the victory to America. Had it not been for this mischance, our plucky vistors would have carried back their fame—scotched, indeed, but still secure. As it is they have the consolation of knowing that the points actually scored by their team exceed by one that made by their opponents. But the ruling out of Mr. Milner's mis-directed shot deprived them of four points, and so decided the contest in favor of America by three points. With such a record, defeat loses all its sting, and the unsuccessful marksmen may console themselves with having merited victory, if they did not achieve it."

"The score made on Saturday has never been equalled in any long range competition, and even the Irish riflemen surpassed all their former efforts. This renders the victory of the Americans the more honourable, while it is an achievement of which the defeated team may be proud."

"There were to riflemen and military men questions of great importance underlying the struggle between the twelve men who were doing battle for the fame of Ireland and America, and to the men who watched closely the progress of the contest the value of the so-called improvements effected of late years in small arms for military purposes must have appeared extremely doubtful. In England for many years there has been in progress a battle between muzzle-loaders and breech-loaders, and each has found its strong supporters. It was at first thought impossible to construct a breech-loading gun that would fire as accurately as the muzzle-loader, but the experiments yesterday showed clearly that this was not quite correct. The trial would, however, have been more satisfactory in its results had not Lieutenant Fulton, who made with the Remington breech-loader the highest score ever made, charged it as a muzzle-loader. In one point the muzzle-loader effectually established its superiority as a military service arm. After every shot the marksmen using the breech-loading rifle were obliged to wipe out their weapons with painful care, while the Irish, who used the Rigby muzzle-loader, fired their whole score without once cleaning out their rifles. Nor did the accuracy of their shooting seem to suffer in the least. On the contrary, their best scoring was made on the last range. It was noticeable that they were able to fire more rapidly than their adversaries. With the breech-loader the marksman is compelled to wipe out carefully his barrel after every shot, under pain of making inaccurate shooting. In target shooting this is not much disadvantage, but in the field it would be impossible for troops to stop and clean out their weapons after every shot. The results would inevitably be that after a few rounds all existing breech-loaders would become fouled and unreliable as the old musket, while troops armed with muzzleloaders would continue during action with the same accuracy as when they first opened fire."

"The outward conditions under which the contest took place were more favorable to the spectators than to the marksmen. From the point where the red flags marked the position to be taken up by the firing squads, spread out an immense rectangular lawn—terminated by a range of targets, behind which rose up the massive earth mounds which the unskillful marksman makes his billet for his lead—smooth, well night, as the face of a billiard board; not a wild flower or a blade of grass peeps up to intercept the vision. Everywhere along the greensward was visible the mark of the mowing machine, that made sad havoc among the humble field flowers. No one, however, seemed to regret the flowers, but every marksman's eye lighted up as he looked along that level track, with outspoken promise of a fair field and no favor. Like most pictures, it had its shady side. The hot sun poured down on the open space with more than September zeal, and the slight exhalation far down near the targets told the practiced eye that the mirage would be likely to bother the riflemen a good deal. What wind there was blew up the range in the direction of the targets, with a scarcely perceptible drift to the right. So far everything was as the American team could have wished it—a total absence of wind and a mirage doubly deceptive to the strangers."

"Under this aspect of affairs the competing teams took their places at the firing-points; the American party having been assigned to 19 and 20, the latter being looked upon as the most favorable to good shooting. On practice-days these targets had been occupied by the Irish, but having won the toss for choice of places they voluntarily chose 16 and 17, the intervening target (18) being thrown down so as to prevent mistakes in firing at wrong targets. The object of the change was made visible during the progress of the match, as by it the Irish team obtained the shelter of a large tree that stands at the 1000 yards range. It was evident from the moment the Irish marksmen appeared on the ground that they suffered considerable inconvenience from the unusual heat. By the aid of friendly umbrellas they endeavored as much as possible to shield themselves from the sun."

"Considerable delay occurred in beginning the firing, both teams being apparently desirous to wait for the other to open fire. Every one busied himself cleaning or discharging his rifle, so as not to have too much the air of waiting for the other. At this time the large crowd of people gathered on the grounds had swelled to at least 8,000. They now gathered closely around the semi-circle of rope which had been placed as a barrier to preserve the firing-parties from interruption. As the preparations to begin proceeded the boisterous conversation gradually ceased, and the immense assemblage waited with bated breath for the shot that should announce that the match was entered upon. Impatient of waiting for the Americans, the Irish, with characteristic pluck, began the contest. The distribution of the marksmen was as follows: Captain Walker, J. Rigby, and J. B. Hamilton occupied 16; J. Wilson, J. K. Milner, and E. Johnson, 17; H.

Fulton, J. Bodine, and L. L. Hepburn, 19; Colonel Gildersleeve, G. W. Yale, and T. S. Dakin, 20."

"The First Shot. Captain Walker of the Irish, was the first to move out and take up position. The captain is a fine looking man, over six feet in height, and heavily built. He fires lying face downwards, his rifle held firmly in the left hand, both elbows resting on the ground. This position in active service would have the advantage of allowing the rifleman to fire with the least exposure of his body. It also enables him to sweep the ground in front, and could be used by huntsmen or soldiers with advantage. For mere target shooting it may be questioned whether it affords the steadiest support for the rifle. It is a favourite position with riflemen of all classes. When Captain Walker moved out and took up his position all eyes were centered on target 16. There was a cessation of conversation, as the result was looked forward to anxiously. But no flag responded to the shot, and a mingled murmur of regret and satisfaction ran through the assembled throng. It was evident that two parties, having diverse interest in the result, were present, and as the day advanced they gradually drifted in the direction of their respective friends. The murmur of satisfaction that ran towards the American targets when no response was made to the first Irish shot burst into applause, which was speedily suppressed by the efforts of Colonel Wingate, captain of the American team, aided by the good taste of the people themselves."

"While this was occurring on the right, Dr. Hamilton had taken up position and fired. Immediately the white disc hid the bull's eye from view, and the friends of the Irish team immediately gave vent to their feelings in loud applause. Major Leach, of the Irish team, was obliged to follow Colonel Wingate's example, and appeal to those present not to disturb the marksmen by any mark of applause or of displeasure. This appeal was good humouredly received, and very generally acceeded to; but as the firing now became general along the line partial manifestations of satisfaction were continued from time to time by the irrepressible spirits on both sides. But after a while the frequency with which the white disc was called up became somewhat monotonous, and the crowd settled down to watch the progress of the match, which from the opening shot seemed to pronounce in favour of the Americans."

"When Captain Walker rose from his first unlucky shot he quietly proceeded to load, simply stopping to exchange a word with Mr. Rigby. It was evident from the gravity of the Irish team, that they were exceedingly annoyed at the inauspicious beginning; but the captain on his second shot scored a centre, and a bull's-eye with his third. It was hoped that all danger of misses was now at an end, as he had secured the elevation, but the sixth shot also passed over the target without eliciting any reply. The shot was watched with close interest, and a murmured "He's missed again" ran through the crowd, but with tones of voice that conveyed different meanings. This second lesson admonished the captain to greater care, and he closed his score with four centres and five bull's-eyes, making a total of forty-six. As the 800 yards range was the favourite American range, the low average made by the captain damaged seriously the chances of an Irish victory. But it is worthy of note that the misses made by the captain were probably caused by the mirage on which the Americans counted with such well-founded hope. Mistake in his elevation was evidently the cause of the misses as his shooting shows very slight deviation. The shots in the centre and bull's-eye are well put on, and goes to show splendid line shooting. By reference to the diagram it will be seen that the mean deviation of the shots which struck the target is very slight, all the shots being centrally grouped."

"It devolved on Dr. Hamilton to arrest the demoralisation which the first shot had evidently caused among his colleagues. Had not Dr. Hamilton stepped into the breech and made good the mistakes of his friends by scoring five successive bull's-eyes, the Irish would have been hopelessly distanced at this range, for the Americans seemed to draw increased nerve and vigour from the mistakes of their opponents. Nothing, however, could have been more in contrast with the characteristics popularly ascribed to Irishmen than that exhibited by the gentlemen of the team. They evidently felt that the battle was going against them, but there was a quiet, unostentatious resolution in their bearing as they stepped out, silently and almost grimly, to take the place of the comrade who had fired. Whatever fortune sent was received with quiet impassiveness. Whatever points were to be communicated were whispered in a few words, and the marksmen lay down, fired, rose, loaded, and prepared to fire, as though they were unconscious of the presence of the thousands who watched these cool, resolute figures as they did their work with a quick intelligence and quiet pluck that eventually lifted them out of the rut into which they had fallen, and brought them to the very threshold of victory. Prominent among this distinguished group Dr. Hamilton attracted general attention. A decidedly handsome man, standing six feet in his stockings, and strongly-built, bold and soldier-like in carriage, he was well calculated to command attention. Looked to as the most skillful shot of the team, he showed how well he merited the confidence of his friends by doing good work just when it was most needed. Thirteen bull's-eyes out of a possible fifteen was his magnificent contribution made to the Irish total at this range."

"It is probable that better shooting has never been made than that shown on the accompanying diagram. Dr. Hamilton adopts the same position in firing as Captain Walker, and the magnificent scoring he makes proves that it is by no means essential to good shootting for the rifleman to twist himself after the manner of one of Michael Angelo's torsi."

"The third figure of the remarkable group forming the left of the line of fire was Mr. John Rigby, of the famous firm of Irish gunmakers whose saw-handled pistols were in pretty frequent requisition in the good old "pistols and coffee time." But though circumstances of the times have changed, the position of the gunmaking firm of the Irish metropolis in reference to the sporting gentry of Ireland has not changed a whit. The sons go to the house for their twist-barreled fowling-pieces and long range rifles, which have superceded the 'saw-handles,' but that is about all. Mr. Rigby must be close on to six feet in height, and is strongly built. He is one of the steadiest and most reliable, though not the most brilliant, shots of the team. Opening with three centres, he at last found the bull's-eye and he succeeded in getting seven shots on the bull's-eye, closing with a score of fifty-two. The shots were well grouped, showing slight deviations. His method of shooting is lying face downward, in the position already described."

"While the gentlemen on target 16 were struggling to make good the points lost in the opening of the match, their comrades on 17 were shooting with splendid precision. J. K. Milner, opening with a centre, followed with a bull's-eye and two centres. Having got his elevation correctly, he then began to score bull's-eyes, and succeeded in closing his score with eleven consecutive bull's-eyes. This was the most brilliant feat of the day, for although both Lieutenant Fulton and Dr. Hamilton made one more point than Mr. Milner at this range, neither of them made so well-sustained an effort. The way, too, in which the shots are grouped on the bull's-eye shows the truest shooting of the day. The eleven shots are grouped closely around the centre of the bull's-eye, showing a marvelous correctness of aim. Mr. Milner's manner of shooting is peculiar. He lies on his back, with the butt of his rifle resting on the hollow of his shoulder, while the barrel rests on his toes. In order to enable him to take aim the back sight of the rifle is placed near the heel plate. The position is neither very graceful nor does it appear very solid. It possesses the disadvantage that the rifleman can only see one object, and in target shooting it exposes him to the danger of shooting at the wrong target. This peculiarity of the posture was illustrated only too forcibly for the comfort of the Irish team by Mr. Milner in the present contest, as it caused him to throw away a shot that would have secured the victory for his comrades."

"One of the men of the Irish team who strove hardest for victory was Mr. James Wilson, one of the younger men grouped at target 17. He had the good luck to open the score with a splendid bull's-eye, and did not make a single outer or miss at any of the ranges. He adopts the mode of lying on his face to shoot, and grasps his rifle with great firmness. He fires slowly and with great deliberation. He proved himself one of the most reliable men of the Irish party. He is of medium stature, strongly built."

"Mr. E. Johnson whose state of health interfered very much with the reliability of his shooting, completed the Irish team. He shoots in a similar position to Mr. Milner. His shooting at this range was very good. He made no misses, and only one outer, making a fair score."

"*The American Team.* During the memorable contest of Saturday the success of the American team depended chiefly on one man, and had he failed to fulfill the expectations formed of him, nothing could have saved the Americans from defeat. Lieutenant Fulton, by profession a civil engineer, had steadily advanced to the front place in the American team, and the wonderful score made by him on the Thursday preceding the match placed him in the front rank of the world's marksmen. But would he be able to sustain the position? Would he repeat that wonderful score? These were the questions which the friends of the competing teams asked each other anxiously when the first shot was fired, and a tall, spare man, clad in blue flannel, rose from his seat and moved to his position at the firing point, looking as cool and collected as if nothing depended on what he was about to do. Lying down on his back and crossing his legs, Mr. Fulton turns slightly to the right, placing the butt of his rifle over his right shoulder, resting against his cheek. The barrel rests in the V formed by his crossed legs, finding a remarkably solid support. The left hand is passed behind the neck, grasping the heel of the butt, holding it firmly against the cheek. In this way the rifle is held as in a vice, and the marksman proceeds to take aim coolly and with the greatest deliberation. When the aim is completed the trigger is pulled by the right hand, kept free for this purpose, and five times out of six the white disc came up in response. Mr. Fulton has shown himself among the most reliable shots that we have any knowledge of. The accuracy of the shooting in the annexed diagram is almost as great as could be obtained by firing the rifle from a vice. The rifle he used is a Remington. He loads it, however, at the muzzle."

"Colonel John Bodine, who was destined by fate to fire the winning shot in the famous International contest, is an old man who must be closing rapidly towards the sixties. He wears blue spectacles while firing, and when cleaning and examining his gun is obliged to use additional glasses, owing to his near-sightedness. He is over six feet in height, and stands as erect as a poplar tree. While firing he adopts the same position as Dr. Hamilton and Mr. Rigby. Like Fulton he shoots with the Remington breech-loader."

"The group firing with the Remington rifle is completed by L. L. Hepburn, foreman of the Remington mechanical department. He shot well, with one outer, making a total of 53. He is well advanced in life, but not old, cool and imperturbable in temperament. On target No. 20 were grouped the three men who preferred to use the Sharp's sporting rifle. At their head was G. W. Yale, an employee of Sharp's factory, a dark, robust-looking man, with plenty of grit in his composition. He made remarkably good shooting, and contributed largely to the victory gained by making the second highest score. The accompanying diagram shows the excellent quality of his shooting. He lies down, slightly turned to the right, and supports his rifle over the left knee. The position looks uncomfortable."

"Colonel Gildersleeve is a young man, in the prime of life. He is of medium height, but powerful frame. He prefers to fire lying on his face. His shooting made a very good average, but showed a tendency to scatter. General Dakin, the sixth member of the American team, is a hearty, well-preserved man of some fifty summers. He shoots lying on his stomach, his rifle grasped firmly in the left hand. He is a steady but not brilliant shot. He made the lowest score in the match."

"The Irish team had finished their score at this range many minutes before the Americans, and notwithstanding the splendid efforts made by some of the Irish team, when the official score was announced they found that they were still some nine points behind. The official score stood as follows:

Eight Hundred Yards.	
Americans	326
Irish	317
	9

"The announcement of this result caused much enthusiasm among the friends of the American team, and a corresponding depression among the friends of the Irish. The members of the team, however, appeared quite unconcerned, and while the spectators thronged about the bulletin-board and read off eagerly the official account, the competing teams retired to a large tent, where a splendid luncheon was prepared for them. Captain Leach took occasion to make a handsome presentation of a silver tankard to the Amateur Rifle Club, and a number of pleasant speeches having been made, the riflemen repaired to their posts to renew the struggle for supremacy. The Americans began to look forward to an easy victory, but in this they were destined to disappointment."

"*At Nine Hundred Yards.* At the 900 yards range the Irish opened with better success, Captain Walker making a bull's-eye. He was followed by Lieutenant Fulton with a centre. The two shots were looked on as fore-shadowing a better score on the part of the Irish, and events justified this feeling. A very serious piece of ill luck befell Mr. J. K. Milner, one of the most reliable marksmen of the Irish team. His method of firing consists of lying on his back with the butt of his gun resting on his armpit, with the muzzle held between the toes, exposes him to the danger of mistaking his target."

"*A Bull's-Eye That Did Not Count.* His opening shot at the 900 yards range was delivered on the wrong target, and the bull's-eye which he made went for nothing. This misfortune occurred once before to Mr. Milner, at Wimbledon. Had it been delivered on the right target the victory would have been on the Irish side, with one point deciding. Lieutenant Fulton made at this range the highest score twelve bull's-eyes and three centres. But notwithstanding this splendid shooting the Irish drew ahead two points, and at the close of the contest at this range the official bulletin announced the Irish team as having scored 312, while the Americans had reached 310."

"The announcement of this result created a profound impression. The shooting on the American side had been magnificent, and at one time the American team stood fourteen ahead of their competitors. The steady, resolute firing of the Irish was, however, telling, and not only did they regain the ground lost at this range, but swept away two of the majority from the first range. They began to have hopes of recovering their lost ground at 1,000 yards, and the magnificent scores by them at this range attested their great skill. The shadows were creeping gradually over the sky, and for a short time the bright hue of the American sky gave way to the cold grey skies resembling those with which the Irish riflemen were familiar. Taking advantage of this familiar light, the Irish fired rapidly, and scored a bull's-eye almost every shot. When they ceased they had drawn ahead of the American team, but several of the latter had not yet completed their score. Word was sent out to the American targets not to lose a point—that the issue was remarkably doubtful. Lieutenant Fulton had three shots to fire, as had Colonel Bodine. The unexpected news so threw the lieutenant off his balance that he finished up with three centres. The fate of the contest hung on the result of Colonel Bodine's last shot. If he should miss, the victory remained with the Irish.

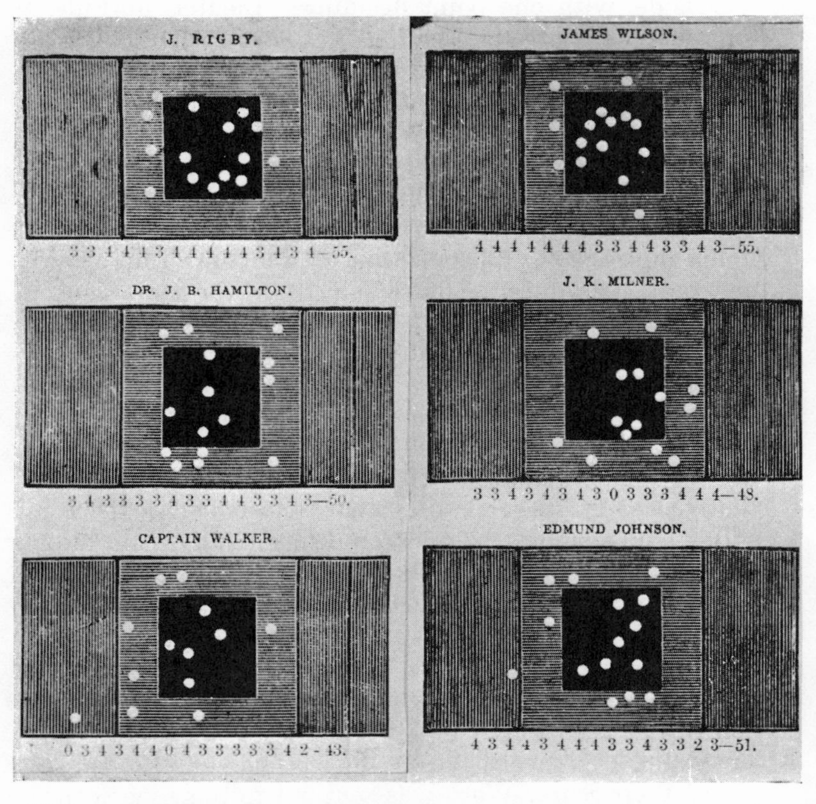

1000 yards Targets shot by the Irish Rifle Team in the International Rifle Match of 1874.

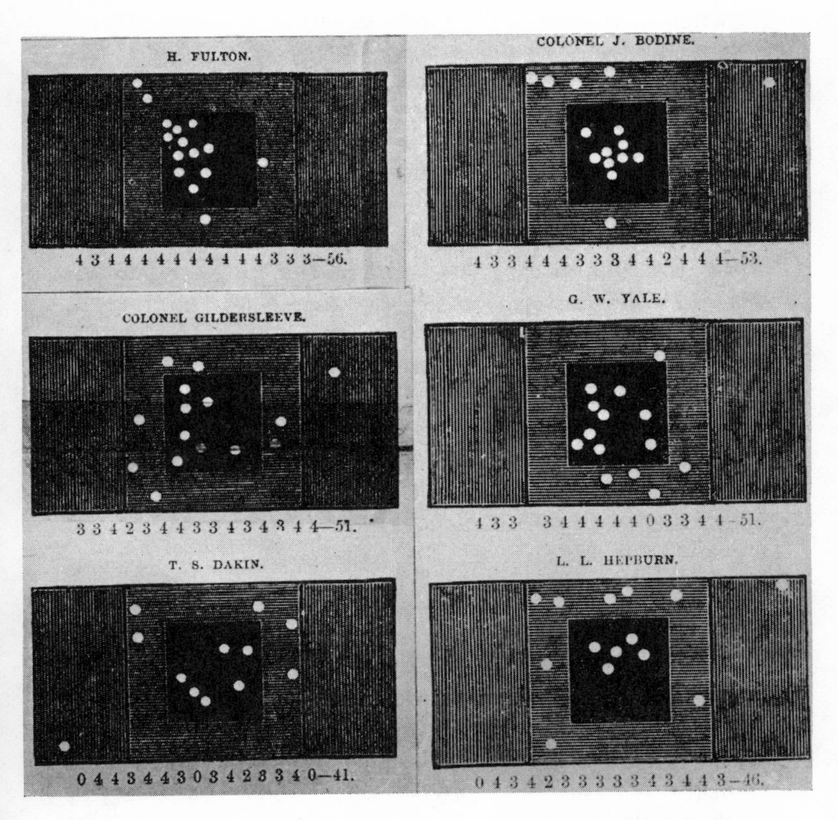

1000 yards Targets shot by the American Rifle Team in the International Rifle Match of 1874.

A moment before this the old marksman had cut his hand with a broken bottle. Having stanched the blood he lay down to take the decisive shot. The state of the case had already been whispered about, and the people crowded in to watch the effect of the last shot. There was an ominous silence among the crowd gazing at the old marksman lying motionless on the ground. At length a white puff of smoke, followed by the sharp ring of the explosion, told that the leaden messenger had sped on its way. Had he missed? "It is on!" broke from a hundred throats, and as the white disc came up telling it was a bull's-eye, the people set up a hearty cheer for the victor, and seizing the lucky rifleman, chaired him as some acknowledgment of the service he had rendered. The enthusiasm among the crowd burst forth in cheers again and again renewed, as if to compensate themselves for the hours of enforced silence they had passed watching the progress of the match. The scores of the final stage were remarkably good, the Irish again beating the Americans, but not making enough points to cover the misses made at the 800 yards range."

"RESUME OF THE SCORES"

Scores of the Irish Team

Name	Target No.	800	900	1000	Total
John Rigby	16	52	56	55	163
Dr. J. B. Hamilton	16	58	52	50	160
Captain Walker	16	46	55	43	144
James Wilson	17	54	51	55	160
J. K. Milner	17	57	49	48	154
Edmund Johnson	17	50	49	51	150
		317	312	302	931
Grand Total of Irish Team					931

Scores of the American Team

Name	Target No.	800	900	1000	Total
Lieut. Henry Fulton	19	58	57	56	171
G. W. Yale	20	55	56	51	162
Col. John Bodine	19	54	51	53	158
Col. Gildersleeve	20	53	51	51	155
L. L. Hepburn	19	53	50	46	149
Gen. T. S. Dakin	20	53	45	41	139
		326	310	298	934

Grand Total of the American Team 934

RECAPITULATION

American Team score in all	934
Irish Team score in all	931
American Team Victorious by......	3

On the day following this match, the American team accepted a challenge by Mr. John Rigby for a match between muzzle-loading rifles of his own make and American breech-loading rifles, for competitors firing twenty-five shots each at 1000 yards without cleaning the rifles. This was a very easy win for the muzzle-loaders, for great as was the reputation which the Sharps breech-loader obtained for itself a few years later, it was at that time wholly unfitted to make fine scoring when not cleaned after each shot. In this match the lowest score made by the Rigby rifle was higher than the highest made by the Sharps rifle. The scores in this match were, according to *The Book of the Rifle*, by Major T. F. Fremantle, as follows:

RIGBY MUZZLE-LOADING RIFLES

Irish Team

Edmund Johnson	84
John Rigby	84
Dr. J. B. Hamilton	77
James Wilson	76
Total	321

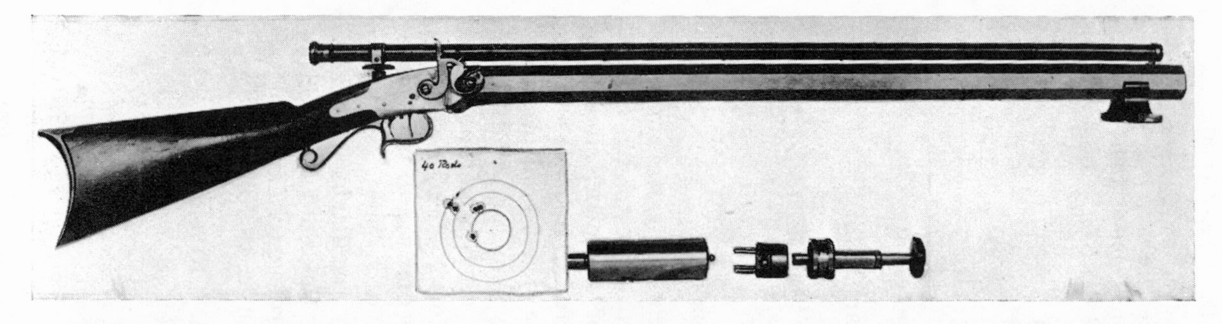

Seth Millard, 45 calibre Match Rifle, Cylindrical Bullet, Paper Patch, 30-inch barrel, weight 20 pounds. Millard Telescope. Group of 5 shots at 40 rods measures 1½ inches on centers. Super-Fine Workmanship on this Rifle and all Accessories. From W. A. Luce Collection.

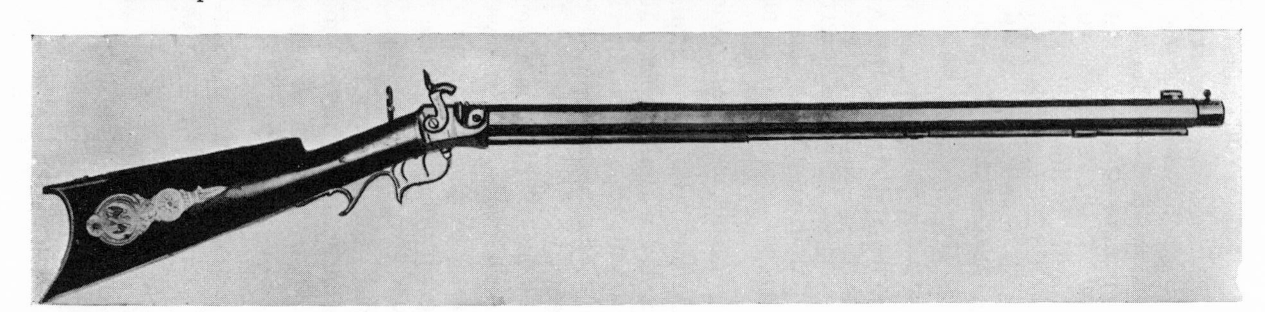

Edwin Wesson 38 calibre Target Rifle, 30-inch barrel, weight 11 pounds. From Shiff the Gunman's collection. man's Collection.

SHARPS BREECH-LOADING RIFLES

American Team

J. Collins	75
Gen. T. S. Dakin	64
Col. H. A. Gildersleeve	49
G. W. Yale	13
Total	201

This shows very conclusively that the Rigby muzzle-loading long range rifles were then much superior in accuracy to the famous Sharps Model 1874 breech-loading long range rifles. The possible score in the above match was 100 as the shooting was on the old Creedmoor target with square bull's-eye counting but 4 points.

It will be noted that the target used in this First International Rifle Match was quite different from those that the great majority of our riflemen today are familiar with as the bull's-eye was square instead of round. The National Rifle Association of America was incorporated on November 24th, 1871, and among the first actions it took was the adoption of a standard target for the different ranges. These were known as the "Creedmoor Target" and all had square bull's-eyes. The target used for 800, 900 and 1000 yards was the same over-all dimensions as the present one for these ranges, being 12 feet long by 6 feet high. The centre portion, 6 feet square, is called a "centre" and counts 3, while inside this "centre" is a black bull's-eye 3 feet square counting 4 instead of 5 as our present bull-eye counts. At each side of the "centre" is a space 2 feet wide by 6 feet high, called the "outer" and counts 2, the same as on our present target for this range. Thus it will be seen that the highest possible 10-shot score on the old Creedmoor Target would count but 40 instead of 50 as at present, while a perfect score of 15 shots, as fired by each man in this

First International Match, would count but 60 instead of 75 as in this match today.

The Creedmoor Targets with square bull's-eyes were used by practically all rifle clubs in this country until April 6th, 1875, on which date the National Rifle Association of America adopted targets having a circular bull's-eye counting 5, surrounded by a circular space counting 4 and called a "centre," while the remaining 6 foot square portion of the long range target was called an "inner" and counted 3. The remaining 2 by 6 foot space at each side of the "inner" remained unchanged and counts 2. Targets with square bull's-eyes were also used by the English, Irish and other foreign rifle clubs until 1875 when the National Rifle Association of Great Britain adopted targets having circular bull's-eyes similar to those adopted by our National Rifle Association, and the Second International Match, at Dollymount, Ireland, in June 1875, was shot on targets having circular bull's-eye counting 5. It will, therefore, be understood why the possible score in this Second International Match counted 75 for the 15 shots while the same number of shots in the 1874 match gave a possible of only 60.

As shown by the foregoing original report of this match, the Irish Rifle Team actually made a total of 935 points for the three ranges, while the total of the American team for these ranges was 934. Therefore, had the bull's-eye that Mr. J. K. Milner made on his first shot at 900 yards been on his own target, the Irish Rifle Team would have been the winners by ONE POINT. This in connection with the fact that the members of the American team cleaned their rifles after each shot while the members of the Irish team fired the entire forty-five shots without cleaning their Rigby rifles, fully convinced them that the muzzle-loading rifles were superior, both in accuracy and as practical rifles, to the breech-loading arms used by the Americans. Before the Irish Rifle Team embarked for their return voyage, arrangements had been agreed upon for the American Rifle Team to shoot a return match at Dollymount, Ireland, during the summer of 1875, and I am glad to be able to show herewith an illustration of the American team that took part in that contest, as copied from the old *Shooting and Fishing* magazine—the "grandfather" of *The American Rifleman*—issue of August 1904. That magazine copied this picture from the old *Harper's Weekly* issue of July 10, 1875.

"The First American Rifle Team to Win Honors Abroad."

This Second International Rifle Match between the Irish Rifle Team and the American was shot at Dollymount, Ireland, on June 29, 1875; the conditions called for 15 shots by each man at 800, 900 and 1000 yards. The target used appears to have been the same as our old Creedmoor with square bull's-eye, as the possible score was but 60 instead of 75, which would have been the possible had the circular bull's-eye target been used. The Irish team again used the Rigby muzzle-loading rifles, while the Americans used Sharps and Remington breech-loading rifles that had been made especially for the team.

The American team won this match with a total of 967 points out of a possible 1080, which was then considered a very remarkable score for those ranges. According to the report of this match in *The Book of the Rifle* by Major T. F. Fremantle, the scores were as follows:

Range.	800	900	1000	Total
American Team				
Col. H. A. Gildersleeve	56	56	52	164
G. W. Yale	57	52	51	160
Major Henry Fulton	58	57	46	161
R. C. Coleman	56	48	52	156

The First American Rifle Team to win honors abroad. On the Range at Dollymount, Ireland, June 29, 1875.

Back row: Capt. L. C. Bruce, Maj. Henry Fulton.
Middle row: Geo. W. Yale, Col. John Bodine, Gen. T. S. Dakin.
Front row: L. M. Ballard, A. V. Canfield, Jr., Col. H. A. Gildersleeve, R. C. Coleman. Bruce was Team Captain, Ballard and Canfield were alternates and did not shoot in the match.

Colonel John Bodine	52	59	51	162
General T. S. Dakin	58	55	51	164
Grand Total				967
Irish Team				
Edmund Johnson	58	54	51	163
James Wilson	58	50	55	163
Dr. J. B. Hamilton	56	54	50	160
Mr. McKenna	52	44	53	149
Major J. K. Milner	55	37	41	133
Mr. Pollock	59	53	49	161
Grand Total				929
American Team victorious by				38 points

Even after this second defeat the Irish riflemen were still firmly convinced that their Rigby muzzle-loading rifles were superior in accuracy and practicability to the American breech-loading rifles, and attributed their failure to win the Second International Rifle Match to the superior ability of the American team in judging the effects of the wind on the bullets at the different ranges. Arrangements were made for the Third International Rifle Match to be shot in the United States during the summer of 1876, the Centennial Year, on the Creedmoor Range. The conditions for this match were as follows: Each team to consist of eight men, each man to fire 15 consecutive shots at 800, 900 and 1000 yards each day for two consecutive days, using "long range rifles," either muzzle-loading or breech-loading, of any make and calibre preferred by the individual members, and using the Creedmoor Long Range Target with circular bull's-eye counting 5. Thus it will be seen that the possible score at each range was 75, which for the three ranges would give a total possible of 225 points for each man each day. The total possible for each man for the two days' shooting at the three ranges would thus be 450, which multiplied by eight (the number of men on each team) equals 3600 points as the possible team total for the two days' shooting.

From the *Harper's Weekly,* issue of September 30, 1876, I quote the report of that match.

"THE GREAT CENTENNIAL RIFLE MATCH"

"The great Centennial International Long Range Rifle Match for the Championship of the World took place at Creedmoor on the 13th and 14th instants and resulted in a grand victory for the American riflemen. Five teams were engaged in the contest, representing Scotland, Ireland, Australia, Canada, and America. The contest was won by 22 points, upon an aggregate score of 3126 out of a possible 3600 points. The Irish team was second, having scored 3104; the Scotch and Australian third, with a score of 3062 each; and the Canadians last, with the score of 2923. The weather, as a rule, was favorable on the first day. The sky was overcast, and there was very little breeze, the banners and flags hanging almost motionless on their staffs. The targets to be fired at were ten in number, two for each team. The Americans drew the windward or west side of the range, and had the Canadians for neighbors on the right. The Irish were next, the Australians fourth, and the Scotch team on the outside. General Joseph R. Hawley, president of the Centennial Commission, was chosen umpire, and General Alexander Shaler and Colonel Cornelius B. Mitchell were selected as referees."

"Soon after eleven o'clock in the morning firing at the 800 yards range was begun. The moment the signal was given, Cruit, of the Canadians, dropped prone on the ground, and, firing the first shot in the match, scored the first bull's-eye. Draper, of the Australian team, fired immediately afterwards, and made a bull's-eye, but unfortunately it was on a Scotch target, and counted for nothing. The Americans were slow in opening fire. They waited some time, and then Fulton lay down on his back, rested his gun-barrel between his crossed legs, grasped the stock with his left hand from behind his head, and his first shot whistled down to the target, but not the bull's-eye. He only got a centre. General Dakin followed with a bull's eye and the crowd cheered. Colonel Bodine followed him, with a centre; Ferwell was fourth, with a bull's-eye; Webber came next, with a bull's-eye; Colonel Gildersleeve followed, with an inner; Allen was next, with a bull, and Rathbone made a centre. The Irish shot well, Johnson making fifteen bull's-eyes in succession. The Australians and Canadians led the range for rapidity in shooting, the Irish kept well up with them, and the Scotch took all the time they wanted."

"In the afternoon the wind increased a little, and was puffy and baffling. At two o'clock the firing on the 900 yards was begun. Major Fulton made another miss on his ninth shot, and Mr. Allen followed his example. Colonel Bodine made a bull's-eye, but it was on the wrong target and went for nothing. Johnson did not do so well as on the previous range, but yet made the respectable score of 67. The highest of the Irish at this range was Rigby, who made 69, While M'Vittie, of the Scotch, made 71, and Thornburn 70."

"The 1000 yards' range firing followed immediately, at a little after four. The shooting opened brisker than ever, the Irish and the Australians leading off, and finishing their rounds within an hour and a quarter. The Canadians and Americans finished about together, but the Scots seemed to shoot lazily. "They're better hurry up," said a prominent rifleman; "the darkness coming on will kill them, sure." But the darker and damper it got, the better shot the Scots, and when at six o'clock they fired their last shot, they had made a total of 523 on the 1000 yards, which made their grand total 1586. The Irish stood next with a grand total of 1582, while the Americans stood third, at 1577. The Australian total was 1545, and the Canadians, 1490. This was the relative position of the contestants at the end of the first day."

"Thousands of spectators were in attendance on the second day, and the excitement was intense. The Canadians opened the ball, and fired several shots before the others pulled a trigger. At the close of the 800 yards' range the American and Scotch teams tied, upon the score of 525; the Australians followed, with 522, the Irish, with 502, and lastly the Canadians, with 492. The firing at 900 yards was begun at two in the afternoon. On this range the Americans dropped 10 points, the Irish 17, the Canadians 27, and the Australians 28, while the Scotch team fell off 63 points, the scores standing as follows: Americans, 515; Australians, 494; Irish, 485; Canadians, 465; and Scotch team, 462."

"The shooting at 1000 yards was opened by the Scotch at half past four o'clock, and was not concluded until nearly six. The Scotch shot badly, as if dispirited; the Canadians and Australians struggled, as if hopelessly; but the Irish and Americans went at the work as if they felt that the contest lay solely between themselves. The shooting was remarkable. Mr. Millner, of the Irish team, made the unparalleled run of fifteen bull's-eyes in succession. No one has ever before made a perfect score at 1000 yards. The firing over, the scores were quickly footed, when Colonel Wingate announced that the Americans had won the match and championship of the world by a score of 3126. At this point the crowd became uncontrollable, and breaking through the lines with cheers and shouts and shaking of hands, they congratulated the Americans on their hard-won fight."

"RESUME OF THE SCORES"

"RESUME OF THE SCORES"

Range	Sept. 13th 800	900	1000	Total	Sept. 14th 800	900	1000	Total	Aggre-gate
American Team									
General T. S. Dakin	69	65	69	203	66	68	54	188	391
L. Webber	68	69	65	202	67	61	65	193	395
Major H. Fulton	66	64	70	200	66	62	58	186	386
R. Rathbone	70	66	63	199	65	72	66	203	402
Isaac L. Allen	68	62	68	198	60	63	65	188	386
Col. H. A. Gildersleeve	70	69	55	194	68	61	71	200	394
Lt. Col. W. B. Farwell	70	66	56	192	68	59	68	195	387
Colonel John Bodine	69	57	63	189	65	69	62	196	385
Grand Total									3126
Irish Team									
V. Rigby	69	65	68	206	62	62	67	191	397
J. Johnson	75	67	64	206	61	62	67	190	396
. K. Milner	67	66	71	204	62	61	75	198	402
ieut. George Fenton	65	66	69	200	68	62	69	199	399
ieut. A. Ward	64	65	65	194	66	54	65	185	379
V. G. D. Goff	64	62	66	192	56	60	59	175	367
Henry Dyas	66	65	61	192	63	62	71	196	388
V. R. Joynt	65	64	59	188	64	62	62	188	376
Grand Total									3104
Scotch Team									
obert M'Vittie	71	71	67	209	60	61	62	183	392
aptain N. Thorburn	65	70	67	202	73	57	64	194	396
r. J. Mitchell	66	62	73	201	63	47	57	167	368
'illiam Clark	65	68	65	198	67	61	61	189	387
eter Rae	71	63	62	196	61	61	60	182	378
avid Fraser	67	67	62	196	70	59	54	183	379
homas Whitelaw	64	65	64	193	65	57	60	182	375
artin Boyd	66	62	63	191	66	59	71	196	387
Grand Total									3062
Canadian Team									
eut. James Adam	69	67	66	202	66	60	64	190	392
Bell	65	64	71	200	63	57	63	183	383
ptain J. J. Mason	63	64	64	191	60	59	61	180	371
ajor J. M. Gibson	64	59	61	184	69	54	60	183	367
orge Murison	64	57	59	180	58	65	59	182	362
orge Disher	62	57	61	180	55	53	55	163	343
eut. William Cruit	67	52	59	178	55	57	54	166	344
ajor W. H. Cotton	67	56	52	175	66	60	60	186	361
Grand Total									2923

U. S. Rifle Team of 1880. Competed in Wimbledon Match with Sir Henry Halford's Team, who won the match. U. S. Team then competed in Match at Dollymount, Ireland and won that match.

Back row: Fisher, Scott, Jackson, Rockwell.
Middle rod: Rathbone, Col. Bodine, Brown, W. Milton Farrow.
Front row: Laird, Clark. This was not an International Rifle Match.

Australian Team									
H. J. King	69	68	69	206	68	61	61	190	396
D. Gee	65	68	68	201	72	62	62	196	397
Major J. T. Sleep	69	69	61	199	64	60	61	185	384
J. S. Lynch	65	64	66	195	61	62	64	187	382
J. J. Slade	63	66	64	193	70	66	69	205	398
Captain B. J. Wardill	71	64	56	191	67	56	54	177	368
Captain J. M.'G. Smith	69	66	52	187	59	67	63	189	376
Lieut. T. T. Draper	60	59	54	173	61	60	67	188	361
Grand Total									3062

These scores in the Centennial International Long Range Rifle Match are quoted from the *Harper's Weekly,* issue of September 30, 1876, and show that this competition was principally between the Irish Rifle Team and the American. In this match the Irish, Scotch and Australian teams used muzzle-loading rifles; those used by the Irish team were made by John Rigby, the noted rifle-maker of Dublin, Ireland, and it will be noted by the scores that the aggregate for the two-days shooting of Mr. J. K. Milner, of the Irish Rifle Team and Mr. R. Rathbone, of the American Rifle Team are the same—402. This shows that the Rigby muzzle-loading rifle was equally as accurate at 800, 900 and 1000 yards as the very best, special Sharps, Sharps-Borchardt, Remington and Ballard long range rifles that it was possible to produce in this country, with which our team was supplied. If Johnson and Dyas of the Irish team had not each shot on the wrong target at 1000 yards during the first day's match, and if Ward and Goff had not made serious mistakes in judging the wind at the 1000 yards range on the second day thereby scoring several "outers"—2's—the Irish team might have won this match. Their Rigby muzzle-loading rifles were used *without cleaning* after each shot while the breech-loading rifles used by our team *were cleaned* after each shot. It is quite certain that had the rules prohibited cleaning the rifle after each shot, the Irish team would easily have won this match.

Riflemen at Vernon, Vt., September 2, 1896. Left to right: R. C. Cressy, Brattleboro, Vt.; M. H. Whitely, West Claremont, Vt.,; H. M. Pope, Hartford, Conn.; D. H. Cox, Neperan, N. Y.; L. Park, Greenfield, Mass.; C. F. Fletcher, Bellows Falls, Vt.; A. D. Spencer, Scranton, Pa. Reproduced from "The American Rifleman," by permission of the Editor.

This, at least, was the report of Sir Henry Halford, the captain of the Irish team, and while it is a fact that each member of the Irish Rifle Team purchased and took home with him, Sharps-Borchardt, Remington or Ballard long range rifles of the latest models, they were still of the opinion that these breech-loading arms were not as accurate at the long ranges as their Rigby rifles.

I can find no record that shows whether the Canadian Rifle Team used muzzle-loading or breech-loading rifles in this match, but it is generally believed that their rifles were muzzle-loaders; however, they may have used the old Snyder 577 calibre breech-loading rifle which was then the service rifle of Great Britain.

The Thirty-Second Annual Meeting of the National Rifle Club was held at Vernon, Vermont, September 3d and 4th, 1889, and from one of Mr. Wm. V. Lowe's note-books, I quote part of the report of that shoot, as follows: "Shooting done at 40 rods, from double rest. Twenty pound guns standard weight. Telescopic sights used, and all targets reckoned in string measure. Guns under 20 pounds in weight allowed 1/8 inch per pound on every string for each pound under weight. We derive certainly *as much* pleasure from the social features of these shoots as from the shooting itself. Who could be otherwise than in good spirits to listen to the buzz of talk in the shooting house? The Club numbers among its members several who are experts with the breech-loader in the style of shooting in vogue on most of the rifle ranges in this country, and the unanimous verdict is that this style of shooting "beats them all." Riflemen who are unacquainted with this style of shooting have missed some of the rarest fun of their lives. Let everyone bring this style of shooting to the notice of their friends, in order that we increase the popularity of this sport. Match to be 5 strings of 10 shots each."

Top: J. Kridder, Match Rifle, 50 calibre, 32½-inch barrel, weight 9¼ pounds. Center: Super-Fine Match Rifle, Unknown Maker, 42 calibre, 31½-inch barrel, weight 12 pounds. Bottom: John J. Wurfflein, Match Rifle, Birds-Eye Maple Stock, 38 calibre, 31½-inch barrel, weight 12¾ pounds. From R. R. Sherman's Collection.

"Shooters	Weight of Rifle	1	2	3	4	5	Total
R. C. Cressy,	19 lbs.	17	8, 3/4	14, 1/4	12, 11/16	18	70, 11/16
E. B. Stephenson,	19	17, 11/16	17, 7/8		15, 1/8	16, 9/16	
N. Washburn,	12	17, 1/16		19, 1/16	19, 7/8		
H. W. Smith,	15	11, 11/16	13, 9/16	22, 9/16	20, 7/16	18, 3/8	86, 5/8
N. S. Brockway,	19	11, 3/8	9, 1/2	9, 13/16	12, 5/16	12, 7/8	55, 7/8
Wm. V. Lowe,	20	10, 1/8	7, 1/4	10, 15/16	12, 13/16	15, 7/8	57
J. Robert Moore,	18	16, 5/16	13, 1/16	19	14, 9/16		
Frank I. Fenn,	18	16, 5/16	14, 1/2	11, 1/2	21, 3/8	24, 7/16	88, 1/8
David H. Cox,	17		22, 15/16				
D. A. Brown,	18	14, 3/16	9, 3/4	11, 7/16		15, 1/8	
L. Park,	20	21	21, 1/2	13, 7/16	18, 1/2	12, 7/16	86, 7/8

Prizes				
N. S. Brockway	won 2 First,	2 Second,	1 Third	There were five prizes in each class; 1st, 2d and 3d.
Wm. V. Lowe	2 "	1 "	1 "	
H. W. Smith			1 "	
R. C. Cressy		2 "		
D. A. Brown			2 "	
L. Park	1 "			
	5	5	5	

The Report was signed, Wm. V. Lowe,
Measurer of Targets."

The last match of this club of which there is any report in Mr. Lowe's note-book is as follows: "The Thirty-Ninth Annual Meeting of the National Rifle Club will be held at Vernon, Vermont, September 1 and 2, 1896. A general invitation is extended to all interested in rifle shooting. Anyone can become a member and is entitled to all the privileges of the Club by paying the $5.00 entrance fee to the match for Prizes and the Club Medal." "The conditions for the match were the same as previously and called for 5 strings of 10 shots each with an allowance of 1/8 inch per pound on each string for rifles under 20 pounds weight."

Shooters	Weight of Rifle	1	2	3	4	5	Total
C. Cressy,	19 lbs.	23, 3/4	21, 3/16	29, 3/4	23, 1/8	19, 15/16	117, 7/8
Park,	20	12, 1/2	13, 9/16	16, 7/8	20, 5/8	19, 1/2	83, 1/16
M. Pope,	15			16, 1/2	16, 9/16	20, 7/16	
H. Cox,	18	17, 3/16	18, 15/16	21, 1/8	19, 11/16	21, 11/16	98, 5/8
H. Whiteley,	16	15	19, 1/2	21, 1/4	9 shots	only	
F. Fletcher,	19	11, 1/2	6, 3/4	11, 3/16	10, 7/16	11, 11/16	51, 11/16
D. Spencer,	15	7, 3/4	8, 15/16	14, 1/4	13, 7/8	16, 7/16	61, 1/4

"Fletcher won the Club Medal for the shortest string."

"Brockway was sick with a fever and did not show up. I went up with camera, but no gun—got pictures of the shooters and these were all spoiled by halation. Whiteley put bullet down without powder and got left."

I believe that this was the last "meeting," or match, that the National Rifle Club held, and it will be noticed that Harry M. Pope shot in this match using one of his breech-muzzle-loading rifles, but fired only 30 shots instead of 50, and while his strings were shorter than those made by some of the other shooters using the cap lock muzzle-loaders they were not as short as Fletcher's and Spencer's. The rifle that Mr. Fletcher used was a Brockway, 38 calibre using the long cylindrical bullet with 2-strip paper patch, and is now owned by Mr. Walter Grote, of Canton, Ohio, or was when this book was written.

With this Brockway 38 calibre muzzle-loader, using a 16 power Sidel telescope, Mr. Grote won the first prize in the Brockway Memorial Match, at Dillsboro, Indiana, in 1937; 10 shots in the prone position with the string of 12 and 31/32 inches. With this same rifle, Mr. Grote won the first prize for the shortest string of 10 shots at 40 rods prone, in the Brockway Memorial Match at Dillsboro, Indiana, on October 9, 1938, with a string measure of 9, 15/16 inches, or a group of 2¾ inches on centers.

On May 26 and 27, 1886, the National Rifle Club, of Vernon, Vermont, held a match at 40 rods rest shooting in which the users of the breech-loading rifles were invited to take part and through the influence of Mr. A. C. Gould, who was then the editor of *The Rifle*, a representative group of riflemen from Boston and a group of muzzle-loader users competed. The muzzle-loaders used the machine rest and telescope sights, while the breech-loader users employed the usual aperture front and rear peep sights, and shot from muzzle rest with the butt of rifle held to the shoulder. In this match a good time was the chief object rather than money and fine-cut tests of the relative merits of the two systems.

N. S. Brockway was the secretary of the club at that time, and asked the breech-loader men to suggest a proper handicap for these rifles. It was proposed and agreed to by the others that the users of the breech-loaders should be allowed a handicap of 10 per cent for each string of 10 shots, to compensate for the difference in the rest, and another 10 per cent for telescopic sights; also an additional allowance of 3 inches for each string. In other words, a total allowance of 1/5 plus 3 inches was to be deducted from each 10-shot string of the users of the muzzle-loading rifles in order to compensate for the different kinds of rests and the lighter weight of the breech-loaders as well as the difference in the sights. One string of ten shots were fired the first day and two strings on the second, making a total of 30 record shots for the two days. The scoring was by the usual string method.

According to Mr. Lowe's report published in *The American Rifleman,* issue of March 1938, the winners for the 30-shots were as follows: D. A. Brown, 35-5/8 inches; C. F. Fletcher, 40-3/8 inches; J. F. Rabbeth, 40¼ inches. Rabbeth used a 38 calibre Remington rifle, Fletch a 38 calibre Brockway muzzle-loader, and Brown a 45 calibre Warner M. L. rifle. In this match there were six men who used breech-loading rifles, as follows: C. W. Hinman, 35 calibre Maynard; G. F. Ellsworth, 38 Ballard; J. F. Rabbeth, 38 Remington (probably a Remington-Hepburn); J. N. Frye, 38 Ballard; H. W. Smith, 45 Ballard; W. Milton Farrow, 32 Farrow. The users of the muzzle-loaders shot with three 38 calibre Brockway rifles, one 39 calibre Brockway, one 42 and one 45 Brockway rifles; one 45 Warner, one 45 Phillips and one 50 calibre Ferris rifles. Therefore, it will be seen that of the nine muzzle-loading rifles used in this match, six of them were made by N. S. Brockway and the shortest string was made with a 45 calibre Warner rifle. The second shortest string with a 38 calibre Brockway and the third best with a 38 calibre Remington breech-loader. The shortest 10-shot string was made by Fletcher with his 38 Brockway rifle, measuring 9-7/16 inches; Hinman's shortest 10-shot string was 10¼ inches; Rabbeth's was 11-5/16 inches.

They all had a good time, the users of the breech-loaders learned a lot about the accuracy of the muzzle-loaders while the muzzle loader men learned that the brech-loading rifles were more accurate than they thought them to be. Mr. Gould took a photograph of the shooters which is here illustrated. Another illustration shows another group of riflemen at that range, including H. M. Pope who appeared to be the only user of a breech-loading rifle attending that match. But, of course, Pope loaded his rifle from the muzzle instead of from the breech. In this match Pope used a rifle of his own make weighing 16 pounds, received an allowance of 5/8 inch on each 10-shot string and in his 30 shots his strings measured, 16½ inches, 16-9/16 and 20-7/16 respectively. The match was won by C. F. Fletcher with his 38 calibre Brockway with a total string of 51-11/16 inches for 50 shots, while his 30 shot scores were 11½, 6¾ and 11-3/16 inches respectively. Fletcher used a rifle weighing 19 pounds and received an allowance of ⅛ inch on each string of 10 shots. I believe this was the last match held by the National Rifle Club, as I can find no records of any later ones.

Some of the most accurate shooting muzzle-loading rifles for 40 rods rest shooting were made by Horace Warner, of Syracuse, New York, who at first preferred the under-hammer type of ignition. With this type of lock, the trigger guard serves as the main spring and, owing to a peculiar arrangement of the parts of the lock, the single trigger works almost as easily as the double set trigger, besides being quicker in action. Warner used the uniform twist of rifling for his barrels; at least I have never seen or heard of one of his rifles that was originally made with the gain twist. But as he was a great experimenter—always trying something new in rifles—it is possible that in his younger days he may have used the gain twist to some extent. Warner was a very skillful workman, very exact and careful in making every part of a rifle, and always seeking methods whereby the *accuracy* of the rifle could be improved. After he located in Syracuse, New York, he shot in a great many rifle matches, both off-hand and with a rest, at ranges from 25 to 40 rods using rifles of his own make of various calibres and weights. However, the greater number of these matches were at 40 rods rest using rifles weighing about 20 pounds, which were usually of 40 or 45 calibre in which the long, cylindrical, composite bullet with oiled paper patch of various types were used. Illustrations herewith show several groups that Mr. Warner shot with rifles of his make.

He was a member of the National Rifle Club, of Vernon, Vermont, for many years and the records of that club show that Warner was often among the prize winners in the matches held by this club, or rifles of his make in the hands of other riflemen sometimes made the smaller groups and won the prizes with their shorter strings. The rifle that Wm. V. Lowe shot in the National Rifle Club matches, and many others, was a Warner 38 calibre using the long cylindrical, composite bullet with oiled paper cross patch, and with it he won many prizes during the years that he devoted to rifle shooting. Illustrations of groups that Mr. Lowe shot with this rifle are shown on another page.

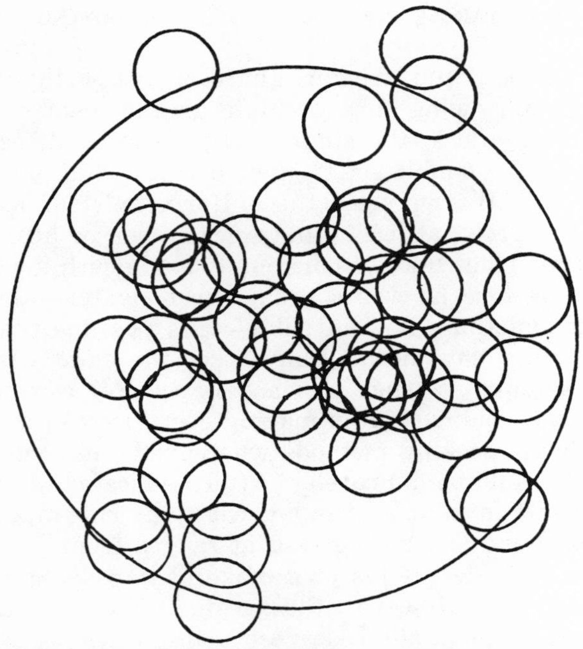

Showing 50 consecutive shots by H. V. Perry, at 220 yards rest, October 28, 1885. String 41, 13/16 inches.

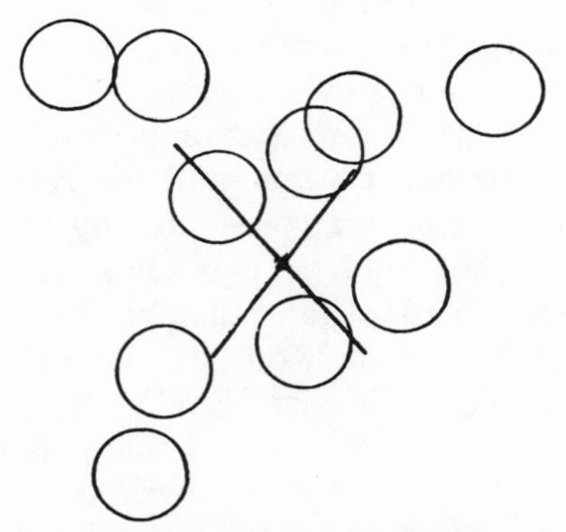

Showing 10 consecutive shots at 40 rods rest, by N. S. Brockway, with 38 calibre rifle using 3-strip Paper Patch, September 8, 1881. String measures 6, ⅝ inches.

In 1887, Mr. Warner abandoned the nipple and percussion cap as a means of ignition for his rifles and adopted instead a device for using the Berdan primer, or certain kinds of shotgun primers, with which hotter, better ignition was secured and thereby the accuracy was much improved. Under date of April 13, 1887, Warner wrote to Wm. V. Lowe as follows: "I have no use for caps or nipples on my guns and probably never will have any more."

Mr. Lowe's rifle was so made that he could use the regular nipple with percussion cap, or remove the nipple and screw into its place the device for using the Berdan primer. From my conversations with Mr. Lowe, I judge that he found the Berdan primer with this device much superior to the percussion cap and nipple in point of accuracy, and used that principally in his shooting with this rifle. Illustrations showing a rifle with this device for using the primer instead of the cap, and groups that were shot with rifles using this primer ignition, are shown on other pages.

Along in the 1880's, H. V. Perry, of Jamestown, N. Y., made many excellent target rifles that gave remarkably fine accuracy at 40 rods rest shooting, and as an illustration of the super-fine accuracy of these arms, I have reproduced from the December 1886 issue of *The Rifle, a* 50-shot group that Mr. Perry made at 40 rods muzzle rest with the butt of rifle held to his shoulder, in a public match at Rochester, N. Y., on October 28, 1885. The string measure of this group is but 41 and 13/16 inches and at that time it was believed to be the *shortest 50-shot string ever made in a public match.* The August 1, 1887, issue of *The Rifle,* reports another 50-shot group made by Perry with one of his rifles in a match at Falconer Crossing, N. Y., on May 19, 1887, that shows a string measure of 45 and 9/10 inches, or an average of .918 inch per shot. A later report stated that this group

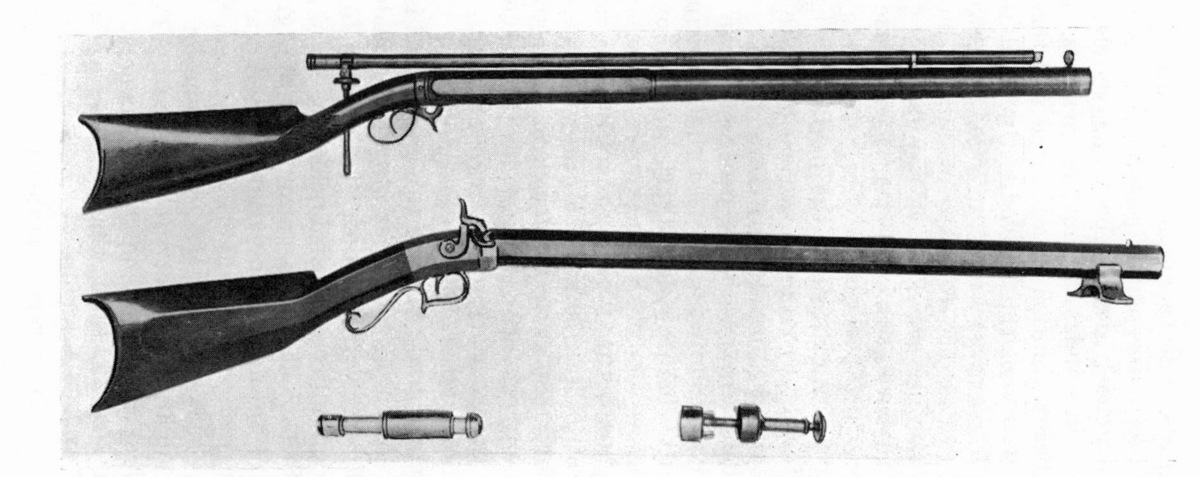

Top: Wm. Billinghurst, Under-hammer Match Rifle, 45 calibre, 30-inch barrel, weight 18 pounds. Billinghurst Telescope.
Bottom: N. Angel, 42 calibre match rifle, 30-inch barrel, weight 20 pounds. From W. A. Luce Collection.

was made with a rifle having a 12-groove barrel of 45 calibre and cut with a gain twist using a cylindrical bullet with a 2-strip oiled paper patch. I believe this is a mistake in stating that the rifle was made with a gain twist; but, of course, it may be possible that Perry was trying out the gain twist in his rifles at that time. Another report in this same magazine stated that in September 1885, Perry made a string of 110 shots at 40 rods with muzzle rest and butt of rifle held to his shoulder, that gave a string measure of exactly 99 inches, and was, doubtless, the *shortest string ever made with that number of shots,* up to that time at least—may even be the shortest on record up to the present date.

Back in 1883, according to reports in the old *Forest and Stream* magazine, Horace Warner and H. V. Perry shot a series of four matches at 40 rods rest, each using a rifle of his own make, for a stake of $100.00 a side in order to prove whether the Warner or Perry rifles were the superior in accuracy. Warner's rifle was cut with the uniform twist of rifling and six or eight lands and grooves, while Perry's had eight, twelve or sixteen grooves and lands with uniform twist. These matches were shot at Falconer Crossing, N. Y., where Warner won the first match by making the shorter string. A few weeks later in the second match, shot on the same range, Perry made the shorter string and won that match. Then the third match on the same range a few weeks later was won by Warner who made the shorter string that time. The fourth match of this series a few weeks after the third, shot on the same range, was won by Perry with the shorter string. Thus this series of matches which were intended to show which of these systems of rifling gave the superior accuracy at 40 rods, failed to prove anything as each man had won an equal number of these matches. Or in other words,

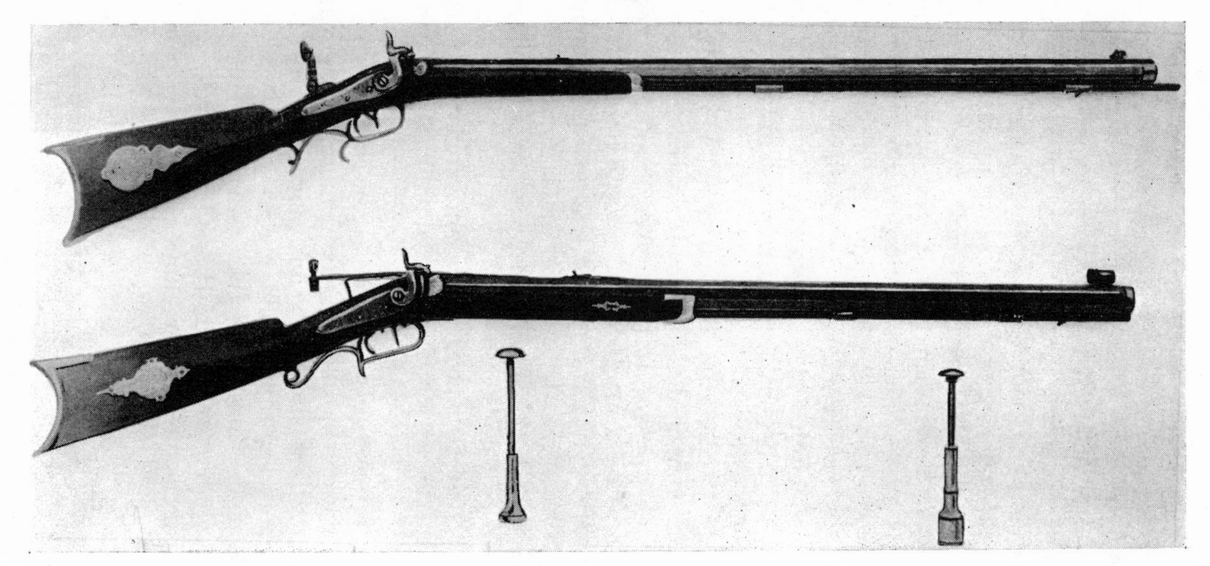

Top: C. Plath Match Rifle, 42 calibre, 31-inch barrel, weight 12 pounds.
Bottom: D. H. Hilliard Match Rifle, 28-inch barrel, 40 calibre, weight 10 pounds. From Dr. P. A. Matteson's Collection.

the Warner rifle had won two of the matches and the Perry rifle had also won the same number of times. From the financial point of view, each man had won and lost the same amount of cash in these matches, and riflemen in general knew no more about the relative accuracy of these two types of rifling than before the matches were shot.

The original report of these matches published at that time stated the stake was $1,000.00 a side, but it is believed that a typographical error was made by which an extra "0" was used in stating the amount, which actually was but $100.00 a side. Another report at the time stated that Perry used the gain twist in the rifle that he used in this match, or series of matches; but this is believed to be a mistake and that Perry's rifle was cut with the uniform twist of rifling. I have never seen a rifle of his make that was originally made with a gain twist, but have heard that he used that system of rifling at one time. Or in other words, I have been told by riflemen that they had owned Perry rifles which were cut with the gain twist. Mr. Walter Grote, of Canton, Ohio, writes me that he has owned nine Perry rifles all of which were cut with the uniform twist of rifling and all with 16 grooves and lands, except one which has eight lands and grooves. He states that he has never seen or heard of a Perry rifle that had a gain twist, but, of course, this would not positively prove that Perry never used the gain twist in any rifle that he made. All of the Perry rifles gave very fine accuracy, according to all reports, and are much prized by the devotees of the muzzle-loading rifle today.

There was great rivalry between Warner and Perry individually, as well as between a group of experts known as "The Warner Riflemen" and another group of experts in Jamestown, N. Y., who firmly believed the Perry rifles to be the more accurate—possibly the *most accurate* rifles made at that time. According to another report in the *Forest and Stream,* issue of December 29, 1887, H. V. Perry, J. Robert Moore and Benj. Garfield, of Jamestown, issued a challenge to Warner & Lowe, of Syracuse, to shoot a match with them at Falconer Crossing, N. Y., to defend the claims that were made in a circular which Warner & Lowe had been sending out which stated: "We claim to be able to make better shooting rifles than can be obtained elsewhere."

The Perry group of riflemen proposed that the match should consist of 3 strings of 10 shots each at 40 rods rest, butt of rifle held to the shoulder, by three men on each team, under the National Rifle Club rules in which 20-pound rifles were the "standard," with an allowance of 1/8 inch added to, or deducted from, each 10-shot string for each pound over or under the standard weight of rifles used by each contestant. The Perry team were to use muzzle-loading rifles made by H. V. Perry while the Warner & Lowe team should use rifles made by that firm. The members of each team were to put up $50.00 each which would constitute a purse of $300.00 that should go to the team that made the shortest aggregate string for the 30 shots. This challenge by the Perry riflemen was not accepted by Warner & Lowe, but instead they proposed that each team should consist of but two men instead of three and that the match should be shot on the Anderson Rifle Club's range near Syracuse. The Perry team declined to accept this change in the conditions of the match, and after some controversy through the columns of the *Forest and Stream* the matter was finally dropped without shooting the match.

Dr. P. A. Matteson, of Bennington, Vermont, owns one of the Warner heavy barrel, muzzle-loading machine rest rifles using the primer ignition, as shown by an illustration on another page, that gives very fine accuracy at 40 rods rest shooting. When he purchased this rifle there came with it in the wooden case, a dozen or more very fine groups that were shot at 40 rods rest with this rifle by Mr. Warner, or the customer for whom it was made. From these groups, I have selected the best, or smallest, 10-shot group and an *average group,* that are illustrated herewith. It will be seen that the smaller group measures but 1 and 6/10 inches on centers of the bullet holes farthest apart, while the other measures 1 and 13/16 inches on centers. There is no record on these groups to show what charge of powder was used or the weight and kind of bullet, but the larger group was dated "Sept. 1885." As before stated, we do not know whether Horace Warner shot these groups in testing this rifle, or if the customer for whom the rifle was made shot these in practice or matches. My, personal, opinion is that they were made by Warner in testing the rifle and were sent to the customer to show that it shot very accurately indeed. Many of the other groups that came with this rifle are as small as the larger one, or smaller, but this 1 and 13/16 inches group may be considered as a fair average of the entire dozen or more groups. There is no doubt that Horace Warner was one of the most noted rifle-makers of his time, and many riflemen in those days believed that his rifles were *the most accurate* ones made.

Another maker of very accurate shooting target and machine rest rifles was Wm. Billinghurst, of Rochester, N. Y., whose rifles were well known throughout this country and even in many foreign countries. One of the most highly prized rifles in the extensive collection owned by Mr. F. E. Dunn, of Glenns Falls, New York, is the heavy 50 calibre Billinghurst rifle illustrated herewith. This rifle was made for Alexander Greer, probably just after the Civil War, and uses a conical, or flat point picket, bullet having a very rounded base, measures .540 inch in diameter, weighs 500 grains, is used with an oiled linen patch and a charge of about 100 grains of powder. The rifle weighs about 35 pounds and gives very fine accuracy at 40 rods rest, as shown by the two groups illustrated, which were shot by John Greer—probably a brother of the owner of the rifle—in 1868. One of these targets bears the notation on the back: "Oriental powder F. g, 3 inches," which was, no doubt, the charge used in shooting all the groups that came with the rifle. There is also with this rifle a diagram of 20 shots at 40 rods rest that gives a string measure of 14 and 7/8 inches which was shot with it in the same year.

Billinghurst made many very accurate shooting target rifles weighing from about 12 to 16 pounds, and I remember that when I was a boy and attended rifle matches with Uncle Alvaro, the man who sometimes won the first prize, or made the shorter string in the matches, used a Billinghurst 38 calibre rifle weighing 16 pounds, according to records that I made at that time. There was much rivalry between this man who owned the Billinghurst rifle—George Peck—and uncle, and in a match where there was a good prize if uncle could make a shorter string than George Peck made, he was practically sure of winning first prize. Uncle's target rifle was made by a man in Ludlow, Vermont, whose name I failed to record, but I think it was made by H. J. Huntoon who made target rifles similar to those of N. S. Brockway. The only target rifles that uncle considered as accurate as his were those made by Wm. Billinghurst, the N. S. Brockway rifle with gain twist and those made by Edwin Wesson, of Hartford, Connecticut, which also were cut with the gain twist of rifling. Uncle was a firm believer in the gain twist and the Billinghurst systems of rifling, and his pet target rifle was made with the gain twist.

During the years that Brockway made rifles he tried out the gain twist, very thoroughly, as he, himself, told me; but it requires much more careful, skillful work to make a gain twist barrel than with the uniform twist of rifling. The gain twist barrel must be cut, or rifled, *very accurately and correctly* as it cannot be leaded, or "lapped," to correct the shape or diameter of the bore. The makers of rifles having the uniform twist of rifling always leaded their barrels after rifling, and they considered this a *very important part* of the work in making an accurate shooting rifle. One of the N. S. Brockway rifles owned by Dr. P. A. Matteson is cut with the gain twist and shows very fine accuracy at 100 yards and 40 rods. However, the majority of the Brockway rifles were made with the uniform twist of rifling as he finally decided that this was the more accurate and easier to make.

Billinghurst also made many light, short barreled rifles, commonly called "buggy rifles" in those days, which gave surprisingly nice accuracy at 20, 30 and even 40 rods when we consider their short barrel and light weight. These buggy rifles were quite popular in those days, especially for shooting squirrels and grouse, as they were so light and handy to carry. One of these by a first-class maker would make one inch 10-shot groups at 75 to 85 yards, about 2½ inch groups at 100, and 6 inch groups at 200 yards when shot from a rest by an expert marksman. Edwin Wesson, of Hartford, Conn., J. E. Gage, of Concord, N. H., and several other rifle-makers besides Billinghurst made a specialty of these buggy rifles during the late 1870's and early 1880's, but those in fine condition are getting very scarce in these days. On another page is an illustration of two fine little rifles that are owned by Mr. W. A. Luce, of Ithaca, N. Y.

Many years ago Mr. Edwin Fay, who sometime in

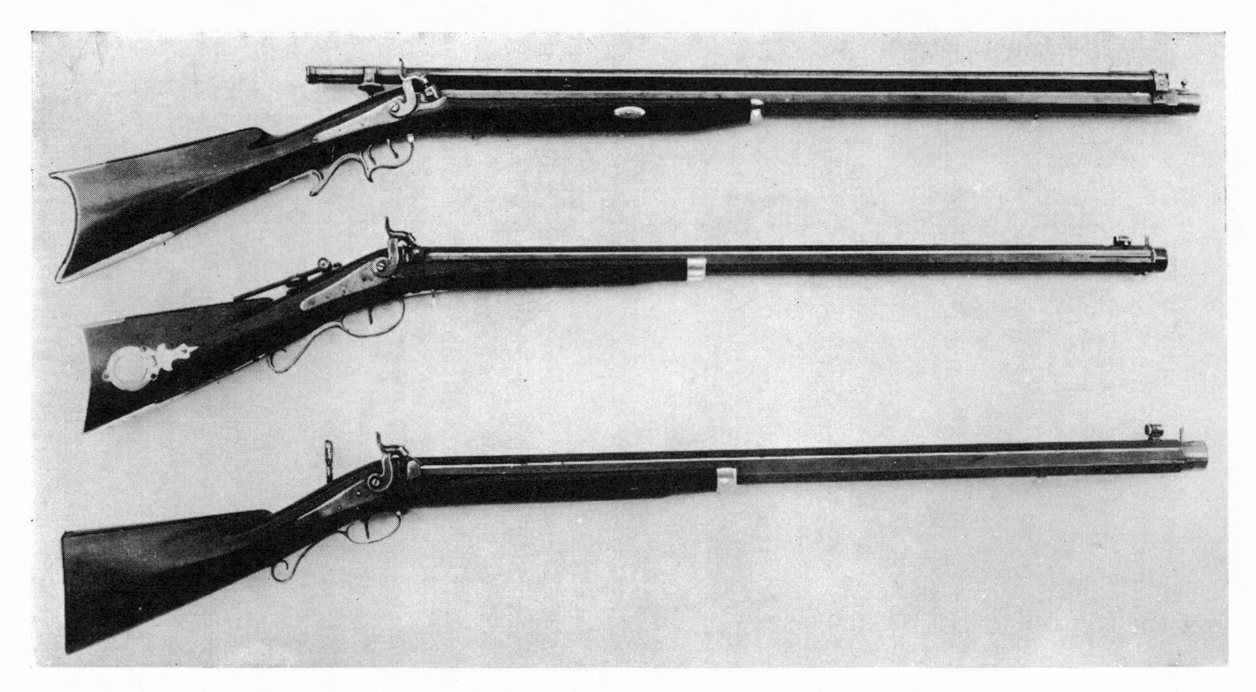

Top: James & Ferriss, 35 calibre Match Rifle, 34-inch barrel, weight 13 pounds, James & Ferriss Telescope. Center: T. Lamson, 42 calibre 33-inch barrel, weight 13½ pounds. Bottom: T. Lamson, 54 calibre Match Rifle, 34-inch barrel, weight 17½ pounds. From Floyd R. Butler's Collection.

the 1890's became president of the old J. Stevens Arms & Tool Company, of Chicopee Falls, Mass., learned rifle-making under Edwin Wesson, then of Hartford, Conn., and during that time he made for his own use, apparently, one of these little rifles having a 12-inch barrel of 31 calibre with false muzzle, which was owned by "Shiff the Gunman," of North Woodstock, New Hampshire, when this book was published. Shiff kindly loaned this rifle to me for test, and with it I made 10-shot groups averaging 3 inches at 100 yards and 7½ inches at 200 yards rest under good weather conditions: that is, when there was little or no wind.

This rifle of Shiff's is a deluxe arm; had a fine grained walnut, detachable stock, silver inlays and silver patch box, gold band inlay in front of the patent breech, a gold eagle inlaid in the barrel near the breech and "Edwin Fay, Hartford, Conn.," inlaid in gold with gold band border in the top octagon of the barrel. This is the only specimen of an Edwin Fay rifle that Shiff has ever seen—and he has handled many thousands of all kinds of arms during his experience as a dealer.

Edwin Wesson of Northboro, Mass., later of Hartford, Conn., was regarded by John R. Chapman, the author of *The Improved American Rifle,* and many other riflemen in the 1840's and 1850's, as making the most accurate target rifles obtainable. Wesson used the gain twist system of rifling, which many experts considered the very best for the finest accuracy in those days and even today, with the lead bullet rifles, is unsurpassed for the finest accuracy. He was a very skillful workman, his rifles were better finished than many of the other rifles of those days, and he made many hundreds of excellent target rifles, as well as hunting rifles, during the many years that he was in business. I have owned three Edwin Wesson rifles, have used several that were owned by friends, and all of these have given better accuracy than many other makes that I have used during the past sixty odd years.

Norman S. Brockway, of Bellows Falls, Vermont, was another noted rifle-maker of the old times, who made principally heavy target rifles and machine rest rifles from about 1867 until along in the late 1880's, when he fell off the roof of the house that he was building at Lake Sunapee, New Hampshire, and injured his spine so that thereafter he was unable to make rifles, himself. After that accident it appears that he formed a partnership with H. J. Huntoon, of Ludlow, Vermont, who continued making the Brockway rifles for about twenty years. This information was given to me by N. S. Brockway himself about a week before his death, and there can be no doubt that it is correct.

There is no doubt that the heavy target rifles that were made by Brockway himself, and those by Huntoon also, were among the *most accurate muzzle-loading rifles* that have ever been produced. The records of the National Rifle Club, of Vernon, Vermont, show that in the twenty matches that were held by this club from their "Spring Meeting of 1886" to and including their "Thirty-ninth Annual Meeting of 1896," rifles made by Horace Warner won the first place by making the shortest string for 50 shots at 40 rods rest in FIVE of these matches; Brockway rifles won ELEVEN of these with the shortest 50-shot strings and rifles of other makes won in FOUR of these with the shortest strings for the 50 shots. Please remember that there is no "hear-say," or "guess work," about this statement; but it is as I have tabulated it from the records of these matches that were kept by Wm. V. Lowe and from those in the Secretary's Book of that club. Therefore, from the above it will be admitted, I believe, that during those ten years the Brockway muzzle-loading target rifles were *the most accurate rifles* for 40 rods rest shooting that were then made, or among the different makes that were shot in those matches.

Among the "other rifles" which won four of these matches, we find a Perry rifle shot by J. Robert Moore, of Jamestown, New York, made the winning score in September 1887, with an actual string measure of 57 and 6/16 inches. Since he used a 19-pound rifle and was allowed ⅛ inch per pound on each string of 10 shots, adding the ⅝ inch to the above gives his "adjusted" string measure as 57, 11/16 inches. That is the only time a rifle by H. V. Perry won any of these matches, unless it was before the 1886 matches. I can find no record of the make of the rifle, or calibre, with which T. Spencer won their first match in September 1858, with the string measure of 54 inches for the 50 shots, but it could not have been a Brockway as he was not making rifles at that time, and I doubt if Warner was either.

Still another quite noted maker of target rifles, as well as other kinds, in those days was Nelson Lewis, of Troy, New York, who during the years he was in this business made a greater number of rifles that any of the other old makers, with the exception of Wm. Billinghurst. Lewis absolutely believed that the gain twist rifling was the *very best for the finest accuracy* and positively refused to make any rifle with the uniform twist. His best grade target rifles always gave very nice accuracy at all ranges including 100 and 200 rods. He was a member of the first rifle club in Troy—known as the "Troy Rifle Club," — which was organized before the Civil War, and was much interested in long range rifle shooting which in those days was usually at 100 to 150 rods—550 and 825 yards. Lewis was a very skillful work-

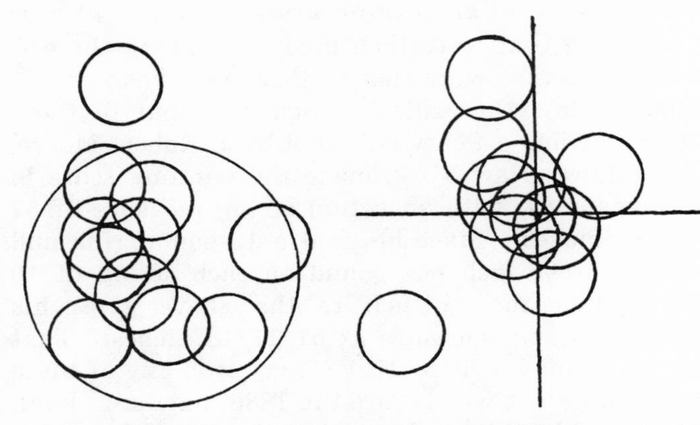

Ten shots at 40 rods, by Morgan James. Group shown full size.

Ten shots at 220 yards, by J. H. Gardner. Group shown full size.

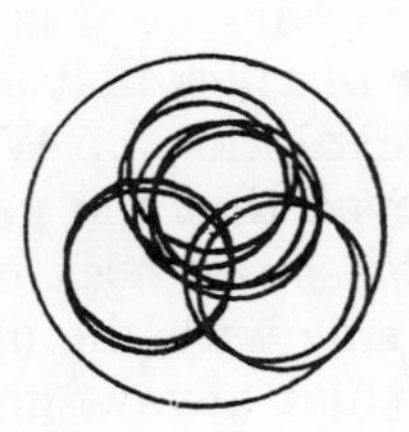

Nine shots at 110 yards by Morgan James. Group shown full size.

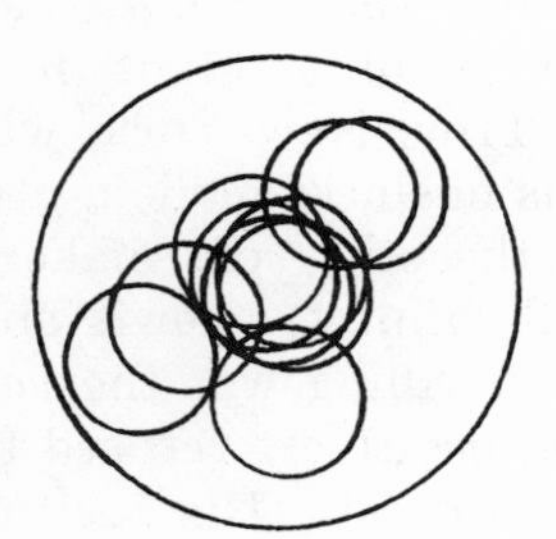

Ten shots at 110 yards by J. H. Gardner. Group shown full size.

man, was extremely particular in making the lock, trigger and in rifling the barrel of his rifles, but did not finish the outside as well as Billinghurst, Morgan James and some others at that time. My friend Floyd R. Butler, a gunsmith of Raceville, New York, has a larger number of N. Lewis rifles than any other person with whom I am acquainted. All of these are in perfect condition inside, nearly all in the same condition outside, and with which we have made many tests at 100 yards rest. Illustrations showing several of these rifles and groups made with them are shown herein.

Morgan James, of Utica, New York, was another of the most noted rifle-makers from about 1835 until after the Civil War, and many expert riflemen considered his rifles superior in accuracy to all other makes. I, myself, have never used a rifle of his make, have seen but very few of them, and when this book was written I was unable to find a Morgan James rifle in any of the extensive collections owned by the numerous riflemen with whom I am acquainted. The reports that I have received regarding this rifle are very conflicting; some riflemen state that all of James' rifles were cut with the gain twist rifling only, while others state that he used only the uniform twist; some state that his barrels were cut with 9 to 12 lands and grooves, while others insist that he used only 6 or 8 grooves and lands of equal widths. However, all these reports agree that he was a very skillful workman, that his rifles were nicely finished, had nice stocks, and gave the *very finest accuracy* at all ranges.

In the *Forest and Stream* issue of November 20, 1890, we find two groups which were shot in 1859, with a heavy Morgan James rifle having a gain twist ending in about 30 inches, using a 210 grain cylindrical bullet with oiled linen patch, and a charge of 90 grains of Hazzard F. g. powder. These groups are reproduced herein for your careful consideration. It will be noticed that the group shot at 20 rods—110 yards—has but nine bullet holes as the tenth shot was omitted for fear of spoiling this splendid group. A circle fully enclosing these nine shots measures but 25/32 inch diameter. The other group at 40 rods—220 yards—includes the "sighting shot," which is the only one outside of the 1 and 23/64 inch diameter circle, while the second circle is the exact size of a silver dollar—before President Roosevelt shrunk it or substituted his "rubber dollars."

Now, you gun bugs who believe that the modern, "latest craze," high velocity rifles are the most accurate arms ever made, just show us any group made at these ranges with your "220 Swift," "22 Varminter," "240 Super-Varminter," 30-06 Springfield, 300 Magnum, or any other pet rifle that has been brought out while this volume was being published, that is as small as these two. As the farmer said about the giraffe: "Hell, there aint no such animile"! Also from the *Shooting and Fishing* issue of May 11, 1893, I have reproduced two groups that were shot with a rifle made by J. H. Gardner, of Scranton, Pa., with a target rifle of his own make weighing 15 pounds, cut with a gain twist and shot from the shoulder with a muzzle rest and using telescope sight. It will be seen that the 10-shot group at 110 yards is slightly more than covered by a half dollar, or is just enclosed by a circle 1, 4/50 inches in diameter, while a circle 1, 27/50 inches in diameter fully encloses the 10-shot group made at 220 yards. Modern rifles, Attention!

George Schalk, of Pottsville, Pennsylvania, was also one of our noted makers of muzzle-loading rifles that were famous for their super-fine accuracy during the years from about 1875 until about 1890. He used the gain twist rifling having eight wide, flat grooves with narrow lands and sharp corners in the grooves. Schalk's earlier rifles were used either with the linen patch or the oiled paper cross patch as desired. The false muzzle of most of his rifles that I have seen have a shallow, circular recess the size of the linen patch, turned in the muzzle end and also have two quite wide, shallow grooves cut at right angles across the false muzzle to hold the paper cross patch when that is used. An illustration herewith shows the Schalk false muzzle for use with either kind of these patches mentioned, and he was the only rifle-maker that I know of, except W. W. Wetmore, whose rifles were so made that one could use both these two types of patches in the same rifle when desired without any change in it. The muzzle of the Wetmore rifle that I had years ago was made in the same way as the Schalk illustrated.

About 1884, following the suggestions of Wm. J. Hayes, of Newark, New Jersey, Schalk abandoned the use of any kind of a patch for his muzzle-loading rifles and adapted it for use with a grooved, lubricated lead bullet. The first rifle of this kind that he made for Mr. Hayes, was a 33 calibre with 30-inch barrel and weighed 16 pounds. This proved to be an especially accurate rifle and Mr. Hayes used it for many years, winning many matches and valuable prizes with it in the German "Schutzenfest" and "Bundesfest" matches of those times. This rifle gave better accuracy, for a long series of shots especially, than rifles using the patch since there was no patch to be torn in loading, or shooting, as well as being easier to load and saved the bother of a patch, according to Mr. Hayes' reports.

A volume could be written on the target rifles and target shooting, but as I have already described the majority of the most noted target rifles of the old times, I will close by giving a brief outline of what I,

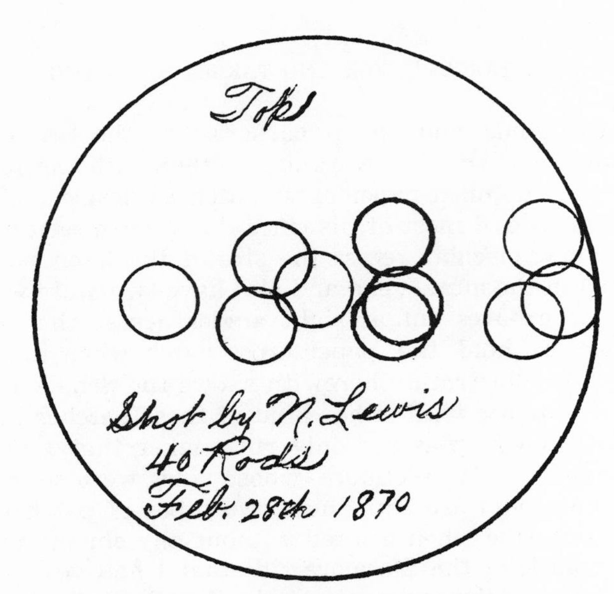

Rifle 45 calibre, 30-inch, weight 16 pounds, string-measures 6, 11/16 inches.

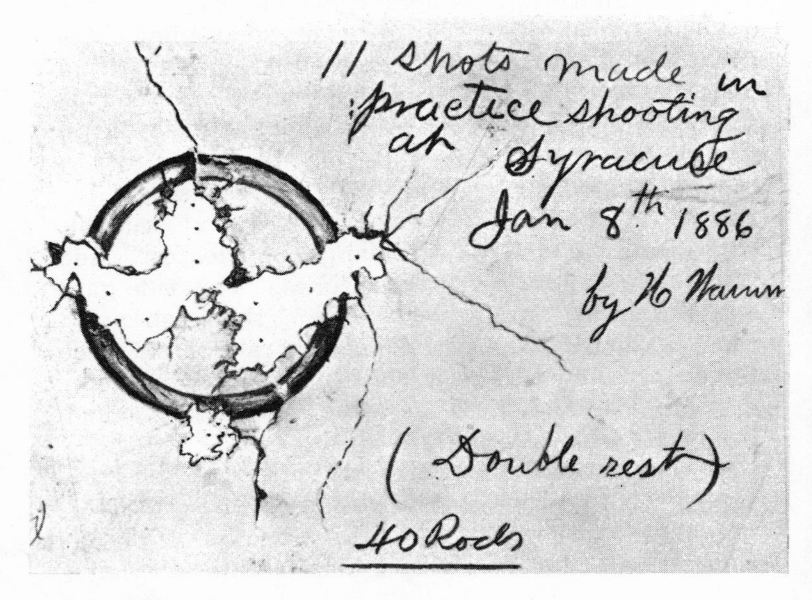

Note that the 11 bullet holes form the letter W—Warner's initial. He often performed this "stunt."

personally, consider the ideal, or best, kind of muzzle-loading target rifle.

My years of experience with the various makes and kinds of those rifles has convinced me that the most practical, most durable, most accurate shooting rifle for both off-hand and muzzle rest shooting at 200 and 220 yards should have a 30-inch octagon, or half-octagon, barrel of good weight but not too heavy, rifled with the Pope system gain twist, with false muzzle and bullet starter, using a 35 calibre bullet weighing about 225 grains, or a 38 calibre with bullet weighing 300 grains, used without any kind of a patch which only wears out the rifling and causes much extra work in loading without in any way improving the accuracy. The ignition should be by means of the Warner or Brockway device for using our present day No. 8½, or 9½ Remington primers, or the No. 115 W. R. A. non-mercuric, non-corrosive primers instead of the old nipple and percussion cap. It should have a shaded aperture front sight with removable discs, a folding peep sight with micrometer adjustments for elevation and windage attached to the tang of the rifle, and base blocks attached to the barrel for use with our modern, short tube telescopes of 5 or 6 power for off-hand shooting and one of 12 to 16 power for rest shooting. The rifle should have a double set trigger, a fore-arm that is easily detachable when using the rifle with the machine rest, or with fore-arm attached for off-hand shooting, and the rifle without telescope should weigh from 12 to 16 pounds depending upon the strength and weight of the man who is to use it.

A rifle of this kind would give as fine accuracy as was ever obtained with the Warner, Morgan James, Perry, or Brockway muzzle-loading rifles, or the H. M. Pope, George Schoyen or A. O. Zischang breech-muzzle-loading rifles; would give its best accuracy with black powder that is reasonable in price instead

Top: N. Lewis, 35 calibre, 24½-inch barrel, weight 7½ pounds. Center: B. W. Amsden, 40 calibre Picket Bullet, 31-inch barrel, weight 9½ pounds. Bottom; B. W. Amsden, Match Rifle, 45 calibre Cylindrical Bullet, 30-inch barrel, weight 12 pounds. All from Floyd R. Butler's Collection.

of requiring the smokeless powder that costs $2.00 a pound, or more. Instead of using metal cased bullets costing from $2.50 to $3.00 a hundred, the cast lead, swaged bullets would be made by the rifleman himself, or if he was too lazy to make them he could buy them at about $15.00 a thousand. There would be no expensive cases to buy, to require washing or cleaning after the day's shooting and to be reloaded before again used, and such a rifle used with good black powder and lead bullets would retain its *gilt-edge accuracy* for 30,000 to 50,000 shots—more than the life-time of a man—instead of becoming "shot out," or eroded like our present high velocity, smokeless

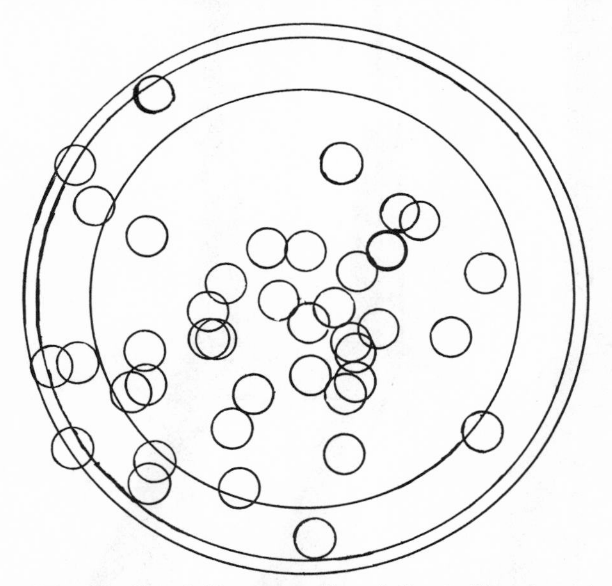

"Fac Simile of 40 consecutive shots at 40 rods rest, by George H. Ferris, Utica, N. Y., in Match with Morgan James for $200.00 a side. Rifle weighed 20 pounds, 45 calibre Picket Bullet. String measures 55, 5/16 inches; James' string measured 81, 6/8 inches." Above quoted from notation on original target. Illustration approximately ½ size.

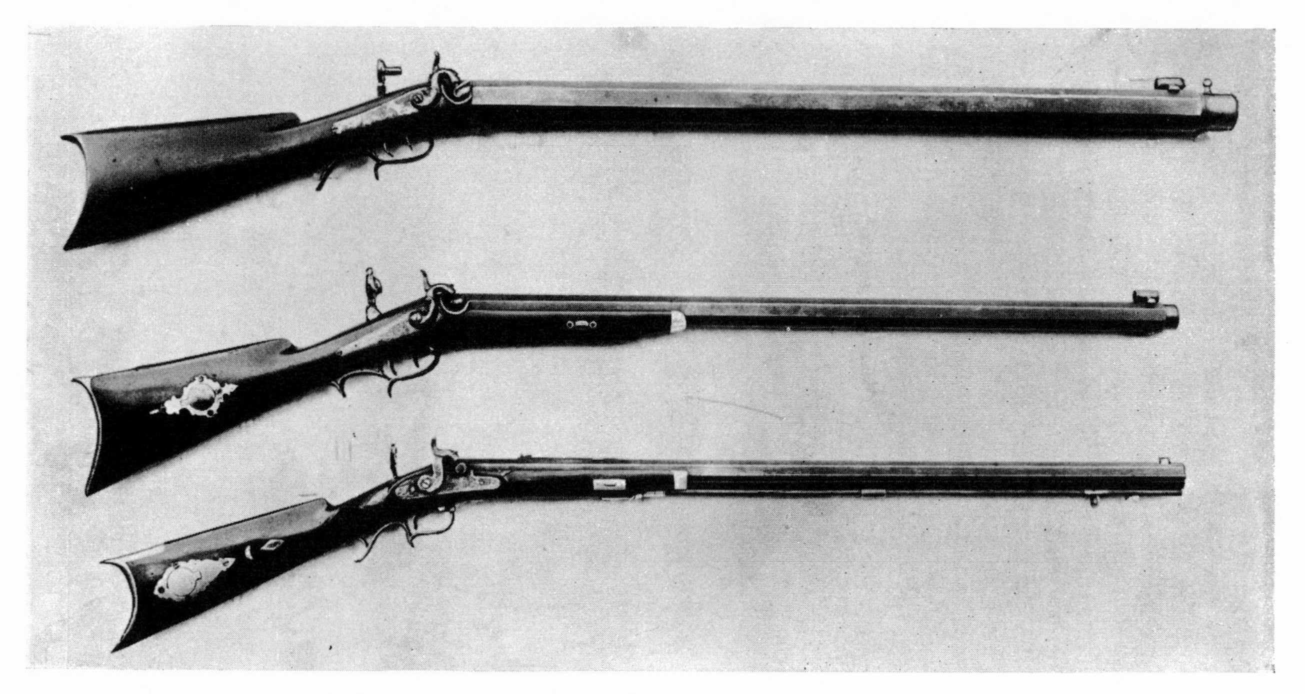

Top: N. Lewis, 50 calibre Match Rifle, Cylindrical Bullet, 33-inch barrel, weight 25 pounds. Center: N Lewis, 50 calibre Match Rifle, Picket Bullet, 31-inch barrel, weight 12½ pounds. Bottom: Warren & Steele, 30 calibre "squirrel Rifle," 31-inch barrel, weight 8 pounds. From Floyd R. Butler's Collection.

powder rifles that lose their finest accuracy about as soon as one "gets well acquainted with them," or after from about 1500 to 3500 shots, as is the case with our modern super-speed rifles of today.

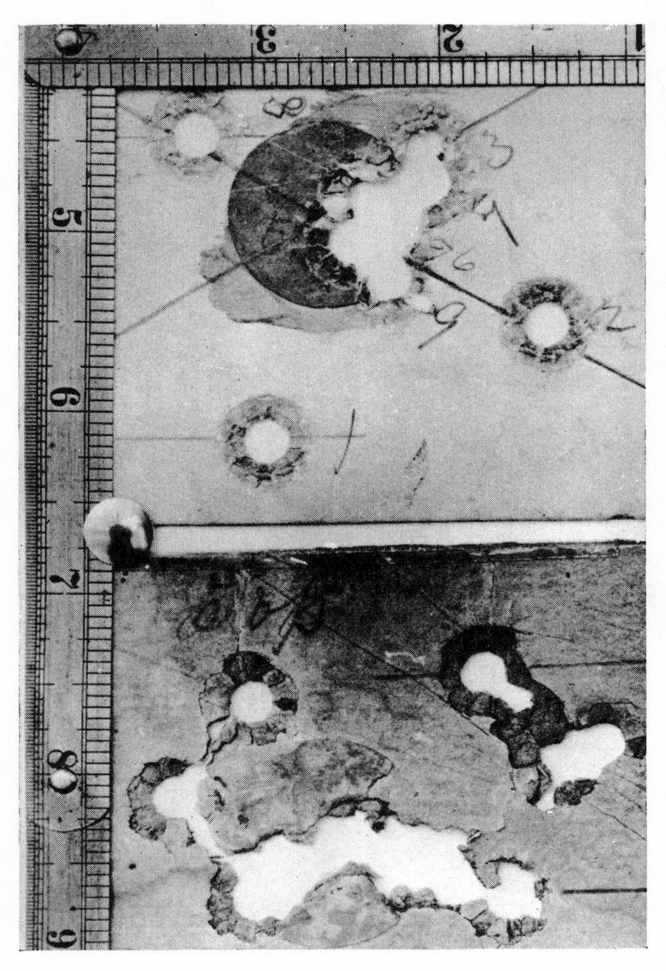

Groups shot by John Greer at 40 rods rest with 50 calibre Billinghurst Rifle owned by F. E. Dunn, in September, 1868.

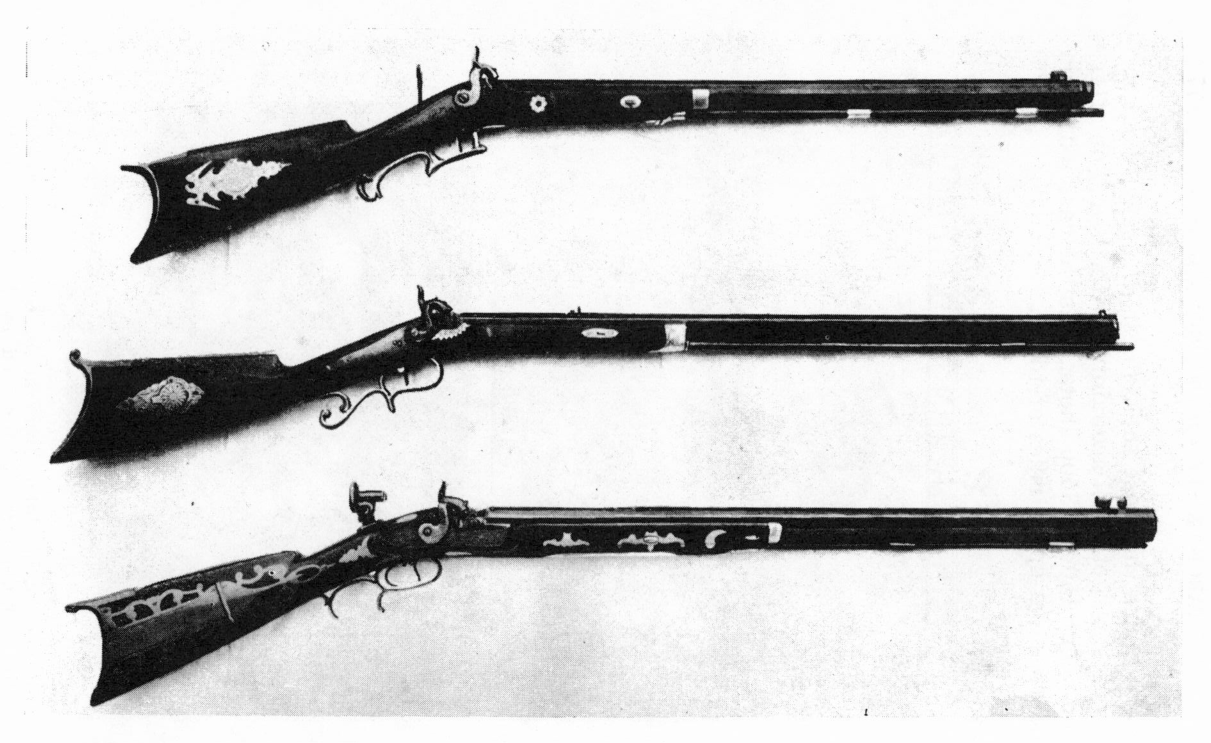

Top: C. L. Clark, 38 calibre Picket Bullet, 24 ½-inch barrel, weight 7 ½ pounds. Center: B. W. Amsden, 36 calibre Round Ball, 27-inch barrel, weight 7 pounds. Bottom: A. Appleby, Silver Mounted, 32 calibre Round Ball, 27 ½-inch barrel, weight 11 pounds. From Dr. P. A. Matteson's Collection.

CHAPTER VII.

THE HUNTING RIFLE

Those who are well-informed regarding the muzzle-loading rifles know that the cap lock muzzle-loading hunting rifles have been made in a *great variety* of *different types* during the years since the percussion cap was perfected. The first, or earliest, of these hunting rifles were long, single barrel, so-called "Kentucky" model that has been made by a great number of rifle-makers all over this country. These were the rifles that were used by the pioneers in the exploration and settlement of the middle-west, southwest and western parts of this country from about 1830 until the Civil War stimulated inventors to give us practical breech-loading rifles using the metallic cartridges.

During those days these pioneers, Indian fighters and hunters were constantly in situations where there was great need of a rifle that would enable the user to fire two or more shots without stopping to reload. This resulted in the development of the double barreled rifle having these barrels side-by-side, with two hammers—one for each barrel—or one barrel above the other fired with one hammer, which after the top barrel had been fired, the lower one was revolved by hand, brought to the top and fired by this one hammer and trigger. This, naturally, was slower in firing the two shots than the double, side-by-side, barreled rifle and someone invented the side-hammer, or "mule ear," rifle having two superposed barrels rigidly attached to the break-off, fired by two hammers placed on the right hand side of the breech with a trigger for each hammer. These mule ear, superposed barrel rifles were very popular in parts of this country, but in New England and New York State the double barreled, side-by-side, with two hammers and two triggers was the more popular.

Then some early genius designed the mule ear, or side-striker, superposed barrel rifle having two hammers and nipples, but both hammers operated with one trigger, which probably were regarded as "marvelous" arms at that time. Thus we see that our double barrel, single trigger arms today are nothing "new," but simply this old single trigger operating two hammers very much improved in design and workmanship.

Not being satisfied with the rapidity of fire with these three types of double barreled rifles, another genius of the old time, Colonel Samuel Colt, invented the well-known Colt Revolving Rifle having one barrel, one hammer and a short revolving cylinder containing five or six separate chambers which was rotated by cocking the hammer and brought each chamber in turn under the hammer ready for firing. During my boyhood days I was told by old hunters and riflemen that when the Colt revolving rifle appeared on the market it was hailed as "the perfect rifle" and with it one could fire the five or six shots in ten to fifteen seconds. It was at first considered *marvelous,* but, like most all other "perfect" inventions, it was soon discovered by actual use that there was much leakage of powder gas between the front of the cylinder and the rear end of the barrel, thereby much reducing the velocity, increasing the trajectory and decreasing the penetration of the bullet. However, H. W. S. Cleveland in his book, "Hints to Riflemen," published in 1864, stated regarding the Colt's Revolving Rifle; "The calibre of the barrel being .02 of an inch less than that of the chambers, the ball is necessarily forced to fit itself exactly to the grooves, which are seven in number and cut with a gain twist.

The excellence of the material and workmanship of these guns require no setting forth at my hands, as the reputation of Colt's arms is established in all four quarters of the globe: but it may not be amiss to state the fact that I have in my possession one of his rifles which I have had in frequent use for more than two years, and from which I have fired over three thousand shots, and it has never been in the least degree out of order, has never been in the hands of the gunsmith, and as evidence that it maintains its precision unimpaired, I may mention the fact that I have recently, with open sights, placed ten consecutive balls in a nine-inch ring at 200 yards. In all my experience I have never known an instance of the accidental discharge of other chambers than the one which is in line with the barrel, nor do I believe it could be made to occur; and I know of no gun which is so safe when carrying, for if the hammer is let down (as it ought to be) upon the bridge between the nipples, there is no possibility of an accidental discharge. To this I will add that I have never used a gun whose performance has proven so invariably satisfactory in all respects as Colt's rifle."

Captain R. B. Marcy, of the U. S. Army, in his "Hand-Book for Overland Expeditions," when giving advice to prairie travelers on the subject of arms states: "For my own part I look upon Colt's rifle as a most excellent arm for border service. It is the most reliable and certain weapon to fire that I have ever used, and I can not resist the force of my conviction that if I were alone upon the prairies, and expected an attack by a body of Indians, I am not acquainted with any arm I would as soon have in my hands as this." Sometime in 1862, according to the report, Lieutenant Hans Busk, of the Victoria Rifles, in England, with a Colt's revolving rifle placed 48 consecutive bullets at 400 yards in a rectangle 21 inches

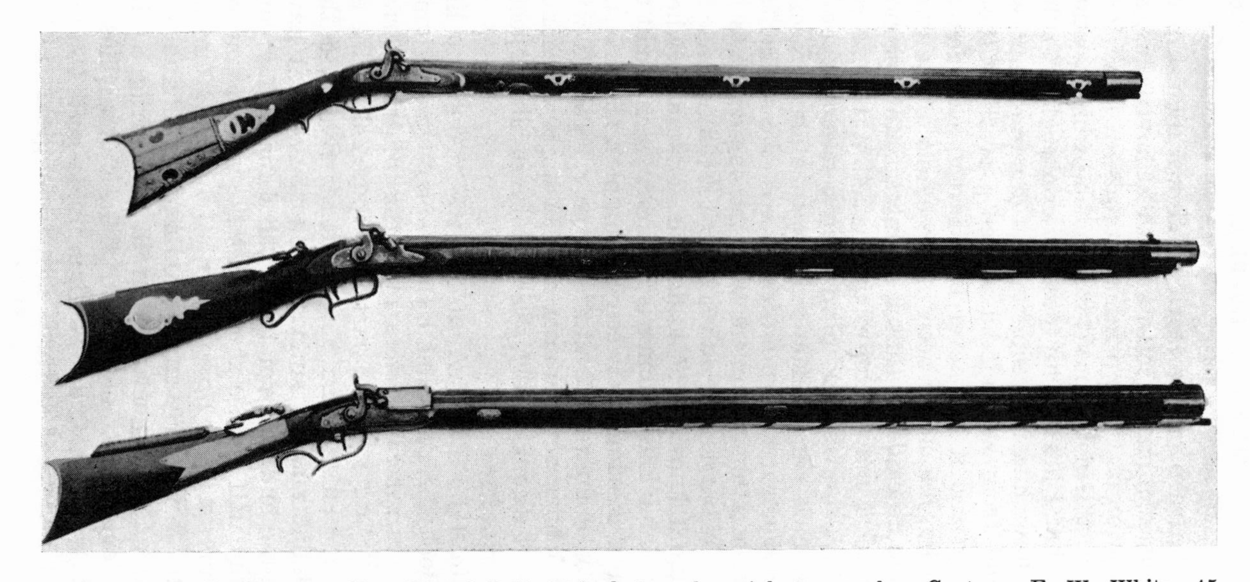

Top: Henry Carlile, 42 calibre Round Ball, 39-inch barrel, weigh 8 pounds. Center: F. W. White, 45 calibre Round Ball, 43-inch barrel, weigh 16¾ pounds. Bottom: B. Musgrove, 60 calibre Round Ball, 43½-inch barrel, weight 19¾ pounds. All from Dr. P. A. Matteson's Collection.

wide by 20 inches high, with 18 of these in or cutting an 8 inch bull's-eye. I have given the foregoing extracts to show the opinion of experts, authorities and Army officers in regard to the Colt's revolving rifle back in the Civil War days in order to call the reader's attention to the fact that in those days this rifle was regarded in much the same way that the present day rifleman considers the "latest fashion, super-speed," bolt action, or semi-automatic rifles; as well as to show that this rifle was a very excellent and practical one for hunting, or war, in those days, even though it is so "archaic" today. It really was a great invention in its day and helped greatly in "civilizing" *lots* of Indians, outlaws and bad-men of those times.

Since there was the same amount of gas leakage between the cylinder and the rear end of the barrel in the Colt's revolving rifle that we have today in our most modern revolvers, the fire-arms inventors designed rifles having three, four, five or six full length barrels that were revolved by hand on a central shaft, or spindle, attached to the break-off so as to bring each barrel in place under the hammer for firing. With these there was, of course, no gas leakage since each barrel is similar to a single barrel arm. But these were heavy, unbalanced, clumsy arms and did not long remain tight on the break-off after much use, which fault seriously affected their accuracy at any considerable range.

John R. Chapman, the author of the book, The Improved American Rifle, was the inventor of a four-barreled rifle of this type that he greatly extolled for use by hunters in the West. This rifle was made with four barrels of cast steel 20 inches long, 90 to the pound gauge, revolving by hand on a 3/8 inch diameter central steel spindle attached to the break-off. The barrels were soldered together in the same way that double barreled shotguns are made, each barrel had a nipple

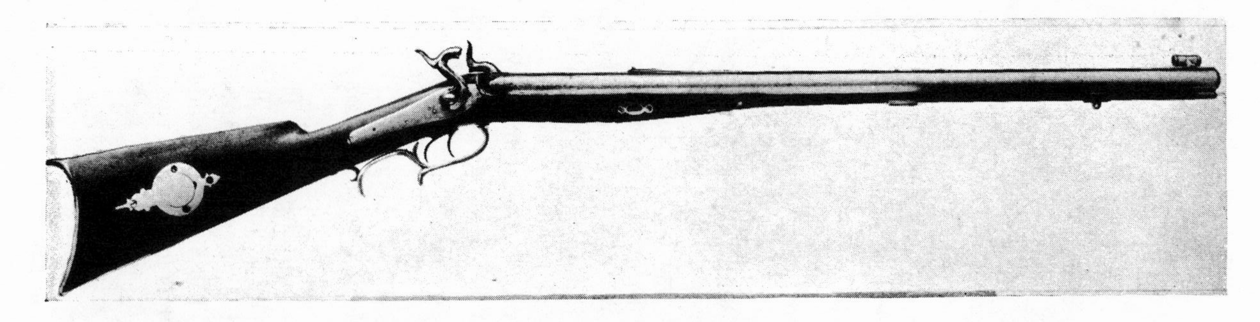

N. Lewis Double Barrel "Deer Rifle," 44 calibre Round Ball, 25-inch barrels, weight 7 pounds. From Dr. P. A. Matteson's Collection.

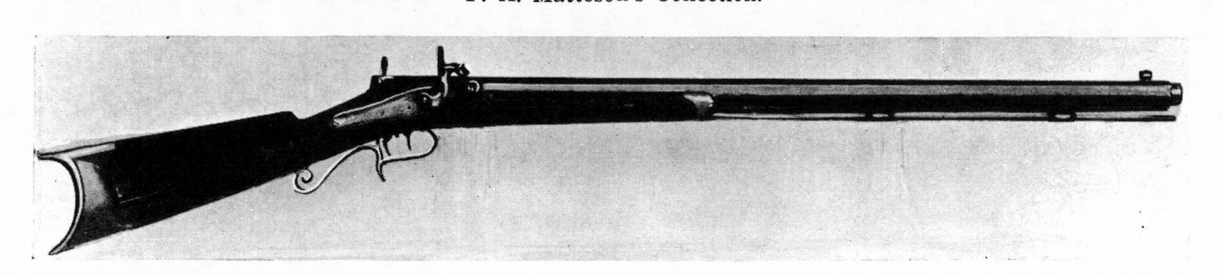

A. Cook Hunting and Target Rifle, 38 calibre, 28-inch barrel, weight 10 pounds. An especially fine balanced Off-Hand Rifle. From Frank K. Lucas' Collection.

in the breech, the action had two hammers and triggers like a double barrel shotgun, and after the two barrels at the top were fired, a catch, or latch, in front of the trigger guard was released and the bottom barrels turned to the top ready for firing.

These four-barreled rifles were made by Morgan James, Wm. Billinghurst and, no one knows how many, other rifle-makers during the late 1840's and early 1850's, but did not prove durable or practical; the barrels became loose from the break-off, thus impairing the accuracy, and these arms soon went out of use. Illustrations showing these 3-barrel, 4-barrel and 6-barrel rifles will be found on another page.

The most practical hunting rifles proved to be the single shot, the double barreled top hammer, and the double over-and-under, side-hammer, or mule ear, arms of various gauges or calibres. These were made by numerous rifle-makers in different parts of this country from about 1830 until in the 1870's when the breech-loading, metallic cartridge repeating rifles came on the market and became popular.

When I was a boy, the Wm. Billinghurst, N. Lewis, Edwin Wesson, and D. H. Hilliard single barrel rifles in 70, 80, 90 and 100 to the pound gauge (.40, .388, .383, and .36 calibres) with a barrel about 30 inches long, using the round ball, or the short, flat-point picket bullet as ordered, were very popular among the hunters where we lived and were excellent hunting rifles. The 100 to 220 to the pound gauge—36 to 28 calibres—were called "squirrel rifles," while the others were considered well suited for shooting deer, bear, caribou and other big game then found in New England and New York States. One bullet from a rifle of these calibres, when placed in the *right spot,* was all that was generally required by a good marksman to kill any of these animals.

Some men who were better able financially, had

Top: N. Lewis, Rifle and Shotgun, Rifle 40 calibre Round Ball, shot barrel, 14 gauge, 27-inch barrels, weight 10½ pounds. Center: N. Lewis, Double Barreled Rifle, 40 calibre Round Ball, 31-inch barrels, weight 9 pounds. Bottom: N. Lewis, 50 calibre Match Rifle, Picket Bullet, 31-inch barrel, weight 16 pounds. From Floyd R. Butler's Collection.

Billinghurst or N. Lewis double barreled rifles usually of 52, 56, 64, or 70 gauge (.45, .44, .42 or .40 calibre) hunting rifles, and these were considered the very *finest, most practical rifles* for big game shooting by those who preferred the muzzle-loaders. These rifles usually had 26 to 28 inch barrels, weighed about 8 to 10 pounds and, firing alternate right and left barrels, would keep ten shots in a 3 or 4 inch ring at 20 rods (110 yards) or up to 125 yards. The Billinghurst double rifles were usually finer workmanship, had better grained wood in the stock, and somewhat better finished than the Lewis double barreled rifles, but seldom gave any better accuracy than the Lewis. Billinghurst generally cut his double barrel rifles with the uniform twist, while Lewis used the gain twist.

Neither of these rifle-makers made so much "fuss" about the "great difficulty" of getting both barrels of these rifles to shoot together with the same sighting, as our present-day rifle-makers talk about; neither did they "rob" a person in their prices of these double barrel rifles. I have before me N. Lewis' price-list of 1876, from which I quote: "Double Barreled Rifles."

"No. 1. Good iron barrels, side by side, good steel locks, plain stocks, brass mounted, plain and globe sights . . . $35.00."

"No. 2. Best iron barrels, German silver mounted, or case-hardened trimmings . . . From $40.00 to $50.00."

Billinghurst's prices for similar rifles with best iron barrels and brass mounted were, $45.00: or with cast steel barrels and German silver mountings, from $60.00 to $75.00.

Just "put that in your pipe and smoke it," you gun bugs. A nice double barrel hunting rifle by two of the best makers in this country, well finished, accurate shooting arms, about 85 to 90 per cent hand work with the crude tools and machines then in use by such makers, all yours including a bullet mould, and swage if needed, for from $35.00 to $75.00. Of course, if you required this rifle all engraved with angels or animals that cost extra, but nothing like the "extra" that one gets "soaked for" today.

On another page will be found illustrations of several N. Lewis double barrel rifles and groups that I shot with some of these in recent years.

Both Billinghurst and Lewis also made "combination, double barreled guns" with the top barrel a rifle of any desired calibre and the bottom one any regular gauge shotgun, or having the two barrels side-by-side. These were considered by many hunters as about "the finest hunting arm," as with such a gun one was always prepared to shoot big game, or grouse, squirrels and other small game. These usually had 28 inch barrels, weighed about 8 to 9½ pounds, depending on the calibre of the rifle barrel, shot accurately with the rifle barrel and gave good results with most all sizes of shot in the shot barrel. The rifle barrel was rifled especially for use with the linen patched round ball, or the short, flat-point picket bullet with linen patch, as ordered by the customer. N. Lewis claimed that his double barreled rifles with gain twist would give *equally as good accuracy* with the round ball or short flat-point picket bullets, but I have never found one of these rifles that actually gave this result at the target. Billinghurst cut the barrels of his double rifles with the uniform twist, but made them with the correct twist of rifling for the round ball, or short picket bullet as the customer ordered, but *did not recommend* the use of both these bullets in the same rifle. I know of no finer muzzle-loading hunting rifle than a Billinghurst double barreled rifle in 70 or 90 gauge (.40 or .38 calibre) using the short, flat-point picket bullet with linen patch, with 26 or 28 inch barrels, and have always wanted one of these for my own use. Years ago when these could have been purchased for about $50.00 I failed to get one, and now these rifles in nice condition with perfect bores are very scarce and command high prices. Billinghurst was a master-rifle-maker, made many different types, or kinds, of muzzle-loading rifles for both hunting and target work, and is regarded by many riflemen as having been the most eminent and noted rifle-maker of his day.

I shot my first "big game" during the spring of 1876, before I was quite ten years old, with my little 30 calibre, muzzle-loading rifle. My father was at that time the manager of the "Maplehurst Farm" at Pittsfield, Massachusetts, where there was a herd of fine, thorough-bred and imported Jersey cattle, and a large flock of thorough-bred—many imported—South-down sheep. The sheep pasture containing some 70 acres was partly on a side hill and bordered on two sides by a quite large tract of woods—several hundred acres in extent—where I had hunted squirrels and grouse with Uncle Alvaro the autumn before and rabbits during the winter.

Early that spring after the sheep were turned out to pasture, uncle—a part of whose work was the care of the sheep at that time—reported to father one morning that during the night some animal had killed several sheep. Father and he examined the slain sheep and father decided they had been killed by a dog, as had happened nearly every year before; but Uncle Alvaro said: "No dog killed those sheep, D. G." (father was always called by his first two initials by all the family and many of the employees) "it was done by some wild animal—probably a lynx." Father was no hunter while uncle was an experienced hunter and trapper and, of course, thoroughly knew the tracks of the different wild animals; but father being

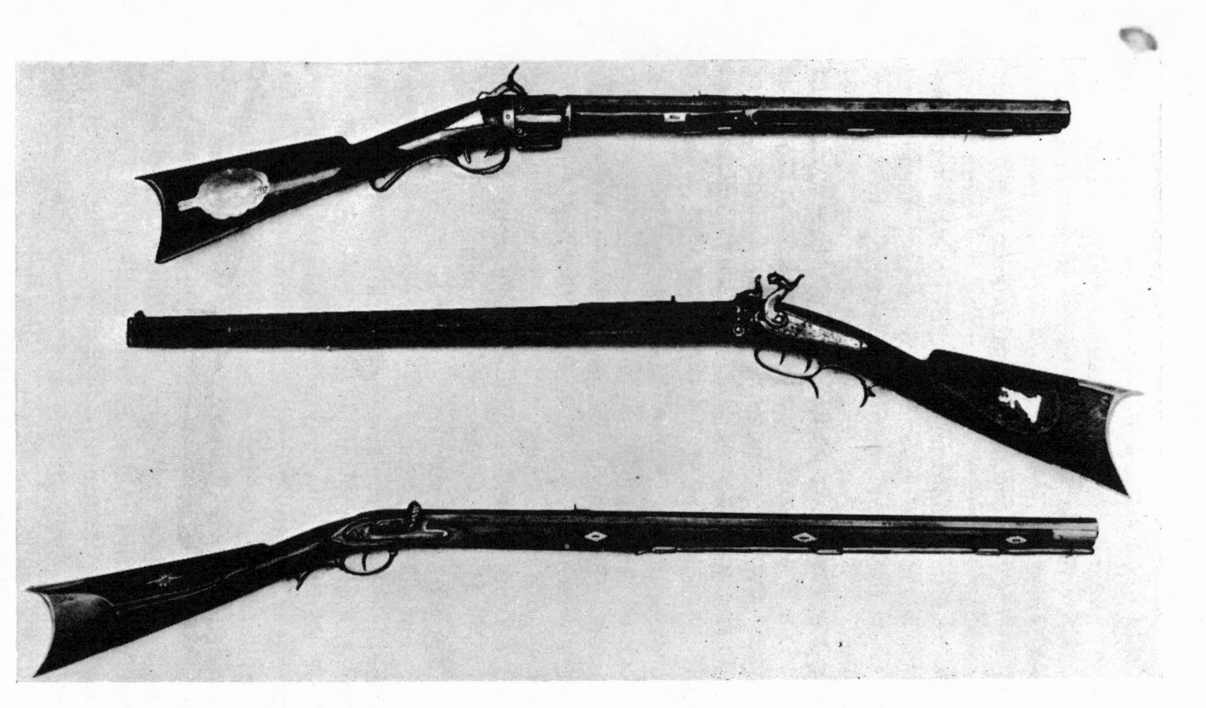

Top: Revolving 6-shot Rifle, 45 calibre, 21½-inch barrel. Front Trigger is lever for revolving the cylinder by hand. Center: J. Buswell Super-Posed Barrels Rifle, 45 calibre, 26-inch barrels, weight 8 pounds. Bottom: W. Raymond, Side-Hammer Rifle, 36 calibre, 29-inch barrel, weight 7 pounds. From F. E. Dunn Collection.

"the boss," and disbelieving uncle's claim that a lynx killed the sheep, told him to get his gun, stay in the sheep pasture all day and shoot any stray dogs that came into it. Our dogs on the farm were imported Scotch-Collies—sheep dogs from Scotland—and would never harm a sheep.

Uncle returned at dark and reported that no strange dogs had been in the sheep pasture that day: he advised that two of the Scotch-Collies—"Jock" and "Lassie"—should be left with the sheep all night, which advice father disregarded. Next morning shortly after daybreak, Uncle Alvaro went to the sheep pasture with several of the Scotch-Collies and returned at breakfast time reporting to father that several more sheep had been killed during the night and stated emphatically that: "A damned lynx killed them."

That interested me, and when father instructed uncle to "get his gun, go to the woods and hunt down and kill the lynx—or whatever animal had killed the sheep," I immediately got my little rifle and ammunition and teased uncle to let me go with him. At first he refused, but more pleadings on my part at least induced him to let me accompany him on this "job." I loaded my rifle very carefully with the conical bullet, which was heavier than the round ball, while uncle got his Billinghurst 40 calibre hunting rifle with the powder flask, bullet pouch and caps, loaded it, and with lunches in our hunting bags we set out for the woods, leaving another man in charge of the sheep. On our way to the woods, Uncle Alvaro questioned me to be sure that I knew what a Canadian lynx looked like and explained that if wounded, one would put up a hard fight. Arriving at the woods, uncle and I hunted together for several hours without seeing the lynx or any animals except squirrels, and about mid-afternoon, uncle directed me to carefully and slowly hunt a certain section while he hunted another part of the woods some three hundred yards east of my section. We were to hunt in a northerly direction parallel to each other and meet at a certain landmark at a certain time that afternoon. The trees in the woods were principally hardwood with a few pines and hemlocks, and uncle had cautioned me *not to venture close* to these evergreen trees as the lynx might be hidden in these tops. Before we separated, uncle explained that I should carefully look for the lynx perched on the limb of a tree and if I saw it I was *not to shoot* at it, but hoot as an owl to call him and watch the animal, keeping well away from the tree, until he arrived.

After we separated I hunted slowly and carefully for an hour or more, carefully examining the trees in my section for the lynx or any animal larger than a squirrel. Sneaking quietly along in this way, I finally saw at a distance of about 100 yards on the limb near the trunk of a hardwood tree, a grey object, which when I had approached to about 50 yards from that tree, a closer examination proved to be the lynx apparently asleep in the tree about 40 feet above the ground. I watched it carefully for several minutes and could plainly see the lynx's head and pointed ears, looking just like the picture of lynx in my "animal book." I carefully removed the cap from the nipple of my rifle, put on a fresh Eley Brothers cap, rested my rifle against the side of the tree behind which I was standing, took careful aim at the animal's shoulder—after I had carefully decided that the shoulder afforded a larger "mark" than the head—and fired. The lynx fell to the ground, kicked a few times and then lay still. While this was happening, I was quickly reloading my rifle where I stood when I had fired.

After the rifle was again loaded, holding it ready for instant use, I carefully advanced towards the lynx that was quiet on the ground and was looking at it when Uncle Alvaro, having heard my shot, came running towards me. On seeing him I shouted, "I've got him! I've got him!" Uncle approached the dead lynx, looked at it and me in silence for a few minutes, then exclaimed: "I've a good notion to give you a damned good licking."

"I told you *not to shoot at the lynx if you saw it,* and *you disobeyed my orders,* you little devil. You deserve a sound licking for disobeying." I replied that I had killed the lynx, and did not deserve punishment for disobeying his orders as I feared the lynx would get away. He answered that if I had only wounded the animal it would have jumped onto me and perhaps killed me before he could have arrived and killed it. After carefully examining the dead lynx he remarked: "That was a damn good shot; just in the right place."

We carried the lynx home without skinning it, while uncle alternately scolded me and praised my good shooting; the scales showed the weight of the lynx as 67 pounds and I felt that I was a "heap big hunter," as the Indian says, I assure you. Uncle skinned the lynx that evening, then tanned the fur with the head and claws on and made it into a rug that I had by my bed for many years, until moths and wear ruined it and it was thrown away.

All this and more, I recorded that night in a small notebook that I kept, and from which I have copied this account of the first "big game" that I shot nearly 64 years ago. That ended the sheep killing, much to my disappointment as uncle said the lynx might have a "mate" in those or neighboring woods, but it proved to be a lone male that had lived well all winter and expected to fatten still more on high grade mutton that spring.

There were more than a thousand woodchucks, or groundhogs, on that farm which included some twelve

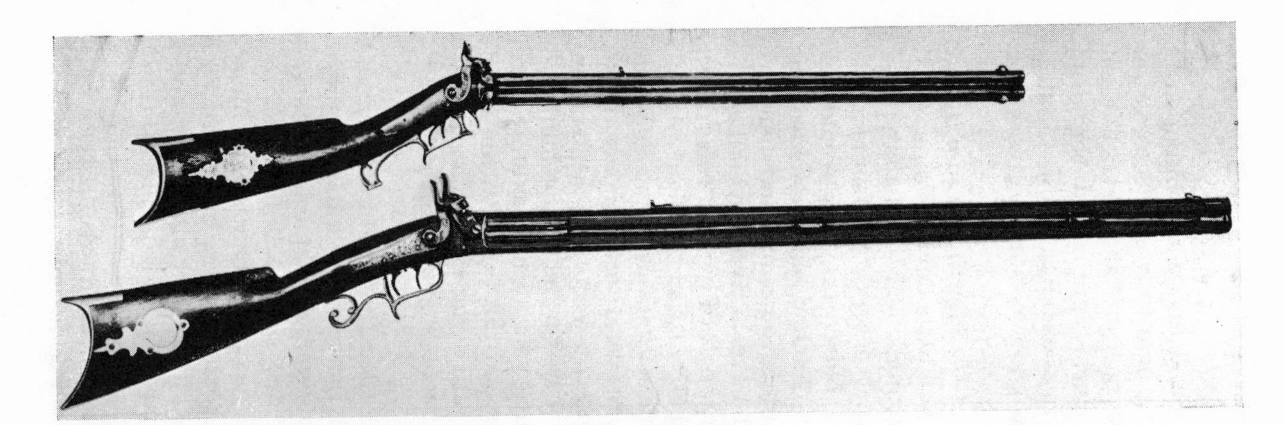

Top: L. L. Hepburn, 4-Barrel Rifle, 36 calibre, 28-inch barrels. Bottom: Abe Williams, Super-posed Barrels Rifle, 40 calibre, 31-inch barrels. From W. A. Luce Collection.

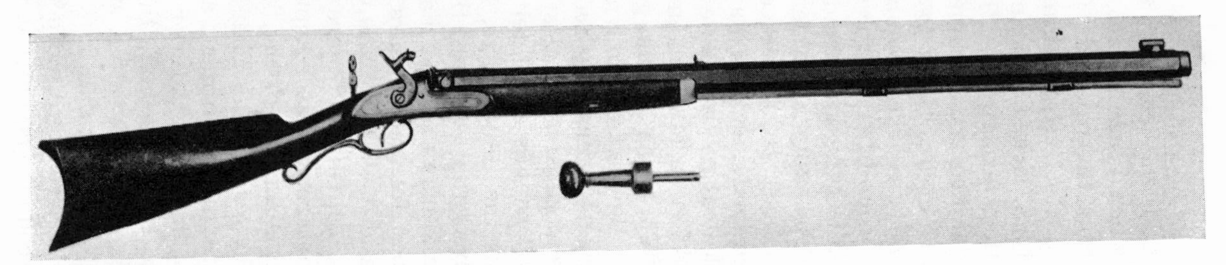

Wm. Billinghurst, 40 calibre Hunting and Target Rifle, 30-inch barrel. From Frank K. Lucas Collection.

hundred acres at that time; when the owner, Honorable Thomas Allen, Sr., arrived from St. Louis for the summer and learned that I shot the sheep-killing lynx, he offered to pay me ten cents a head for all the woodchucks that I could shoot or trap on that farm. Before his arrival, I had commenced shooting these at every opportunity with my little rifle, and the money that I thus earned went mostly for powder, caps, and linen for patches for my rifle, but I started laying aside some of this cash with which to later buy a larger calibre, heavier and better muzzle-loading rifle, like uncle's Billinghurst hunting and target rifle.

Early in October 1879, after I had recovered from a severe illness, my parents allowed Uncle Alvaro to take me with him to Campton, New Hampshire, in the White Mountain region, on my first deer hunt. Mother had relatives, Mr. and Mrs. Alvin Houston and two daughters, living on a farm, part of which was in Campton and part in Waterville, and uncle and I visited these relatives to hunt deer in that section. Waterville, New Hampshire, was then and still is a "back town" well off the main highway, about ten miles up the valley of the "Mad River" surrounded by mountains, and with but few inhabitants. That part of Campton and all of Waterville, then was, and now is, excellent country for white tail deer and black bear; there we spent more than two weeks hunting these animals.

As my 30 calibre rifle was too small bore for killing deer or bear, a friend of Uncle Alvaro's loaned me his muzzle-loading hunting rifle, a 42 calibre with 28 inch barrel weighing about 9 pounds, using a short, flat-point picket bullet with linen patch and made by Geo. O. Leonard, of Keene, New Hampshire. I also took with me my 30 calibre muzzle-loader to use in shooting squirrels and grouse, but before we returned home I killed my first black bear with one conical bullet from

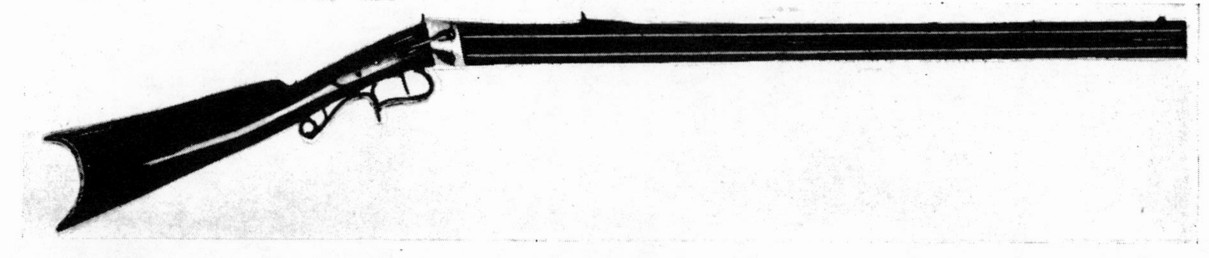

Unknown Make "Mule Ear" Rifle, 44 calibre, 30-inch barrels, weight 10½ pounds. From Shiff the Gunman's Collection.

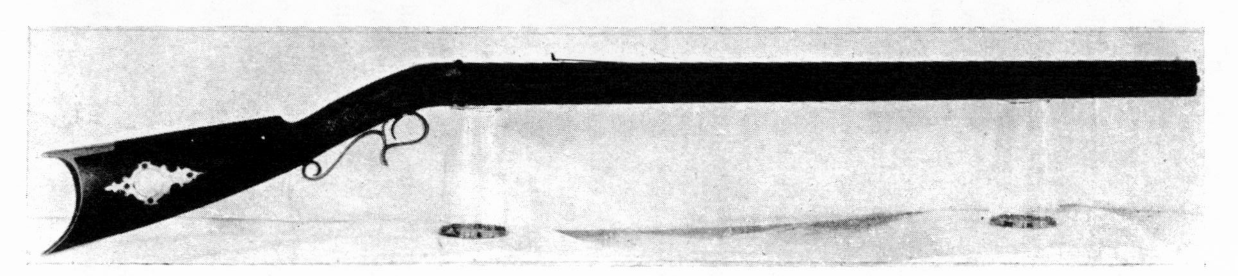

S. Vosburgh, "Mule Ear" Rifle, 35 calibre Round Ball, 31¾-inch barrels, weight 11 pounds. Single Trigger fires top barrel with first pull; second pull fires the bottom one. From Frank K. Lucas' Collection.

it, placed at the base of the bear's ear. This bear had been killing sheep and young cattle belonging to a farmer in Waterville, who set a trap for the bear, near sheep it had killed a day or two before; the bear walked into the trap and as uncle and I had spent the previous day hunting with this man, and spent the night at his house, we accompanied him the next morning to look at the bear trap. As I had never seen a wild bear, he promised to let me shoot it if there was one in the trap.

On arriving at the trap, there was a large black bear in it with the chain and toggle fast between two trees. Uncle had his rifle with him, in case he might need it, but let me serve as the bear's executioner after telling me where to place my bullet. At a range of about 25 feet, the 30 calibre bullet at the base of the bear's ear dispatched it as easily as I could have killed a rabbit. I remember that at the time I thought it was a great feat, but later I realized that shooting a trapped bear was no sportsmanship. Rather a dirty trick on the bear, but he was the aggressor in that case and well deserved his fate. My notebook gives the weight of this bear as 450 pounds—not dressed, of course.

A few days after we arrived in Campton, uncle and I were hunting near the base of Mount Tecumseh late in the afternoon where we surprised a bunch of several deer feeding on acorns. Among these were two bucks, and uncle gave me the first shot at one that I selected: we each aimed at a buck about 65 yards from the fir balsam trees that concealed us, at a whispered "now" from uncle, I fired at my buck, followed almost instantly by the report of uncle's rifle. His buck dropped from a neck shot, while my buck ran a short distance and fell dead from a bullet through the heart, and when I saw the deer fall, kick a few times and then lie still, I was so excited that I had difficulty in reloading my rifle before approaching the deer.

Every day, sometimes several times a day, uncle had warned me: "When you shoot at a deer, or animal, *immediately reload your rifle before stirring out of your tracks,"* and I obeyed those instructions in this case without being prompted, but with much nervousness and especial difficulty in getting the cap onto the nipple, as uncle jokingly reminded me later. After dressing and hanging up the deer it was then nearly dark and as we were ten miles or so from the house, uncle decided to camp there that night. I helped build a brush "lean-to" with fir-balsam beds; then uncle taught me how to build a "cooking fire," we then heated water in the tea pail, cleaned our rifles and reloaded them. Then we cooked and ate venison with pilot bread and tea that we had in our packs; after which we made a "night fire" as the night in the mountains would be cold, talked over the events of the day by the glow of the fire, then slept soundly on the balsam beds till sunrise. Next morning uncle said all the camp lacked was some wolves howling in the distance, but every time I awoke in the night I heard the owls hooting which satisfied me as well as howling wolves would have. Some years later when I was traveling in the Hudson's Bay Country of Canada where the wolves would howl at night as my Indians and I sat around our campfire or lay in our sleeping bags, I often thought of that first night's camp with Uncle Alvaro in the White Mountains of New Hampshire, and wished that he was with me to enjoy ? the wolves that were doing their best to sing us to sleep.

While on this hunting trip, in addition to shooting my first white tail deer with the 40 calibre Leonard muzzle-loader, and black bear, I also shot a good number of grey squirrels and grouse with my 30 calibre rifle. In those days these were very plentiful.

especially in that section, and several grouse would sit in a tree while one shot the head off of a bird. Usually the others would fly but a short distance to another tree and thus by careful stalking, more grouse were easily killed with the rifle.

We also learned while on this trip that black bear were quite numerous in Campton, Thornton, and Waterville, and could easily be shot during the "Berries-Ripe-Moon," as the Indians call it; that is, in late August and early September. In places along the Mad River Valley and at the base of some of the mountains there grew great quantities of blueberries and blackberries, where when these were ripe one could be practically sure of finding bears busily picking berries and one could walk up within a few yards—often a few feet—of the bear, if one was careful to keep the wind in his favor. These blackberry patches were often several acres in extent, with the briars growing very close together and six to eight feet high, among which the bear trails wound like cow-paths in a pasture.

After hearing Cousin Alvin and the neighboring farmers tell how plentiful the bears were in that section and how easy it was to shoot one when blackberries were ripe, uncle and I planned to visit this relative again the next year during the blackberry season, and "exterminate" some of these bears that killed so many sheep and young cattle every spring and autumn.

While the single shot muzzle-loading rifle is all right for shooting deer that even when wounded run away instead of showing fight, the wounded black bear nearly always proceeds to "make it interesting" for the hunter who wounds it. Therefore, Uncle Alvaro said we would trade for two good double barreled rifles during the winter, come to that section the next year in early September and shoot some bears—make a "wholesale slaughter" of them and thus the cash we got for the hides would pay for our new rifles and expenses of the trip. There was also a bounty of ten dollars, at that time, paid by the State for each bear killed, so that with the bounty and the money for the bear hides, uncle and I figured that we would kill enough bears to enable us each to buy several new rifles. In fact, during the winter of 1879—'80, I laid plans to "practically exterminate" all the bear in Campton and Waterville, buy a Sharps breech-loading 44-90-470 rifle, a Winchester, Model 1876, 45-75-350 repeater, a Colt's 44-40 revolver and go to the West, and clean up the remaining bad Indians, buffalo and grizzly bears; thereby, incidentally, making my fortune as well as getting acquainted with "Buffalo Bill," "Kit Carson" and other noted scouts, hunters and Indian fighters.

Before Christmas 1879, Uncle Alvaro ordered a Billinghurst double barreled rifle in 45 calibre with 28 inch barrels to use the short, flat-point picket bullet with linen patch, and finally found a man who would trade his Wm. Read double barreled 44 calibre muzzle-loading rifle for one of uncle's double-barreled muzzle-loading shotguns and twelve dollars cash "to boot." Uncle made this trade and I was to pay him the twelve dollars as I earned it.

During the winter, uncle taught me how to trap foxes, then in the spring he showed me how to catch muskrats—that then sold at 25 to 35 cents—and in this way with other money that I earned in various ways during the summer, I had paid him the twelve dollars "boot" on the Wm. Read double rifle and he made me a present of his remaining share in it. Thus by August 1880, with uncle's new Billinghurst 45 calibre and my Read 44 calibre double barreled, muzzle-loading rifles, with a good supply of ammunition for each, it "looked bad" for those bears in Campton and Waterville.

Both the Billinghurst and Read double rifles proved very satisfactory; the Billinghurst was, of course, the more accurate, but was considerably heavier, weighing over ten pounds, which uncle considered just right for such a rifle. The flat-point picket bullet weighed 350 grains and was used with 80 to 90 grains of powder. My Wm. Read double rifle had 27 inch barrels, weighed 8½ pounds, used a flat-point picket bullet weighing 275 grains with a charge of 65 to 80 grains of black powder, but I generally used 75 grains only. Both these rifles were cut with a slow twist of rifling and with the Curtis and Harvey "Diamond Grain" No. 6 black powder, required no cleaning between shots and would give as fine accuracy after fifty shots as with the second. On another page are shown two groups that were shot with these rifles at 15 rods using a sand-bag rest, which shows as good grouping as is obtained with our best lever action hunting rifles today.

At last September (1880) came, I was given permission to be absent from school for two weeks on condition that I should make up the work on returning to school. Uncle Alvaro and I, with our double barreled rifles and hunting equipment, boarded the train for Campton, New Hampshire, where after nearly two days travel on the slow, dusty trains of those days we arrived at the little station in the woods where some member of the family met us with a horse and wagon, and after a pleasant drive of several miles we arrived at the farm where we were welcomed by Cousin Alvin and others of his family.

That evening we were told that there were lots of blackberries, that bears were very plentiful and we certainly ought to have no trouble in shooting several of them. Cousin Alvin had arranged his work so as to go hunting with us next day and show us the best places for bear.

After a good night's rest we were up early next morning to help with the necessary farm "chores" and after those were finished and a hearty breakfast eaten, Cousin Alvin, with his 56 calibre Spencer breech-loading, Civil War carbine, Uncle Alvaro and I set forth on "the great bear hunt," that I had planned about and dreamt about for nearly a year.

The Bear Hunt of 1880. After traveling several miles up the valley of the Mad River and hunting several blackberry patches where bears had been feeding only a short time before, but had evidently gotten our scent and left hurriedly before we sighted them, Cousin Alvin guided us to a very extensive blackberry patch near the base of a mountain where the blackberry briars were six to eight feet tall. Keeping the wind in our faces, we carefully approached this blackberry patch through which we found bear trails winding and twisting in every direction where the bears had fed on the blackberries that grew there in great quantities. Halting at the edge of this briar patch to look and listen, we plainly heard several bears breaking down the blackberry bushes as they ate the berries. We looked at our rifles to be sure they were ready for instant use, then with Uncle Alvaro in the lead, myself next and Cousin Alvin in the rear, we silently followed one of the bear trails as it twisted among the briars and after slowly and very carefully traversing this for about two hundred yards we arrived at a sharp turn where we saw the briars being shaken violently and heard the bears. Uncle raised his hand as a signal to be very quiet, then carefully and quickly stepped around the turn in the path, with me close behind him, and there but a few yards in front of us we saw two large black bears standing upright on their hind feet busily eating blackberries. Uncle quickly raised his rifle, aimed at the bear's heart and fired both barrels in quick succession. The bear dropped to the ground with a hoarse growl, kicked spasmodically a few times and lay still. As soon as uncle had fired his second shot, he bent forward from the hips and said to me: "Shoot, shoot." Aiming quickly at the chest of the second bear, that still was standing upright looking at us apparently in great surprise, I fired the right barrel of my rifle, at which the bear clumsily jumped into the briars, stumbled as I fired the second shot, went a few feet and fell dead, much to my delight.

All this happened in a few seconds and we each had killed our bear, which appeared to us to have been very easily done, but Cousin Alvin said the second bear must have been a fool to stand there after the first bear dropped and let me shoot it. He said that was very unusual behavior for a bear under such circumstances. When I saw that my bear was dead, I had an attack of "buck fever," or "bear fever," and trembled so violently that it was with much difficulty that I finally reloaded both barrels of my rifle.

Those bear trails among the briars were so narrow that two men could not stand side by side in them, in most places, and the briars were so large and thick that one would have required a suit of armor if he attempted to penetrate them. Thus one was obliged to walk through these briar thickets by following the bear trails only.

Here is where our double barrel rifles had shown their advantages, as we each had killed our bear with the two shots without giving either bear time to put up a fight, as might easily have happened had we used single shot rifles. Our next big job was dressing these bear in that briar thicket where they had fallen, and uncle and I proceeded to dress his bear while Cousin Alvin went to the nearest farm to borrow a horse and farm wagon with which to draw home the bears, which was finally accomplished after much hard work, and long after dark we arrived back at the house with our two bears.

The next day we were all busy skinning, cutting up the bears, trying out the bear's oil and stretching the hides. Bear's oil sold readily to the apothecaries in those days, and all hunters and riflemen considered it the *very best* for lubricating the rifle after cleaning it, for oiling the linen patches for the hunting rifles and the paper patches for the target rifles. Bear's oil when properly tried out and filtered is water-white, practically odorless, does not thicken, or "gum," is an excellent rust preventive and really is about the *best* gun oil that I know of; but is difficult to obtain, in the majority of places, in these modern days. The bear that uncle shot was a female and weighed 283 pounds after removing the entrails, while the bear that I shot was a male weighing 312 pounds, according to my records.

Uncle and I had killed these first two bears *so very easily* that I, in my ignorance of bear hunting, thought it would be easy for us to each kill about a dozen bear on this trip, but uncle and Cousin Alvin both said we had encountered "two fool bears" that time and the next ones we met probably would not be so easy to kill. That prediction proved correct, as later events demonstrated.

On the morning of the second day after we had killed these bears, Uncle Alvaro and I took a horse and farm wagon, drove up the Mad River valley road for several miles, forded the river to the west side at a point about a mile from the place where we had killed the other bears, tied the horse to a tree and proceeded on foot quietly to the blackberry patch, confident (I was, at least) that we could each kill another bear in that same place. However, the wind proved wrong, was very "shifty," or changeable, and while we started two or three bears that were feeding on the blackberries, we actually saw but one as it plunged out of the trail into the briars after getting our scent. We each fired at it as it disappeared in the briars, but only slightly wounded it, the bear escaped and we were obliged to return to the house without any bear that day.

On the next day, uncle killed another large female bear in this same blackberry patch and I shot the lone cub that was with its mother eating berries. The female weighed 325 pounds after the entrails had been removed, while the cub that I shot only weighed 90 pounds, according to the records I made at that time.

After that, the bears all "got wise" to the fact that they were being hunted in that blackberry patch and kept away from it, or came there only very early in the morning or late at night, so that we failed to get another bear from that place. We hunted hard every day, each shot a nice white tailed buck and plenty of squirrels and grouse, but the bear that we located in berry thickets got our scent and escaped unharmed.

One day during the second week of this hunt, Cousin Alvin accompanied us on a trip up the Waterville valley to Mount Osceola to hunt bear in a new place. We left the farm early that morning with a horse and farm wagon, drove to the end of the highway, then followed an old logging road for several miles to a point where we ate our lunch, tied the horse to a tree, fed and left it, and then hunted several "likely places for bear" near the base of that mountain. About mid-afternoon as Cousin Alvin and I were carefully following a bear trail in a blackberry patch while Uncle Alvaro hunted in another direction, I turned a sharp corner in the trail and there faced a bear at about five yards range walking towards me. On seeing it, I fired too quickly with the first barrel, wounding it high in the left fore-shoulder, when it advanced quickly a few steps, rose on its hind feet growling savagely, when at a range of about ten feet I fired the second barrel aiming at the bear's chest, at which it dropped to its four feet and came at me. Just as I was wondering what to do next, the report of Cousin Alvin's 56 calibre Spencer carbine close to my head almost deafened me as his bullet caught the bear in its open mouth, shattering the brain, and the bear dropped dead.

"That was a close call," he remarked as we looked at the bear that lay almost near enough for me to have kicked its head. I agreed that it was plenty close. An examination showed that my second bullet had hit the heart, torn it in pieces, but still the bear kept coming savagely at me until Cousin Alvin's bullet in the brain stopped it.

While we were dressing my bear we heard uncle shoot once in the near distance and later found him dressing a large male bear that he killed with one bullet at the base of the right ear, at a range so close that the powder had singed the bear's fur. We had difficulty in getting that horse near enough to the bears to drag them out to the wagon, and then when he was hitched to the wagon with two bears on it, the horse tried several times to run away while traveling the logging road. Finally we arrived, late at night, back at the house with two more bears.

The rest of that week was spent in skinning these bears, cutting up the meat, trying out the oil, stretching the hides, and getting ready for our return trip to Pittsfield, Massachusetts, with our bear hides, a small quantity of the bear meat, which neither uncle nor I liked to eat, several gallons of fine bear's oil, and thirty dollars each in cash that we had collected as bounty for killing these bears. We sold some of the bear's oil to an apothecary in Pittsfield, kept more than a gallon each for our own use, Uncle Alvaro sold two of his bear hides, I sold the bear cub's hide for $5.00 and one of the others for $10.00 Thus with the $30.00 bounty, $15.00 for the two bear hides sold and $5.00 for my share of the bear's oil sold, I received $50.00 in cash as the result of my first bear hunt. I was a sure "heap big bear hunter," when I returned to school after that hunting trip, and if any of the pupils or teachers wanted to know anything about black bears, or hunting them, they knew just where to get "first hand information" on that subject.

My good mother was much worried when she heard of my narrow escape from "being killed by a bear" when I shot the last one on that trip, allowed me to keep $10.00 of the money received and put the balance—$40.00—in my savings bank account. Thus my plans for buying the Sharps and Winchester rifles, the Colt's revolver and going West to become "a great hunter and Indian fighter" fell flat; thereby, doubtless, saving many an Indian from losing his scalp and allowed the few remaining buffalo to live a little longer.

During the winter of 1880-'81, uncle and I frequently discussed our two hunting trips in the Campton-Waterville territory of New Hampshire, the rifles we had used on those trips, their killing power on big game. their faults or defects, etc., and boy-like, I decided that I must have a breech-loading, repeating rifle for shooting bear.

Since I had failed to kill, with the two shots from my double barreled rifle, the last bear I had shot at that autumn, and might have gotten killed myself had not Cousin Alvin with his 56 calibre Spencer seven-shot repeating rifle finished the bear, I argued that no muzzle-loading rifle was really the *right* one for shooting black bear. Uncle still maintained that if a man could not kill a black bear with a good double barreled muzzle-loading rifle with its two "lightning-fast" shots, he was a poor shot, or a poor hunter—or both. His long experience as a hunter and as a sharpshooter in war had taught him to be cool and steady in the face of danger, so that shooting a charging bear had little more effect on his nerves than shooting a deer or squirrel. But as I had not his steady nerve in facing a dangerous animal nor his skill in placing my bullet *right* when a wounded animal showed fight, I felt the need of a breech-loading, repeating rifle with five or more shots ready for use almost instantly. This resulted in his decision that in my case the repeating rifle might be best for hunting bear, and early that spring he purchased for me a Model 1873 Winchester repeating rifle, 44-40 calibre, with 24-inch half-octagon barrel, half magazine holding six cartridges, and having the "Rocky Mountain" front and the full "California buckhorn" rear sights. This rifle with the six cartridges in the magazine weighed under eight pounds, balanced nicely, provided seven shots that could be fired very rapidly and at 100 to 150 yards shot as accurately as I could hold in off-hand shooting or from the sitting position. I was so pleased with this 44-40 Winchester rifle that I gave uncle my Wm. Read double barreled rifle in exchange for the Winchester, that cost him $19.50 cash, a Winchester reloading tool, Winchester bullet mould, a canvas case for the rifle and three hundred cartridges. Thus I acquired my first breech-loading repeating hunting rifle that I was certain would prove a better rifle for me to use in shooting bear than any muzzle-loading rifle. The next October when uncle and I again made a hunting trip to the Campton-Waterville country to "exterminate" more of those black bear, I used my 44-40 Winchester repeater while uncle stuck to his Billinghurst double barreled 45 calibre muzzle-loader.

But this book deals with the muzzle-loading rifle

only; therefore, I will briefly state that on that hunting trip I killed but one bear, weighing 300 pounds, with my 44 calibre Winchester, wounded four or five others, most of which Uncle Alvaro killed with his double barreled muzzle-loading rifle after I had "pumped" five or six shots into them. Thus uncle proved his claims that the double barreled 45 calibre muzzle-loading rifle with its 350 grain bullet backed by 80 or 90 grains of powder, in the hands of a good hunter who was also a good marksman, was a far better killer on bear than the 44-40 Winchester repeater in spite of its seven shots that could be fired so rapidly. That cartridge used too small powder charge and the bullet was too light—lacked knock-down, killing power—to be effective on black bear even at short range, while the heavy 45 calibre soft lead bullet from uncle's Billinghurst double rifle literally knocked a bear off its feet and killed splendidly.

Thus I know from actual experience that the double barreled muzzle-loading rifle of 44 or 45 calibre with a soft lead picket bullet weighing from 275 to 350 grains backed by 75 to 90 grains of good black powder, in the hands of an experienced hunter-rifleman is a very effective killer on deer, black bear, caribou and moose, all of which I saw Uncle Alvaro kill with that Billinghurst double rifle before he adopted the breech-loading hunting rifle.

I still have a "friendly feeling" for those Billinghurst, N. Lewis, and other good double barreled muzzle-loading rifles and know that they are good killers on big game.

Probably the most noted muzzle-loading, single shot, big game hunting rifles in the old times were the famous Hawken "plains rifles." From an article by the late Horace Kephart published in *Shooting and Fishing* in 1897, and from Mr. L. O. Holman, of Trumansburg, N. Y., I find that the two brothers, Jacob and

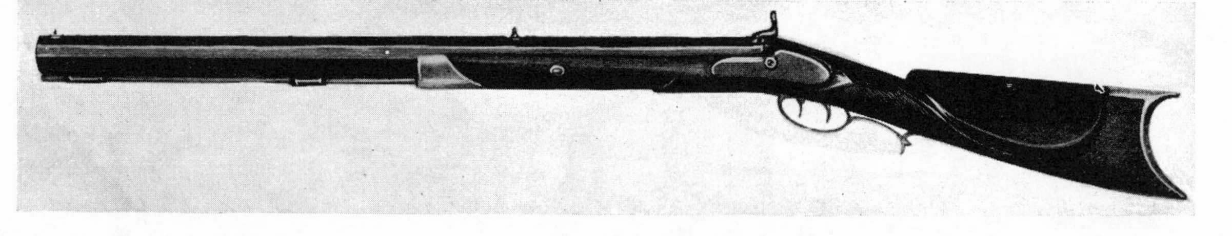

Jacob Hawken, Silver Mounted "Plains Rifle," 45 calibre, 28-inch barrel, weight 12 pounds.

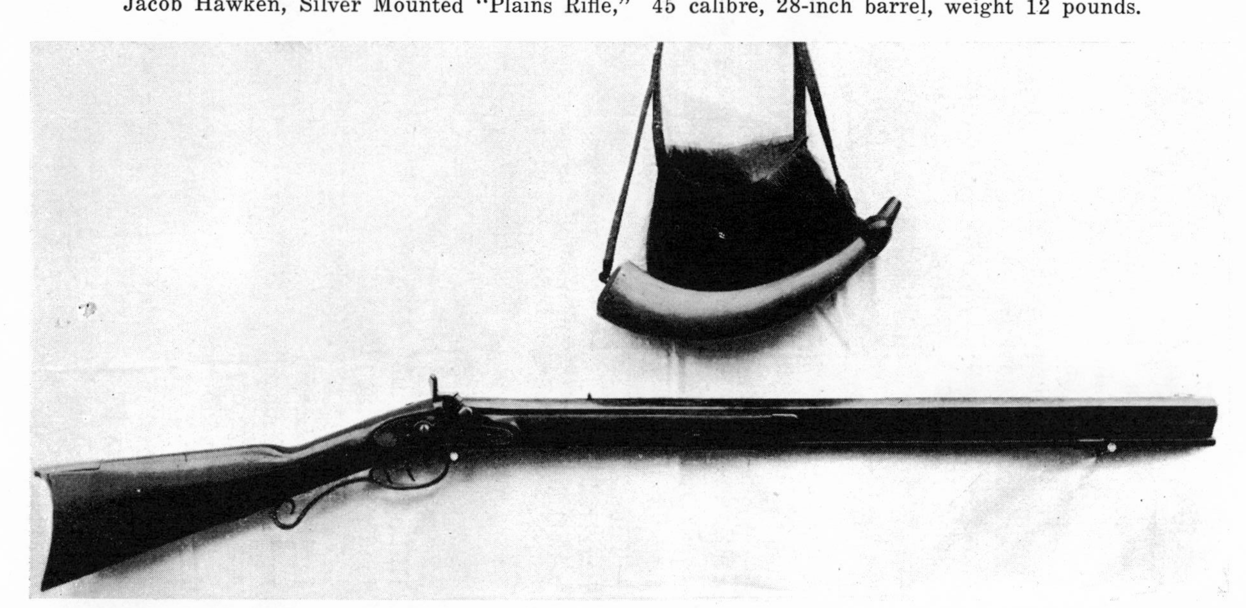

"S. Hawken, St. Louis," Plains Rifle, 45 calibre, 28-inch barrel, weight 10¼ pounds. Old Beaver Skin [illegible] that have seen much use in the old days on the Plains and Rockies.

Samuel Hawken, were of Pennsylvania Dutch ancestry. Jacob Hawken was born in Hagertown, Maryland, in 1786, but it is not known when he moved to Missouri. However, the first St. Louis directory of 1821, lists: "Hawken, Jacob, gunsmith, 214 North Main Street," Samuel was born in Hagerstown, October 26, 1792, came to St. Louis in 1822 and became a partner with Jacob where they made rifles for the old mountain men and trappers for nine or ten years; then the shop was moved to 33 Washington Avenue, St. Louis, where they made rifles until sometime in 1862. The business was then sold to John P. Gemmer, who had been one of the Hawken workmen and knew all about those rifles, who continued making the Hawken type of rifles in St. Louis for fifty-three years, retired from business in 1915 and died sometime in 1919 or 1920.

For more than half a century preceding the Civil War, the Hawken rifle was the most noted, most desirable, and the *best big game, single barrel hunting rifle* in existence. It was *the rifle* among the old mountain men, trappers, explorers, and Indian fighters from the time General Ashley built his first fort on the Yellowstone River to the last days of Kit Carson, at Taos, New Mexico. During all that time, the *Hawken was the one rifle that these men swore by,* and the majority of them would have no other make if it was possible to get a Hawken. The name was frequently misspelled "Hawkins," the mountain men and trappers generally mispronounced it as "Hawkins," but the correct spelling is *Hawken.*

Horace Kephart and I carried on a somewhat interrupted correspondence for some thirty years, from which I know that sometime during the 1890's he purchased from William Albright, of St. Louis, a Hawken rifle that had remained unsold and had never been fired, except when tested by one of the makers.

As the rifle had no maker's name stamped on it,

Mr. Kephart took the rifle to one of the old surviving Hawken's workmen, Charles Siever, to ascertain if it was a genuine Hawken. Quoting from Mr. Kephart's letter: "Siever examined the rifle carefully without comment, then he removed the lock, examined that and then answered: 'Dot iss shenuine Hawken rifle. Py golly, I make dot lock mineself more as forty year ago.' Therefore, it is certain that this rifle is a genuine Hawken."

Mr. Kephart's Hawken rifle was practically 53 calibre, had a 34 inch heavy, full octagon barrel, half stock, with low silver bead front (3/16 inch high) and "buck-horn" rear sights, double set trigger, a light weight stock with the crescent-shaped butt plate and weighed 10½ pounds, most of the weight being in the barrel. The barrel was rifled with a very slow twist, rather shallow grooves, to use a pure lead, round ball weighing 217 grains with a greased linen patch and a charge of about 60 to 200 grains of black powder, and gave nice accuracy with any of these charges at ranges from 50 to 250 yards.

According to the report in the old *Shooting and Fishing* magazine, Mr. Kephart tested this rifle at 200 yards with the 217 grain round ball, fine linen patch greased with vaseline and 41, 82, 123, 164, and 205 grains of F. F. F. g. "Deadshot" powder. That report stated: "With 41 grains of powder there was no perceptible recoil; with 82 grains it was about the same as that of a 32-40 of like weight; with 123 grains it seemed about as heavy as that of a 38-55-330; with the 164 and 205 grains I experienced less shaking up than with a Springfield 45-70-500 fired in the same position. My arm was neither lamed nor discolored. The results satisfied me that a muzzle-loading rifle of 10½ pounds can be fired with a ½ ounce round bullet and all the powder that accuracy will permit, without any recoil that a hunter or soldier would notice. This test gave me the impression that on a calm day I could keep in a 12 inch bull, which is all that I would guarantee to do with any gun fitted with such sights."

In this test Mr. Kephart shot in the off-hand, hip rest position with the butt plate resting against the arm just above the biceps.

Jacob Hawken was the more celebrated rifle-maker of the two, and any plainsman or mountain man who had a rifle made by "Old Man Hawken" or "Jake Hawken," as those men often called him, owned an arm that was as noted in those days as the H. M. Pope, George Schoyen or A. O. Zischang breech-loading, single shot target rifles were in the 1890's or today.

According to records, the famous Kit Carson used a Hawken rifle that at his death was given to the Montezuma Lodge, F. & A. M., of Santa Fe, New Mexico, where it is on exhibition, but this rifle is marked "Samuel Hawken."

Some of the Hawken rifles were not marked, or stamped, with any maker's name; some in the earlier days were made with a full stock clear to the muzzle, but later the fashion changed to the half stock as it was lighter. The majority of these rifles were 36, 34, or 32 round balls to the pound (50, 52, or 53 calibre), but they were also made in 56, 48, and 40 gauges (44, 46, and 48 calibres) for customers who so desired. For ordinary shooting, the customary powder charge was half the weight of the ball, or 108 grains, the recoil with it was unnoticeable and it shot practically "flat" up to 150 yards, while with 164, 180, 200, and 210 grains of powder it would shoot nearly "level sighted" at 200 to 250 yards with *good accuracy* and great killing power. These rifles required no cleaning for an entire day's shooting regardless of the number of shots fired and gave as good accuracy with the last shot as with the second.

The Hawken plains rifle was the *ne-plus-ultra* big game hunting rifle of the West in those days. On another page will be found an illustration of one of these rifles, and an average group that was shot with it.

One of the hunting stories related to me when I was a boy, by William Story, one of the "old settlers," before mentioned, of Dunbarton, New Hampshire, is quoted below from the notes I made at that time: "My other gun thar in the corner is a 'smooth-bore rifle,' 36 to the pound, made by John Butler, of Lancaster, Pennsylvany, was a flint-lock when fust made but I hed her changed to a cap lock afore the Mexican War, because the cap is surer fire than a flint. She shoots good with a round ball an greased patch, or with buck shot or small shot. When a feller hez to shoot nigh dark or in a hurry he hez a better chance to hit with ther smooth-bore loaded with buck shot than with a rifle that hez but one ball.

"One day when I was a young feller an we was bout outer deer meat, I tuck 'ole Betsey' (his smooth-bore) one arternoon an went out to shoot a deer at a place whar they hed been workin. When I got to that place thar want no deer an I set out to another place whar I knowed thar was some a few days afore. Wal, when I got to that place I seed a passel o deer an shot three; then I went to work a dressin an hangin them up high enuf in a tree so that ther wolves couldn't git em. I took two o ther hams and some meat wropped up in a deer hide an struck out fer home just as it war gettin dark. Wal, I hedn't gone fur when I heared some wolves a howling back whar I hed killed my deer, an purty soon I heared them cusses a follerin arter me. It was a gettin dark by that time an I hurred along best I could, but I soon seed it wan't no use an them cussed wolves would soon ketch up to me. I hed to do somthin purty quick, an I knowed a little gully with high sides whar them wolves would pass thru an I could git up on the top an shoot them when they come along thar. By that time I was a runnin to keep ahead o ther cusses an I run thru the gully, got up on the high side that hed a purty high ledge on top, with ole Betsey ready to shoot the fust wolf that come into it. Bout that time the fust wolves got there an I let drive with my gun an killed two o the cusses. Then I hurried to load my gun agin an got her loaded an shot two more wolves that time. Then I hurried to load her up agin an when I felt in my huntin bag for a cap thar wan't none left. I must a spilled them when I was a running. Now this was a purty fix; them wolves was a comin closter an it was so dark bout all I could see was their eyes an their white teeth. Wal, I knowed the only thing to do was to git up a tree, so I picked out a good tall chestnut an clum up about 30 foot. I hed to leave ole Betsey down on the ground as I couldn't git up that tree with her an the deer meat. Bout as soon as I got up that tree to a big limb them cusses was all round that tree a jumpin up an a howlin because they smelled that meat; but I wasn't agoin to let them devils get that meat, no, sir-ee.

"Wal, I tied myself to the trunk o the tree with a piece of rope I hed in my pocket so as not to fall off if I fell asleep in the nite, an them cussed wolves staid round that tree all nite a lookin at me an a howlin. I wish't I had my gun an some caps up thar in that tree so I could a shot some more o those critters, but I couldn't do nothin only set up in that tree till mornin when the cussed wolves would go away an I could come down an go home. Them wolves just staid round that tree all nite an didn't go away till long arter sun-up. Then when I was sure them cusses was all gone, I come down that tree an I was purty stiff an cold arter a settin up thar on that limb all nite. But I purty soon get limbered up an hurried along towards home, when arter a ways I seed two o my neighbors with their guns a comin out to hunt me up. Wal, I hedn't had nothin to eat since dinner the day afore, so we kindled a fire an cooked some deer meat an et it. Then we went back to the place whar I had killed the deer an hung em up: we took em down an cut em up, an packed the meat in the deer hides, tuck em on our backs an struck out fer home. My wife was purty glad to see me again, an arter that I seed that I didn't git caught out a huntin arter dark an that I had plenty o gun caps with me whar they wouldn't git spilled or lost when I was a runnin."

When I asked, "About what year was that?" Mr. Story thought a moment and said: "Bout the fall o 1850, I guess."

Mr. Story was 80 odd years old when he related this to me and might have been wrong about the date of this experience, as his memory was, of course, failing somewhat. He was a great hunter, a skilled marksman with the rifle, and had many thrilling experiences during his younger days.

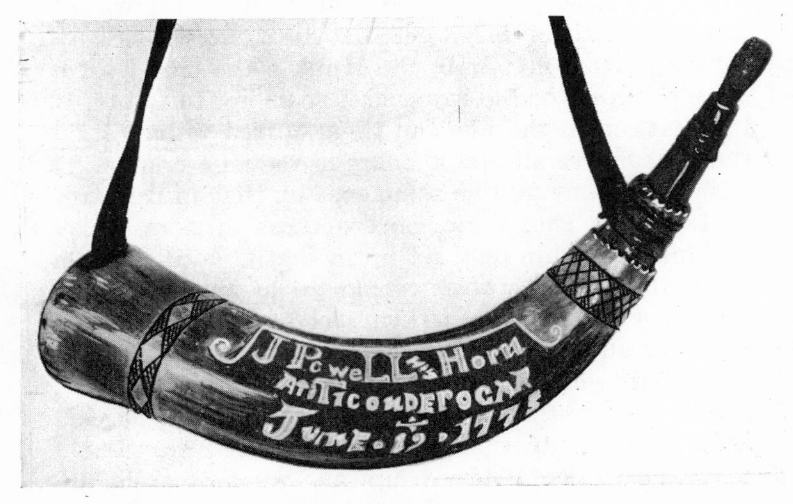

Powder-Horn used by Continental Ranger at Fort Ticonderoga, N. Y.
Owned by W. T. Brodeur.

CHAPTER VIII

TOOLS USED BY THE OLD-TIME RIFLE-MAKERS

The old-time rifle-makers were, unquestionably, very ingenious indeed, and the work they did was really remarkable, considering the crude tools which they had to work with and the fact that they were obliged to make all these tools themselves. I believe it is a fact which cannot be disproved, that a present-day mechanic having been educated in our schools and colleges today, would be absolutely unable to make a rifle or shotgun with only the very few tools that the old-time riflesmiths had. Even with his superior education, he would be unable to make the necessary tools for making such an arm.

For instance, what would a modern mechanic, or machinist, do without a micrometer caliper? Yet the early rifle-makers up to about 1850, when the micrometer caliper was invented, managed to make many very accurate shooting flint-lock and cap lock rifles without any micrometer. Also, it is well known that the early German, Swiss and Pennsylvania Dutch riflesmiths back in the early 1700's did not have a lathe with which they could turn a piece of iron, cut a thread or drill a hole, or do any of the hundred-and-one operations that are done with the lathe by rifle-makers today. Yet in spite of these handicaps, they managed to make every part of a rifle—barrel, lock, sights, stock—assemble these together and thus turn out the completed rifle which gave the finest accuracy with the round ball that had ever been produced until about 1835.

Referring again to Horace Warner, who when he was a young man living in the wilderness of Ridgeway, Pennsylvania, having no tools except a draw-

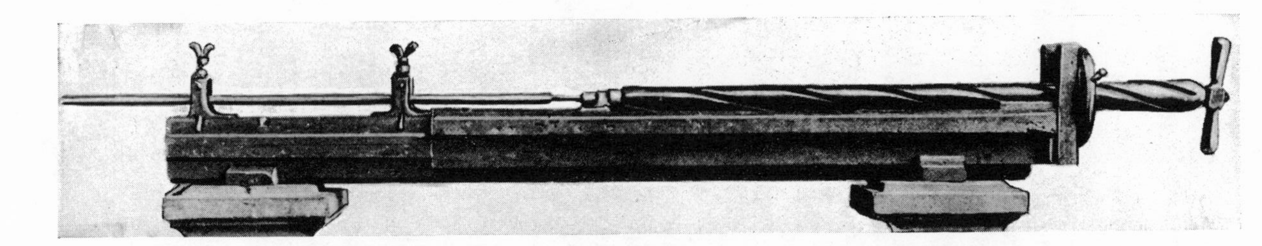

A Fine Rifling Guide and Bench used in Virginia in 1800. Reproduced from "The Kentucky Rifle" by Permission of the Author.

knife, pocket-knife, a few chisels and files, but not even a vice, made the necessary tools and substitute for a vice in which he fastened his old, rusty rifle barrel and proceeded to "freshen her out" so that it thereafter shot much more accurately and loaded easier. Just show us the town or city-bred young man, with his boasted modern education, who could do that "stunt" today. That certainly required genuine ingenuity, patience and determination.

Norman S. Brockway told me that he made the great majority of the tools that he used during the years in which he made those *super-accurate* muzzle-loading rifles for which he was noted. With the early riflesmith and the pioneer, necessity was the mother of invention. If he needed a cabin in which to shelter his family and himself, he made this from the trees in the forest with his ax, saw, possibly an adz, and an auger. When the cabin was finished, he made the necessary tables, chairs and other furniture; all by the use of these few tools. When he needed a plow or a cart, he went to work and made it—all with the half-dozen crude tools that he had.

Many of these pioneers, when their rifle became "shot out," made the necessary tools for use in "freshening it out," or even re-cutting it. In the latter case this necessitated making first a rifling guide and bench, unless he was able to borrow a rifle barrel to serve as a guide for rotating the saw, or cutter, with which he re-rifled his own rifle and sometimes those for his neighbors.

A description of the simplest kind of wooden rifling guide is given in chapter I, and an illustration, copied from *The Kentucky Rifle* by permission of the author, shows one of these home-made wooden rifling guides with which John Selvidge, of Bradley County, Tennessee, rifled hundreds of arms in 1795 and along in the 1800's. Another illustration, copied from this same book by Captain Dillin's permission, shows a rifling guide and bench constructed entirely from bronze and iron. With this simple type of rifling guide it was, of course, impossible to cut more than one pitch of rifling with the same guide. Therefore, it was necessary for the riflesmith to make as many different rolls, each having a different pitch of rifling, as was needed for cutting barrels with different twists of rifling that he used in making his arms.

The barrels for the flint-lock rifles, as well as those for the early cap lock arms, were made by welding short strips of iron around a "core rod," as described in the first chapter, and repeating this process until an iron tube, or barrel, of the desired length had been formed. That having been completed, the next step in making the barrel was the boring operation; which was done with the "short bit." This bit has a short piece of the end left square, not twisted, so that it will follow the hole in the welded barrel without running off, in order to enable the riflesmith to bore from both ends of the barrel with the certainty that the two holes would meet exactly in the middle of the barrel. In this way the barrel was "first bored," or "rough bored," for its entire length, after which it was smooth reamed with the "long bit" having a hickory guard on the off side of the cutting edge to prevent the borings, or chips, from scratching the bore. The long bit was rotated by the hand-operated boring machine while the barrel, sliding in a fixture on the bench, was fed by hand from the breech end onto the bit and thus smooth reamed for its entire length. The barrel was next straightened, as described in the first chapter, and was then ready for shaping the outside. Wooden plugs were fitted in each end of the barrel which was taken to the grindstone and fastened into a frame so adjusted that the center of the barrel would come within one-half of its desired diameter against the stone. The barrel was worked back and forth against the grindstone until the octagon flat had been ground its entire length and the right width. Then the barrel was turned to the next octagon, ground in the same way and so continued until all eight flats had been ground.

The barrel was next taken to the rifling bench, clamped in two fixtures for holding it with the bore in line with the rifling rod; the hickory rifling rod with the "saw," or cutter, set into it at one end while the other end was attached to a steel rod the length of the barrel was clamped into the rifling guide. The cutter was kept well oiled, pushed back and forth by means of the rifling guide, the grooves of which sliding through the dialed head-piece was revolved thus rotating the rifling rod in the bore and cut one groove at a time. When one groove had in this way been cut until the saw no longer cut, the dial was turned one notch and another groove cut in this same way. This was repeated until all seven or eight grooves had been cut. The saw was then taken out of its bed and elevated by placing a piece of paper under it, again inserted in a groove in the barrel and this work repeated over and over until all the grooves were as deep as desired. I am told that with good smooth-grained iron and a sharp cutter, a barrel can be rifled in this way in about two or two and a half hours.

After the barrel was rifled it was leaded, or "lapped," with a lead plug charged with emery powder, as described in chapter I, until the burrs left by the rifling cutter were smoothed off, the bore polished and given its finished diameter and shape. Browning the barrel, stocking the arm, fitting the lock, mountings and sights came next in the order mentioned; then the rifle was ready for range tests by firing at a mark to ascertain whether or not it gave

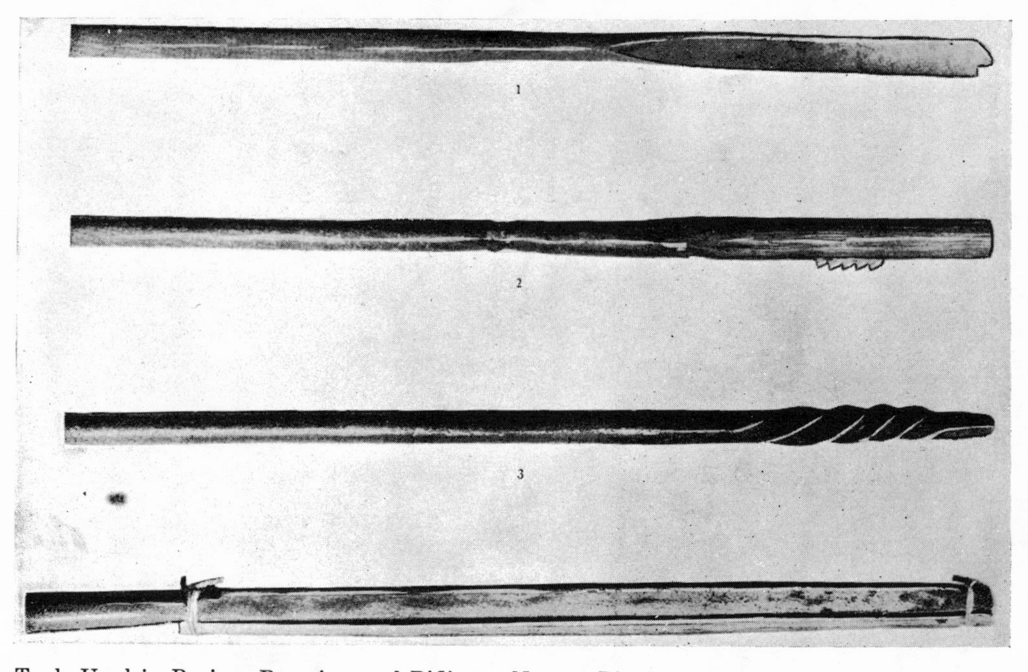

Tools Used in Boring, Reaming and Rifling. No. 1, Bit for boring channel for ramrod. No. 2, Rifling Rod with Saw set in hickory rod. No. 3, Short Bit for rough boring the barrel. No. 4, Long Bit for smooth boring the barrel. Has hickory guard on off side of cutting edge to prevent borings from scratching the bore. Reproduced from "The Kentucky Rifle," by Permission of the Author.

the desired degree of accuracy. If it did not show satisfactory accuracy, the barrel was "worked over," with the leading bolt on the leading rod and in this way was generally made to shoot accurately. Sometimes it happened that the rifle could not be made to shoot accurately; then the barrel was discarded and a new one made, although this seldom occurred if the smooth reaming and the rifling had been correctly performed.

Illustrations herewith show the short bit, the long bit, rifling rod and saw, or cutter, copied from *The Kentucky Rifle,* by permission of the author.

Very few tools were used by the old riflesmiths in making the stock for the rifle, inletting the lock, trigger and guard and fitting the mountings. Planes, draw-knives, chisels and gouges, a few bits and drills, several rasps and files, saws, the pocket-knife and a small ax, were the principal tools used by these men. It is surprising how much of the "roughing out" of the stock some of these old-time stockers could do with the hand ax, or hatchet as some call it. More than fifty years ago I knew an old gunsmith and rifle-maker, H. W. Jackson, who was then more than seventy years old, and I often spent a day in the shop watching him work on repairing, re-cutting, rifling a barrel, or stocking a rifle. I made notes of his methods at the time and still have these. The first time I saw him attack a fine-grained piece of tiger-flame maple plank from which he made a stock for a muzzle-loading rifle, I almost held my breath as he made the chips fly with a small ax. I half expected to see him strike into a cross-grained spot and ruin the stock; but nothing of the kind happened and soon he had it hewed out to a point where it looked much like a rough turned stock as it came from the old Blanchard stock turning lathe years ago. Jackson then remarked; "Thar, that is

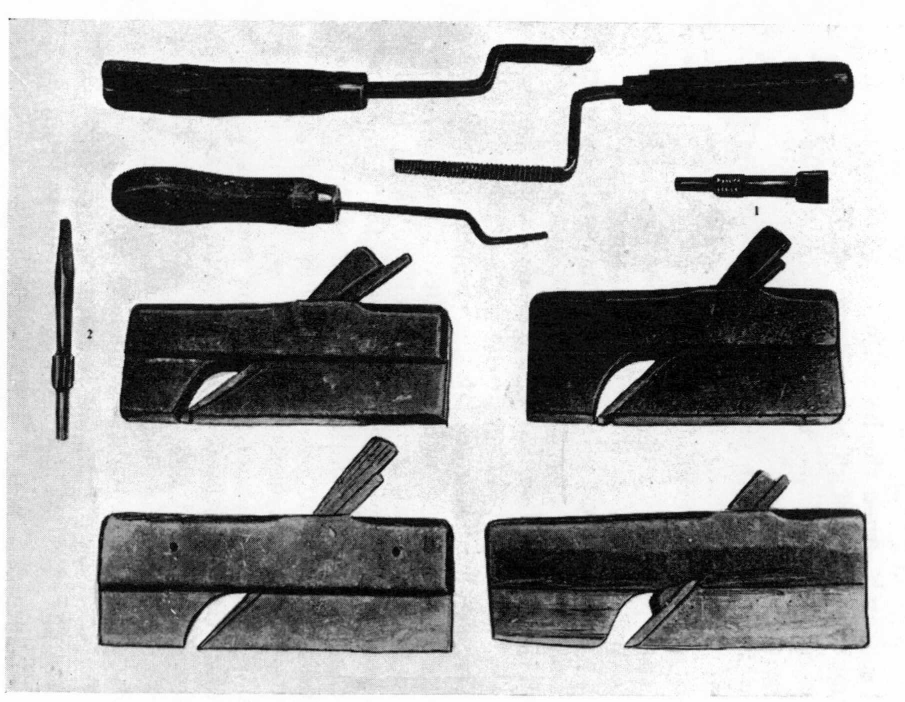

Tools Used by the Old Riflesmiths. Were used by John Selvidge, Bradley County, Tenn. No. 1, is tool for threading the barrel for breech plug. No. 2, Reamer for preparing the breech for threading with No. 1. Others are hand-made planes, gouge, chisel and rasp used in making stocks. Reproduced from "The Kentucky Rifle," by Permission of the Author.

about all I can do with the hand-ax; now I'll fit in the barrl."

Fastening the rough stock in a vice, he planed the top smooth and straight from the small of the stock to the muzzle, then he laid out a center line from the butt to the end of the full length stock, scratching this quite deep with a scratch-awl. Then, with different sized chisels, the octagon barrel was inletted, the channel for the octagon flats was smoothed with a plane, rasps, files and sandpaper. He next screwed in the breech-plug and nipple, and with small chisels, a pocket-knife, files and drills, the breech-plug and the upper tang was fitted nicely into place. The lock was next in a similar way, set into its place, the set trigger properly fitted into the wood and the trigger guard likewise fitted. That having been completed to his satisfaction, he worked down to size and shape the outside of the long forearm and stock, using planes, rasps, files, pieces of glass as scrapers, and lastly sandpaper of different grades.

The last work that Mr. Jackson performed on the stock that day was to wet the outside of the stock and forearm thoroughly with water, dry it quickly over his forge, then rub it down with fine sandpaper to "take the whiskers off," as he said. This was repeated half a dozen times or more until the stock had a fine velvety smoothness when he remarked: "Thar, she's as smooth as a gal's leg; I'll ile her and leave till to-morrer." A heavy coat of raw linseed oil was given the stock, after first giving it several coats of a mixture of about 1/3 turpentine and 2/3 raw linseed oil which dried in quite rapidly and filled the pores of the wood before applying the heavy linseed oil. The stock was then hung up to dry until the next day when he would rub it down, apply more linseed oil, allow it to dry and rub it down again, and repeat this process until he had secured the desired polish.

Cherries used by N. S. Brockway in cutting Bullet Moulds. All were Hand-Made by himself.

I often spent the entire day from soon after breakfast until nearly dark, watching Jackson at work, observing the way in which he performed the different operations, talking rifles and rifle shooting with him, etc., made notes of all this in my note book and I have always remembered those days as very interesting ones as well as days in which I learned a lot that I could not have gotten from any books.

After the barrel had been completed, browned, the stock fitted, lock and trigger set in place, the patch-box made and set into the stock as well as any silver or other metal ornamental inlays properly inletted, and while the stock was being oiled and rubbed down, the riflesmith usually made and fitted the sights. The slots near the muzzle and at the proper distance from the break-off were cut with three-cornered files; then a low, flat-topped rear sight with V notch, or other desired shaped notch, was filed out of a piece of soft iron. But the notch in the rear sight was purposely left a trifle too shallow so that it could be filed down to the right degree in order to "shoot center" when the rifle was tested at the target. If the arm was a hunting rifle, the low "barleycorn," or "knife-blade," front sight was carefully filed out of a piece of soft iron and blued, or filed from a piece of brass or silver, according to the customer's order. As before stated, the front sight for the hunting rifle was always a very low one—seldom over 3/16 inch and often but ⅛ inch—and the majority of these were the barleycorn shape, as that appears to have been the most popular in the early times. The method of making and attaching the sights for the target rifle is given in detail in chapter II. The barrel was fastened in a vice, the breech-plug removed, and by sighting through the bore the barrel was aligned on a black spot painted on the wall at the far end of the shop. Then the rear sight was carefully driven into the barrel slot, using a hardwood, or brass, drift to prevent battering it, until it was in the center of the barrel. The front sight was next driven into the front sight slot, using the drift to prevent battering the base, until the two sights were correctly aligned on the spot on the wall; thus the rifle was "bore sighted," or the sights correctly aligned latterally, ready for shooting at a mark after the stock was finished and dried.

When the stock was ready for use, the rifle was assembled, a bench with a sand-bag as a rest for the forearm was arranged from which the riflesmith fired at a target, or mark, placed at 100 or 110 yards—usually—in order to enable him to file down the notch in the rear sight until the balls were well centered in the bull's-eye, and the front sight correctly adjusted latterally by tapping it to the right or left as required in order to center the point of impact of the balls, or bullets.

Cherries of various sizes and shapes were hand-made by the riflesmith, being turned in the lathe to nearly the desired shape, then filed or ground to the exact shape and diameter, making proper allowance for shrinking in hardening. They were then hardened and the cutting edges honed sharp, when they were ready for use in cutting the mould; which was often made from bronze instead of iron as that was easier to work, generally cast a better bullet as the bronze cut smoother and does not rust if neglected. However, some of the riflesmiths always made their bullet moulds from iron, and all these early, or older, moulds had plier-shaped iron handles which were mighty uncomfortable to work with, as I know from experience. Why they did not put wooden handles on these has always been a mystery to me.

Even as late as 1836 when the Colt revolver was placed on the market, practically all the bullet moulds were still made with iron handles, but a few years later, or before 1840, many of the rifle-makers improved their moulds by fitting them with wooden handles, which certainly was a distinct improvement and enabled the rifleman to cast bullets more rapidly and comfortably. After about 1840 all moulds were made with comfortable wooden handles, all makers had adopted some form of a cut-off for their moulds and various improved models, including moulds for casting the parts of the two-piece, composite, bullets for the target rifles, fitted with wooden handles, were furishe by the rifle-makers.

Back in the early days, the late 1700's and early 1800's, the great majority of the rifle-makers did not have a lathe, but by about 1820 the makers of the higher grades of rifles used lathes having a treadle and operated by foot-power—like the early sewing machines. Of course, the larger firms of rifle-makers having small factories with steam or water power for operating their machines, operated their lathes and other machines then in use, by power. Even as late as 1887, that noted rifle-maker Harry M. Pope, made the first Pope barrel on a lathe operated by foot power, according to his own statements. When I was a boy the majority of the small rifle-makers and gunsmiths used foot operated lathes as their shops were not equipped with power.

The early riflesmiths in the days before the Revolutionary War drilled the holes in metal parts with the hand-drill or the bow-drill, but after the breast-drill came on the market this was used in drilling these holes. Later, probably about 1825, larger upright drills attached to a timber supporting the roof of the shop, operated by a crank turned by hand, were used for drilling the holes in all metal parts by the small rifle-maker. Of course the small factories that made rifles had upright drills of large size operated by steam or water power, but this chapter deals only with the individual rifle-maker who made arms only in a small way—the "custom rifle-maker" as they are called today.

Even as late as 1860, the really skillful rifle-maker was obliged to know how to make most of the tools that he used in his work, and when I was a boy old men told me that they were required to learn, during their apprenticeship, how to make these tools, and they actually made many of their saws and hack-saws by filing the teeth in the edge of sheet steel of the desired thickness, tempering these and then "setting the teeth" and filing them sharp so as to cut properly. As late as during my boyhood days, I was taught to properly set and file a saw, and any man who called himself a carpenter who could not set and file his own saws would have been the laughing stock of the community.

The old-time rifle-maker with his ingenuity and skill, his old, hand-made tools, and his methods and workmanship, are gone from most parts of this country, and today one must go far back into the mountain sections or the rural districts far back from towns in order to find even an old-time, "honest to God" carpenter. Even the old blacksmiths have gone from most of our country, their descendants have largely read Sears, Roebuck & Company's catalog, bought a few modern automobile mechanics tools and the blacksmith shop is now a "garage", where you get your Ford, or what-have-you, automobile repaired, ? your tires inflated, wheels changed, etc. The present day boy who wants a bit, drill, saw, or other small tool buys it at the "10 cent store", and when this tool is too dull for further use he pays some one to sharpen it, or throws it away and buys a new one for another dime that "dad" gives him.

I half expect that in a few years we shall see "Woolworth's 5 and 10 Cent Stores" selling the cheap 22 calibre rifles at "cut rates."

We surely shall if Mosberg, Stevens, Savage, Remington, Winchester, Marlin and other great arms manufacturers continue bringing out new and cheaper 22 calibre rifles. Then the riflesmiths will disappear, as if anything goes wrong with this rifle it will be thrown away and the owner will buy a new one at the same store for about "$1.98 marked down from $4.63." However, the anti-gun laws enacted by the anti-gun cranks will have taken away even your muzzle-loaders and your 22 calibre rifles in another decade, and then there will be no need of gunsmiths or gunmaker's tools.

CHAPTER IX

SOME NOTED MAKERS OF MUZZLE-LOADING RIFLES AND THEIR RIFLES

WILLIAM BILLINGHURST

"Wm. Billinghurst, Rochester, N. Y.," as was stamped on the barrels of his rifles, was undoubtedly the most widely known and one of the most skillful of the old-time rifle-makers. According to the records that I have found, he was born in Monroe County, New York, in 1807, but we do not know in what town; he died in Rochester, N. Y., on March 4, 1880.

Very little information is obtainable in Rochester or vicinity about Billinghurst, in spite of the fact that he was in business there as a rifle-maker for more than 40 years. It appears that he came to that city sometime in 1838. The oldest Rochester City Directory in the Rochester Public Library is dated 1841, and in that we find: "William Billinghurst, gunsmith and rifle-maker, 43 Main Street." In that directory for 1853, we find the following advertisement: "William Billinghurst, Main Street, Rochester, New York. The subscriber is largely engaged in the manufacture of Rifles on the most improved principles with which few are practically acquainted. Rifles, Target Rifles, Repeating Rifles, or Seven-Shooters, Double Barreled Rifles, One-Above-the Other, Rifle and Shot, Double Barreled Guns, Telescopic Sights for Rifles made to order. Repairing of all kinds done to order."

During the years that Billinghurst was in business as a rifle-maker, he designed, or invented, several different types of rifles among which we find the "Seven-Shooters," which were first made in the pill-lock ignition type and later changed to the cap-lock.

From the *Rochester Daily Democrat* of August 10,

1852, I quote the following: "'A Revolving Rifle.' Yesterday we were shown a revolving rifle made by Mr. William Billinghurst, a veteran gun manufacturer whose fame is only hindered by a modesty which equals his genius. The complete and beautiful firearm is constructed upon a principle long well known here. A cylinder about 4 inches long contains 7 barrels which receive the charge through the long barrel like other guns, the cylinder being turned, by hand, as each charge is deposited. When loaded and primed the gun may be carried safely for any length of time and the charge will not suffer from dampness even if exposed to rain or thrown into the water. The whole 7 can be fired in 1/4 of a minute by an expert shot. Attached to the gun below the rifle barrel is another barrel for shot, which extends to the breech through the cylinder and is entirely disconnected. It operates separately and may be fired at the same time as the rifle or afterwards. Such guns, excepting the shotgun part, are not very novel in this region where Mr. Billinghurst has made them for some time. This rifle was patented by Mr. Miller, the inventor, but the patent expired and the patentee dying, it was not renewed. The principle was subsequently adopted by Colt and others in making revolving pistols and rifles."

On another page is shown an illustration of this Billinghurst "Seven-Shooter." From the foregoing report it appears that Mr. Miller (whose first name I was unable to learn) invented the revolving rifle some years before Colonel Samuel Colt invented his revolver and that Mr. Miller had taken out a patent on his invention at that time. However, when Mr. Miller died his heirs did not renew the patent, which allowed any one to adopt as much of Miller's invention as desired.

It is very doubtful if any of the other old-time makers of muzzle-loading rifles were so noted that their fame as rifle-makers extended to foreign coun-

Billinghurst 42 calibre Target Rifle, 30-inch barrel, weight 14 pounds. From Frank K. Lucas' Collection.

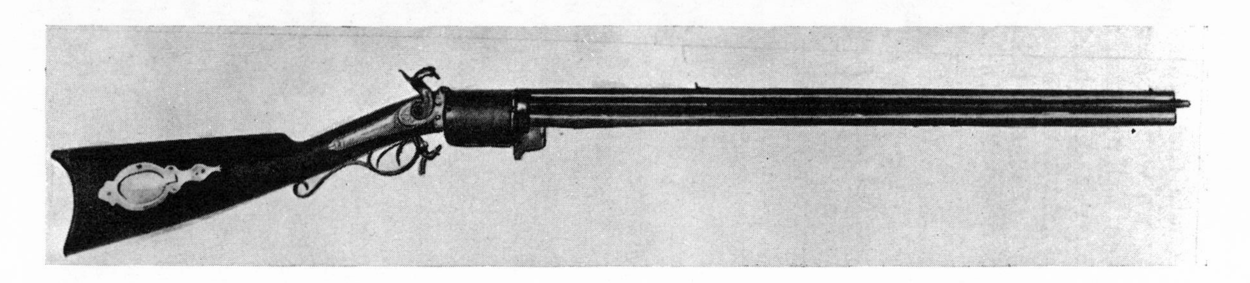

Wm. Billinghurst, Pill Lock, 7-shot Rifle, 40 calibre round ball, with 14 gauge shot barrel underneath, as mentioned on preceding pages. Made later in Cap Lock Model. From W. A. Luce Collection.

tries, as was the case with William Billinghurst. Records have been found which show that he received orders for rifles from titled noblemen and others in Brazil, India, Scotland, England, France and Norway. Therefore it will be seen that his reputation as a most skillful rifle-maker was widely known. I believe it is a fact which cannot be disputed that our other noted rifle-makers, Horace Warner, Nelson Lewis, Morgan James, H. V. Perry, N. S. Brockway, Edwin Wesson, nor any of our other well-known makers of muzzle-loading rifles, never received orders from abroad as their reputation did not extend to foreign countries; while Billinghurst's reputation brought him many orders from abroad, as will be seen by the following report that I copied from the *Rochester Daily Democrat* issue of August 2, 1841.

"William Billinghurst of this city has received an order from Don Pedro d' Alcantara, the Young Emperor of Brazil, to make a rifle for him. Mr. Billinghurst is regarded as one of the best rifle-smiths in this country and will, we doubt not, execute the order as satisfactorily to the Emperor as creditably to himself. The rifle will probably be finished in about 3 months and will cost $400.00."

Also from the *Rochester Daily Democrat* issue of August 22, 1843, I quote the following: "Our friend, William Billinghurst, who made a repeating rifle for the Emperor of Brazil a year or two ago, has just completed one for the Maharaja of Bombay, India. It is designed for the demolition of Tigers, and carried but 16 balls to a pound, probably the largest ever made in this city. It is a beautiful piece of workmanship with remarkable engraving; and it is highly creditable to Mr. Billinghurst and this city that orders for work of this description should be received from so great a distance."

In this same paper a few months later, I found a

short report to the effect that this large bore rifle that Billinghurst made for the Maharaja of Bombay was so satisfactory and pleased his highness so much that Maharajas of two other provinces of India had commissioned Mr. Billinghurst to make rifles for each of them. In later issues of the Rochester daily papers I found reports that Billinghurst had received orders for double barreled rifles, single shot rifles, and repeating rifles from titled noblemen and emenient sportsmen in the other countries mentioned.

There is no question that Billinghurst was a very skillful rifle-maker. His rifles were generally stocked with better wood and better finished than most of our other famous makers with which I am familiar. I have frequently heard it said that Billinghurst never made rifles with the gain twist but always used the uniform twist. However, I know that this is not correct as I, myself, have owned one Billinghurst target rifle and one of his hunting and target rifles that were both cut with the gain twist. Also, more than 50 years ago my Uncle Alvaro had Billinghurst make for him a double barreled, 45 calibre rifle that was cut with the gain twist. It is true that the majority of his rifles were cut with the uniform twist, but as he was a great experimenter, he, of course, tested out various twists and methods of rifling during these experiments, and made rifles with either the gain twist or the uniform twist as desired by his customers.

Some of the finest, most accurate, medium weight and heavy target rifles that I have ever seen or used were made by William Billinghurst. Illustrations herewith show several of his rifles and groups that were shot with them.

A diligent search in Rochester and vicinity failed to locate a photograph, or picture, of Mr. Billinghurst; I, myself, have never seen a picture of him during the years past and it is very doubtful if there is any photograph of him in existence.

NELSON LEWIS

Nelson Lewis, rifle-maker of Troy, New York, was one of our well-known makers of muzzle-loading hunting rifles, single shot hunting rifles, double barrel rifles, double barreled rifles having the barrels superposed, "combination" guns having a rifle barrel and a shot barrel side by side, as well as light weight, medium, and heavy weight target rifles of various calibres. I think it is undoubtedly true that Lewis made a greater number of rifles than any of our other noted rifle makers, with the exception of William Billinghurst. According to Mr. Fred L. P. Mills of Deerfield, Massachusetts, Nelson Lewis was born in 1811 near Speigletown, New York, a few miles north of Troy. As a young man he followed market hunting—then a legitimate business and highly remunerative if a man was a good hunter and a good shot; and Lewis possessed both of these qualifications.

The business of hunting took him to the shop of J. M. Caswell, in Lansingburg, New York, who was a skillful gunsmith and made both rifles and smooth-bore arms for the Militia that was then being organized around Troy and the members of which had to furnish their own arms. Lewis, being fond of guns and of a mechanical type of mind, decided to quit market hunting and learn the gun-making business, apprenticed himself to Caswell and did the stocking for him for a year or so. He was naturally a keen observer and in that way learned a lot about making rifles and guns during his apprenticeship, so that in 1843 he commenced business for himself in a shop on the corner of Congress and Church Streets, Troy, New York, where he made rifles, guns and pistols for more than 40 years.

During the time that Lewis' shop was located here a number of empty powder kegs lined the sidewalk as seats for his customers and a wooden gun 12 feet long hung from iron brackets over the sidewalk as his only sign. The front part of the building was used by Lewis as a store where guns, rifles, ammunition, etc., were displayed, and the back part was equipped with tools and the few machines of those days as the shop in which Lewis made his rifles and other arms, made repairs, etc. On the wall back of the counters were displayed record targets and groups that were shot by Lewis in matches, or in testing his rifles, or by members of the National Rifle Club of which Lewis was a member.

Lewis, like all the old-time gun makers, had a surprisingly small number of machines in his shop as the major part of the work in making a gun or rifle was done by hand. A boring machine for smoothing or reaming the bore of the barrels and a "rifling bench" with "rifling guide" were practically all the machines found in these old rifle-makers shops in those times. Lewis bought his barrel blanks from E. Remington & Son, using the cast steel for rifle-barrels, which he smooth-reamed inside, rifled, finished, fitted the lock and stocked in an excellent manner.

Lewis always cut his rifle barrels with a gain twist and absolutely refused to accept an order for a rifle to be made with the uniform twist. His "standard" type of rifling was equal width of grooves and lands and both cut with square corners.

I have examined several Lewis rifles that were rifled with quite wide grooves and narrow lands, but these are exceptions—not his regular standard rifling. If the rifle was a target arm with false muzzle, Lewis ordered the blank to be sent from the Remington factory with the pins fitted before it was sent to him and thus, in his case, the nice snug fitting pins that hold the false muzzle in place were fitted by E. Remington & Sons—not by Lewis. Lewis did not even have a lathe in his shop, but all such work as making bullet swages, bullet starters, threading the patent breech, and end of barrel was done by "Bill" Hart in his machine shop which was near Lewis' shop.

The fine engraving that is seen on Lewis rifles was done by John Wolfe, a German, who worked for Lewis and was his only employee except his son Kilby. The majority of the stocking was done by Kilby, and all this very fine fitting of the stock to the break-off, letting in the lock, trigger guard, patch-box and all ornamental inlays were his work—all done with the chisel or carving tool by hand. Most of the Lewis rifles are cut with 6 grooves and lands but occasionally we find one with 8. During the 1870's, Lewis worked considerably in developing "long range" rifles for target work at ranges over 100 rods—550 yards—in his endeavors to provide rifles that would give better accuracy than the Sharps and Ballard breech-loading, single shot rifles that were then so popular. However, we can find no record that he ever produced a rifle that was as accurate at 800, 900 and 1000 yards as the Sharps and Ballard long range rifles.

Lewis was very particular in the rifling and accurately fitting the bullet to the bore of his rifles, and never let a rifle go out of his shop until he, himself, had developed an accurate load for it by range tests. If he could not make the rifle shoot very accurately, he "worked it over," or even partly re-rifled it and in this way made it shoot as accurately as desired. If this could not be done, he made a new barrel that was *right* and never let an inferior shooting rifle go out of his shop.

Mr. Floyd R. Butler, of Raceville, New York, has a larger number of fine N. Lewis target rifles, hunting and target rifles, double barreled rifles and "combination" rifle and shotgun, of various calibres, than any other person with whom I am acquainted. In the tests that he and I have made with these rifles we found them to be exceptionally accurate at ranges including

40 rods. The Lewis best grade, heavy target rifles are regarded as being as accurate as those made by N. S. Brockway, Horace Warner, Wm. Billinghurst, or any of the other makers of super-accurate muzzle-loading target rifles. Illustrations showing several types of rifles made by N. Lewis, as well as groups shot with these at various ranges are given herein.

A long search in Troy and vicinity failed to locate any photograph, or picture, of Nelson Lewis; I was unable to find any person who had ever seen a picture of him and we do not believe there is one in existence.

NORMAN S. BROCKWAY

We find today many experienced users of muzzle-loading rifles who regard Norman S. Brockway as the most remarkable rifle-maker of his time, they consider him as having been fully as noted in his day as Harry M. Pope was from the 1880's to about 1900, and still is today. It so happened that about a week before Mr. Brockway's death, I had the pleasure of spending several hours with him talking rifles and rifle shooting; I was the last person outside of his immediate family that he was able to see and talk with for any length of time, and from the notes that I made at that time, I submit the following sketch of his life and career as unquestionably one of the most noted makers of the *most accurate shooting rifles* of this kind that have ever been made in this country.

Mr. Brockway was born in South Charlestown, New Hampshire, on March 13, 1841, and his family moved to Bellows Falls, Vermont, in 1844, where he grew to manhood. When the Civil War broke out he went to Springfield Armory where he worked as a filer on mainsprings at first. At that time the Armory employed three hundred forty-nine filers in making the various parts for the old Springfield rifled musket, as it was called. After a few months he was ill and obliged to stop work for a time, but on his return he was put to work on the two-leaf rear sight for that arm, and continued on that work until February 1864, when he went to work for the Norwich Arms Company, of Norwich, Connecticut, which had a Government contract for making rifles, and Brockway was placed in charge of the mainspring work. His father was also employed by this same firm and worked principally on stocking these arms.

In March 1865, Brockway was engaged by Smith & Wesson, as the operator of a turret lathe in cutting out the steel blanks for revolver cylinders, where he worked when President Lincoln was assassinated. He said the shop and all business was closed the next day and there was great excitement in that city.

In May 1866, Brockway went to Bellows Falls, Vermont, to help his father build his house, and when that was finished he built his own shop and nearly all his tools. He said: "I even built my own engine as I wanted a small one with more horse-power than was then regularly made and I knew that I could make this engine for about one-quarter of what it would cost to buy it." When I asked if he also built his own boiler, he answered: "No, I bought one that had been used a little and re-built it so that it was better than when new." He commenced the rifle-making business on the first of May 1867, and specialized on heavy muzzle-loading target rifles with the false muzzle, bullet starter, bullet moulds, swage and all the other accessories that were required with such rifles. He made all his own tools for making these rifles as well as for making the telescopes that he made in later years.

He told me that he made all his barrels from "the best English cast steel, when I could get that, or from cast steel that I bought from E. Remington & Sons when I could not get the English steel," quoting his words. Again quoting Brockway's words: "I bored all my barrels with a regular twist drill as they did not have the barrel drilling machines then that we have now. I welded a twist drill to a shank, the breech end of the barrel was held in the lathe chuck, the muzzle end supported by a steady rest, the drill was run through a lignumvitae steadying block held in the tool post, and was fed by the tail stock of the lathe. I made a tool somewhat like a pair of wooden pliers that was clamped around the shank of the drill to prevent it from turning, but if it got jammed it was instantly released and turned with the barrel. Every half inch, sometimes every quarter of an inch, the drill had to be withdrawn and the chips removed, and a mirror was used with lights thrown into the bore to see if the drill was running straight in the center of the barrel. If it was not, I ran the lathe very slowly to see just where it was out of line, marked that spot, took out the barrel, laid it on the anvil and struck it with a lead hammer hard enough to straighten it. Then I put the barrel back in the lathe and drilled some more. It was necessary to withdraw the drill, examine the bore with the mirror and lights, and straighten it if necessary, from 60 to 80 times in drilling a 32 inch barrel, and that was the *toughest job*—and the longest—in making a barrel."

"After the barrel was drilled and reamed slightly, I fitted the false muzzle; drilled the holes, fitted the steel pins to hold this in place, then clamped the false muzzle in place and finished reaming the bore. Then I planed, or ground, the barrel to octagon shape and the desired size. I used the 'long bit'—a square reamer—backed with a piece of wood in reaming my barrels, the same as all rifle-makers in those days—and there is nothing better today, if a man knows how to use this *right*." When I asked if he had found the gain twist or the uniform spiral the best—made the most accurate shooting rifles, he said: "When I first started making rifles I did not have a rifling guide and I borrowed a gain twist guide from L. M. Amidon who was a jeweler in Bellows Falls, and an enthusiastic rifleman, and for several years all my barrels were gain twist. I experimented extensively with the gain twist and the uniform twist of rifling and finally decided that the uniform twist was the best—gave the better accuracy at 40 rods—and the gain twist is much more difficult to cut RIGHT than the uniform twist, so I quit making rifles with the gain twist. You can't lead a barrel that is cut with the gain twist, but have to cut it *right* the first time trying, and can't change it much after the barrel is rifled." "Then I made myself a rifling guide that was somewhat like those used at Smith & Wesson's when I worked there, but had some improvements of my own, with the uniform twist of rifling and used that in cutting my barrels after that." I experimented a lot with different twists, widths and depths of grooves, and found that one turn in 18 inches was best for most calibres. I found that the number of grooves and lands has *very little effect on the accuracy,* but the *width of the grooves does have a great deal to do with the fine shooting* of a rifle. The wide grooves and narrow lands are the best for the finest accuracy. I tried both six and eight grooves and lands and liked the eight grooved barrels the best."

When I inquired about what calibre he had found the best—most accurate at 40 rods,—he answered: "The 38 calibre with a long cylindrical bullet using the paper 2-strip, or 3-strip patch, or the 35 calibre with the same kind of bullet and paper patch, is the best, and will make smaller groups at 40 rods than any larger or smaller calibre."

I asked him to give me the finished dimensions of the bore in his best 38 calibre rifles, and he let me take a note-book from which I copied the following:

NORMAN S. BROCKWAY

Noted Maker of super-accurate Target Rifles.

The last Rifle that Brockway made; 38 calibre Cylindrical Bullet for 3-strip paper patch, using primer ignition. Brockway telescope. Weight of Rifle and telescope, 18 pounds. Owned by W. T. Brodeur.

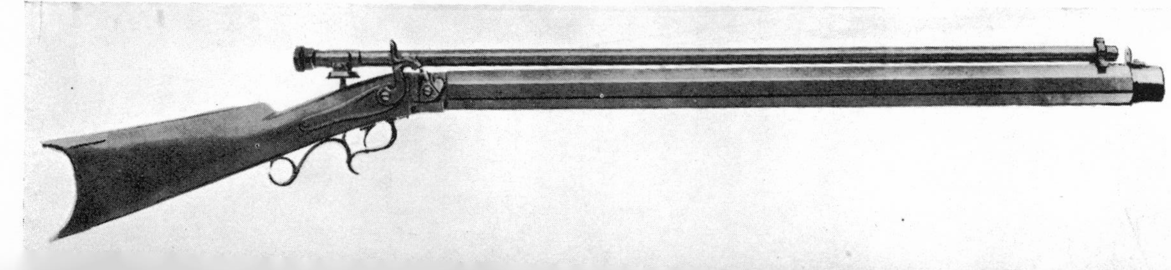

"Bore, .380 inch; pitch of grooves, one turn in 16 or 18 inches (he thought the 18-inch pitch was best); width of grooves, .145 inch; widths of lands, .058 inch; depth of grooves, .005 inch." Regarding the best weight of a rifle, he stated: "For off-hand shooting, about 12 or 13 pounds; for rest shooting at 40 rods, from 16 to 20 pounds was best." I asked if the 20-pound rifles gave very much better accuracy than a 16-pound one, and he answered: "A 16-pound rifle of my make in the 38 calibre for the 3-strip paper patch, when shot from a good machine rest by a man who is experienced in rest shooting, will make just as small groups as any 20-pound gun." He further stated: "A 30 or 40-pound rifle will not give any better accuracy at 40 rods than a 20-pound one—or even a 16-pound gun." Brockway said that he had not found the one-piece cast bullet to be as accurate as the two-piece having the base part of pure lead and the front of hardened lead, or "babbit metal" and swaged together.

He stated further: "The bullets cast in a mould and swaged together are not as accurate as a bullet that is swaged out of cold lead wire or rod. Then I made a machine to use with hydraulic pressure with which I could swage bullets from lead rods that I bought from the National Lead Company. I cut this lead wire into the right lengths for different weights of bullets, weighed every piece on fine scales so as to have them all the same weight, and all that were *exactly the same weight* I swaged into shape in my hydraulic press. In that way, I got every bullet alike, none of them had any 'bubbles' inside and these were the very BEST bullets that can be made today for lead bullet rifles." These bullets were made from lead that was only slightly hardened; he thought they were about one to 50, but he said: "A man in Philadelphia wanted me to make him a thousand bullets from much harder lead—

about 1 to 20 or 25, I guess—so I got the lead rod from the National Lead Company, cut it up into pieces the right weight and started to swage them up in my hydraulic press. About the first bullet I swaged, I put on so much pressure that it burst the 6-inch thick cast steel swage piece of this machine, a piece of which went past my head mighty close and stuck into one of the beams overhead so hard that I couldn't pull it out. If it had ever hit my head it would have killed me instantly—I never would have known what hit me." "I didn't try making any more bullets from such hard lead as that."

As related in chapter 2, Brockway made his own telescope sights during the last few years that he made rifles, but during the earlier years he used those made by L. M. Amidon of that same city. Brockway's barrels were all made with the "choke bore," the last two inches of the muzzle being about .002 inch smaller than the rest, as this shape of bore gives the best accuracy and is easier to load the bullet without deforming it. This choke was put into the barrel by leading the bore with the leading rod and emery, and Brockway said this was the *most important part* in making a fine shooting rifle, even more important than rifling it. He further stated that a rifle with the re-cut, or relined, barrel always gave finer accuracy than it did originally, and he had proven this repeatedly. He relined, or "bushed," as he called it, many rifles by drilling out the bore to a larger diameter, then soldered in the relined barrel. He said that these relined and re-rifled barrels gave so much better accuracy that many riflemen sent their rifles to him to be relined, or re-rifled, and in every case the accuracy was thereby *much improved.* In re-rifling a barrel, Brockway said that he reamed out the original rifling, then smooth-reamed so as to make the bore a true cylinder, after which he rifled it the same as a new barrel and leaded it. Some call this "re-cutting," a barrel, which is quite different from relining a rifle. He believed that the chief reason for the improvement in the accuracy of a re-rifled, or relined one, was that shooting the rifle before this was done, developed so much pressure in the bore that the metal of the barrel was condensed, rendered more homogenous, and finer grained so that after re-rifling, the pores of the metal were much smaller, the inside of the bore much smoother by being thus condensed, and in this way the accuracy was much improved. This in some way affected the liner containing the rifling that was soldered inside the original barrel and thus improved the accuracy.

When I asked Brockway for his "rule" for determining the correct charge of powder for a rifle, he said: "I shot the rifle over snow in winter, or at other times with white wrapping paper spread on the ground in front of the rifle, started shooting with a charge that I thought would be about right and after firing that I looked to see if there were unburned powder grains on the paper, or snow. If there were none, I increased the powder charge and shot again and again examined the paper for unburned grains of powder; in this way, increasing the charge for each shot, I found a charge which did not all burn—left some unburned powder grains on the paper or snow. Then I reduced that charge a few grains so that it would just *all burn completely* when the rifle was fired, and that was the *right charge* for that rifle. I then made the charger to exactly hold that quantity of powder by 'stricken measure,' from a tin or brass tube cut to the right length and having a cork fitting tightly in one end, and sent that with the rifle. If the customer did not want to use quite as much powder as the charger held, he could push the cork in a little ways so as to reduce tne charge, but I was always sure that the rifle gave the best accuracy with the charge that just filled the charger sent with the rifle."

An inquiry about the best kind of black powder for rifles was answered as follows: "I tried all kinds of powder and all the different grains of each. I liked the English, Curtis & Harvey 'Diamond Grain' No. 6 and it gave fine accuracy in my rifles, but I had so much trouble in getting it except in New York or Boston that I used the Hazzard 'Kentucky Rifle' F. g, or F. F. g, mostly, and it gave practically as good accuracy as the Curtis & Harvey, but did not burn quite as moist in hot weather as the English powder." He further said: "All black powder should be sifted through a fine sieve before using so as to get out all that is too fine and thus have all the powder as nearly the same size grains as possible. That improves the accuracy quite a lot."

During the last few years that Brockway made rifles he adopted the device for using the Berdan primer as a means of ignition instead of the nipple and cap, as the primer gave considerably better ignition and resulted in a decided improvement in the accuracy of the rifle. He considered this far superior to the percussion cap ignition.

Brockway said that he made quite a lot of breech-muzzle-loading rifles also; that is, he fitted one of his barrels to a Winchester, Ballard, Sharps-Borchardt, Farrow or other breech-loading, single shot actions; rifled these barrels the same as for muzzle-loading having the false muzzle, bullet starter, swages, etc., the same as the Pope, Schoyen and Remington-Walker rifles of this type. These showed very nice accuracy at 40 rods—as good as the muzzle-loading cap lock rifles, and were easier to load and to clean after each shot. He stated that he liked the Farrow action best for such rifles as it was very much stronger than the Ballard, and as strong as the Winchester or Sharps-

Borchardt single shot actions. A few of the breech-muzzle-loading rifles were equipped with a mechanical bullet seater that Brockway made, by means of which the bullet with its patch was forced through the false muzzle into the bore of the rifle the length of the starter plunger; then the mechanical bullet starter was removed and the bullet pushed home with the loading rod. This type of bullet starter was very expensive to make, required especially skillful workmanship in making, but is the very BEST method of entering the bullet into the bore of the rifle *without in any way deforming the bullet,* or upsetting it. Even the ordinary bullet seater used in connection with the false muzzle, causes a *very slight upsetting of the bullet* in striking the knob of the starter plunger when only ONE blow is used, while if the starter knob is struck several blows the bullet is upset by every blow, and the finest accuracy thereby decreased to a certain extent.

"Uncle Norman" Brockway was the last of that group of highly skilled workmen back in the percussion lock period who gave the American riflemen the American target rifle, a remarkably super-fine, precision rifle which gave a degree of accuracy that has never been surpassed even up to the present day. He died at West Brookfield, Massachusetts, on July 25th, 1936, at the age of 95 years and 4 months, but the fame of his rifles, and many of the rifles themselves, will live after him and be used for many years to come by those who love and appreciate them. Mr. Brockway himself will long be remembered as one of the world's master rifle-makers, a remarkably expert rifleman and a straight shooter in every way.

Illustrations showing a Brockway rifle, several groups shot with his rifles, and a picture of him are shown herewith.

HORACE WARNER

The subject of this sketch was born in a town near Hartford, Connecticut, about 1832, and died at Williamsport, Pennsylvania, in 1893. When he was 16 years old his family moved to Ridgeway, Pennsylvania, which was then a wilderness, where he grew to manhood. He was the oldest of a family of eleven children. When the Civil War broke out Horace Warner and his two brothers Hiram and Robert, enlisted in Berdan's Sharpshooters, while his brothers William and Simon enlisted in Company C, 105th Regiment of Pennsylvania Volunteers.

Having grown up in the wilderness where schools were few, Horace Warner attended school but very little, yet through self-education when a young man, he became very well educated in a practical way, his penmanship was fine and his letters were quite models of English.

Wm. V. Lowe was an intimate friend of Warner's from the early 1880's until his death, was in partnership with him under the firm name of Warner & Lowe for several years, and Mr. Lowe kindly furnished me this data regarding him.

When the family moved to Ridgeway, his father bought Horace an old rifle; game of many kinds was plentiful, bears were common and were always shot as a protective measure since they killed hogs, young cattle and sheep, and bear's grease was desired for cooking and the oil was also of value. This gun was so rusty and in such poor condition that Warner went to work improving it on rainy days. He had no tools—not even a vice or screwdriver—and was obliged to make whatever he needed himself. He partly split a big log to fasten the gun barrel in, and with a draw-knife, pocket-knife, chisel and files, made the necessary tools and "freshened out" this gun so that afterwards it loaded much easier and shot pretty well.

The boys in the neighborhood heard about Warner's repairing his own rifle and brought their guns to him to be fixed. Thus he acquired experience in this work, and as he was very ingenious, in three or four years he became quite a "gun-tinker" and a very good rifle-shot.

About that time a somewhat noted gun-maker had established himself in a town about 30 miles away, and Warner decided that now he would have a *good* gun. So he went to Pittsburgh—180 miles distant—on a raft, bought a steel barrel and, traveling on foot, carried it all the way home on his shoulders. The next day after he got home he walked 30 miles to the gun-maker, who made gain twist rifles, carrying the gun barrel and left it there with orders to make the best rifle possible out of it. When the rifle was finished Warner walked again the 30 miles to the rifle-maker's place, got his rifle and carried it home, with great expectations.

The neighbors all came to see this wonderful rifle shot, and Warner was much disgusted to find that it was not as accurate as his old rifle that he had "worked over." Warner swore that he could make a better shooting rifle himself, at which the neighbors laughed, and then he swore that he *would* make a better, more accurate rifle. He made another trip by raft to Pittsburgh and bought another barrel, but as he had not enough money to pay for a steel rifle barrel he bought a good iron one that was cheaper. Then he walked home again carrying the rifle barrel—180 miles.

Then he went to work and made his rifling guide and rifling bench, as well as all the tools needed—made all these with only the pocket-knife, chisels, draw-knife and files—and completed his rifle with all the trimmings; made his own lock and every part of the rifle. When this rifle, made with these very few, crude tools, was finished, he showed the neighbors that this rifle

HORACE WARNER

Master Rifle-maker and noted expert rifleman.

Warner holding a gun invented by himself. Top barrel Rifle, lower for shot, fired by one hammer according to position of rods in breech.

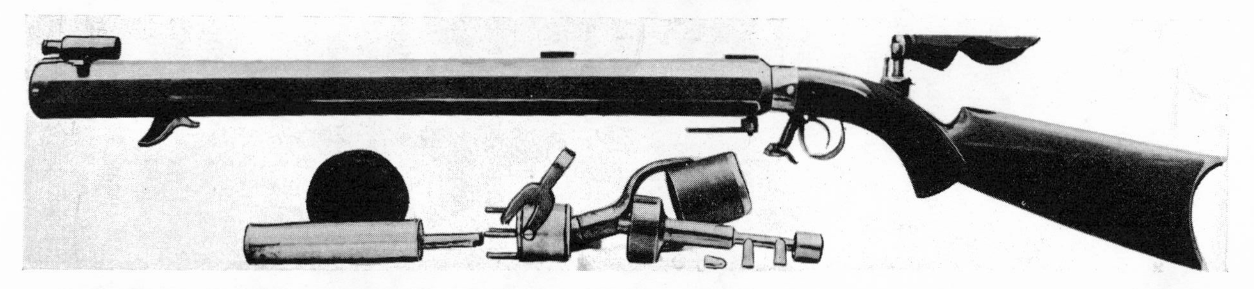

Dr. R. A. Mattesen's 45 calibre Horace Warner, Machine Rest Rifle, 27-inch barrel, weight 35 pounds. Primer he had made *actually was more accurate* than the one by the noted rifle-maker. After that he went to work on the gain twist rifle that the rifle-maker had turned out for him and made that shoot very accurately.

In this way Warner got started in rifle making without ever having "learned the trade" or ever having spent an hour working in a gun shop. He never had lived in a place where he could get an education on rifle-making or guns, where he could learn about their shooting qualities, etc., but had always been obliged to work out his own problems by the "trial and error method." Warner was very strong, and as a young man had exceptionally keen eyesight and hearing that had been developed by his life in the wilderness.

Once he shot a three-day match at 25 rods (138 yards) with a friend, in which Warner shot off-hand while his friend shot from a rest. There was a 25-cent stake on each string, the shortest string measure to win, and Warner won the match. The target used was a white bull's-eye set on a black background and one bull's-eye had 13 bullet holes in it, cutting it almost to pieces. Warner's wife placed a teacup on this group and it completely covered all the 13 shots. The next day they shot at 40 rods and Warner won the matches that day; then the other man proposed shooting at 80 rods on the third day under the same conditions—Warner to shoot off-hand and the other man with a rest. The third day was so windy that Warner could not hold well enough for good accuracy and the other man gained on him so that when they quit shooting at dark they were about even on the score.

Warner moved to Syracuse, New York, about 1880, and had a shop in part of the Lefever Arms Company's factory where he carried on his work as a rifle-maker and gunsmith until a short time before his death.

Soon after Warner located in Syracuse, the riflemen

in that state and New England learned that his rifles gave very fine accuracy and were in much demand by experts for 200 yards and 40 rods shooting. He was a member of the National Rifle Club, of Vernon, Vermont, where he shot in their matches for many years and he, or his rifles used by other shooters, won many prizes.

He was a great experimenter, always seeking ways to improve the accuracy of the rifle, tested thoroughly many different types of rifling, different depths and widths of grooves, widths and shapes of lands, different twists of rifling, etc.

During the latter years that he was in business he made many heavy target and machine rest rifles, some weighing 40 to 60 pounds, in 50 to 60 calibre. He preferred the under-hammer lock and the device for using the Berdan primer ignition for his rifles, as this had proven superior in accuracy to the nipple and percussion cap. During the years before about 1882 or '83, Warner also made some of the hunting and target rifles without the false muzzle, but having the muzzle of the barrel turned cylindrically to fit a bullet starter. These rifles usually weighed from about 9 to 12 pounds and were usually of 38, 40, or 42 calibre using the short cylindrical bullet, or the flat point picket bullets. I do not think he made many rifles of this kind, but I have seen a number of these that he made while in Williamsport. After locating in Syracuse, he specialized principally on the target rifles weighing from about 15 to 25 pounds or more. He cut his barrels with the uniform twist of rifling, generally with 8 grooves and lands in which the grooves were somewhat wider than the lands. However, I have seen numerous Warner rifles in which the grooves and lands appeared to be of equal widths.

The heavy Warner rifle that Dr. P. A. Matteson owns (herewith illustrated) is an extremely accurate shooting arm as shown by the groups illustrated. But I, personally, do not like these very heavy rifles; to my way of thinking they are but "light field-pieces," or artillery, needing automobile wheels on them for transportation purposes. I strongly dislike handling and shooting this type of rifles and have never shot this Warner rifle of Dr. Matteson's.

There is no doubt that the Warner target rifles weighing about 18 to 20 pounds were extremely accurate at ranges from 40 to 100 rods and that many matches were won with these rifles. Warner, himself, shot in a great many rifle matches during the 1880's and '90's, and usually was the winner or among the high score men in these matches.

An account is given in Chapter VI, of one of the series of matches that were shot by Warner and H. V. Perry, many years ago. We find numerous reports of matches in the old *Forest and Stream* and *Shooting and Fishing* magazines in which both these men took part, and were generally among the prize winners in these during the years mentioned. There appeared to be more rivalry between Perry and Warner than between the other expert riflemen of those days.

Horace Warner was a fine gentleman, a remarkably ingenious, skillful workman, an exceptionally fine marksman, and one of the most noted makers of super-accurate muzzle-loading rifles of his time.

H. V. PERRY

During the years from about 1850 until in the early 1890's there were many riflemen in this country who stoutly insisted that the *most accurate* muzzle-loading rifles were those made by H. V. Perry, of Jamestown, New York. As with the other old-time rifle-makers, very little information regarding Perry is obtainable today from the Jamestown Public Library or other sources. It is believed that he commenced business as a rifle-maker about 1840, and was at first located in Fredonia, N. Y., as all the earlier rifles of his make give that as his address. All of the 3-barrel Perry rifles that I have seen were stamped "Fredonia, N. Y.", and were made before the Civil War.

I am told that he removed to Jamestown early in 1850, and we know that he continued business there until poor health obliged him to retire from business. No one appears to know where or when he was born, but we have records which show that he died on May 7th, 1897. He had very few advantages for education in his early life, and was obliged to earn his own living from an early age—when a mere boy—on account of the death of his parents. He inherited a love for the rifle, which he learned to use when quite young, and as he was very ingenious—like practically all the old riflemakers—he learned rifle-making when a young man and followed that business until about a year before his death.

During the 1870's and 1880's there was quite a group of expert riflemen in Jamestown who were staunch advocates of the Perry rifles, and who shot with him in many matches. Perry preferred team matches instead of individual ones, and the "Perry Rifle Team," as he and his shooting companions were called, were always ready to shoot matches at 40 to 100 rods with other teams and experts. When this book was written I was unable to find an H. V. Perry rifle in any collection in New England or New York State; therefore, I am unable to show an illustration of one. Mr. Walter Grote writes me that he has owned nine Perry rifles, which with only two or three exceptions, were all cut with the uniform pitch or rifling and had 16 grooves and lands. These few exceptions had 8 grooves and lands with uniform twist of rifling.

Years ago when Perry was in his prime, there was, as before stated, great rivalry between him and Horace Warner. As a result of this these two experts shot many matches, usually at 40 rods rest, in their endeavors to prove which of these two makes of rifles were the superior in accuracy. Warner preferred to shoot from machine rest, while Perry preferred the muzzle and elbow rest with the butt of the rifle against the shoulder. He considered this the more practical method of shooting as it demonstrated the skill of the shooter better than by the use of the machine rest.

It is believed that after about 1875, Perry made but few of the various types of hunting rifles, but specialized on the target, or match, rifles weighing from about 12 to 16 or 18 pounds, as well as the so-called "long range rifles" in 40 or 45 calibre weighing just under 10 pounds to comply with the National Rifle Association rules. The old *Forest and Stream* magazines back in the 1880's, *The Rifle,* and *Shooting and Fishing* during those years and the 1890's report many very small groups having been made by Perry himself with his own rifles, or by users of his rifles, in matches at 40 rods rest shooting. Scores of 10 shots each measuring but a little over 6 inches and those of 7 inches were quite frequently reported in these magazines. Groups of 50 consecutive shots at 40 rods muzzle and elbow rest, were reported as having been shot in numerous public matches, with string measure as short as 41, 13/16 inches. One of these groups copied from *The Rifle,* issue of December 1886, is illustrated on a preceding page. Some of the early *Forest and Stream* magazines report even shorter 50-shot strings as having been made by him in matches, but were not illustrated.

There are abundant records to prove, beyond all doubt or question, that Perry was an unusually skillful marksman, and that he made some of the *most accurate rifles* that have ever been made—not excepting the modern high velocity rifles. He was a very particular and skillful workman and his rifles were much better finished than the majority of the rifles of those times.

CARLOS GOVE

Among the noted old-time makers of muzzle-loading rifles of many different kinds should be included Carlos Gove, of Denver, Colorado. Mr. Gove was born in Wentworth, New Hampshire, on April 19, 1817, and died in Denver on July 14, 1900, at the age of 83. He came of sturdy old revolutionary stock, his ancestors being Americans and his grandfather was a soldier in General Washington's army. He never used tobacco nor whiskey, which stamped him at that time in the West as somewhat of a curiosity. When he was 16 years old he ran away from home to enlist in the First U. S. Cavalry and served with it through the Seminole Indian Wars in Florida, and then on the Western frontier. It has been said that at the time of his death he was one of the oldest U. S. regular soldiers. Mr. Gove was connected with the Indian Department of the U. S. Government for many years as an Indian Agent at different Posts, as he understood and spoke nearly all of the Indian languages in the West, as well as being fluent in the Indian sign language. Records show that he was one of the *honest* Indian Agents, which is more than can be said for many of those agents.

Carlos Gove commenced his business career as a rifle-maker and gunsmith in St. Joseph, Missouri, in 1847, and continued business there until 1854, when he moved to Council Bluffs, Iowa. He also owned and operated gun stores at different times in Cheyenne, Wyoming, and Ogden, Utah. He was a natural mechanic, very ingenious and a very skillful workman and became quite noted in the West as a very skillful maker of *super-accurate rifle*. He was connected with the Great North American Fur Company for a number of years, during which time he hunted and trapped on the Great Plains where the Indians and bison were numerous.

After the great excitement occasioned throughout Colorado and the West by the finding of gold in the sands of Cherry Creek, the town of Denver grew rapidly and it soon became apparent that it would be the coming center for supplies for a large section of the country. Mr. Gove was quick to realize this and while other merchants hurried to the new town with stocks of dry goods and wet goods, he crossed the plains in 1860 with an assortment of firearms that ex-

CARLOS GOVE

Expert Rifle-Maker, Big Game Hunter and Expert Rifleman.

perience had taught him would sell readily to the hunters, trappers and miners then hastening westward to grow up with the country. The next year he settled in Denver as a rifle-maker and gunsmith and continued in this business until in the 1880's when he retired.

He was assisted in his work by George C. Schoyen who, about 1862, came from Chicago and entered Mr. Gove's employ when quite young. Mr. Schoyen's workmanship was of the very highest order and while some of his skill came to him naturally from his Norwegian ancestors, much of it was, no doubt, due to the very thorough and careful training he received at the hands of Mr. Gove.

It is doubtful if any man in the West sold more firearms than Mr. Gove and many of those that he sold were of his own make. His sole amusement was hunting and rifle shooting, and rest shooting with the heavy muzzle-loading rifle appealed most strongly to him. His skill at 200 yards off-hand was high, but his best shooting was done at 200 or 220 yards rest with a muzzle-loading rifle. He shot and won many matches of this kind using rifles of his own make as well as those made by Wm. Billinghurst, who was one of his firm friends, until the latter died. When long range rifle shooting was in vogue he became much interested in that, made several muzzle-loading rifles especially for shooting at 800, 900 and 1000 yards, and was one of the most reliable long range shots of the Denver Rifle Club, of which Mr. Gove was the first president and a life member. Through his business and mining investments he became quite wealthy, and was mayor of the City of Denver for several years.

The Republican-Gazette of Gove City, Gove County, Kansas, under date of April 20, 1833, states: "Carlos Gove made good Guns. He made a rifle with octagon barrel for Buffalo Bill, with the famous scout's name

Carlos Gove 42 calibre Long Range Rifle, 31-inch barrel, weight 27 pounds. Gove Telescope.

inlaid in silver on the top flat of the barrel, which was used by him for many years on the Plains for shooting buffalo and Indians."

An article in *Outdoor Life* for October 1933, regarding Carlos Gove states: "He was a thoroughbred when it came to sport, and thought no more of shooting a match for $100.00 or $500.00 a side than our later-day sportsmen do of going into a little sweepstake event. In '63 he shot a rifle match with M. L. Rood, at 100 rods, a 10-shot string for $1,000.00 a side, besides some good-sized side bets. Gove won easily." "One day in '73 a man walked into Gove's store on Fifteenth Street and offered to bet $2,500.00 that he could beat Gove in a match at live birds, shooting at ten birds. Gove accepted the wager, the money was put up and the match shot, with the result that Gove won by the score of ten to seven. Mr. George Schoyen was a witness to this match and can vouch for this account of it."

Herewith will be found an illustration of a heavy, long range muzzle-loading rifle that Mr. Gove made many years ago, now owned by one of his relatives in Brandon, Vermont. This is 42 calibre, the barrel is 31 inches long, full octagon of very large size and the rifle and telescope weigh 27 pounds. I also illustrate a group that my gunsmith friend, Floyd R. Butler, shot with this Gove rifle at 100 yards rest quite recently, as well as a group at the same range that was shot by Mr. Gove in 1891. I am glad to be able to also reproduce a photograph of this noted riflemaker and sportsman.

EDWIN WESSON

Back in 1835 to about 1850 some of the finest, most accurate target rifles, as well as lighter weight hunting and target rifles, were made by Edwin Wesson, of Northboro, Massachusetts, and Hartford, Connecticut.

My first target rifle for 40 rods shooting which I acquired in 1881 or '82, was made by him, gave nice accuracy and I used it for a number of years; derived much skill and a *lot of pleasure* from its use.

I am indebted to Colonel Douglas B. Wesson, of Springfield, Massachusetts, for the following information regarding Edwin Wesson, who was a distant relative of his. "Edwin Wesson was the elder brother of my grandfather, D. B. Wesson, who was the founder of this company (Smith & Wesson, the famous revolver manufacturers—N. H. R.) and made rifles at Northboro, Mass., from about 1835 to 1840, when he moved to Hartford, Conn., where he continued making rifles until 1850, when he died. Edwin Wesson was also a brother of Frank Wesson who made breech-loading pistols and rifles at Worcester, Massachusetts, from about 1865 to well along in the 1880's."

I have recently seen it stated that Frank Wesson made muzzle-loading rifles, but this is certainly a mistake as Colonel Wesson writes me that the *first* firearms that Frank Wesson made, about 1860, were breech-loading pistols to use the then new 22 calibre rim fire cartridge. The first of these 22 calibre R. F., pistols were made for Frank Wesson by B. Kittridge & Company, of Cincinnati, Ohio, about 1859, and later Wesson established his factory at Worchester, Mass., where he made them himself. Later, after the Civil War, he made breech-loading rifles of various calibres and the so-called "pocket rifles," also some certain types of shotguns—principally single barrel arms.

Edwin Wesson was regarded by John R. Chapman as the *best rifle-maker,* or the maker of the *most accurate shooting* ones, in this country from about 1844 to along in the 1850's, according to his book, *The Improved American Rifle.* All of his rifles were cut with the gain twist rifling, and he was *so positive* that this gave the *best accuracy* that he refused to make any rifles with any other rifling.

During the years that he was in business he used two different methods of attaching the barrel to the break-off of his rifles and, necessarily, in stocking these. Both of these types are here illustrated, but my first Edwin Wesson rifle was stocked with a forearm, like one of these shown. I have always liked the second type of his rifles—the model without forearm—best for target shooting and think it rather strange that it was not adopted by other makers as it was a stronger method of attaching the barrel and break-off than the taper pin method that was used by others. But if one wanted a rifle to use for hunting as much as for target work, the model having the usual walnut forearm was much the better. If you have any doubts about that, just go hunting some morning in winter when the thermometer is well below zero and see how nice? and warm? that steel barrel, without wood forearm, feels in your hands when you are carrying or shooting it. I will wager that you would then "cuss" both the maker and yourself.

D. B. Wesson, the grandfather of Colonel Wesson of today, also worked with his brother Edwin at Hartford, Conn., where he was superintendent of the shop, and made some muzzle-loading rifles that were occasionally marked with his name. Dr. P. A. Matteson formerly owned a very fine 44 calibre round ball rifle which had inlaid in gold on the top octagon flat, "D. B. Wesson, Hartford, Ct." with a gold band border surrounding these words. I believe that Colonel Wesson now owns this fine specimen—in almost new condition—that his grandfather made so many years ago.

Herewith is illustrated a group that I shot with the Edwin Wesson rifle that was owned by "Shiff the Gunman" when this book was in preparation, and shows that this rifle will "still shoot fine." I regret that I was unable to find a picture or photograph of Edwin Wesson.

MORGAN JAMES

Morgan James, of Utica, New York, was another of our most noted and skillful makers of muzzle-loading rifles that gave the very finest accuracy.

A long search in that city for information and data regarding him and his work, proved fruitless. The Utica City Directory of 1859, lists: "Morgan James, gunsmith, corner Fayette and Seneca Streets," and continues listing him in this way each year until and including 1866.

That is absolutely all the information that I was able to obtain about him from any publication in the Utica Public Library, or from any person in that city or vicinity, except the following. An old gentleman in that city from whom I inquired stated: "Yes, I remember Morgan James and his shop where he made remarkably accurate shooting heavy target rifles, as well as many lighter single barrel hunting rifles and double barreled rifles that were very popular with hunters. His double barreled rifles were especially popular among hunters in the Adirondacks and the West. Many of his double rifles were used on the plains for shooting buffalo and Indians and were carried by pioneers to California and Oregon during the 'gold rush'."

This man had never seen a picture of Morgan James, did not believe he ever had one taken and doubted if I could find one. This proved true, as no book or magazine could be found that contained his picture.

Another old gentleman told me that he remembered that during the Civil War, Morgan James made a number of heavy "Sharpshooters rifles" with full length telescope sights for Berdan's Sharpshooters and the U. S. Government. John R. Chapman in his book, *The Improved American Rifle,* states that James made fine target rifles and the *best* telescopic rifle sights that were to be had during the period from 1844 to 1848.

Charles Winthrop Sawyer in the book, *Our Rifles* mentions Morgan James' rifles as being *remarkably accurate* at 40 rods rest shooting, and the groups that I have illustrated in Chapter 9 show beyond all doubt that his rifles were *absolutely unsurpassed* in accuracy— possibly unequalled by any other maker. The reader will be obliged to search for a *long time,* and part with many of his hard earned dollars, before he finds *any rifle,* of any make, kind or calibre, old or the most modern, which will shoot a 10-shot group at 40 rods that is entirely enclosed in a circle but 1 and 27/50 inches in diameter and the eleven shots all hitting a silver dollar at that range. When you find such a rifle, just follow the example of the wise man in holy writ: "Who when he had found one pearl of great price, went and sold all that he had, and bought it."

And, permit me to add, when you have searched the world over and found a rifle that is as accurate as this—the "one pearl of great price"—*hang right onto it,* "till death you do part," as you will never find another that equals it—probably. The old *Forest and Stream* magazine, and Sawyer's book, *Our Rifles,* state that Morgan James cut his rifles with a gain twist, but we do not know the number and shape of the lands and grooves that he used in these.

No one that I could locate has one of his rifles and I am, therefore, unable to illustrate this.

We do not know where or when he was born, but I was told by people in Utica that he died about the close of the Civil War.

GEORGE H. FERRIS

Among the noted rifle-makers from about 1850 to 1890, we find George H. Ferris, of Utica, New York,

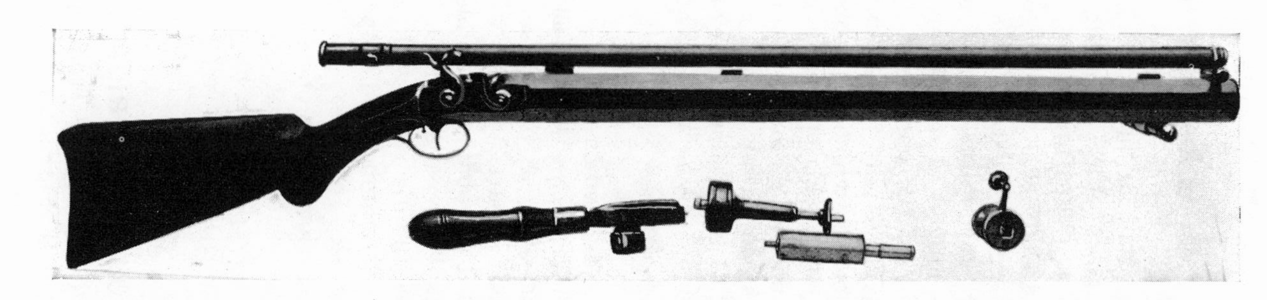

George H. Ferriss 48 calibre, Heavy Match Rifle, 30-inch barrel, weight 28¾ pounds. Ferriss Telescope. Photograph by Courtesy of E. M. Farris, Secretary, National Muzzle-Loading Rifle Association.

but like so many of these old-time makers very little information about him is today obtainable. I went to Utica and made a diligent search for data regarding his history and work, but very little is known there about him.

The Utica City Directory of 1850 lists: "Ferris, George H. riflemaker and gunsmith, 40-Lansing Street." It also stated that he was associated with Morgan James in making rifles, guns and telescopic sights until 1859, when Ferris appears to have continued in this business alone until 1866, which is the last time his name appeared in any directory of that city.

Whether Ferris died at that time, or retired from business, I am unable to state as no records are available.

When his name first appeared in the directory of Utica, he spelled it Ferris and continued to spell it that way until 1863, when he changed it to "Ferriss."

This directory also lists a gunsmith by the name of Fred G. Ferris for 1859 and '60, when he went into some other business and changed his name by spelling it "Ferriss," and it appears that soon after this George H. also adopted that way of spelling his name.

I could find no person in that city who knew anything about George H. Ferris, or "Ferriss," except that several remembered that: "I have often heard my father speak of his shop where he made very fine rifles before and during the Civil War, but I know nothing about his rifles or him except this."

When I was a boy there were quite a lot of his rifles in use; they were nice workmanship and gave nice accuracy at ranges including 40 rods which is the longest range at which I ever saw them used. Some riflemen and collectors state that the Ferris rifles were cut with the gain twist and 8 grooves, while others are positive that he used the uniform pitch of rifling with a larger number of grooves and lands. I made no records of this matter years ago when I often saw rifles of his make and now the information I receive about this is quite contradictory.

The only George H. Ferriss target rifle that I have seen during the past twenty years, or more, was owned by E. M. Farris, the Secretary of the National Muzzle-Loading Rifle Association, a few years ago. I took a photograph of it at that time and it is shown herewith.

It is to be regretted that records were not kept, in the years past, regarding the personal history, and the rifles that were made by these old rifle-makers, as well as all the details regarding the method of rifling they used in making their rifles, number of grooves and lands, width, depth and shape of these, etc. Such detailed records would be of much interest and value today, but they are not to be had as these rifle-makers and their immediate relatives appear to have all died and almost nothing is now known about these men.

James & Ferris, Utica, New York, also made many fine medium weight target rifles weighing about 10 to 14 pounds, and I have owned two of these in years past. At present my friend Frank K. Lucas, of Webster, New York, owns the rifle of this make herein illustrated. This barrel is cut with the uniform twist of rifling, has 6 grooves that are ⅛ inch wide and 6 lands 1/12 inch wide. These grooves are rather shallow,—about .005 inch as near as I can measure them.

This may be the system of rifling, depth of grooves, etc., that George H. Ferris used in his rifles—and it may not be, no one appears to know. I do not believe this is the Morgan James type of rifling as it is generally believed that he used the gain twist only. Whether the firm of James & Ferris consisted of Morgan James and George H. Ferris, or James and Fred

G. Ferris, or some relative of Morgan James and either or both of these men by the name of Ferris, or "Ferriss," no one now living really knows. At least, I have been unable to find any book, magazine or person who can furnish this specific information. This James & Ferris rifle that friend Lucas owns is a very nice one, 36 calibre, weighs 13 pounds, which I have used for a year, or more. The workmanship on it is fine and the accuracy is good. The full length telescope is the type that was invented by John R. Chapman and made by Morgan James, but this one is stamped: *"James & Ferriss,* Utica, N. Y.," while the barrel is stamped *"James & Ferris,* Utica, N. Y. Remington cast steel." Note that the name is spelled both ways on this rifle and telescope—so as not to show any partiality in spelling, I suppose.

GEORGE SCHALK

Years ago, back in the late 1870's until well along in the 1890's, one of the widely known makes of rifles that were noted for their *fine workmanship* and *splendid accuracy* would have the words "George Schalk, Pottsville, Penn.," stamped on the top of the barrel. I well remember having met Mr. Schalk in the summer of 1883, at Newark, New Jersey, where he shot in one of the German "Schuetzen" rifle matches with a rifle of his own make, about 38 calibre, using the circular linen patch with short, flat point conical bullet.

Wm. J. Hayes, one of the most noted experts with the Schuetzen rifle, also shot a Schalk muzzle-loader of 38 or 40 calibre in this match and was among the winners and high score men. Schalk cut his barrels with a gain twist having wide grooves with square corners and narrow lands, and many of his rifles were in use by Schuetzen riflemen in New Jersey, Pennsylvania and other states.

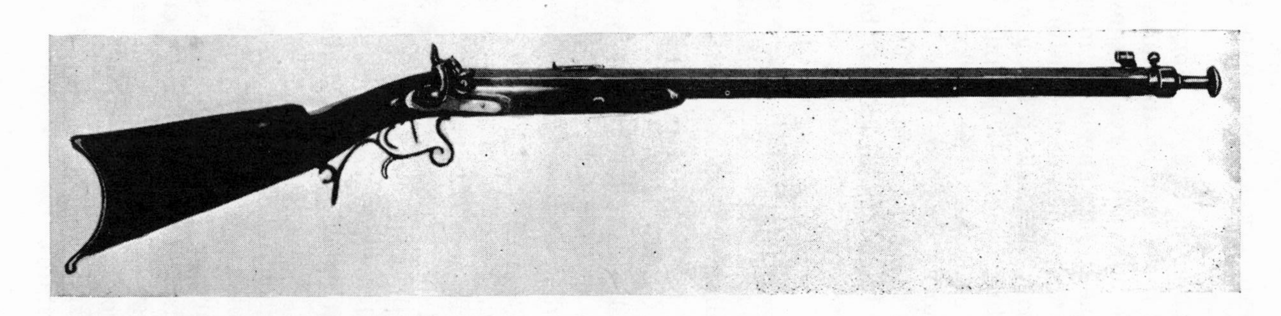

George Schalk, Target Rifle, 35 calibre Cylindrical Bullet used with either linen or 2-strip paper patch, weight about 14 pounds. Photograph by Courtesy of Livingston L. Johnson.

I believe that Schalk was born in Germany, or Austria, and probably learned his trade as a rifle-maker before coming to this country. The trigger guard found on most of the Schalk rifles is of a German or Austrian design, which would also indicate that he learned rifle-making in one of those countries. He was a remarkably *skillful workman* and every part of his rifles was finished very nicely as well as being *very accurately made.*

Sometimes in 1884, at the suggestion of Mr. Hayes, Schalk made for him a 33 calibre muzzle-loading rifle for use without any patch, but using a grooved, lubricated bullet which was easier to load by means of the false muzzle and bullet starter than a bullet having a patch of any kind, as well as saving the trouble of cutting and using the patch. This rifle that Mr. Hayes used gave better accuracy than any of the different rifles he had tested with which a patched bullet was used and with it he won many prizes and matches. With this Schalk 33 calibre rifle, Mr. Hayes won the King's medal in the Western "Bundesfest" at Indianapolis, Indiana, in 1885, with a score of 220 out of a possible 225 points on the German ring target at 200 yards off-hand. During the summer of 1887, Hayes shot in a series of three competitions of 100 shots each at 200 yards off-hand on this same target and scored 2196 out of a possible 2500 points in the first match. The second one at Newark, N. J., on August 7th, he won with a score of 2211, and he won the third at Union Hill, N. J., a few weeks later with the score of 2216. The Schalk rifle in Hayes' hands easily won the 300-shot match, in which a splendid silver trophy was the prize, with a score in the second and third matches that were several points higher than had ever before been made in a 100-shot match on that target. This shows that the Schalk rifle certainly was a very accurate one as well as that Mr. Hayes was an exceptionally fine off-hand shot.

A number of years ago Mr. H. A. Donaldson, of Little Falls, New York, had a Schalk rifle of 40 calibre or larger, that he had owned for many years and with which he had made many fine groups at 100 and 200 yards rest shooting. This rifle of Donaldson's used some kind of a patch with the bullet instead of the lubricated, grooved lead bullet. Mr. L. L. Johnson, of Washington, D. C., owns the only Schalk muzzle-loading rifle that I was able to locate at the time this book was published. This is a 35 calibre using either the circular linen, or the oiled paper cross patch, and the false muzzle is so made that either kind of patch can be used as desired by using swages that leave the finished bullet the correct diameter for these two patches. That is, one swage makes the bullet the correct diameter for use with the linen patch, while the other swage makes it a few thousandths of an inch larger so as to be correct for the thinner paper patch.

I believe that numerous tests and experiments with the muzzle-loading rifles using the grooved lubricated bullet without any patch have proven conclusively that a patch of any kind is *wholly unnecessary* for the finest accuracy, serves no useful purpose except to wear out the bore of the rifle, and gives *finer accuracy* than any rifle using the patched bullet, as well as giving a much longer accuracy life of the rifle.

As a proof of this statement, allow me to call your attention to the group of 10 shots made at 200 yards rest with the butt of the rifle held to the shoulder, shot by the late C. W. Rowland, of Boulder, Colorado, with his H. M. Pope, 32-40 calibre, 17-pound rifle using a 200 grain bullet which was muzzle-loaded and used with one cartridge case that was reloaded after each shot in the usual Schuetzen way. Yes, this group by Mr. Rowland with his Pope breech-muzzle-loading rifle is *actually smaller* than the group shot with a Morgan James rifle before mentioned and illustrated, and this is NOT a "freak" group that could not be duplicated as Mr. Rowland made many such groups—as small as, or even smaller than, this one shown.

Who, may I ask, has ever made *more accurate shooting rifles* than Harry M. Pope? Answer—*nobody.* I believe that our skillful makers of today should adopt the Schalk, or Pope, system of rifling as it appears to be the ideal type for muzzle-loading rifles, gives equally as fine accuracy as the rifles using any kind of a patch, is considerably easier to load, and has a longer accuracy life.

Schalk rifles in fine condition are now very scarce and are highly prized by those who are so fortunate as to own one. I believe that Mr. Schalk died during the late 1890's or early 1900, and it is to be regretted that no one now makes muzzle-loaders with this system of rifling.

B. W. AMSDEN

From information furnished by my friend Floyd R. Butler, of Raceville, New York, I learned that B. W. Amsden, of Saratoga Springs, New York, whose house and shop was on the corner of Lake Avenue and Hodgman Streets, made hunting rifles, target rifles, shotguns and pistols in that city during the period from about 1860 to 1880. It has been stated that he also made some heavy sharpshooters rifles for the United States Government during the Civil War, but I can find no record of any such rifles that he made.

Amsden bought the cast steel rifle barrel blanks all drilled from E. Remington & Sons, and reamed, rifled, finished and stocked them himself using the old hand tools then in use, most of which he made himself the same as other rifle-makers of those times. He was a very skillful workman and his rifles were very well finished. His target rifles, as well as those of other types, used the oiled linen patch, although he may have made some that used the paper cross patch, but I have never seen any of his rifles which used the paper patch. The barrels for his rifles were cut with a right-hand, uniform twist of rifling to use the conical, or flat point picket bullet, generally cast in one piece, and gave nice accuracy at ranges up to 40 or 60 rods, but were not usually very accurate at longer ranges. We find many of his rifles of 38 calibre using bullets that weigh from about 170 to 225 grains, and many in 40, 42 and 45 calibre, target or match rifles with heavy full octagon barrel.

The front sight on the Amsden target rifles was usually the shaded pin-head of very small size indeed, which were made from a pig's bristle with a "bead" formed by slightly burning the bristle with a red-hot iron, then this pin-head was dyed black and set into a piece of soft pine, like a match stick, and then screwed into the base piece so as to extend the correct height into the shade.

The rear peep sight on his target rifles was nearly always made with a square stem sliding through the upper tang and fastened in position by a small set screw instead of being threaded through the tang, as in most other makes of rifles. The windage adjustment on his rear peep sights was made by means of a horizontal piece sliding in a slot cut in the rear sight disc, and many of these were provided with screw adjustments which enabled the user to make more accurate and closer adjustments than could be made by the older method of driving the front sight to the right or left of the center with a small hammer.

Amsden also made many combination guns, having a rifle and shotgun barrel side by side. The rifle barrel was usually of 38 or 40 calibre with a 14 or 16 gauge shot barrel, and these had a ready sale in those days for hunting purposes. I have also seen quite a number of double barreled rifles that Amsden made which were 38, 40, or 42 calibre.

We were informed that Amsden's characteristic "trade mark" was a silver eagle inlay on the cheek rest on the target rifles of his best grade, on his hunting and target rifles, and combination guns. I have never seen a picture or photograph of B. W. Amsden, although I have made a diligent search to find such. It is very doubtful if there is any photograph of him in existence. I understand that he was a rather heavily built, stocky man weighing in the vicinity of 200 pounds, was about five feet nine or ten inches in height and wore the usual full beard of those days.

PETER A. REINHARDT

Peter A. Reinhardt was born in Neidernberg, Bavaria, Germany, in 1827, and when five years old came with his parents to Columbus, Ohio, where at an early age he was apprenticed to Cornelius Jacobs to learn the gun-making business.

At the age of twenty-two Reinhardt married Catherine Clee who came to Delaware County from Prussia in 1840, and that same year he moved to Loudonville, Ohio, where he worked for a time in a shop with a man by the name of Sprague, but he soon went into business by himself as a rifle-maker and gunsmith.

He was a very fine and skillful workman, made many fine rifles and really spent his life in making and shooting them. According to history, Reinhardt was the only rifle-maker in Ashland County, Ohio, in 1849. After being in business for 7 years he closed his shop in Loudonville and went to Rochester, New York, where he took a "post-graduate" course in rifle-making under that master-rifle-maker William Billinghurst, where he remained for several years.

Reinhardt must have got what he needed from his work with Billinghurst, as after his post-graduate course with him he returned to Loudonville and again commenced making rifles that began to "bring home the bacon" in big time competitions as the results of his years of training and experience, and his rifles sold very readily.

Rifles with the name "P. A. Reinhardt" and the two Masonic emblems that usually marked his product began to figure in shooting competitions of national importance. At South Vernon, Massachusetts, with 28 states represented in the entries, a Reinhardt rifle carried off top honors. At Dayton, Ohio, in 1877, Reinhardt won first place and a prize of $75.00 in gold. At Fort Wayne, Indiana, in the same year he again won first money which was $50.00 in gold. A year later in a match at Tiffin, Ohio, Reinhardt won a gold watch and $60.00 in gold. At Warren, Ohio, in a match with L. W. Rogers of Tiffin, Ohio, he won over $100.00. He was always willing to back his own rifles with his skill and his money. He was not only an expert craftsman but an expert rifleman as well. In a private 10 shot match at 40 rods with John W. Adams, of West Virginia, he won a prize of $100.00, with a string that measured just 11¼ inches, which shows the *fine accuracy* of his rifle. In another private match, Reinhardt won a hundred dollar purse from John W. Johnson of Wheeling, West Virginia. In another important match with many of the best shots in the country entered, he won, with one of his own rifles, a ten-shot event at 40-rods, with a string measuring exactly 10¼ inches.

Reinhardt made rifles in Loudonville until 1896, when he moved to Dayton, Ohio, where he continued his work until advancing years caused his retirement.

Dr. P. A. Matteson has owned a number of Reinhardt rifles which I have tested at 100 to 200 yards and found that they gave very nice accuracy. His round ball rifles appeared to be especially accurate at

60 to 100 yards. I have been unable to find a picture or photograph of Reinhardt although I have made a careful search for one.

We sometimes find his name spelled "Reinhard," and as "Reinhart"; both are wrong as the correct spelling is *Reinhardt.*

I am indebted to *Muzzle Blasts,* issue of March 1940, and Mr. Stuart Martin for the principal part of the above information regarding Mr. Reinhardt.

Among the other noted makers of muzzle-loading rifles are Abe Williams, of Owego, New York, L. W. Tisdel, of Philadelphia, John Meunier, of Milwaukee, Wisconsin, and N. G. Whitmore, of Pottsdam, New York. All of these men made fine rifles of various types and calibres, and they all gave fine accuracy. However, very little information is now available regarding any of them.

Abe Williams, of Owego, N. Y., specialized in the heavy octagon barrel, under-hammer, machine rest rifles. During the Civil War, he made "sharpshooters" rifles for the U. S. Government; many of these were extremely heavy arms weighing 50 to 60 pounds in some cases. An account of the shooting of a Confederate General during the Civil War, by Captain John Metcalf, 3d, of the U. S. Army Signal Corps, at a range of more than one mile (measured range, not guessed at) with one of these heavy Abe Williams rifles, is given in chapter VI.

My dentist friend, P. A. Matteson, D.D.S., of Bennington, Vermont, has owned for several years one of these heavy rifles by Williams, which is in practically new condition, inside and out; and the doctor claims it shoots extremely accurately at the longer ranges. I have never fired it myself, as I dislike using those extremely heavy rifles in spite of the fact that they shoot remarkably fine. An illustration of this Abe Williams rifle is shown herein. I have been unable to

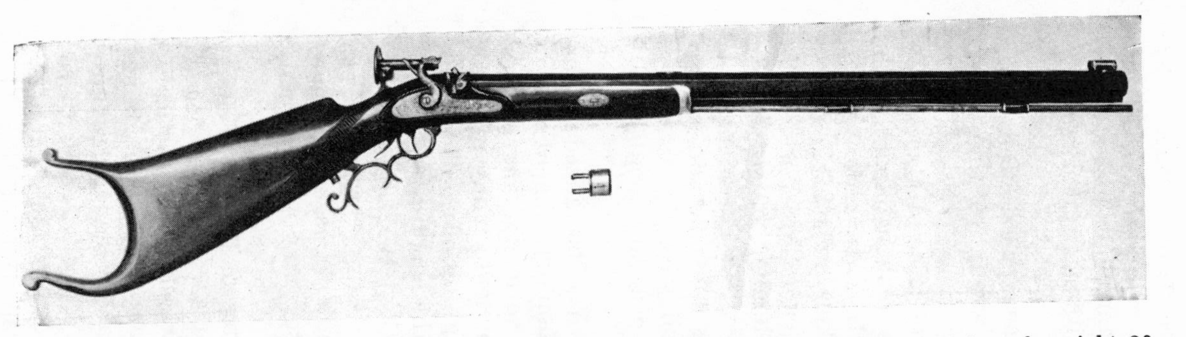

John Meunier, 38 calibre Target Rifle, using 330 grain Lubricated Bullet; 28¾-inch barrel, weight 20 pounds. Remarkably fine workmanship on this rifle. Note peculiar location of Set Trigger.

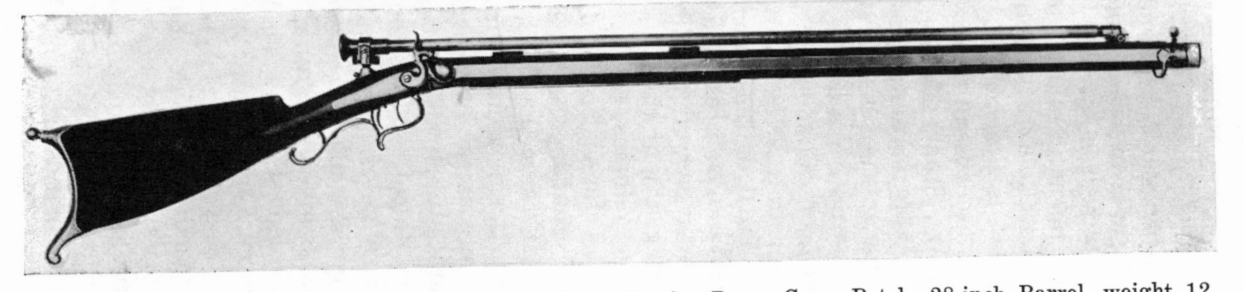

L. W. Tisdel, 40 calibre Target Rifle, Cylindrical Bullet for Paper Cross Patch, 28-inch Barrel, weight 12 pounds. Tube sight. Both rifles from Dr. P. A. Matteson's Collection.

obtain any information about Williams, of his birthplace, when he was born or when he died. My inquiries about him in Owego, only brought the information above given and he was commonly referred to in that city as "the wandering gun-maker." It is thought that he died sometime in the 1870's. I do not think that he made a great many rifles for private individuals, but most of his arms were made for the Government from about 1862 until the close of the Civil War. Sawyer's book, *Our Rifles,* gives Abe Williams' address as Covington, Kentucky, and it is possible that was his birthplace, or where he lived when he died.

L. W. Tisdel, of Philadelphia, made many fine target rifles of various kinds, weights and calibres. He was a *fine workman,* his rifles were finished in a better manner than most of the rifles of those times and they were noted for their *fine accuracy.* Dr. Matteson also has a fine Tisdel rifle, 40 calibre, weighing about 12 pounds, that I have used considerably and found it to be superior in accuracy at 100 to 150 yards to most other rifles of this weight and calibre.

Inquiries in Philadelphia regarding Mr. Tisdel failed to produce any information about his life, place and date of birth, where or when he died; although several persons in that city "thought he died along in the 1880's, in that city." It is also reported that L. W. Tisdel and his brother—whose name was Samuel, I believe—owned and operated a sporting goods store and a gun shop in Ithaca, N. Y., where they made rifles for some twenty years. That is all the information that was obtainable about these men in that city, except that those from whom I inquired who really knew about Tisdel and his brother, all stated; "They made fine rifles that shot very fine at 40 rods or more."

John Meunier, of Milwaukee, was—in all probability—born in Germany or Austria, and there learned his trade as a rifle-maker, no doubt. He was an especially fine, skillful workman, and made many of the *very finest muzzle-loading rifles* that have ever been produced in this country. By that, I mean the *finest workmanship*. They were also very accurate shooting rifles at 200 yards, or more, according to all reports. One of these rifles that was owned by Dr. Matteson until recently was in my care for about a year, during which time I shot it considerably at 200 yards rest, and made very small groups with it when it was used with the lubricated, grooved bullet. It was supposed to have been made for use with the linen patch, but I was unable to get anything but "fair accuracy" with the patched bullet at any range. When I commenced using the lubricated grooved bullet in it, there was a great improvement in the accuracy obtained at both 100 and 200 yards. I have always considered this Meunier rifle as one of the "prize arms" of the doctor's fine collection, but he let somebody "hornswaggle" him out of it about a year ago. It will be a long time before he finds another one that equals it in both workmanship and fine accuracy, I think.

Back in 1931 and again in 1935, according to reports in *The American Rifleman,* a rifle by N. G. Whitmore, of Pottsdam, New York, won the first prize in the Rising Sun, Indiana, muzzle-loading rifle match at 100 yards rest. That rifle was then owned by Walter Cline, of Chattanooga, Tenneesee, I believe, and is the same rifle that was used by the late Captain Quayle, of the Peters Cartridge Company, in making the tests for accuracy at 186 yards rest, on January 15, 1930. This test is described in *The American Rifleman,* issue of May 1931, and shows a 5-shot group which measures 1-1/8 inch horizontally by 7/8 inch vertically, made with a telescope sight, of course. The bullet used was a 225 grain picket with linen patch, backed by 65 grains F. F. g, Kings Semi-Smokeless powder and gave an average velocity of 1638 ft. sec., according to the report published. The Whitmore rifle is generally regarded as one of the *very finest*, both in workmanship and accuracy, but very few of them are to be found today.

My friend Howard M. Irish, of Buckfield, Maine, picked up one of these rifles of 45 calibre a few years ago, with all the accessories; rifle and all in very fine condition inside and out, but at the time this was written, neither Mr. Irish nor I had tested this rifle for accuracy. A man that I knew many years ago had a 40 calibre Whitmore rifle which used a long cylindrical bullet with paper cross patch, that gave very fine accuracy at 200 and 220 yards rest. This rifle was so famous for its fine accuracy that it was often barred at "turkey shoots," because the owner won all the trukeys with it and the other shooters did not have a chance to get one. An illustration of the Whitmore rifle owned by Mr. Irish, is shown herewith. The man who today owns one of these N. G. Whitmore rifles in fine condition, with all the accessories, surely has a "prize" in the muzzle-loading rifles.

CHAPTER X

THE MOUNTAIN RIFLESMITHS

The great majority of the riflemen, especially the younger ones, throughout this country except in several of the Southern states, no doubt believe that all our accurate shooting rifles are made only in modern factories, by the use of the most modern machinery operated by experienced machinists, under the supervision of college educated mechanical and ballistic engineers. They would not believe it possible that an uneducated man with no knowledge of machinery, or training in the use of machines, and without a rather complete outfit of modern machinists' tools, could make a rifle that would shoot accurately at 100 yards or more. Comparatively few of these modern sportsmen know that a few of the descendants of the old riflesmiths are still living among the mountains of Kentucky, Tennessee, North Carolina and Maryland, and are now making very accurate shooting, muzzle-loading rifles in the same way that these arms were made by their fathers and grandfathers a hundred years ago, or more. Yet such are the facts.

Some thirty years ago, I first visited one of these old riflesmiths, who lived in a house of hewn logs, back in the mountains of Kentucky about twenty miles from the railroad and fourteen miles from the nearest town, with whom I spent part of my vacation and learned a lot of very interesting things as I watched him daily at work making rifles, re-rifling barrels and making repairs on guns. I was greatly surprised when I first entered his shop, to note that he had no lathe, and I wondered how he could cut the threads on the breech plugs, or patent breech, of the rifles that he made. Later I learned that he made these from old bolts a little larger diameter than was required for the finished breech plug. He filed the threads off the bolt, worked it down to the right diameter, all by hand with the file, and then cut the threads with a screw-cutting die held in the die-stock, after drilling and reaming out the cone of the patent breech. Before doing this he cut off the head of the bolt with the hack-saw and forged part of the bolt to form the upper tang of the rifle, leaving the other end of it to be fitted as the breech plug. After forging the tang it was shaped and finished with the file and emery cloth.

I was also much surprised to note the very few, simple, old-fashioned tools that he used in making these fine shooting, round ball rifles. He had comparatively few "boughten" tools in his shop, but made more than half of these himself; made his own planes, plane-knives, chisels, cold-chisels, and draw-knives out of old pieces of iron or steel that he picked up. In one corner of his shop was a pile of old scrap iron, odds and ends of most everything, and if he wanted a chisel, gouge or draw-knife, he picked out a piece of iron or steel from this junk pile, forged it into shape, filed and ground it nearly to an edge, then tempered it and ground it sharp. And his edged tools held a sharp edge and cut better than our factory-made ones today as he was an expert in tempering these. When I asked where he learned to temper steel he said: "All I know about this I learned from my pappy years ago."

This man made his own forge of stones from his fields, set these in cement, made the flue and the chimney, and even made the bellows for forcing the draft of the forge—all by hand from materials gathered from the forest and fields, with the exception of the cement which he purchased by barter—not with money—from the country store in the distant town.

The mountain riflesmiths are natural born mechanics, they somehow know how to perform most

any necessary work from building a house or barn to repairing an automobile. Yes, most of these riflesmiths back in the mountains have a Ford automobile, an old model to be sure, but it takes them wherever they want to go, whenever they please, and they keep it in repair themselves instead of running to the garage with it every few days as you probably do with your latest model car. These men seem to possess the peculiar ability of being able to make most anything out of almost nothing, from no suitable materials as we would say, by the use of the fewest and simplest tools, of any people on this continent. The articles they make are generally remarkably well made, well finished and very durable. They are, undoubtedly, the most ingenious, self-reliant, independent upon others, of any class of people in the United States and are in this respect like the pioneers who explored and settled this country.

Some of these mountain riflesmiths use the wooden rifling guide sliding on a bench, like that illustrated on page 16, in rifling the barrels for their guns. Others use an old rifle barrel, having the desired pitch of rifling, for rotating the hardened lead bolt that carries the rifling rod with its saw attached to one end of this bolt and pushed and pulled back and forth through this barrel by a rod attached to the other end. If the riflesmith makes rifles with different twists of rifling, it is, of course, necessary to have rifle barrels that are cut with these different twists for use in rotating the rifling rod and saw.

Quite recently I had the pleasure of accompanying friends on a visit to Elmer Wolf, who lives in the mountains of Thurmont, Maryland, and is one of the few remaining riflesmiths still living in that section. Mr. Wolf's father was a riflesmith in that region many years ago; Elmer learned rifle-making from him and although he is now over 70 years old, he still makes

new rifles, re-rifles old, shot-out ones, makes repairs, new stocks, etc., in the same old way and turns out thoroughly well-made, accurate shooting rifles. An illustration herewith shows Elmer Wolf and his method of utilizing another barrel in rifling, or re-rifling, a rifle barrel. The cap lock rifle shown on his bench is one of that Mr. Wolf had nearly finished for a customer. Yet, with these primitive tools and methods, he makes very accurate shooting round ball rifles. His barrels are cut very slowly, the saw taking but a very light cut each time it is passed through the bore, thus the barrels are cut very smoothly and require little or no leading, or emerying, after rifling. Like all the other old-time riflesmiths, he uses a surprisingly small number of tools, principally of the old-fashioned, home-made kinds, in his work.

I am told by modern rifle-makers that after a barrel has been rifled, if by accident it is bent, it can not be straightened and must be discarded. I was shown a rifle for the 25-20 S. S. cartridge which went through a fire, the barrel was bent, damaged in other ways and the stock burned off. The remains of this rifle were then given to Mr. Wolf, who proceeded to straighten the barrel, re-cut it to 27 calibre, chambered it for the 25-20 S. S. case expanded to handle a 27 calibre 86 grain bullet, fitted this barrel into the action and now uses it as his "squirrel rifle." He says it shows very nice accuracy at the usual hunting ranges, in spite of the fact that it went through the fire and was then thrown away as useless. Of course, it was necessary for him to make a new cherry for this odd sized bullet in order to cut a new bullet mould for this 27 calibre bullet; all of which was easy for Mr. Wolf to do.

Elmer Wolf also relines muzzle loading rifles with steel liners that he buys and then rifles himself, and I am told that these relined rifles of his gives as good accuracy as those relined with the most modern, machine-made liners used by Diller and others. When we visited Mr. Wolf he was considering relining a muzzle-loader with a bronze tube and rifling that, as he felt confident this would produce an accurate shooting rifle with a barrel that would not rust if neglected or left uncleaned for any length of time. This appears to be quite a radical idea, but rifled arms, both long guns and pistols, were undoubtedly made in Europe during the 16th century, and this may be worth trying again. Who knows?

The mountain riflesmiths make the patch box, trigger guard, side plates, rod pipes or thimbles, butt plate and ornamental inlays usually from brass which they sawed and filed to the desired shape and size, but sometimes these were made of German silver, or sterling silver when the customer wanted an especially fine rifle. The front sight is almost invariably filed out of silver, usually of the caterpillar type of bead and set low on the octagon barrel. The various forms of rear sights are filed out of soft iron and then browned, or blued, after the rifle has been targeted at 60 or 100 yards and the rear sight notch adjusted to the correct height. These rear sights always had but a single leaf which was adjusted for a certain range, as the pioneer riflemen always used the same charge of powder and through long practice knew just how much to hold over on an animal, or mark, beyond that range for which the rifle was sighted. They were experts at this and did not require a rear sight that was adjustable for longer ranges; they probably never would have used the adjustable rear sight even if such had been furnished with the rifle.

The mountain riflesmiths today stock the majority of their rifles with black walnut, as this grows in the forests where they live, instead of the tiger flame maple. The fine grained maple with which the riflesmiths a hundred years ago stocked their rifles is now scarce in those sections and difficult to obtain from other sections, and while most of them prefer the tiger flame maple for stocks they seldom use it for the above reason only.

The walnut, maple, or other wood for stocks was sawed into planks 2 or 2½ inches thick, then stacked out of doors and air-dried for a year or more, after which it was stacked in the shop, or other building, and dried for another year or two. I am told that it required about four years to properly air-dry the wood used for stocks by the old riflesmiths. Elmer Wolf stated that he seldom made tiger flame maple stocks now as this is so difficult to obtain, and he had a good number of walnut planks air-drying outside and inside his shop, which he will later use in stocking rifles for his customers. These old riflesmiths generally make only the round ball rifles, usually of large bore—36, 28 or 23 round balls to the pound, 50, 55, or 60 calibre—with long, heavy, full octagon barrels. Most of these makers and their customers are very partial to very long barrels, from 48 to 60 inches, or even longer, as they believe these burn the black powder to better advantage and thus give finer accuracy than the shorter barreled rifles.

These extremely long barrels also give a very long distance between the front and rear sights, which affords more accurate sighting with accompanying improvement in accuracy. Many of the mountain riflemen affix sheet metal shades a foot or more in length over both the rear and front sights in order to reduce the light reflection and improve the definition of both the sights and the target. Shooting matches, usually at 60 yards, with these long barreled rifles are very popular among the mountain riflemen in many sections of that part of the country. The targets used in these matches are usually a board blackened by burning over a fire, as a charred board is intensely

Elmer Wolf, Riflesmith, left; Major Jerome Clark, U. S. Army, Retired, right. Each are holding rifles just finished by Mr. Wolf.

black, having a white card with the shooter's name thereon fastened to this as an aiming point. Each man has two practice shots, as they call them, at his own board, after which he examines his board, moves the white aiming point if desired, and makes his "cross" on the board by two knife cuts crossing each other, or by a black cross on the white card. Then each shooter fires his three or five shots, according to the conditions of the match, and when all have fired the targets are brought in and measured. The shooting in these matches is always in the prone position with the rifle resting on a log, a square timber, or other rest, on the long fore-stock at a point about six inches from the muzzle. The fore-stock of many of these rifles is made with a rectangular projection of wood, flat on the bottom, for this purpose.

In measuring the targets, dividers are used to measure the exact distance from the center of the cross on each man's target to the center of the bullet holes, these measurements recorded in inches and sixteenths and the total gives the string measure for each group. It usually requires the very finest accuracy, having all the bullets cutting closely into the cross, in order to win first, or even second, prize in these matches. If a bullet strikes near enough to the exact center to cut all four lines it is called a "four-point center", and in order to win the first prize in many of these matches it requires at least three "four-point centers" with the other two bullets nearly cutting the center. It sometimes happens that a 5-shot string with three four-point centers only wins second prize as some other marksman makes a group with four balls each counting as four-point centers and the fifth very nearly cutting into the hole made by these four balls.

Thus it will be apparent that only the most accurate shooting rifle, with an expert marksman behind, it has any chance of winning a prize in these mountain rifle matches today even though the shooting is done with the old—archaic as some would call them—muzzle-loading rifles. Up to the limit of their accurate range, and their best accuracy appears to be at 60 yards, these long rifles made by the mountain riflesmiths will shoot as small groups as the *very best* modern, high velocity rifles today. The prize in these mountain rifle matches is frequently a beef steer which is divided into five parts, or "choices" as they call them; two fore quarters, two hind quarters, and the hide and tallow. In that case each shooter has one shot for each "choice" in his 5-shot string, and the man making the shortest string for the five shots wins the first prize, or first choice, which is one of the fore quarters. The man who has the second shortest string takes the other fore quarter, and so on until all the choices have been assigned to the marksmen who make the five shortest strings.

Back in the old days—75 years ago or more—these riflesmiths made their own locks for their rifles, but now Elmer Wolf and others buy them from dealers in gunsmiths's supplies in the larger cities as they can buy the locks cheaper than they can make them, and these are thoroughly well-made, good locks at that. It is also very doubtful if any of the mountain riflesmiths today make their own barrel blanks, but instead they buy the unrifled barrel blanks from the arms manufacturers, then anneal these blanks by old-time methods and rifle and finish them, instead of making these by hand as was the custom one hundred years ago. However, many of the rifles made by these men are made from old rifle barrels that are sent to them by the customer, which they rebore to larger calibre, smooth ream with the long bit and then re-rifle as in the case of new barrels. These rifles made from old barrels thus re-rifled generally give better accuracy than those with new barrels, according to all reports.

Practically all the mountain riflesmiths are expert marksmen with the rifle, they learned to shoot the rifle when a boy, they love the rifle and love to shoot them, they make rifles principally for this reason and not because they expect to get rich in the business. Like Elmer Wolf, if they can "make day wages by making good shooting rifles" they are satisfied; and "day wages" with them does not mean fifteen or twenty dollars a day net profit that most of our modern rifle-makers in the cities require on account of "high over-head, high rent, high wages, etc". The only "over-head" that these mountain reflesmiths know about is the roof of their house, or the blue sky over their beloved mountains. They have no worries about "labor troubles, sit down strikes, or the stock market", but are plain, old-fashion, thoroughly honest craftsmen who earnestly endeavor to make the very best muzzle-loading rifle—"the best I know how"—in the old-fashioned way.

And when you see and shoot the rifles these rifle-smiths turn out back in their mountain shops, with their few, primitive tools, it makes one stop and think about this "modern civilization with its city dwellers, planned economy, regulation and regimentation of business", etc. In a few more decades all of the mountain riflesmiths will have passed on to the better world, and they will then be only a memory like the pioneer, the buffalo and the passenger pigeon, and the world will have lost more of the old-time geniuses.

CHAPTER XI

MISCELLANEOUS HINTS AND SUGGESTIONS

Before Mr. Wm. V. Lowe commenced making rifles and early in his rifle shooting career, he carried on an extensive correspondence with the late Horace Warner, of Syracuse, New York, and the important parts of these letters from Mr. Warner were recorded by Lowe in his note-books on rifle-making and rifle shooting. Many years later, these note-books with much other data was sold by Mr. Lowe to Mr. Walter Grote, Canton, Ohio, and through the kindness of Mr. Grote, I have been allowed to publish whatever I chose from these records. I find that many most important matters in connection with rifle-making and rifle shooting are very fully covered and explained by Mr. Warner in these letters; therefore, I am including in this chapter the major part of Warner's answers to Lowe's inquiries, as I am sure that these will prove of great value to the younger men who may engage in rifle-making, as well as being especially important to the users of the muzzle-loading rifles in general.

Extract from Horace Warner's letter dated April 3, 1887. "In answer to your question why does your gun shoot weak against cross wind; it is evident that the bullet has a staggering motion; i. e. does not spin evenly—point not true to line of flight. This may be due to: Too much choke; Too little choke; Imperfect choke; Too loose at breech; Too much bearing; Too little bearing; Bad form of bullet; Too much polish on inside of barrel, and some other things. You can take your choice. Fix up one thing at a time till you strike the right one, and then if you have not spoiled it on some other point, you may find out just what the trouble was. That is the way a gun tinker has to do to find out what the matter is, and it takes lots of time and ammunition. Since you are trying to shape up your gun, I will tell you as well as I can how I go to work to do it, and it may help you out a little, in fitting a new barrel.

The form at first is a cylinder, of course; then I work it large up to within 2½ or 3 inches of end of lands proper, tapering this choke to within about an inch of the end of barrel. Then leave the last inch and Patent Muzzle straight out. From the commencement of the choke to the breech make it as near one size as possible. When that is enough larger than the muzzle to let a *naked bullet* (*that is a proper fit for the gun*) which has been put through the Patent Muzzle, drop of its own weight as soon as it gets to the lower end of the choke, you have enough. Then take off the Patent Muzzle and work out the front end of the choke in the barrel by pushing your emery bolt through from the breech end till you have made the choke in the barrel enough larger than it is in the Pat. Muzzle so you can blow the naked bullet out of the end of the barrel, with your breath by blowing a quick, hard puff—just as hard as you can. Keep trying it from time to time till you can *just do this.* Your gun must be wiped *clean* and *dry* when you try it and you must stop the breech with a wad when you put the bullet in the muzzle so that it cannot drop out, and just as soon as you can blow the naked bullet clear out through the muzzle, you have it about the right shape. This is the right shape when you are to use linen patches. The bullet should drop *freely* from choke to breech; but for paper patch (especially thin paper) it should not drop quite so quickly and if it will travel slowly along the barrel and keep going till it gets to the breech, it is loose enough, and the chances are that you cannot quite blow it out. For the friction along the barrel will prevent its gaining so much impetus.

For a large bored gun and a linen patch, the Pat. Muzzle needs to be about 1/1000 inch smaller than the breech where the bullet lies, and the muzzle end of the barrel 1/2000 inch (.0005, N. H. R.) smaller than the breech. For paper patch, a trifle less choke than for linen. After all, you have to depend a good deal on the sense of touch and feeling, and *this must be acquired by practice.* After you have it shaped up as above, try a bullet with patch on. If your starter rod puts it to the bottom of choke (and it should very nearly) you ought to be able to shove the bullet down with the thumb and finger after it is 6 inches from the choke, and shove it back toward the muzzle nearly as easy till it gets within 3 inches, or 2½, of end of muzzle, then should begin to tighten and gradually increase the pinch until at the last inch it should go about as hard as you can push with *one* hand. Of course, all this test of pushing and blowing depends on how strong a man can do it. I have given you my rule and practice, and if you can impart about the same strength to these movements it will work pretty well for you. End of first lesson." "P. S. as your gun is already choked, try it by putting ball in. If it drops too freely, take choke out of Pat. Muzzle till it drops about right; then begin blowing ball back and relieve muzzle of barrel till you can blow it out."

Extract from Letter from Horace Warner dated April 13, 1887.

"I have shipped your gun to you today by Express. I have taken great pains with the gun and I do not know of a better one in the world. Think it will hold good for a long time if properly treated, for I have finished the inside with a hardening process peculiar to me which to a great extent does in advance what the force of the powder would eventually; i. e., condenses the metal on inside surface to the depth 1/60 inch or more." * * * "Have made two nipples for the gun and besides a device for using primers, which although it is rather 'outlandish' in appearance, I predict will win your confidence after receiving a fair trial. . I have *no use for caps* or nipples on my guns and probably never will have any more. With primers there is no hang-fire and scarcely ever a snap—a great advantage in shooting from the shoulder. You may be bothered to work yours at first but will soon master it if patient. The cap which holds the firing-pin and primer in place is also the tool for de-capping. It may be an eye-sore to you at first, but you will become reconciled to it with better acquaintance. After the primer is in place, put the cap on with the fingers; when down to place, wiggle and work it carefully till the screw takes position and then give the handle of the wrench a quarter turn to the rear, or until the cap comes taut. The extracting process you will soon master, and then you will be able to do it without much more delay than the ordinary nipple, and it is so much surer to go quick and clean. Then besides, it does not dirty your telescope and barrel with smoke, which is a great nuisance, especially to clean up around the 'snail' after every day's shoot. I put in a charger, or rather for you to measure a charge by, of the Hazzard's F. g. Sea Shooting powder. I turn the powder slowly and carefully from my flash top into the charger which fills it to within about 1/16 inch of the top. You can order primers from the Union Metallic Cartridge Co., Bridgeport, Conn.; order the thin No. 2 primer then you get a thin and strong primer not liable to burst through. The Winchester No. 2 primer is the same size, but being copper metal is not so stiff or strong. Have to write you another letter soon about how to cast bullets for the new style swage as the swage makes them now."

Extract from Mr. Lowe's note-book dated April 22,

1887. "Went to Boston to see Mr. Smith (Hiram W. Smith, N. H. R.) and found him in; also William Farrington and his son. Mr. Farrington only stopped a few minutes as Mr. A. C. Gould came in. While there however, Mr. Farrington said: "When Wetmore and I worked together we could make 12 guns that would positively shoot the first time out. Once in trying a new gun he said, I am going to beat 10 inches the first string (40 rods). Some one bet him a quarter he would not; bet taken and he easily beat 10 inches." "William Farrington in his best days was probably one of the very best target rifle makers; none were his superior and few his equal. Since he gave up rifle shooting about 1866, is now running telegraph lines. Is now 62 years old and climbs poles as readily as ever."

Extract from Mr. Lowe's note-book dated, Saturday May 14, 1887. "Went to Falconers, New York, and on way stopped at Jamestown and went in to see Perry who kindly showed me all around the city. Went to Falconers at 4 P. M., Eastern or Boston, time and walked from depot to shooting house with rifle and traps. Was introduced to Mr. Horace Warner by H. V. Perry. We had long chats together in the sitting room after supper. During the conversation he said that when a gun shoots better when hurried and shot fast, it shows too loose a fit at breech and the reverse when it scatters when it heats up. There may be a point between where it will not make much difference whether shot fast or slow."

The following extract from Mr. Lowe's note-book is of interest, in my opinion at least: "Tuesday Evening, June 22, 1887. Went up to visit Brockway. Got to Bellows Falls about 11 P. M. Went to his shop early the following morning, and after some conversation on various topics, Mr. Brockway swaged some bullets and then hired a team to take us up to the shooting grounds. Got there about 11 A. M., put up target and commenced with the new 32 calibre. Tried different thicknesses of patches and different styles of bullets, all of no avail. Thursday it rained. Brockway told me how he laid out the curve on a wooden rifling roll."

"In the first place have the roll as large as possible so as to minimize any error as much as possible. Suppose we want to make a regular twist; have our roll, for simplicity, as long as the distance we wish to make one turn in. For example, a 30-inch twist."

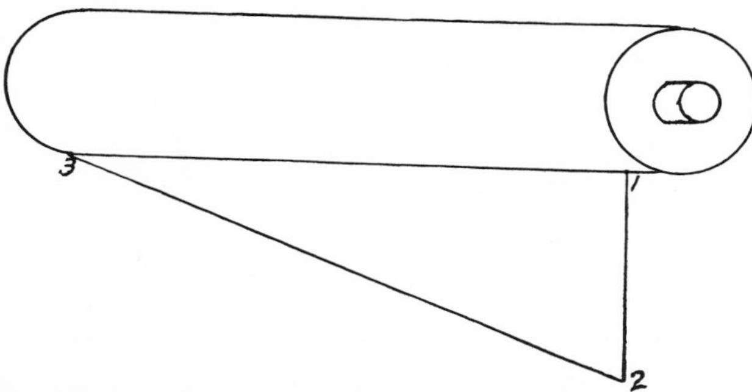

"Suppose 3—1 be laid off on a line parallel to the axis of the cylinder just 30 inches long. Take a piece of wire, 1—2, just equal to the circumference of the roll. Hold this wire at right angles to the surface of the cylinder, 3—1. Now stretch a piece of wire, 3—2, from 3 to the extremity of wire 1—2. Now, turn the cylinder slowly winding up the two wires, 1—2 and 2—3.

The wire 2—3 will then be wound spirally around the surface of the cylinder. Now, with a light hammer, carefully drive this wire into the surface of the wooden roll. Then cut out the grooves to conform to these marks." This completes the roll for the rifling guide with the uniform twist of rifling.

Also, on another page Mr. Lowe gives Brockway's

instructions for making a rifling guide for the gain twist, as follows: "Now suppose we wish a gain twist; suppose you want a 30-inch twist ending with a 10-inch twist."

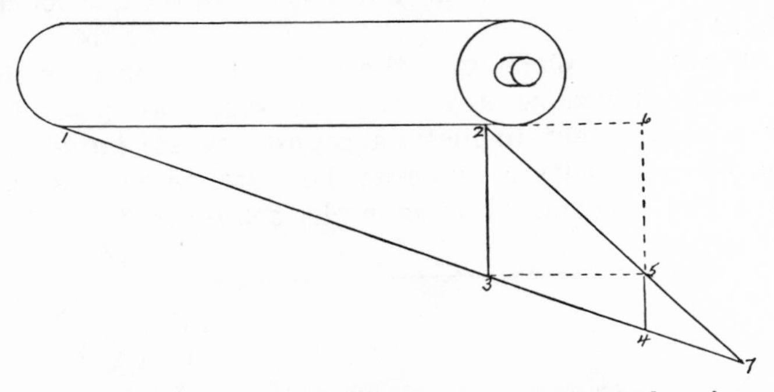

"Lay off 30 inches, set off a point, 3, just the circumference of the roll from 2; from this point measure off 10 inches in a direction parallel to the cylinder, 3—5 and in line with 1—3 set up a point 4 and fasten the wire at 1. Draw the wires through 1—3 and 2—5. Where they intersect set up a pin, 7, and let wire draw over this when winding it up, and this will give the rate of twist required. With a light hammer, proceed as before; that is, drive the wire carefully into the surface of the wooden roll; then cut out very carefully the grooves to conform to these marks around the cylinder." "It will readily be seen that the generating line is parallel to the curve generated on the cylinder at any portion of this curve."

Thus you will readily see how simple it is to lay out a rifling guide—a wooden one—for either the uniform or gain twist types of rifling, and here you have the method that Brockway used in making his rifling guides.

Peculiar Shaped Bullets for Muzzle-loading Rifles.

The old adage: "There is nothing new under the sun" most aptly applies to the shape, or form, of bullets for rifles. When anyone states that "this shape of bullet never has been tried, or tested," he is making a very unwise statement at least, as no one really knows ALL the different shapes of bullets that have been designed and tested during the years since the invention of the rifle. As an illustration of this fact, and to show that the so-called "boat-tail" bullet is nothing at all new, let me state the following: In 1904 when I lived in Winsted, Connecticut, and was a member of the rifle team of Company M, First Infantry, Connecticut National Guard, on an occasion when this rifle team was shooting in a match in Hartford, myself and another rifleman were talking with an old Civil War veteran whose name was Merrill and who had been a gunsmith before that war. During our conversation regarding rifles, bullets, etc., he showed us a bullet that he and another gunsmith had designed and tested somewhat in 1861 and '62 before he enlisted in the Army. I made a sketch in my notebook of this bullet and its paper patch. Mr. Merrill's bullet was 40 calibre, the body of the bullet was 1.08 inches long, from the end of the boat-tail to the point it measured 1.14 inches, and weighed 390 grains. The patch which is similar in shape to the usual cross patch used in muzzle-loading rifles, has a hole in the center of the cross which fits over the boat-tail of this bullet in loading, while the other parts of the patch fit up around the bullet in loading in the same way as the 2-strip and the cross patches.

Mr. Merrill said that he and his friend made two of the rifles for use with this bullet, which were cut with a gain twist commencing with 48 inches and ending with 15 inches. The charge of powder was 2¾ inches of the bore, or from 90 to 100 grains weight, of Kentucky rifle F. g., and the rifle gave fine accuracy at all ranges including 1000 yards and 200 rods—1100 yards. By "nice accuracy," he meant that they had made 15-shot scores of 57 and 58 out of a possible 60 at 1000 yards on the old Creedmoor target with square bull that counted 4. When we asked him if he continued making rifles for this bullet after the war, he answered: "My friend was killed at Gettysburg and when the war was over I had done all the shooting that I wanted to for a long time. Then the breech-loaders came into use and I never made another rifle for this bullet."

I have often thought of having some rifle-maker make a rifle for me to use this bullet and patch, but have never done so. I believe it has great merit, should give super-fine accuracy at all ranges from 200 to 1000 yards, and it would be well worth while for some rifle-maker to make a rifle for this bullet and give it a thorough trial.

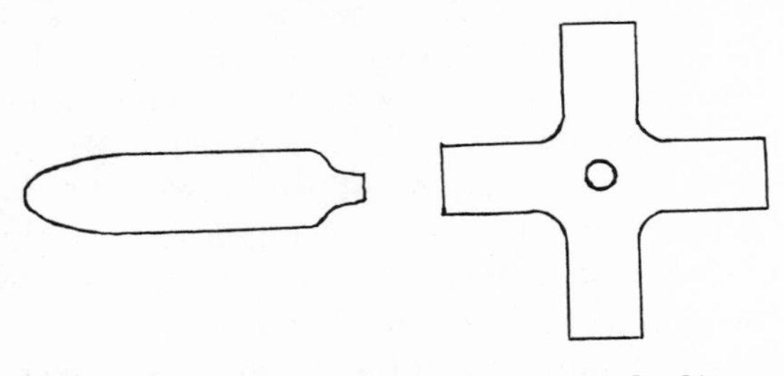

In loading, the hole in center of patch fits over the boat-tail of the bullet.

Bear's Oil as a Lubricant. When I was a boy all the old riflemen and hunters insisted that pure bear's oil is the *very best* for oiling the linen or paper patches for the muzzle-loading rifles, as well as for lubricating the rifle after cleaning. My Uncle Alvaro also regarded it as the best for this purpose, but bear's oil was not always obtainable even in those times, while sperm oil could be purchased everywhere. For that reason both uncle and I, as well as the majority of riflemen, used the sperm oil for lubricating the bore and outside of the rifle and for oiling the patches of either kind.

After uncle and I went on our first bear hunt to the Campton-Waterville country of New Hampshire, we always kept a good quantity of bear's oil on hand for our own use, as well as to sell in small quantities to other riflemen who preferred it to the sperm oil. Bear's oil when properly tried out and filtered, is water-white, practically odorless, is a fine lubricant for the bore and outside of the rifle and does not thicken, or "gum," after standing a long time. Therefore patches that are lubricated with it will not be sticky, or gummy, after having been oiled for a long time. In this respect, I think bear's oil is better for oiling the patches than any other oil we have. All the old-timers said: "If you clean your rifle with bilin water, let her cool a leetle, swab her out good an ile her with bear's ile, yor rifle will keep all right an never rust." If you live where bear's oil is obtainable, try it for oiling the patches for your muzzleloader and you will find it the BEST for that purpose, but as a rust preventive and lubricant for the bore of the rifle there are several oils on the market that are superior.

Some of the old riflemen and hunters also used skunk's oil for lubricating the patches, chiefly because it was always obtainable; but they always preferred the bear's oil when they could get it.

In chapter 1, I mentioned the beautiful butternut brown finish that most of the old-time rifle-makers used on their best grade rifles, and mentioned that I had tried for many years to obtain the formula that these makers used for this browning. Just recently Mr. L. O. Holman, of Trumansburg, New York, furnished me this formula which was used by Reuben Harwood, who wrote very interesting articles for *Shooting and Fishing* during the 1880's and early '90's, under the pen names of "Iron Ramrod" and "Aberdeen." Mr. Harwood was a gunsmith, a small bore rifle crank who was very fond of hunting small game with the rifle, and was a skillful workman. He was then located in Somerville, Massachusetts, and originated the "Hornet" cartridge for use in small game shooting, vermin and target work. Harwood used this formula in putting this beautiful browning on rifle barrels in those days; Mr. Holman has also used it for many years in browning barrels, and I know that it works splendidly.

Reuben Harwood's Formula for browning plain steel barrels:

"Nitric acid, ½ ounce; Spirits nitre, ½ ounce; Spirits wine, 1 dram; Blue stone, 2 drams; Tincture steel, 1 dram; Rain water, 1 quart."

"Mix in a clean bottle, cork tightly and leave it at least one week to thoroughly amalgamate before using. Keep in a warm place; freezing spoils it. After the old finish has been scoured off with emery cloth moistened with oil (not kerosene) and the barrel thoroughly polished, wipe it thoroughly with clean, dry rags. Then apply whiting, powdered chalk, or plaster of paris on a dry cloth to absorb and clean off all remaining grease. From now on *do not allow the fingers or bare hands to touch the surface,* but handle the barrel only by the wooden plugs fitted tightly into both breech and muzzle. The secret of success, if there is one about it, now is: *Keep the hands from the barrel;* handle by the long plug in the barrel and stand it up on the shorter plug in the other end. If the barrel must at any time be lifted otherwise than by the plug, use a piece of clean cotton cloth to grasp it with; but handle it only by the plugs. After wiping over thoroughly with the powder—whiting—we are ready for the browning fluid. Should by accident any oily substance or the hands come in contact with the barrel after applying the whiting, or during the process of browning, it will cause a spot different in color and very undesirable. In that case stop; scald the barrel well with boiling water poured down the outside from a teakettle, use No. 120 emery cloth to remove the browning and start anew. Have a plug projecting 2 inches from the muzzle and one 5 inches long from the breech. Hickory, white oak, or any tough hardwood will answer well for plugs."

"Pour a small quantity of the browning solution into a small glass or earthen vessel and apply to the barrel with a soft cotton rag, putting it on lightly lengthwise of the barrel. Wet the surface thoroughly and well, but not enough to run, holding the barrel vertically by the longer plug, allowing it to rest on the shorter one. Keep it always in the same position while browning. Stand away in a warm, dark place over night. Much depends on the temperature; it should be even and never at the freezing point. Barrels brown quicker and better where it is warm, but not hot. A coat of red, blue, or greenish corrosion will be found, which, when dry enough, is carded or scratched off, always remembering to work lengthwise of the barrel. A steel wire scratch brush may be used, but not too stiff one. Hold the short plug in one hand and with the other use the card or scratch brush lightly and quickly as long as the rust will fly from abrasion."

"The barrel is usually ready for the first scratching after standing over night, say twelve hours; but if the temperature is below 60 degrees F. it must stand longer; at any rate until a dry rust has formed. Do NOT let the hands touch the card or scratch brush, or get any oil or grease on it. After the first scratching, the process may be repeated three times a day—morning, noon and night—until the color suits. The longer it is in the process the darker the color will be. It varies somewhat according to circumstances, but approximately forty-eight hours will give a chestnut brown, which grows darker until the fourth day, when a purple commences. When the color is dark enough to suit, scratch off thoroughly with a soft scratch brush or steel wool and pour a teakettleful of boiling water down the barrel over the browning. That stops the action of the fluid; the heat will dry it off. Then scratch lightly as before. Next give the barrel a light, even coat of boiled linseed oil applied with a clean cotton rag. Wipe well, remove the plugs, and it is done and can be handled. Better let it stand a few days before using much so as to further harden the browning."

Individuality in Rifles. It is a well-known fact among makers of muzzle-loading rifles and those who have had much experience in shooting them, that each rifle had certain peculiarities, or individualities, which are different from all others. We invariably find that two muzzle-loading rifles by the same maker, of the same calibre, same weight, same model or type and same length of barrel, will not give the same degree of accuracy with exactly the same charge, or size of grain, of powder. In the rifle family we find as many individual traits, and degrees of excellence in accuracy as we find among members of the same family. During my experience as a teacher I have had hundreds of cases in which two children from the same family were as unlike as day and night; one child was studious, careful, thoughtful and accurate in his work, while the other was very careless, thoughtless, inaccurate and would not study. Two muzzle-loading rifles of the same make, weight and calibre are often as different as these two children cited.

In *Shooting and Fishing,* issue of August 13, 1891, is an article by Horace Warner on this subject, from which I quote the following: "Given good material to commence with, the excellence of the weapon will depend entirely upon the ability of the maker to harmonize all its combinations with reference to the peculiar work for which it is designed, and to finish in detail all the parts of the piece and adjuncts, up to the highest standard of workmanship. And right here the trouble commences. What is the standard for inside shape and finish of the barrel? What for length, form and temper of bullet? Is the standard for inside shape and finish generally adopted by the leading manufacturers, the one that will give the best possible results if strictly followed? If so, can the manufacturers themselves produce the same features in every piece?"

"Decidedly not. If they could, every piece of the same material and dimensions would perform equally well. They make each piece so like all the others that the eye cannot detect any difference; even their instruments for taking measurements might not record any difference, yet, when we know that a difference of 1/3000 of an inch in the inside of either breech or muzzle end of the barrel may make the difference between an ordinary and a fine shooting rifle, it will not be difficult to comprehend why all the rifles turned out from any factory should not shoot equally well. No man and no machine can, at every trial (even upon the same material), make a rifle so nearly like its predecessor that it will, with certainty, give the same or equally good results in shooting."

"But let us suppose that a skillful hand-workman, who is conscientious and determined to put out nothing but good work, has made a target rifle for a patron who wants nothing but the best. He finishes the rifle in as good style as he knows, and goes out to test it, finds that it is all that he expects (A No. 1), and sends it to his customer who is delighted with it.

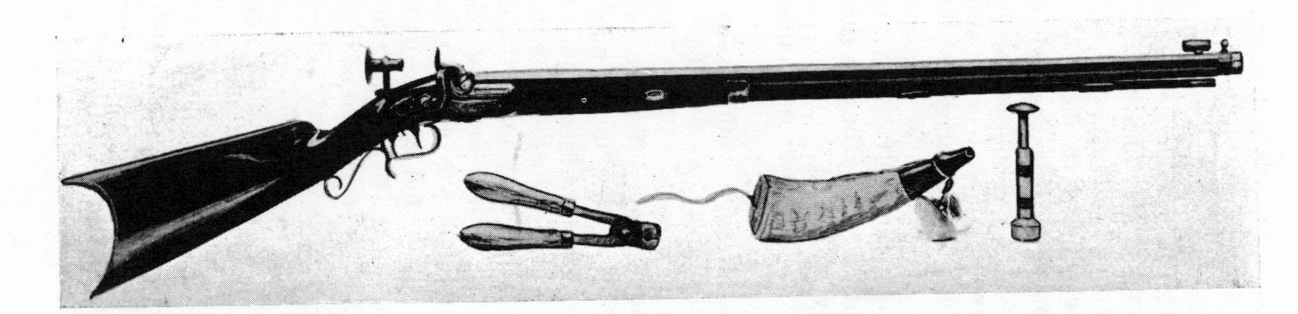

F. Wasmann, Target Rifle, 40 calibre, 31½-inch barrel, weight 12¼ pounds. From Dr. P. A. Matteson's Collection.

A neighbor of his customer who witnesses the performance of the rifle, orders one for himself just like it. The maker goes to work on another; makes it in every respect as nearly like the first one as he possibly can. When he puts it upon trial he cannot keep all his shots in the 7 circle at 200 yards with good rest and fair weather. The rifle is decidedly bad; will not fill the order. What shall be done? Shall he make another and another until he gets one that will, or shall he try to make that one work satisfactorily?"

"Having a little pride and determination in his make up, he decides that he will make that one shoot, or wear it out in trying to; so he goes to work at it again, changing the form of inside slightly, and finds some improvement in the shooting; keeps to work on it, making changes little by little in the barrel or ammunition, with steadily improving scores until, in about a week's time, he brings it up to the required degree of excellence, easily keeping all its shots within the 11 and 12 ring. There it is; a fine shooter, and no mistake. It has passed through all the gradations, from intolerably bad to extremely fine; all the improvement due to well directed labor. What shall be said of the individuality of the piece from first to last? It has just what the maker gave it; nothing more, nothing less. The same may be said of all the rifles (or shotguns) made. None are so poor, and very few so good, as not to be susceptible of improvement."

"I have known one rifle at least which, for a limited time, would or did deliver 10 consecutive shots at 40 rods from double rest with such uniformity that every shot broke into the hole made by the preceding shot, as long as the direction of the aim was unchanged. Three changes of aim were made during the time in an effort to place the shots a little nearer the centre of target, and the string was completed by placing the last three shots in one hole so exactly on the centre that it was difficult to tell which was the better of the three, and all three measured less than 3/16 of an inch, centre to centre. This performance might be regarded as a scratch, a freak, a combination of good luck and good management, or even a mark of individuality in the rifle itself. The latter conclusion might be accepted with a certain degree of complacency were it not for the fact that the rifle would not retain *that degree of accurate and uniform delivery* for any considerable length of time. One hundred to 150 shots from it would suffice to destroy its 'gilt edge' qualities. After that its work would be for a time fair, then ordinary, and soon inferior. Then it must be again worked over and given the proper form and finish inside, when it would, for another interval, resume its former excellent work. For four or five times during my ownership of the rifle this process was repeated, and always with the same results. The gilt edge quality could not be retained for any great length of time; neither could it be secured at every trial in working the rifle over, for the success depends entirely upon one's ability to decide when the inside form and finish are correct. This is a matter so difficult to determine that the operator must depend as much upon luck in suspending his labors at just the proper time as he can upon any positive knowledge he possesses. He might have had the piece in *just the right condition* a half dozen times during the operation but *he did not know it,* and perhaps quit the work at a time when it was a little at fault; and so it goes with rifle work. No man is smart enough to tell when a rifle is at *its best,* for he can scarcely tell what the best would imply."

"He knows the best he has seen and can take that as his standard, and strive to equal it. He may excel it or he may come short of it, when he can only try again. The excellence of the shooting so entirely depends on the perfection of the form and style of finish inside, both of which will be constantly, though perhaps slowly, changing by use that there will come a time when the two conditions will be so changed that the performance of the rifle will not be up to its original standard, and may go far below it. Two rifles, one of which may be extra fine in shooting qualities, the other only ordinary or even inferior, may, by constant use in a year or two, have their relations to each other exactly reversed—i. e., the poorer of the two may become in that time the better rifle; all owing to some changes of inside form and finish wrought by the action of the powder and bullet."

"To sum up I will reiterate what I have already stated, that the characteristics of all firearms are due entirely to the manner in which they have been made, and all may be changed or modified by intelligent effort; and further, that all will be changed to a certain extent by continued use, so that none can be relied upon to do the same quality of work throughout a long period of service."

From the foregoing it would appear that if you actually possess a muzzle-loading rifle which has *gilt edge accuracy,* you should shoot it just *as little as possible* since after one or two hundred shots that *super-fine accuracy* will, probably, have disappeared and its performance will thereafter be somewhat below its former degree of excellence.

The Pitch, or Twist of Rifling. Even the most experienced, skillful rifle-makers, and expert riflemen of many years' experience, often desire some sort of a formula, or table, by which the approximately correct twist, or pitch, of rifling for a certain calibre of rifle may be ascertained before ordering a barrel made for it. Of course, you can if you "have money to burn," leave this all to the man who makes this barrel, who probably really knows no more about the matter than you do, but has a "standard" of his own which he will follow in making the barrel unless you specifically state the pitch of rifling that he must use. Numerous formulas have been devised during the years past by which it was supposed that the correct pitch, or twist, of rifling for any given calibre of rifle could be determined. The majority of these were of little or no practical value and seldom enabled the rifleman to ascertain in advance just what twist of rifling would be the best—give the best accuracy—in a certain calibre.

An English scientist, Professor Greenhill, early in 1830, established a formula for determining the necessary pitch of rifling for cannon, and from this Major J. P. Cundill, R. A., some years later, calculated a table of twists for small arms projectiles, which has given the most reliable data on this subject of any yet devised, and which is here given.

"Table of Twists for Small-Arms Projectiles, by Major J. P. Cundill, R. A."

Length of Bullet in Calibres	Length of Twist in Calibres	Length of Bullet in Calibres	Length of Twist in Calibres
2	84.29	4.0	36.43
2.1	78.98	4.1	35.43
2.2	74.32	4.2	34.49
2.3	70.20	4.3	33.59
2.4	66.53	4.4	32.74
2.5	63.24	4.5	31.94
2.6	60.26	4.6	31.21
2.7	57.55	4.7	30.44
2.8	55.09	4.8	29.74
2.9	52.72	4.9	29.07
3.0	50.74	5.0	28.44
3.1	48.82	5.1	27.83
3.2	47.04	5.2	27.24
3.3	45.38	5.3	26.68
3.4	43.84	5.4	26.14
3.5	42.40	5.5	25.63
3.6	41.05	5.6	25.13
3.7	39.79	5.7	24.66
3.8	38.61	5.8	24.20
3.9	37.48	5.9	23.70
		6.0	23.33

Again quoting from Mr. Lowe's note-book on this subject of pitch of rifling: "Warner and I went into such matters as the best twist of rifling for different conditions, and the correct length of bullet for uniformly reliable results. A long, heavy bullet has an advantage, as the resistance of the air is largely on the point of the bullet, and with a longer, heavier bullet we have a better chance to beat the wind. We considered many rifles, and the data on rifles which had showed especially well were as follows:

Calibre	Twist of Rifling in Inches; One turn in	In Calibres; One turn in	Bullet Length In Inches	In Calibres
32	14	40¾	1- 1/8	3.5
32	13	40-2/3	1- 3/16	3.7
35	14	40	1- 3/16	3.4
38	15	39½	1- 3/8	3.6
38	14	37	1- 7/16	3.8
45	20	44½	1-11/32	3.0

Swaging Bullets. In order to obtain the best accuracy — make the smallest groups — with the muzzle-loading rifles using the picket, conical, sugar-loaf, or cylindrical bullets (sometimes called the "slug balls"), as well as the composite, two-piece bullets, it is necessary to true these up, compress the lead, bring them up to the correct diameter, make the base and point of the correct shape if the bullet is cast in one piece, or firmly secure the parts of the two-piece bullets together and make them of the desired shape and diameter, by the process known as "swaging." As before stated, the bullets that are cast in one piece as well as those cast in two pieces, are practically never of the correct shape of point and base, or the correct diameter, as these come from the bullet mould. Therefore, it is necessary to swage these into the correct shape and diameter in order to get accurate shooting from them.

Various types of bullet swages are described and

illustrated in chapter III, but the older, or earlier, type of swage was made in two pieces—the body and plunger—with no provision for expelling the swaged bullet from the body of the swage. It was supposed that if the swage was properly polished and finished inside, the bullet would come out after being swaged by striking the swage with a hammer so as to jar it and thus cause the bullet to drop out. But, as all users of the muzzle-loading rifles well know, this often does NOT cause the bullet to come out of the swage; then repeated attempts to jar it out by striking the swage on the bench, or with the hammer, sometimes fail to make the bullet drop out, thus causing much trouble and annoyance to the rifleman.

This induced N. S. Brockway to design the swage having a small plunger in the base to form the point of the bullet and expel the swaged bullet by a light tap on this plunger, and was a great improvment over the old type of swage. However as there are many of the old swages still in use and causing trouble because the swaged bullet will not come out easily, it is well to know an easy method of getting the bullet out of the swage. Mr. R. R. Sherman, of McLean, Virginia, discovered that if the bullet will not come out of the swage by jarring it, heating the swage will cause the bullet to drop out easily. Hold the body of the swage in the flame of a blow-torch until it gets quite hot—about as hot as a flatiron when in use; then the bullet will "pop" out of the swage without injuring either the swage or the bullet. While the swage is hot, other bullets are swaged and drop out easily by slightly jarring the base of the swage; when it gets cold, heat the body of the swage again and the bullets practically drop out after being swaged. This "hint" will save riflemen much "cussing," time and trouble when using the old type swages; but if you are having a new swage made it is wise to have it made with the plunger for expelling the bullet—the so-called "Brockway type" of swage.

Correct Fit of Round Balls. It frequently happens that one obtains a round ball rifle without the original bullet mould and has difficulty in deciding upon the proper diameter of the bullet before ordering a new mould for it. Therefore, N. S. Brockway's "rule" for this will enable one to ascertain the correct diameter of mould to order. His method was as follows: "The round ball as it drops from the mould should be the *bore diameter of the rifle plus one thickness of the patch material.*"

As an illustration of this, suppose you have a 70 gauge round ball rifle for which you desire a new mould. The bore diameter of the 70 gauge barrel should be .400 inch; let us assume that the linen which you are to use for the patches measures .009 inch in thickness; your bullet mould should be cut to drop a bullet .400 inch plus .009 inch, or .409 inch diameter. A bullet this diameter will load properly and give the best accuracy with this rifle.

If the rifle for which you desire a new mould uses the picket, sugar-loaf, or conical bullet with cloth patch, this same rule is used in ascertaining the correct diameter of the bullet as it comes from the mould; that is, the bore diameter of the barrel plus one thickness of the material used for patches. However, if the rifle uses the long cylindrical one-piece, or two-piece, bullet with paper patch, Mr. Brockway stated that the bullet as it comes from the swage should be the bore diameter of the barrel plus *one-half the thickness of the paper used for the patches.* In other words, if the bore diameter of your rifle is .380 inch and the paper from which the patches are cut is .002 inch thick, the swaged bullet should be .380 inch plus .001 inch, or .381 inch diameter as it comes from the swage. Mr. Brockway also stated that he tested the bullet fit by putting the swaged bullet in its paper patch through the false muzzle into the barrel, remove the bullet starter, insert the loading rod, start the bullet down the bore by holding the loading rod with the thumb and forefinger only and after pushing the bullet about six inches down the bore, let go of the rod and its weight should cause the bullet to slowly slide down the bore to the breech. When the bullet fits this way the rifle should give its finest accuracy. Of course, this means that the bullet should be cast from pure lead—not hardened.

Were the Old Kentucky Rifles "Sighted High?" This is a question often asked by the inexperienced users of the round ball rifles, who forget that the law of gravitation absolutely applies in this case as well as in all others concerning falling bodies. In spite of the mythical statements often made that the Kentucky rifles "shoot flat" at 60 to 100 yards, the real facts are that *they do nothing of the kind* as that is an absolute impossibility with rifles of that velocity, or any other. It is true that the Kentucky rifles have very low front sights, generally extremely low ones, and the rear sight is also apparently a very low one; but if the breech plug is removed from the barrel and then it is bore sighted on a black bull at 60 yards range, a glance through the sights will show that the line of sights points some distance above the line of the bore and thus allows for the drop of the ball in travelling the 60 yards so that it will "shoot center" at that range, or at 100 yards if the rifle was sighted by the maker for this longer distance. Bear in mind the undisputable fact that *regardless of the velocity it may have,* any and all bullets will drop 16 feet during the first second after leaving the muzzle of the rifle, and it matters not whether the arm be a Kentucky round ball rifle, the 30-06 Springfield, the 220 Swift, the 240 Super-Varminter, or whatever calibre or velocity of rifle you may use on this earth. Scientists tell us this does not apply in the moon, but we know of none of our "gun bugs" who have been there to test this matter as yet.

Loading the Powder into the Target Rifle. When I was a boy many of the most expert shots with the muzzle-loading cap lock target rifles always used a tin or brass tube a little smaller diameter that the bore of the rifle and about an inch longer than the barrel, with one end funnel shaped through which the powder was poured down the barrel of the rifle. After carefully wiping the bore after each shot, this long tube was inserted in the bore nearly to the breech and held with one hand while pouring the powder into it with the other hand. In this way, no grains of powder adhered to the side of the bore, but the entire charge was deposited in the cone of the patent breech and base of the bore so that none of the grains were crushed in seating the bullet. This tube was then withdrawn and the bullet loaded through the false muzzle with the bullet starter as usual. These men firmly believed that by loading the powder through this long tube in this way they secured finer accuracy and made somewhat smaller groups at all ranges. Uncle Alvaro and many other experts called this "an old maid's idea," said that it *did not improve the accuracy,* and only caused so much more work in loading and so much more equipment to carry around. Be that as it may, we noticed that these men who used these long loading tubes very seldom made any smaller groups, or won any more matches, than the riflemen who did not use them in loading. Of course, it is possible that these advocates of the long loading tubes did not have as super-accurate rifles as the others even though their rifles were by the best makers—Brockway, Edwin Wesson, Horace Warner, George H. Ferris, Billinghurst, and others of the best grade in those days.

However, it is a hint worth trying, especially if you are in the habit of leaving the bore of the rifle somewhat damp after cleaning for each shot.

RESTORING THE GILT-EDGE ACCURACY OF A RIFLE

After a rifle has been fired from a thousand to several thousand times the barrel becomes highly polished, or "glazed" as some rifle-makers call it, the sharp corners of the lands are rounded off, and the fine shooting is gone. Horace Warner devised a method of "recutting," as he called it, such barrels by the use of the special tools shown in the sketch herewith, and in this way restored the original fine accuracy. Sometimes a barrel after being recut in this way showed even firner accuracy than when new, according to reports of riflemen who had their rifles recut by Warner.

In order to properly control the action of the cutter in the barrel, Warner mounted the cutter in a bolt of lead-and-tin mixture, which was cast in the barrel around a wooden core which is shown in No. 2 in the sketch on page 30. The middle portion of this core was made wide, and the sides set at an angle to correspond with the angle of the rifling. A mortise was cut through as shown, to let the metal flow through. The wood at one side was then cut out to form the recess for the cutter, this recess being kept at the correct angle. The floating out cutter is shown at 7.

When a barrel was so badly rusted and pitted that recutting would not restore its accuracy, Warner "floated out" the rifling with tool 6. This consists of a piece of hardwood snugly fitted in the bore, and carrying the rifling cutter 7, set in the recess shown. After all the rifling was removed with the floating out tool, a bolt of lead was cast in the bore, as described

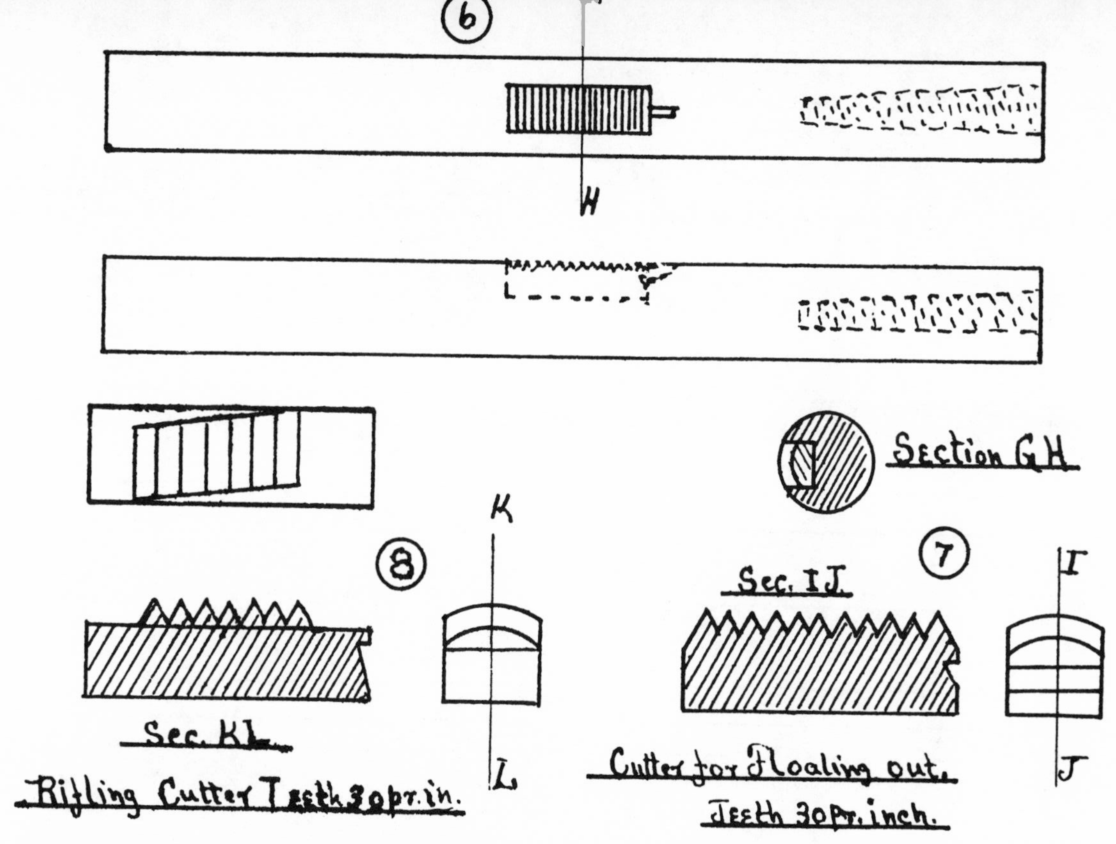

Sketch of Tools for Floating Out and Recutting Rifle Barrels. Sketches by Wm. V. Lowe, From "The American Rifleman," by Permission of the Editor.

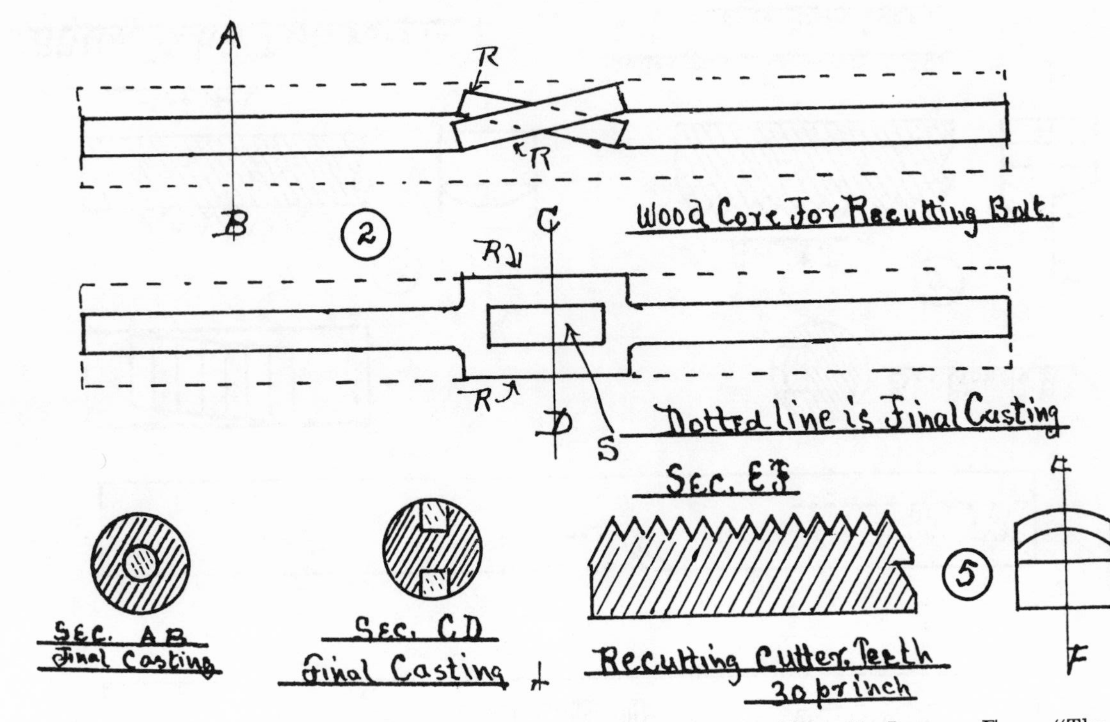

Sketch of Tools for Recutting and Re-rifling Barrels. Sketches by Wm. V. Lowe. From "The American Rifleman" by Permission of the Editor.

in chapter I, and the bore leaded out until it was smooth and round, which usually enlarged it about 1/100 of an inch. The barrel was then ready for re-rifling to larger calibre, by the use of the rifling machine in the same way that a new barrel was rifled. After re-rifling to a larger calibre, the barrel was leaded in the same way as a new barrel, which operation is described in detail in chapter I.

For some unknown reason a re-rifled barrel practically always gives better accuracy than when new, as has been repeatedly proven. N. S. Brockway told me that frequently his customers used a new rifle but a few weeks before having it re-rifled to the next larger calibre. If the customer wanted a 38 calibre rifle, he ordered it originally made as a 35 calibre, used it a short time and then had Brockway re-rifle it to the desired 38 calibre, and in every case this considerably improved the accuracy. Brockway stated that he could not recall a single instance in which this did not prove true with a re-rifled barrel as well as with the relined barrels that he made.

WIPING THE BARREL AFTER EACH SHOT IN TARGET SHOOTING

The experts of the old days always wiped according to the weather; that was their rule. If one was shooting on a hot, dry day in July or August, the best accuracy will be obtained by using cleaning patches that are quite wet and leaving the bore a trifle damp when reloading for the next shot. Or when shooting on a damp day when there is much moisture in the air, the wiping patches should not be at all wet, but only damp enough to soften the residue and make it easy to remove. Then the bore should be left quite dry when loading for the next shot.

Regardless of the weather conditions great care

should be used in wiping the bore *precisely the same way* after each shot. If the bore of the rifle is wiped perfectly dry for one shot and left somewhat damp, or wet, for the next one, it is *impossible* that these two bullets will have the same point of impact at the target. Thus a very small group may be much enlarged and a valuable prize lost simply by slight carelessness in wiping the bore of the rifle. All the old-time expert riflemen were *extremely particular* about this point.

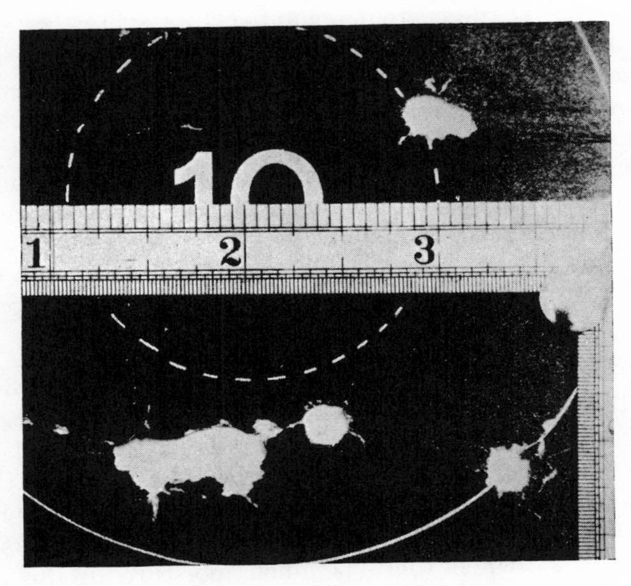

Five shots at 40 rods rest, by Walter Grote, with Brockway 38 calibre Rifle, Tube Sight, in Match. String measure 7¼ inches.

CHAPTER XII

A PARTIAL LIST OF OLD-TIME MAKERS OF MUZZLE-LOADING RIFLES

I believe it is a very conservative statement when I state that it is today impossible for any author to compile a *complete list* of the men who have made muzzle-loading rifles in this country since the percussion cap was perfected. Fifty years ago this would have been possible, but today it cannot be done, because there were many men throughout New England and New York States who made rifles occasionally, or as a "side line" in connection with the operation of a small machine shop, and even a blacksmith shop, who have been dead for many years, and those elderly people residing in these places who knew about the men who made these rifles are also dead. No one thought of keeping any record of these old rifle-makers as that business was nothing unusual in those times; now both these rifle-makers and those who were acquainted with them and their work are long since dead. Every few weeks I hear of some one who made muzzle-loading rifles that I had never before heard of, or see an old rifle of this kind that was made by a man that we never heard of before. Gun collectors are frequently finding specimens of this kind that were made by a hitherto unknown rifle-maker in some village in New England or New York State, Pennsylvania, Kentucky, Ohio, Tennesee or some other state. As an instance of this kind, I may mention that about forty years ago a gunsmith by the name of Parkhurst had a small shop on the main road from Bedford to Amherst, New Hampshire, where he made excellent muzzle-loading rifles. Uncle Alvaro and I often visited his shop, saw him making new rifle barrels, making stocks, re-cutting barrels, etc., and on several occasions we shot a rifle of his make that he had just finished, or re-cut, on his range back of his shop. Today, I am unable to find any person in Amherst who remembers Parkhurst, his shop or the rifles that he made and I have never seen his name in any list of makers of muzzle-loading rifles. The same is true in many villages in Vermont, as years ago there were a great number of gunsmiths who made rifles for the hunters and riflemen in the surrounding towns; made good hunting rifles especially, some also made target rifles that had a local reputation as being very accurate arms. Today it is difficult to find any person in those villages who remembers these old rifle-makers. Therefore, it is obvious that any list of makers of muzzle-loading rifles, must, necessarily, be incomplete.

C. B. ALLEN,
Springfield, Mass.

ETHAN ALLEN,
Grafton, Mass.

G. F. ALLEN,
Utica, N. Y.

A. APPLEBY,
Portsmouth, Ohio.

B. W. AMSDEN,
Saratoga Springs, N. Y.

L. M. AMIDON,
Bellows Falls, Vt., made telescopes principally, but also made rifles.

HENRY ALLEN,
New York.

N. ANGEL,
Erieville, N. Y.

OLIVER ALLEN,
Norwich, Conn.

E. ANSCHUTZ,
Philadelphia, Pa.

ALLEN & THURBER,
Norwich, Conn., about 1842 to 1847, Worcester, Mass., 1847 to 1856. The "Allen" of this firm was Ethan Allen.

ALLEN & WHEELOCK,
Worcester, Mass. Ethan Allen again in this firm.

JOHN ARMSTRONG, JR.,
Gettysburg, Pa.

S. ADAMS,
Battle Creek, Mich.

WILLIS AVERY,
Salisbury, N. Y.

CYRUS BARKER,
Providence, R. I.

MOSES BABCOCK,
Charlestown, Mass.

WILLIAM BILLINGHURST,
Rochester, N. Y.

E. BERQUR,
Detroit, Mich.

L. BUTTERFIELD,
Lynn, Mass.

NORMAN S. BROCKWAY,
Bellows Falls, Vt.

JOHN BROWN,
Fremont, N. H.

G. L. BRAMMER,
Chesapeake, Ohio.

T. BIDDLE,
Philadelphia, Pa.

W. BERRY,
Poughkeepsie, N. Y.

CYRUS BARKER,
Providence, R. I.

BEUTTER BROTHERS,
New Haven, Conn., also Meriden, Conn.

D. H. BISBEE,
Norway, Maine.
ANDREW BROWN,
Fremont, N. H., also Poplin, N. H.
J. BEAN,
Address unknown.
J. F. BROWN,
Haverhill, Mass.
JOHN BROWN,
Poplin, N. H., also Fremont, N. H.
REUBEN BROWN,
Nicholville, N. Y.
W. C. BIDDLE,
Philadelphia, Pa.
BARTLETT BROTHERS,
Binghampton, N. Y.
S. S. BAIRD,
Chittenden, Vt.
J. BUSWELL,
Glenns Falls, N. Y.
WILLIAM R. BURKHARD,
St. Paul, Minn.
H. A. BUCK & CO.,
West Stratford, Conn.
A. H. CHAPIN,
Earlville, N. Y.
ROSWELL F. COOK,
West Potsdam, N. Y.
LYMAN CHAMBERLAIN,
Ellisburg, N. Y.
CARLOS C. CLARK,
Windsor, Vt., also Manchester, N. H. Claimed to have invented the false muzzle for target rifles in 1836, but this was patented by Alvan Clark, a cousin of Carlos Clark's father, in 1840. Carlos Clark also claimed to have been the inventor of one of the first telescopic sights for rifles, but this is very doubtful.
ANSON CHASE,
Hartford, Conn., also New London, Conn.
J. M. CASWELL,
Lansingburg, N. Y.
E. W. COOK,
Lockport, N. Y.
ASHABEL COOK,
Clayton, N. Y.
WILLIAM CRAIG,
Allegheny, Pa.
N. H. CHOATE,
Auburn, N. Y.
H. COLEMAN,
Boston, Mass.
C. CHURCHILL,
Albany, N. Y.
HENRY T. COOPER,
New York, N. Y.
HENRY CARLILE,
———? Pa.
W. F. CRANDALL,
Gowanda, N. Y.
RICHARD CONSTABLE,
Philadelphia, Pa.
F. DAVIDSON & CO.,
Cincinnati, Ohio.
JOHN DERR,
Lancaster, Pa.
EBENEZER DELONG,
Parishville, N. Y.
HENRY DERINGER,
Philadelphia, Pa.
R. DEWARSON,
Boston, Mass.
H. E. DIMMICK,
St. Louis, Mo.
WILLIAM DIXON,
Adams, N. Y.
J. S. DUTTON,
Jaffrey, N. H.
R. DEWARSON,
Boston, Mass.
H. D. DWIGHT,
Belchertown, Mass.
J. M. ESTABROOK,
Milford, Mass.
J. EATON,
Concord, N. H., also Boston, Mass.
A. G. EASTMAN,
Rochester, N. Y.
SAMUEL EGGERS,
New Bedford, Mass.
GEO. EASTMAN,
Concord, N. H.
WM. B. FARRINGTON,
Concord, N. H., also Lebanon, N. H.

EDWIN FAY,
Hartford, Conn. Later, President of J. Stevens Arms & Tool Co., Chicopee Falls, Mass.

GILMAN B. FOGG,
Manchester, N. H.

A. B. FAIRBANKS,
Boston, Mass.

GEORGE P. FOSTER,
Taunton, Mass.

GUSTAV FISCHER,
New York, N. Y.

H. ? C. ? FISH,
New York City. Initials may have been W. G., or W. E. Not sure about this.

GEORGE H. FERRIS,
Utica, N. Y., also spelled his name Ferriss.

FRED G. FERRIS,
Utica, N. Y., also spelled it "Ferriss."

THOMAS FRENCH,
Canton, Mass.

CHARLES L. GARDNER,
Rochester, N. Y.

J. N. GARDNER,
Scranton, Pa.

J. E. GAGE,
Concord, N. H.

E. GILBERT,
Rochester, N. Y.

G. W. GEMMEL,
Troy, N. Y.

JOHN P. GEMMER,
St. Louis, Mo.

J. F. GEHRETT,
————? Pa.

JAMES GOLCHER,
Philadelphia, Pa.

JOHN GOLCHER,
New York, N. Y.

GEORGE GOULCHER,
New York, N. Y.

CARLOS GOVE,
Denver, Colo., also St. Joseph, Mo., and Council Bluffs, Iowa.

HENRY GROOT,
Pittsfield, Mass.

ALBERT ("PUT") GOVE,
Lincoln, Vt. This was "Danvis" in the book, "Uncle Lisah's Shop" and in "A Danvis Pioneer."

JOHN GRAINGER,
Toronto, Ontario, Can.

GROVER & LOVELL,
Boston, Mass.

JOSEPH GOULCHER,
also spelled Golcher, Philadelphia, Pa.

GEORGE GUBB,
New York, N. Y.

H. B. HARRINGTON,
Lebanon, N. H.

E. L. HALL,
Springfield, Mass.

J. HARDEN,
Lock Haven, Pa.

LUKE HARRINGTON,
Sutton, Mass.

WARREN HATCH,
Plattsburg, N. Y.

WARREN HATCH,
Burlington, Vt.

L. L. HEPBURN,
Colton, N. Y.

D. H. HILLIARD,
Cornish, N. H., also marked "Cornish Flats, N. H."

P. HOBBS,
Monterey, Mass.

CHARLES HOLMES,
Colton, N. Y.

AUSTIN HORR,
Cape Vincent, N. Y.

W. L. HUDSON,
Cincinnati, Ohio.

PHINEAS HULET,
Shaftsbury, Vt.

HARLEE J. HUNTOON,
Ludlow, Vt.

P. HOBBS,
Monterey, Mass.

R. W. HOUGHTON,
Norway, Maine.

RUFUS J. HOWLAND,
Binghampton, N. Y.

J. HENRY & SON,
Boulton, Pa.

NATHANIEL H. HARWOOD,
Brookfield, Mass.
JOSHUA HAYNES,
Waltham, Mass.
W. L. HUDSON,
Cincinnati, Ohio.
JOEL HAPGOOD,
Shrewsbury, Mass.
LUKE HARRINGTON,
Sutton, Mass.
JACOB HAWKEN,
St. Louis, Mo.
SAMUEL T. HAWKEN,
St. Louis, Mo., also Denver, Colo.
J. B. HOGAN,
North Adams, Mass.
BROWN INGALL,
Portland, Maine, also Andover, Maine, and Bucksport, Maine.
MORGAN JAMES,
Utica, N. Y.
JAMES & FERRIS,
Utica, N. Y.
JAMES H. JOHNSTON,
Pittsburgh, Pa., proprietor Great Western Gun Works.
LEVI? JORDAN.
South Adams, Mass.
JOHN H. JOHNSTON, or JOHN H. JOHNSON?,
Waynesboro, Pa.
NICANOR KENDALL,
Windsor, Vt.
N. KENDALL & CO.,
Windsor, Vt.
KENDALL & LAWRENCE,
Windsor, Vt.
JOHN KRIDDER,
Philadelphia, Pa.
P. H. KLEIN,
New York, N. Y.
L. M. LELAND,
Augusta, Maine.
THOMAS LAMSON,
Bennington, Vt.
GEORGE O. LEONARD,
Keene, N. H.
NELSON LEWIS,
Troy, N. Y.
A. LEONARD,
Saxons River, Vt., also A. Leonard & Son.
RICHARD LAWRENCE,
Windsor, Vt.
RICHARD S. LAWRENCE,
Hartford, Conn.
JOHN P. LOVELL,
Boston, Mass.
JOHN P. LOWER,
Philadelphia, Pa., also Denver, Colo.
HENRY E. LEMAN,
Lancaster, Pa., also "Lehman."
LANE & READ,
Boston, Mass.
JOHN P. LINDSAY, or LINDSEY?,
Windsor, Vt.
SIMEON MARBLE,
Sunderland, Vt.
J. MARSH,
Binghampton, N. Y.
A. C. MCGIRR,
Marietta, Ohio.
JOHN MILLER,
Penfield, Mich., also Munroe, Mich.
SETH P. MILLARD,
Lock Port, N. Y.
S. C. MILLER,
New Haven, Conn.
JOHN MEUNIER,
Milwaukee, Wis.
WM. D. MILLER,
Pittsfield, Mass.
JOSEPH MEDBERRY,
Rochester, N. Y.
ALLEN MERRITT,
East Randolph, Mass.
W. W. MESSER,
Boston, Mass.
JOHN P. MOORE,
Union, N. Y.
R. MOORE,
Cincinnatus, N. Y.
R. A. MOORE,
New York, N. Y.
THOMAS MORSE,
Lancaster, N. H.
CHAS. MILLER,
Honeoye, N. Y.
W. P. MARSTON,
Toronto, Ontario, Can.
JOHN MULLIN,
New York, N. Y., also J. & P. Mullin, New York, N. Y.

SAMUEL B. MUSGROVE,
Ironton, Ohio. Name may have been Samuel S. Musgrove.

HITCHCOCK & MUZZY,
Address unknown.

W. E. OGDEN,
Owego, N. Y.

M. L. OLMSTEAD,
Auburn, N. Y.

A. B. PARKER,
Three Mile Bay, N. Y.

H. V. PERRY,
Jamestown, N. Y.

DANIEL POTTER,
Hartford, Conn.

P. W. PORTER,
New York City.

HENRY PRATT,
Roxbury, Mass.

H. POTTER & CO.,
———, N. Y.

C.? E.? PARSONS,
Plattsburg, N. Y. Initials may have been E. C., or C. W.

C. PASSAGE,
Rochester, N. Y.

C. PLATH,
New York City.

WM.? PARKHURST,
Amherst, N. H. Not sure about first name; might have been Henry.

PARKER,
Ludlow, Vt. Initials may have been G. H., C. H., or E. H. Not sure.

ALVAN PRATT,
Concord, Mass.

ELIAS PRISLEY,
Hooversville, Pa.

T. B. PURMONT,
Heuvelton, N. Y.

C. V. RAMSDELL,
Bucksport, Maine, also Bangor, Maine.

P. A. REINHARDT,
Loudonville, Ohio. Last name also spelled "Reinhart" or "Reinhard."

WILLIAM READ,
Boston, Mass., also William Read & Co.

B. RIGGS,
Bellows Falls, Vt.

RIPLEY BROTHERS,
Windsor, Vt.

ELIPHALET REMINGTON,
Ilion, N. Y., also Herkimer, N. Y.

J. H. ROCKETER,
Syracuse, N. Y.

HENRY RICH,
Canton, N. Y.

ROBBINS & LAWRENCE,
Windsor, Vt.

C. A. & J. H. RECTOR,
Syracuse, N. Y.

A. H. ROWE,
Hartford, Conn.

CHARLES ROTH,
Wilkes-Barre, Pa.

WM. ROBERTS,
Danville, N. Y.

THOMAS RIGGINS,
———?, Tenn.

O. A. RICHARDSON,
Lowell, Mass.

W. G. ROBBINS,
Windsor?, Vt.

H. A. RUGGLES,
Stafford Hollow, Conn. Not sure about initials; may have been B. A., or W. A.

JOHN SHERRY,
Lancaster, Pa., also later in Beaver Township, Pa. Claimed to have invented the gain twist rifling and the segmental type of rifling. Both of which known and tried early in 1700, before Sherry was born. Sherry was born in 1797.

WILLIAM R. SCHAEFER,
Boston, Mass.

SCHAEFER & WERNER,
Boston, Mass.

GEORGE SCHALK,
Pottsville, Pa.

CHRISTOPHER SCHALK,
Williamsport, Pa.

JOHN SHELL,
Leslie County, Ky., was 134 years old when he died as established by records; the late President Calvin Coolidge

sent his physician to investigate Shell's age and record who found this correct. He was born in Tennessee in 1788, paid taxes in 1809 as shown by Tax Receipts, was too old for service in the Mexican War—1846—and died in July, 1922. It is stated that he made one or more cap-lock rifles in 1920. The major part of the foregoing is quoted from "The Kentucky Rifle," by permission of the author, Captain John G. W. Dillin.

LOREN SOPER,
Theresa, N. Y.

JOHN SMITH,
Exeter, N. H.

H. SUMERS,
Barnet, Vt.

JAMES A. SCRIVNER,
Auburn, N. Y.

J. P. SCHENKL,
Boston, Mass.

C. C. SIEBER,
Columbus, Ohio.

H. SLOCUM,
Worcester, Mass.

EUGENE SMART,
Dover, N. H.

MARTIN SMITH,
Greenfield, Mass.

ARGULUS or ANGLUS? SMITH,
Buffalo, N. Y. Not sure about first name.

P. SMITH,
Buffalo, N. Y.

CHAUNCEY SNELL,
Auburn, N. Y.

SLOTTER & CO.,
Philadelphia, Pa.

ABEL SPAULDING,
North Buckfield, Maine.

DWIGHT SPENCER,
Hartford, Conn.

E. S. SWETT,
Kalamazoo, Mich.

JOHN SEAVER,
Vergennes, Vt. Not sure if first name was John or James.

SARGENT & SMITH,
Newburyport, Mass.

ASA STORY,
West Parish, Vt.

CHARLES STUART,
Binghampton, N. Y.

H. STEVENS,
Watertown, N. Y.

HORACE SMITH,
Springfield, Mass. Later of the firm of Smith & Wesson.

A. W. SPIES,
New York City.

———— SPENCER,
Windsor, Vt.

C. C. SIEBERT, or SIEBER?,
Columbus, Ohio.

H. L. SIEBERT,
Cincinnati, Ohio.

L. W. TISDEL,
Scranton, Pa.

TRUITT BROTHERS & CO.,
Philadelphia, Pa.

THADDEUS THAYER,
Norwood, N. Y.

BENJAMIN THOMAS,
Hingham, Mass.

MARSHALL TIDD,
Woburn, Mass.

JOSEPH TOOKER,
Carthage, N. Y.

GEORGE W. TRYON,
Philadelphia, Pa. Also Geo. W. Tryon & Son, and George W. Tryon & Co.; Geo. W. Tryon Son & Co.

JOSEPH TONKS,
Boston, Mass.

ARGULUS TAYLOR,
Ira, N. Y.

HENRY TOMES & CO.,
New York City.

S. VOSBURGH,
West Rush, N. Y.

S. VAN VALKENBURG,
Albany, N. Y.

PROSPER VALLEE,
Philadelphia, Pa.

DAVID M. VARNEY,
Burlington, Vt.

JOHN VANDERHEYDEN,
Auburn, N. Y.

HORACE WARNER,
Williamsport, Pa., also Syracuse, N. Y.

JAMES WARNER,
Springfield, Mass.

EDWIN WESSON,
Northboro, Mass., also Hartford, Conn.

DANIEL B. WESSON,
Northboro, Mass., Hartford, Conn., Worcester, Mass., and Springfield, Mass. Later of firm of Smith & Wesson.

H. G. WHITMORE,
Boston, Mass.

ANDREW E. WHITMORE,
Somerville, Mass.

D. WHITTEMORE,
Cambridge, Mass.

H. W. WHITE,
Jackson, Mich.

ELI WHITNEY,
Whitneyville, Conn., also New Haven, Conn

LOREN H. WRISLEY,
Norway, Maine.

BEN. WHITMAN,
Stillwater, N. Y.

ABE WILLIAMS,
Owego, N. Y. Made heavy "Sharpshooter's" rifles for the U. S. Army during the Civil War.

N. G. WHITMORE,
Pottsdam, N. Y.

N. N. WILMOT,
Boston, Mass.

B. C. WOOD,
Painted Post, N. Y.

ASA H. WATERS,
Millsbury, Mass.

A. H. WATERS & CO.,
also A. Waters & Son, Sutton, Mass.

J. S. WARE,
Worcester, Mass.

ORLANDO WARE,
Worcester, Mass.

F. WASSMANN,
Washington, D. C.

CHARLES WERNER,
Rochester, N. Y.

W. W. WETMORE,
Lebanon, N. H., also Windsor, Vt.

H. B. WEAVER,
Windham, Conn.

T. S. WHIPPLE,
Cambridge, Vt. Made heavy "Sharpshooter's" rifles for the U. S. Government during the Civil War.

O. W. WHITTIER,
Enfield, N. H.

W. N. WOOD,
New York City.

——— WINGERT,
Detroit, Mich.

LOOMIS S. WRIGHT,
Waddington, N. Y.

J. J. WURFELEIN,
Philadelphia, Pa.

H. WHITE,
Jackson, Michigan.

——— LAWRENCE,
Laconia, N. H.